The Dependency Movement

The Dependency Movement

Scholarship and Politics in Development Studies

Robert A. Packenham

Harvard University Press
Cambridge, Massachusetts
London, England
1992

This book is printed on acid-free paper, and its binding materials
have been chosen for strength and durability.

Library of Congress Cataloging-in-Publication Data

Packenham, Robert A.
    The dependency movement : scholarship and politics in development studies /
    Robert A. Packenham.
        p.   cm.
    Includes bibliographical references and index.
    ISBN 0-674-19810-7
        1. Dependency.   2. Economic development.   3. Latin America—Dependency on
    foreign countries.   4. Latin America—Economic policy.   I. Title.
HD75.P3   1992
338.9—dc.20

91-27689
CIP

Preface

In the late 1960s the dominant theoretical and methodological approaches to Third World development—modernization, functionalist, structuralist—came under challenge from *dependencia* writers from Latin America and elsewhere. Dependency ideas, a blend of Marxism and nationalism, entered the mainstream and eventually transformed a number of scholarly fields: Latin American, African, and development studies, much of comparative politics, international political economy, and comparative sociology, among others.

This book describes, analyzes, and evaluates dependency ideas and their consequences in Latin America and the United States. It is, I believe, the only study of the dependency movement as a whole and the first comprehensive assessment of it by a non-Marxist scholar. As such, it tends to criticize the utopianism, nonfalsificationism, and especially the politicization of dependencia approaches more than their substantive hypotheses. While some of the latter seem to me to be mistaken, others appear to be empirically sustainable; in fact they deserve more attention than they have lately received.

In criticizing the politicization of scholarship I do not take the naive view that scholars can or should proceed in a political vacuum. That is impossible. But taking into account the scholar as a political being should not be confused with the intentional subordination of scholarship to political struggles. Scholars in democracies are relatively free of politicizing pressures to conform (unless they choose not to be), whereas scholars in authoritarian and totalitarian regimes and movements are not. Thus scholarship in the democracies of contemporary Latin America, Western Europe, Japan, and North America is much less politicized than it is in, say, Fidel Castro's Cuba. To conflate the two very different definitions of politicization is an intellectual obfuscation and a calamity in terms of scholarship, political arrangements, and economic and social policies.

This distinction informs, in the words of one reader, the "passion and conviction" that underlie this book. It is worthwhile to note specifically what the passion and conviction are about. They are not about any particular articles, books, or authors. Nor are they an excuse to avoid traditional scholarly conventions requiring documentation and citation and prohibiting personal attacks or ad hominem arguments; to the contrary, I honor those conventions and try, to the best of my ability, to follow them scrupulously. Rather, my main concern is the dependency movement's politicizing imperatives, practices, and effects. These features violate the most basic value in the academy: the freedom to go where facts, logic, and reason lead, unfettered by political pressures and fears of being politically incorrect.

In the university, that freedom must be the highest value. It can prevail only when the scholarly and political vocations are separate. Some scholars accepted and benefited from that separation when dependency ideas were insignificant and disparaged it when they became prominent. That pattern of thought and behavior is not only morally wrong but pragmatically short-sighted. Today's majority is tomorrow's minority and vice versa. To disdain the insulation of scholarship from political pressures now is to deprive oneself of the protections that insulation provides later.

Sooner or later all researchers need such protections. To the extent that the dependency movement has broken down the separation of scholarly and political vocations, it has also eroded those vital safeguards. Scholars need to defend and affirm the academic freedom that benefits all researchers and also society as a whole. My approach here is to use the tools of scholarship themselves and to be as clear and direct as possible about the issues. Because I address the issues explicitly, some readers may see the book as polemical, but that is not my intention. In this connection I am gratified that the reader who noted the book's "passion and conviction" also found it to be "unwaveringly disciplined."

A word is in order about the timing of the book in relation to broader trends and events. I finished the first complete draft of the manuscript in June 1989. Thereafter I tightened it considerably and added some new references, but all the main arguments were in place before the vast events in Eastern Europe and the USSR that began in August 1989 and have had such far-reaching consequences.

Dependency debates have been heavily influenced by academic fads and fashions. Since the beginning of my work on this topic, therefore,

I have always addressed not only the ideas themselves and their effects, but also, and centrally, the larger issues raised by the dependency movement. Otherwise, I knew, the work would be partly hostage to those notoriously unstable fads and fashions. As it happens, the dependency movement has lasted far longer—and not only in the United States—than I or anyone else predicted. In July 1991, for example, at the World Congress of the International Political Science Association in Buenos Aires, leading dependency authors restated the arguments they had advanced almost a quarter century earlier; the large audience responded enthusiastically and gave one of them a ten-minute standing ovation. In the United States dependencia rhetoric and scholarship continue to flow freely—now often without the dependency label, but frequently still with it.

Thus, reports of the death of the dependency movement are premature. The politicization and nonfalsificationism it engendered and nourished are still very strong in the academy. What has weakened is the movement's appeal as an explicit set of substantive hypotheses. This trend is ironic and revealing. It occurs just when the actual dependence of Latin American countries on the United States (and also interdependence within Latin America) is tending to increase. The paradox is partly explained by the diminished appeal of socialism as a model for development in many parts of the world, including Latin America. Taken together these trends are further confirmation, if any were needed, that the dependency movement has always been about capitalism versus socialism more than about dependency versus autonomy.

Fellowships from the Woodrow Wilson International Center for Scholars and the National Fellows Program of the Hoover Institution greatly facilitated my work on this book in its initial and middle stages, respectively. Smaller grants from the Carnegie Endowment for International Peace and the Institute for the Study of World Politics were also helpful. The Instituto Brasileiro de Relações Internacionais (IBRI) of the Fundação Getulio Vargas in Rio de Janeiro, the Instituto Universitário de Pesquisas do Rio de Janeiro (IUPERJ), the Institute of Latin American Studies (ILAS) of the University of London, and the Centro de Estudios Internacionales (CEI) of El Colegio de México in Mexico City generously provided office space and a congenial scholarly *ambiente* during my stays in their countries.

At Stanford University, the Center for Research in International Studies, the Center for Latin American Studies, and the Department of Political Science provided modest but vital financial and logistical support at various moments. The Department's administrator, Arlee Ellis, was helpful and resourceful. Willa Leonard and Yvonne Nakahigashi did some of the word processing. John Cardenas and Cristina Llop helped with the references.

I am grateful to the publishers of the following journals and books for permission to use passages from my writings that appeared previously in their pages: *Latin American Research Review* (17:1, 1982), in chapter 1; *New World* (2:1/2, 1987), in chapters 2 and 12; *North/ South Relations* (1983, Praeger), eds. Charles Doran, George Modelski, and Cal Clark, in chapter 6; *Brazil in the Seventies* (1976, American Enterprise Institute for Public Policy Research), ed. Riordan Roett, in chapter 6; *Journal of Interamerican Studies and World Affairs* (28:1, 1986), in chapter 7; *Dominant Powers and Subordinate States* (1986, Duke University Press), ed. Jan Triska, in chapter 7; *Political Liberalization in Brazil* (1986, Westview), ed. Wayne Selcher, in chapter 9. In all cases these materials have been revised for use in this book.

At Harvard University Press, Aida Donald gave early encouragement to the project and wise counsel and firm support until it was completed. Elizabeth Suttell and Anita Safran managed to be simultaneously efficient and diplomatic: Betty as the able coordinator of almost everything and Anita as a sensitive and skillful copy editor.

In the years during which I have worked on this book many people have provided ideas, information, criticisms, and professional and personal support. I thank them all most sincerely. With apologies to those whose names do not appear, I must express my explicit appreciation to the following colleagues and friends whose comments, criticisms, and support were, in various ways, especially important: Gabriel and Dorothea Almond, José Murilo de Carvalho, Wanderley Guilherme dos Santos, Javier Elguea, Carlos Fuentes, Lincoln Gordon, Samuel Huntington, Alex Inkeles, Helio Jaguaribe, Juan and Patricia Lindau, Seymour Martin Lipset, Scott Mainwaring, Lucian Pye, Jeffrey Seward, Thomas Skidmore, Josefina Zoraida Vázquez, and Robert Ward.

Rio de Janeiro
August 23, 1991   R.A.P.

Contents

Tables

If they say, "Come with us . . .
    let us wantonly ambush the innocent . . . "
. . . my son, do not walk in the way with them,
    hold back your foot from their paths;
For . . . these men . . . set an ambush for their own lives . . .
they shall eat the fruit of their way
    and be sated with their own devices.

The Proverbs of Solomon

Introduction

Nineteen sixty-five was a watershed year in North American society and politics. In April U.S. Marines landed in Santo Domingo. In August Watts exploded. Throughout the year the war in Vietnam escalated, and political protests and movements swept the country. A country shaken by the murder of its President began to wonder whether its pathologies were systemic. "The sixties," which started in earnest only in 1965, had begun. The sixties witnessed a deep crisis in the field of development studies in the United States. Concepts and theories that only a few years earlier had seemed important contributions to knowledge and policy were now challenged and attacked from nearly every ideological and scientific direction. By the end of the decade, the field of development studies was a shambles. Liberal ideas in particular were out. It was less clear what was in.

In Latin America the sixties were also a turning point but for somewhat different reasons. Latin Americans were little concerned with Vietnam, the Cold War, or the kinds of urban and ethnic issues that preoccupied North Americans. Latin Americans were concerned with political authoritarianism, socioeconomic inequalities, poverty, appropriate forms of economic growth, and external constraints on national autonomy. Liberal approaches to development, while by no means unknown, did not have the same degree of influence there as in the United States. In the mid-sixties the structuralism of Raúl Prebisch and others associated with the Economic Commission for Latin America (ECLA, or CEPAL in its Spanish and Portuguese acronym) had been the most influential Latin American approach to development, but it and others were increasingly under attack.

These were the circumstances in the United States and Latin America when a set of writings, ideas, and authors that came rapidly to be known as the dependency school, theory, or, as I prefer, approach or perspective, came into being. Like the contributors to some other "schools" or perspectives of this sort, dependency writers did not necessarily work together or even know one another—although many of them did, especially in Santiago de Chile between 1964 and 1967. Certainly they did not agree on everything, but they agreed on a great deal. This book is a study of dependency ideas, their influences, and their implications in the United States and Latin America.

As a study of the ideas themselves, it addresses three questions, in ascending order of intellectual and social importance though not necessarily of length of explicit treatment in the text. First, what is the substance of dependency ideas? That is, what did dependency authors claim to know about dependent capitalism and what did they propose as an alternative to it? Second, what were the ways of knowing, the epistemologies, of dependency authors? Third, what were their premises about the relationship between scholarship and politics—between their ideas and ways of knowing, on the one hand, and social, economic, and political forces, on the other?

As a study of the influences of these ideas in Latin America and the United States, the book treats the spread of dependency thinking as a significant episode in inter-American cultural relations that needs to be analyzed comparatively and sociologically. In particular it pays attention to the different kinds of influence dependency ideas have had in the two areas and the reasons for these differences.

Finally, as a study of the implications of these ideas, the book uses the dependency movement as a window through which to view topics of even broader and deeper significance.

Why Study the Dependency Movement?

A study of dependency ideas and their influences is important because of the sheer magnitude of the impact of these ideas in Latin America and the United States. Of all the approaches to development, particularly Latin American development, of the last twenty-five years, none has had deeper or more pervasive influence, especially in the United States, than the dependency perspective. It has influenced every social-science discipline, some of the humanities, and various applied and professional fields. It spawned or helped to spawn other areas of scholarly inquiry that became major fields of specialization in their own right—in political science, for example, bureaucratic-authoritarianism and the political economy of development. Countless books, monographs, readers, articles, textbooks, symposia, special issues of scholarly journals, prizes, and other forms of scholarly activity and recognition have been devoted to dependency ideas and authors.

What began in the late 1960s as a minority protest or challenge entered the mainstream and in some scholarly areas became the new orthodoxy. Dependency ideas also became influential beyond the scholarly world. Falcoff (1980, p. 797) noted that "dependency explanations . . . are no longer confined to academic sanctuaries; they are now the common currency of a growing body of generals, bishops, editors, chiefs of state, even Latin American businessmen." He was writing about Latin America; a similar point has been made about various sectors of North American society and government (Schoultz, 1987, pp. 21–23). The influences of the dependency movement are by now sufficiently broad and deep that even when specific studies and authors are no longer widely remembered and cited, which is very far from being the case so far, its effects on the language, premises, and hypotheses of scholarly discourse and the world of affairs would still be significant. In other words, as its proponents have suggested, even if the dependency perspective were to vanish as a conscious, explicit approach this subtle legacy would ensure that it had not lived—or died—in vain.

A second reason to undertake an analysis of the movement is that, for all their influences, dependency ideas are still widely and seriously misunderstood. To the extent such confusion persists, the intense, unproductive controversies that have occurred are inevitable and will continue. Some scholars, for example, have sought to test dependency ideas without fully understanding them. This point applies most obviously to many cross-national quantitative studies but also to some single-country case studies and conceptual critiques. As defenders of dependency ideas delight in pointing out, such studies have often not been salutary. But one also needs to state immediately the other side of the coin, which is that no one has done a good job of explicating the issues between proponents and critics of these writings, or even of identifying clearly their essential features.

In short, confusion about the dependency perspective is widespread among both critics and defenders. It occurs not only at the level of substantive claims, but also, and even more so, at the levels of epistemology and premises about scholarship and politics. Until dependency ideas are understood better, debates and attempts to test them will continue to generate more heat than light. Ignoring the controversies and conflicts, while tempting, is no solution. They and their effects exist. It is better to address them explicitly and systematically than implicitly, haphazardly, and polemically.

There is therefore a need for an analysis of dependency ideas that is scholarly, informed, *and* willing to explore critically the fundamental claims and premises of the approach. The most frequent and influential criticisms of *dependencia* ideas have come either from debates among dependency writers or from Marxist scholars who share many dependency premises. But these are essentially debates within the overall perspective rather than assessments of the perspective itself. Most scholarly commentary has been either uncritical in any significant sense or unable to understand what dependency ideas are about.

Furthermore, success in finding alternatives to the dependency approach—ways to maximize its strengths and minimize its weaknesses—rests crucially on the degree to which there is an informed understanding of the approach itself in the first place. The dependency perspective has many interesting features. It has a manifest appeal. Many dependency ideas are plausible. Some are correct. But there are always, in any approach, more plausible ideas than tenable or correct ideas. Unfortunately, given its premises, there is no way within the dependency approach to say that any of its plausible ideas is incorrect; if one cannot do that then one cannot say which are more likely to be correct. The only way to have a base from which to construct a valid alternative to the dependency approach is to understand it accurately and thoroughly.

Broader Issues

The dependency movement is significant not only in its own right but also as a window through which to view broader issues. First, it is a notable episode in the history of social thought in Latin America. In the United States, Latin American social theory has been a relatively neglected field of scholarly study in recent decades. This is regrettable, for it is a fascinating area in its own right and much more laden with implications for behavior and institutions in the region than is usually recognized. (Latin American scholars, fortunately, have been more attentive to the subject.)

The dependency movement is also a notable episode in the history of social thought in the United States. Studying the dependency movement extends earlier efforts to understand the nature and the roots of the thinking of U.S. and other First World social scientists regarding Third World development. In particular, we try to describe some of the elements of continuity and change in U.S. perspectives on this subject from the sixties to the present.

Third, and most important, the dependency movement raises a number of fundamental scientific, ethical, and political issues that have arisen across the social sciences and humanities in the post-sixties. Of these the most crucial is whether social science and scholarship should be insulated from political forces or willingly and intentionally subordinated to them. The former is the classical conception that has been traditional in the United States and elsewhere. The dependency movement challenges that view head-on and advocates the latter conception. Clearly this shift has wider implications, and not just for the social sciences.

How the Book is Organized

The first five chapters deal with dependency ideas themselves. They correct a number of misconceptions that are widespread in the scholarly literature. For example, the main dependency approaches were misnamed: they are much more fundamentally about capitalism versus socialism than about national dependency versus national autonomy. An adequate understanding of these approaches, here called, collectively, holistic dependency, requires attention to their central features and levels of analysis: substantive holism, substantive utopianism, epistemological holism (nonfalsificationism), and the premise of politicized scholarship. These chapters are based on analyses of the most influential dependency texts and neglected sources in Portuguese and Spanish; they also include an appraisal of the intellectual origins of the dependency movement and a new typology of dependency and dependency-related approaches.

Chapters 6 and 7 consider dependency ideas from a different angle of vision. Focusing on two concrete situations of dependency, one capitalist (Brazil) and the other socialist (Cuba), these chapters use an alternative approach, analytic dependency, to explore holistic dependency's substantive research program and to set its assumptions and methods into sharper relief.

In chapters 8 through 12 attention shifts to the influences of dependency ideas in Latin America and the United States. Claims that dependency writings were manifestations of increasing intellectual and psychological autonomy in Latin America are misleading. The most innovative, constructive, and promising theoretical and policy perspectives in recent years in Latin America have come from outside the dependency movement. In the United States, the net effects have also been negative but in different ways. The dependency movement made some positive intellectual contributions, but it also contributed greatly to a costly politicization and theatricalization of U.S. scholarship and to a damaging impasse in the field of development theory.

1 The Dependency Perspective: Origins, Themes, Variations

The dependency perspective expresses both continuities and changes in the history of attempts to interpret Latin American development. It emerged in Latin America in the second half of the decade of the 1960s as, among other things, a critique of theoretical and practical orientations prominent at the time. In this sense it represented change. In a deeper and ultimately much more significant sense, however, the dependency perspective was a restatement of ideas that had recurringly been influential in the region and whose real origins lay elsewhere.

Continuities

To a much greater degree than is frequently realized, in Latin America dependency ideas have been manifestations of continuity rather than profoundly new developments. (In the United States, these ideas were much more an expression of change and discontinuity.) Where, in terms of specific authors and intellectual currents from the past, do these ideas come from and what continuities do they express?

In the first place, and most important by far, they are part of the Marxist tradition of Latin American thought. More than anything else, the dependency perspective restates Marxist ideas about Latin American development that have a long history in the region, that remain influential in various sectors, and that probably will continue to be influential no matter what happens to the dependency "school" per se. Fernando Henrique Cardoso's comments on the historical origins of dependency ideas deserve to be quoted at length:

> The analyses of dependency situations in Latin America done in the second half of the sixties did not represent new methodological propositions. What happened was that a current which was already old in Latin American thought managed to make itself heard in the

discussions that were taking place in institutions normally closed to it: ECLA, the universities, some goverment planning agencies, and—last but not least—the North American academic community.

As for the renovating influence of the North American neo-Marxian current, if it was real (principally the contribution of Baran), it was certainly not greater than that of Marx himself, and it did not "reveal" anything not already present in the perspective of critical Latin American thought before 1960 . . .

A study of the history of ideas in the twentieth century would show that each generation of critical intellectuals seeks to revive Marxism with a new breath of life . . .

Studies of dependency, then, constitute part of this constantly renewed effort to reestablish a tradition of analysis of economic structures and structures of domination; one that would not suffocate the historical process by removing from it the movement which results from the permanent struggle among groups and classes . . .

Studies of dependency continue a live tradition of Latin American thought, reinvigorated in the 1960s by the proposition of themes and problems defined in a theoretical-methodological field not only distinct from what inspired Keynesian and structural-functionalist analyses (the theory of modernization, and of the stages of development that would repeat the history of the industrialized countries), but radically distinct with respect to its inherent critical component. (Cardoso, 1977a, pp. 9–10, 17)

One can quarrel over details, nuances, and minor exaggerations, but these passages are essentially correct. And very important.

A second source of ideas and inspiration for dependency writers has been the works of Lenin and others about imperialism (Palma, 1978, pp. 890–898; Evans, 1979, pp. 14–35). Marx had no theory of imperialism. His writings deal poorly with the phenomenon of nationalism. For Marx, classes were by definition primary: nations "expressed" class relations. Lenin did not have much of a theory of imperialism either—widespread misconceptions to the contrary notwithstanding—but he had more to say than Marx. Drawing on the writings of the liberal Hobson and the Marxists Hilferding and Luxemburg, Lenin wrote his famous pamphlet on imperialism in 1916. In it he elaborated a notion of imperialism that involved both class and national aspects. Thus Cardoso writes that Lenin "formulated with simplicity what would be the core of the dependency analyses: the forms of articulation between the two parts of a single mode of production, and the subordination of one mode of production to another" (Cardoso, 1972, p. 4; also Palma, 1978, p. 890).

In this fashion Lenin anticipated the dependency idea of the "anti-nation inside the nation" of Cardoso and of all other dependency writers. This notion is crucial in the dependency perspective. It links the national and the class aspects of the analysis. It subordinates the former to the latter, as Marx did, but it pays more attention to the national unit than Marx did. It makes, or rather appears to make, the two aspects of the analysis entirely compatible. It locates the unique solution to the linked problems of class exploitation and national imperialism in the overthrow of capitalism and the installation of socialism. It provides an epistemological device which prohibits the theoretical content of the perspective from being falsified. In these and other ways Lenin's ideas also form part of the background to, and are a source of, dependency ideas.

A number of European and North American Marxists may also have had an impact on the emergence of dependency ideas. For example, Cardoso (1977a, pp. 8–12) has named the Frenchmen Jean Paul Sartre and Louis Althusser, the Hungarian Georg Lukács, the Italian Antonio Gramsci, and (more ambiguously) the North Americans Paul Baran and Paul Sweezy as authors whose works influenced dependency thinking. The pattern of references and citations in Cardoso's own studies tends to support these claims but with important qualifications. Before his study with Faletto on dependency appeared, Cardoso had already co-authored or authored three books. Cardoso and Ianni (1960), writing about race relations in Florianópolis, make no references to the European and American Marxists, but Cardoso's other early books, on capitalism and slavery in Southern Brazil and on Brazilian entrepreneurs and development (Cardoso, 1962, 1964), both cite frequently and draw heavily on the works of Baran, Lukács, Marx, Sartre, and Sweezy; Marc Bloch, Maurice Dobb, and C. Wright Mills are also cited. The 1969 edition of Cardoso and Faletto refers to none of these authors, however, and the 1979 edition refers, among them, only to Marx. Other major dependency works also cite the classic Marxist sources but few of the contemporary ones. For instance, Sunkel and Paz (1970) have twenty-three index references, some of them very lengthy, to Marx, Engels, and Lenin, but of the contemporary Marxists just mentioned they cite only Lukács (twice) and Sweezy (twice).

Some dependency writers have suggested links between their work and that of a number of Latin American Marxists, neo-Marxists, and other "radical" writers who preceded them in writing "critically" about Latin America: historians Sergio Bagú and Caio Prado, Jr., sociologists Florestan Fernandes, Pablo González Casanova, and Jorge Graciarena, and economists Armando Córdoba, Antonio García, and Alonso Aguilar (Cardoso, 1977a, p. 9; Evans, 1979, pp. 25–26). Clearly, dependency writings express continuity with these earlier Latin American intellectual currents. The question of influence is more complicated. In the case of Cardoso, the influences of Florestan Fernandes and Caio Prado, Jr. are manifest. These two giants of "critical" social science in Brazil are cited prominently and used in each of Cardoso's major works (1962, 1964, and Cardoso and Ianni, 1960) leading up to his book with Faletto. The 1962 book is dedicated to Fernandes. Cardoso's early works also cited the Brazilian historian Nelson Werneck Sodré who also belongs to this "critical" tradition. But the other authors mentioned by Cardoso in his 1977 article are seldom if ever mentioned or cited in his works in the 1960s. The same is true for other dependency authors. For instance, of the "critical" authors mentioned by Cardoso the only one listed in the index to Sunkel and Paz (1970) is Bagú, and he only once.

Surprisingly, the Peruvian Marxist José Carlos Mariátegui (1894–1930) is rarely cited by dependency authors on such lists, even though he would seem to occupy a prominent position in this regard. A journalist, essayist, and political activist in Peru in the late teens and the twenties, Mariátegui was one of the first Latin American intellectuals—if not the first—to adapt Marxist and Leninist ideas sensitively and creatively to Latin American realities. He was, according to John Womack (1980, pp. 170–172), "probably the intellectual equal of his contempories Gramsci and Mao . . . He should interest the left around the world . . . [He was] the most significant Latin American socialist of his generation—one of the most creative in the world in the 1920s." What made him important was that he made "the connection between nationalism and socialism" in a way that "still bears practical meaning today."

There are indeed a number of parallels between Mariátegui and the dependency writers. Both he and they fought a two-front battle against conservative and liberal perspectives on the one hand and "vulgar" interpretations of Marx on the other hand. Both urged studies of "concrete situations"—and Mariátegui actually did them. Both sought to link nationalism and socialism. Both insisted that "autonomous capitalism" was no solution for Latin America and that the only real solution lay in socialism. Both agreed with Marx that the purpose of social analysis is not only to interpret reality but to change it.

One can thus make a good case that the most important Latin American "father" or "grandfather" of dependency writings was Mariátegui. Yet his name has been mentioned relatively infrequently in this regard. A few authors have acknowledged him (Cotler, 1979), but most have not. None of Cardoso's four books published in the 1960s (and none of his articles in the seventies) cites Mariátegui. The 1979 edition of Cardoso and Faletto mentions him only once in passing (p. 121) in the context of a discussion of politics in Peru rather than as an intellectual forebear. Sunkel and Paz do not cite or mention him. Neither does Palma in his analysis of the Marxist and Leninist antecedents of dependencia writings. Of the major works on dependency, the only one I have found which cites Mariátegui is Frank (1967, pp. 123, 285). Ironically, according to many interpretations, Frank did not adequately acknowledge his debt to the Latin American roots of dependency thinking. Yet in respect to Mariátegui, Frank acknowledges that debt more fully than most dependency writers or commentators.

The omission of Mariátegui from Palma's article is notable because Palma focuses on historical origins and writes specifically about the 1920s as a turning point in Marxist analysis of Latin America. According to Palma (1978, pp. 896–897): "Only around 1920 did a new vision of capitalist development in the backward nations begin to be developed within Marxist thought (see Lenin, 1920). It would be formulated explicitly at the Sixth Congress of the Communist International (the Comintern) in 1928. This approach differs from that which preceded it in that in its analysis it gives more importance to the role played by the traditional dominant classes of the backward countries." Palma quotes a passage from a statement presented at this Congress: "When the dominant imperialist power needs social support in the colonies it makes an alliance first and foremost with the dominant classes of the old pre-capitalist system, the feudal-type commercial and money-lending bourgeoisie *(sic)*, against the majority of the people." And Palma then comments: "In my opinion this Congress [in 1928] may be considered the turning point in the Marxist approach to the concrete possibilities of the historical progressiveness of capitalism in backward countries."

There is no doubt that the ideas Palma describes here, this "new vision" as he calls it, are parallel to the ideas of dependency writers— the stress on the internal as well as the external manifestations of dependency, the "alliance" of interests between the two aspects of dependency, and so on. It is equally certain, however, that everything Palma says here about a new vision was also present in Mariátegui's writings. Yet Palma ignores the Peruvian and instead locates the "turning point in the Marxist approach to the concrete possibilities of the historical progressiveness of capitalism" in a Congress of the Comintern that met in Moscow in 1928—the same year that Mariátegui's most important book, the collection of essays about Peru that he wrote for Peruvian journals in the period 1925 to 1928, was first published as a single volume (see Mariátegui, 1971, p. xxix).

One other broad source of continuity, different from all the rest, must be mentioned. Many non-Marxist authors and sources, from a variety of perspectives, are cited by dependency writers and have influenced them. Among these are the Economic Commission for Latin America (ECLA, or CEPAL in its Portuguese and Spanish acronym), whose ideas were partly accepted, partly criticized, and partly extended by dependency writers; liberal modernization and development theorists, whose ideas were even more sharply criticized by dependency authors; and other non-Marxists who do not fit neatly into either of these two categories. We shall have more to say about the ECLA and modernization theorists in the next section, on discontinuities, where they are more appropriately considered; but it is well to note here that dependency authors express continuity with as well as criticisms of these authors and ideas.

An excellent example of a writer who mixes Marxist and non-Marxist ideas and sources from various disciplines is Cardoso. Cardoso's first book (Cardoso and Ianni, 1960) is dedicated to Roger Bastide and Antonio Cândido, and these authors, plus other non-Marxists such as Donald Pierson and Gunnar Myrdal, are prominently cited. His second book (Cardoso, 1962) draws on Celso Furtado, Sérgio Buarque de Holanda, Raymundo Faoro, Gilberto Freyre, Claude Lévi-Strauss, Talcott Parsons, Robert Merton, Charles Wagley, Max Weber, among others. His book on enterprenurs (Cardoso, 1964) has an extremely long list of non-Marxists as sources, including Raymond Aron, Reinhard Bendix, A. A. Berle, Peter Drucker, ECLA, Furtado, John Kenneth Galbraith, Albert Hirschman, Bert Hoselitz, Helio Jaguaribe, Clark Kerr, John Maynard

Keynes, Abba Lerner, Karl Mannheim, Parsons, Walt W. Rostow, Joseph Schumpeter, Werner Sombart, and Weber.

Some of the other dependency writers have also been eclectic. For instance, Sunkel and Paz (1970) cite frequently a host of non-Marxist economists, such as Albert Baumol, Evsey Domar, Roy Harrod, J. R. Hicks, Hirschman, Nicholas Kaldor, Keynes, Oskar Lange, Alfred Marshall, David Ricardo, Schumpeter, and Adam Smith. Jaguaribe (1973) and O'Donnell and Linck (1973) have been even more eclectic.

Strictly in terms of numbers of citations, in fact, the non-Marxist are cited more often than Marxist sources in the works of Cardoso, Sunkel, and others. But one must not put excessive weight on the *number* of citations in interpreting intellectual antecedents. For one thing, the non-Marxists are often cited as objects of criticism rather than sources of ideas. Second, and even more important, given the Marxist premises which undergird and inform the dependency perspective, non-Marxist influences are possible only up to a certain point. They can never be controlling. Assignment to the category of a "true" dependency writer turns more than anything else on the question whether one is perceived to have allowed too much of a non-Marxist mode of analysis to have entered one's writings. Cardoso and Sunkel stretch eclecticism to the outer limits of tolerance; for some Marxists, in fact, they exceed those limits. Jaguaribe and O'Donnell are even more eclectic and are even more criticized for it.

In sum, non-Marxist authors have also influenced dependency writers, many of whom are intellectual eclectics. Their eclecticism, however, while sometimes perceived as valid and useful, also creates tensions. Marxism is the base. It is inviolable. Its tenets are "commonplaces" that are "obvious." All discussion must go on within these terms. Here is Cardoso (1972, pp. 4–5, emphases added) on these matters; notice how much is taken to be obvious and commonplace:

[In assessing criticisms of dependency analyses, mainly from others in the Marxist tradition] the problem, in fact, is not, it seems to me, in knowing if dependency analyses constitute the last cry of independence of the ideology embedded in Latin American economic patriotism following the failure of attempts at autonomous national development [under capitalism]. Nor is it, to take another criticism, to know if in the final analysis *dependency is merely a*

> *consequence of the present stage of development of international capital in the monopoly phase.* Nor is it in repeating that *"the motor of history is the class struggle"* and therefore that *the only perspective adequate* for the analysis of the historical process in the dominated countries *is one that assumes the "class perspective."* *These affirmations are commonplaces,* with the virtues and the limitations of the *obvious:* they contain grains of truth which are lost in the confusion of a lack of theoretical structure [perdidos en la confusa amalgama de la inestructuración teórica].
>
> Obviously the capitalist economy is becoming increasingly internationalized; *obviously societies are divided into antagonistic classes; obviously particular cases [lo particular] are conditioned by generic factors [lo general].* Given all this, the correct question is, why can one not go beyond partial characterizations of the situation and the historical process in Latin America—"partial" used here in the Marxist sense of abstract, that is, based on partial and indeterminate relations?

It is affirmations such as these that establish the limits within which the non-Marxist influences are permissible in the works of dependency writers.

Discontinuities

Dependency ideas expressed change as well as continuity. They were reactions against ideas that were prominent in the mid-sixties. The objects of such criticism may be categorized in three groups, some of which were more heterogeneous than others: "liberal" ideas about development, "structuralist" ideas about development, and "vulgar" Marxism.

Dependency as a Critique of Liberal Ideas

Dependency writings were, in the first instance, a critique of "liberal" theories of economic, social, and political development. Simplifying greatly, it is possible to identify three clusters of such liberal theoretical perspectives that dependency writers criticized.

One cluster includes the classical, neoclassical, or orthodox theories of economic development of writers as traditional as Adam Smith and as contemporary as Walt W. Rostow, Wilbert Moore, and Clark Kerr (Cardoso and Faletto, 1979, p. 11). From the dependency perspective, such authors "justified the nonindustrialization of the [Latin American] region in view of the comparative advantages that might be obtained with agricultural production for export" (Cardoso, 1977a, p. 9). For dependency authors, this principle of comparative advantage was a damaging myth that covered up and justified the inherently exploitative nature of international (and intranational) capitalist economic relations. Whereas liberal theorists of economic development emphasized productivity and aggregate national product, dependency writers emphasized more equitable distribution among classes, regions, and sectors. Whereas the former accepted conventional, Western definitions of economic development as appropriate for Latin America and the Third World generally—definitions based on wants of individuals considered largely outside their class context—the latter insisted on definitions appropriate, in their view, to the Latin American reality. This meant definitions based on needs of individuals in classes as identified by the dependency analyst rather than mere wants.

A second target was so-called modernization theories elaborated by contemporary sociologists and political scientists mainly from the United States. These writers, many of whom were North Americans, tended to find the socioeconomic conditions of political democracy in such factors as increased industrialization, expanding middle classes or "sectors," and certain value orientations such as a "civic" political culture. Another variant of modernization theory was offered by structural-functional theorists, who specified universal functions for all social and political systems and sought to identify the ways these functions were performed in different societies.

The dependency writers challenged modernization theorists on a number of grounds. Whereas the modernization theorists tended to treat national units as autonomous, dependency authors stressed the international context of national development, underdevelopment, and distorted development. Whereas modernization theorists used European and U.S. cases as examples to be followed in Latin America, dependency writers rejected those models as inappropriate. Whereas modernization theorists expected political democracy to accompany socioeconomic modernization, dependency and "bureaucratic authoritarianism" writers came to argue the opposite, namely, that increases in modernization were associated with increasing political authoritarianism. In this respect the military coups in Brazil in 1964, Argentina in 1966, and Chile and Uruguay in 1973 were decisive events affecting the evolution of theoretical perspectives (Collier, 1979b, pp. 3–5). Among the theorists criticized by dependency and "bureaucratic authoritarianism" writers are Robert Merton, Talcott Parsons, Robert Redfield, Daniel Lerner, David McClelland, Everett Hagen, Jacques Lambert (Cardoso and Faletto, 1979, pp. viii–ix, 8–9); Robert Dahl, David Easton, Gabriel Almond, and Sidney Verba (Cardoso, 1971b, pp. 24–42); Seymour Martin Lipset, Philips Cutright, and James S. Coleman (Collier, 1979, pp. 3–4; O'Donnell, 1973, p. 4)

The classical and modernization streams of liberal thought overlapped with each other and with a third stream, namely, the ideas of policymakers in the U.S. government and elsewhere engaged in economic and technical assistance programs in Latin America. The U.S. Alliance for Progress and, to a lesser degree, the U.N. Development Decade, were examples of programs that were particular targets of the dependency writers. All three liberal clusters of thought preferred incremental change to radical change and valued freedom no less than equality. In varying ways dependency writers tended to criticize those liberal preferences.

Dependency as a Critique of ECLA Ideas

Dependency writers were not the first or the only social scientists in Latin America to challenge the principle of comparative advantage. Besides the writers in the Marxist tradition mentioned earlier, such authors as Raúl Prebisch, Celso Furtado, Aníbal Pinto, among Latin Americans, and "along with or before them" Ragnar Nurkse, Hans Singer, Gunnar Myrdal, and Albert Hirschman, had also challenged that principle in varying ways and degrees (Cardoso, 1977a, p. 9; Cardoso, 1979b, pp. 58–60). In the fifties and early sixties the most influential author in this group was Prebisch, the intellectual leader, and after 1950 the director, of the Economic Commission for Latin America (Hirschman, 1961, pp. 12–13). Prebisch argued that real world economic relations between the mainly industrial "center" and the mainly agricultural-and-extractive "periphery" (terms made famous by Prebisch) did not conform to the principles of classical or neo-classical theory. In his view a better metaphor, doctrine, principle, or theory for characterizing these relations was "unequal exchange" (Love, 1980).

Prebisch argued that center-periphery relations were asymmetric, and that orthodox liberal economic theory, most notably the principle of comparative advantage, underemphasized this asymmetry and its consequences. Prebisch contended that the gains from trade were divided unequally between center and periphery: specifically, that the terms of trade tended to move systematically against the periphery countries. In effect this meant that the center *exploited* the periphery (although Prebisch did not use that term), that development in the center and underdevelopment in the periphery had roots in the international trading system, and that development in the center and underdevelopment in the periphery were not isolated phenomena but functionally related phenomena (Hirschman, 1961, pp. 14–17; Love, 1980, p. 46).

Dependency writers both endorsed and criticized the ideas of ECLA. They agreed with most or all of the ECLA arguments just described, so far as they went. Their critique was that ECLA analysis did not go far and deep enough. ECLA had proposed a number of solutions to the problems they diagnosed. Among these were industrialization through import substitution, expanded regional economic organization (for example, Central American Common Market, Latin American Free Trade Association), more foreign aid, more "reliable" foreign investment on better terms for borrowing countries, and greater attention to government intervention and economic planning (Hirschman, 1961, pp. 14–23; Kahl, 1976, p. 137). The dependency writers argued that such proposals, when implemented, only deepened national dependency, increased socioeconomic inequalities, and fostered authoritarian politics. (Cardoso and Faletto, 1979, p. viii; Kahl, 1976, p. 137; Palma, 1978, pp. 906–909). ECLA supposed there were "obstacles" and "distortions" on the periphery which could be reduced or eliminated under capitalism (Cardoso, 1977a, p. 9), but in the dependency view this premise was a snare and a delusion. ECLA only attacked the symptoms, not the real problems.

Dependency as a Critique of "Vulgar" Marxism and Imperialism

If dependency was more than anything else a part of the Marxist tradition, and as such a critique of both liberal and ECLA ideas, it was also an effort to criticize certain features of Marxist thought and practice which dependency writers regarded as vulgar, outdated, incomplete, or faulty in some other way. The degree to which these allegedly errant features actually existed and the degree to which dependency writings eliminated them are debatable matters. Even Cardoso concedes (1977a, p. 10) that "The crust of so-called 'vulgar Marxism' . . . is so recurring that it must have something to do with Marxism itself." For the moment it is enough to note that dependency writers perceived such features in Marxist and Leninist thought and practice and believed they were making improvements in them. Let us see what those perceived features and suggested improvements were.

First, dependency writers sought to change the emphasis of Marxist theories that viewed imperialism primarily from the point of view of the center. Dependency writers wanted to look at imperialism from the periphery. This meant paying less attention to the causes of imperialism in the center and more attention to the effects of imperialism and dependency on underdevelopment, development, and distorted development and to the causes of dependency in Latin America (Cardoso, 1977a, pp. 18–19; Bodenheimer, 1971; T. dos Santos, 1980, pp. 301–302; Kahl, 1976, p. 16). In the eyes of many this is the main contribution of dependency writings.

Second, dependency writers opposed "'vulgar' . . . analyses that regarded imperialism and external economic conditioning as the substantive and omnipresent explanation of every social or ideological process that occurred" (Cardoso, 1977a, p. 12; also Kahl, 1976, pp. 16, 177). The key criticisms they made of such "vulgar" conceptions were that they ignored the internal aspects of dependency and the ways political and social aspects interacted with economic aspects in dependency relationships.

Third, dependency writers sought to revise those Marxist perspectives on imperialism which, while more sophisticated than the vulgar ones just mentioned, were still, in their eyes, out of date or simplistic or both. For instance, writing in the fifties, Paul Baran (1957; also Evans, 1979, pp. 19–24) had constructed an elegant argument purporting to show why center countries had an interest in keeping periphery countries from industrializing. The view the dependency writers sought to correct has been summarized as follows by Cardoso (1977a, p. 18):

In Latin America up to the end of the decade of the 1950s there was a deeply rooted conception that the international economic trusts were not interested in the industrialization of the periphery, since they exported finished goods there; their fundamental interest was the control and exploitation of primary agricultural and mineral products. The theory of imperialism reinforced this point of view . . . [From this point of view] the anti-imperialist struggles were at the same time struggles for industrialization. The local states and national bourgeoisie seemed to be the potential historical agents for capitalist economic development, which in turn was looked upon as a "necessary stage" by a considerable part of critical opinion.

Dependency authors did not reject this perspective entirely. After all, it was for them a view "consistent, at least in part, with what happened up to that point" (Cardoso, 1977a, p. 18). Rather they sought to revise and supplement it. They argued that important features of imperialism had changed. The "international economic trusts" were now multinationals no longer interested mainly in primary products. Industrialization was occurring on the periphery. The "local states" and the "national bourgeoisies," instead of being potential allies in struggle against imperialism, were now precisely the main components, along with foreign capital, of the "triple alliance" that constituted the newest form of imperialism in Latin America— the "new dependency" of "dependent development" (Cardoso, 1977a, pp. 12–14, 18–19; Cardoso and Faletto, 1979, pp. xxiii– xxiv, 149–176, 209–216; Evans, 1979, passim; Kahl, 177; Cardoso, 1972, p. 23).

Thus despite their criticisms of certain features of Marxist thought and practice, dependency writers did not reject Marxist thought itself. Their criticisms were directed at vulgar Marxists and outdated conceptions of imperialism from Lenin, Baran, and others. They were not directed at the basic concepts, methods, theories, and assumptions of Marxism itself.

Was There a Thunderclap? Who Was the Thunderclap?

Although the dependency perspective has roots in the Marxist tradition, it was and still is an intellectual current in its own right. It is widely perceived in those terms. Certainly it is viewed that way by the dependency writers themselves. In the next sections we discuss main themes, variations, and representative writers, and whether it is permissible to speak of "the" dependency perspective. Here we address briefly the question, who if anyone is properly said to be the founding father or fathers of the movement? Was there an historic moment of conception? Of birth? Are these matters important, and if so, why?

Dependency writers and others have been intensely concerned about the question of priority—even though at times they deny it or make light of it. For example, Cardoso has explicitly minimized the importance of the question of who wrote what when ("the question of in whose head the thunderclap was produced" [Cardoso 1977a, p. 8]). But in the same article he also repeatedly stakes a claim to his own priority: "my own book on slave society in Southern Brazil . . . [was] already published when Gunder Frank discussed his thesis on 'feudalism' and 'capitalism' . . . The draft version [of the 1967 ILPES manuscript] was distributed in Santiago in 1965 . . . Theotonio dos Santos . . . presents a similar view in the study he wrote after the discussion in Santiago of the essay written by Faletto and myself" (Cardoso 1977a, pp. 22–23, nn3–6, 8, and 13). Later Cardoso again stated flatly (1979b, p. 316) that it was he who founded the dependency school: "The first version of dependency studies in connection with development was a report that I presented at ILPES in 1965. Following this report Enzo Faletto and I published *Dependencia y Desarrollo en América Latina*, whose first complete version was circulated in 1967, at ILPES" (Instituto Latinoamericano de Planificación Económica Social).

Palma, Kahl, and the Valenzuelas endorse Cardoso's claims. Palma (1978, p. 909) makes a point of referring to "the completion in 1967 of *Dependencia y Desarrollo en América Latina*." He also follows Cardoso in arguing (p. 911) that Cardoso's work on Brazilian slavery (Cardoso and Ianni, 1960; Cardoso, 1962) "foreshadowed" his work on dependency in general and his "rejection of the stagnationist thesis" in particular. Similarly, Kahl states (1976, pp. 137–138) that "By 1967 Cardoso and Faletto had finished a document that was circulated in mimeographed form and published two years later (after some hesitancy with ECLA about its suitability) as *Dependencia y Desarrollo en America Latina*." Kahl also writes (p. 137) that "dependency was a phrase then [1964–67] gaining currency in Chile, although used by other men in somewhat different ways"; in a footnote to this statement Kahl adds (p. 189) that "Two books in English give alternative approaches to that of Cardoso but within the broad dependency framework; both authors were in Santiago in the middle 1960s: Andre Gunder Frank (1969) and Keith Griffin

(1969)." By stating that Cardoso "wrote the first paper using that term in 1965" (p. 136), stressing that Cardoso and Faletto finished their work in 1967, noting that Frank was in Santiago in the "middle 1960's," and dating the publication of Frank's book in 1969 instead of 1967, Kahl seems to invite the inference that the work by Cardoso and Faletto preceded Frank's work and that the former might have influenced the latter. Valenzuela and Valenzuela (1978, pp. 536, 553) state flatly that Frank was merely an "interpreter" of the work "of important authors in the field such as F. H. Cardoso, O. Sunkel, and T. dos Santos." Frank's interpretations, they write, were "oversimplified and often distorted views of much of the Latin American contribution," but "Because of the language 'barrier' . . . Frank is often thought to be the founder of the dependency school."

Disclaimers to the contrary notwithstanding, there is thus manifestly much concern—and conflict and confusion—among dependency writers and others about the date and the author or authors of the "thunderclap." The confusion on this point is greater still because some scholars (see Bath and James, 1976, pp. 6–10) consider such authors as Raúl Prebisch, Aníbal Pinto, and Celso Furtado to be dependency writers. If they are so classified, then they are indeed founding fathers, for they definitely wrote much earlier than Cardoso, Frank, dos Santos, Sunkel, et al. But in our classification Prebisch et al. are clearly part of the ECLA school rather than the dependency perspective. Others agree. For example, even as he praises the writings of Furtado, Pinto, and Prebisch, Cardoso (1977a, p. 9) carefully distinguishes them from his own.

As the statements noted above indicate, much of the debate over priority focuses on the question of Cardoso versus Frank. It is possible that this focus gives insufficient attention to claims for paternity that can plausibly be made on behalf of other authors such as Theotonio dos Santos, Osvaldo Sunkel, Rui Mauro Marini, and Thomas Vasconi. Several of these authors (Frank, Cardoso, dos Santos, Sunkel, perhaps others) spent most of the middle or late sixties in Santiago de Chile. They were in contact with each other there, although the role, if any, of such interaction in the evolution of their thinking about dependencia is unclear. A valuable list of citations to works written in 1966 and 1967 on dependency by authors such as dos Santos, Marini, Quijano, Sunkel, Vasconi, and others is given in T. dos Santos (1980, pp. 300–301). A semi-serious, semi-whimsical claim to "grandfatherhood" has also been staked by Albert O.

Hirschman (1978, 1980) on the basis of his book *National Power and the Structure of Foreign Trade* originally published in 1945 and republished in 1980. In that pioneering book Hirschman identified ways in which powerful countries could use trade systematically to exploit weaker units. While in some respects these views are broadly consistent with ECLA and dependencista ideas, Hirschman did not reject as fully as they did the main principles of neoclassical economics. In general Hirschman's ideas are very different from dependency ideas; he is an avuncular, constructive, and firm critic more than a doting grandfather.

What does the evidence indicate about the main claims to priority? Cardoso and Faletto's *Dependencia y Desarrollo en América Latina: Ensayo de Interpretación Sociológica* was first published in 1969. In all the fifteen printings of the Spanish edition of this book that were published from 1969 through 1979, Cardoso and Faletto say they wrote it "between 1966 and 1967" (p. 1). In the revised and expanded English edition (1979, p. vii) they say "We wrote this book . . . between 1965 and the first months of 1967." The earliest date of any publication on dependency by Cardoso or Cardoso and Faletto that I have been able to find is 1968 (in Jaguaribe et al.). My conclusion is consistent with the detailed bibliography on Cardoso in Kahl (1976, pp. 190–193). A mimeographed version of a draft of the first two chapters of the eventual book was distributed by the Instituto de Estudios Peruanos in Lima in March 1967 (Cardoso and Faletto, 1967). Cardoso (1977a, p. 22n6) and others have cited a mimeographed document by Cardoso and Faletto, with the same title as the eventual book, coming out of the Instituto Latinoamericano de Planificación Económica Social (ILPES) in Santiago in 1967. Whether this is a draft of the entire manuscript, or the same draft of the first two chapters as the one distributed in Lima, I have not been able to determine.

Gunder Frank's book *Capitalism and Underdevelopment in Latin America: Historical Studies of Chile and Brazil,* was first published in January 1967. Frank reports that he wrote his book "between 1963 and 1965" (1974, p. 89). According to Frank, Faletto read Frank's manuscript in draft and provided written comments on it which Frank incorporated into his book sometime before July 1966 (1967, pp. xv, 65–66). Cardoso and Faletto do not discuss the influence if any of Frank's book on their book and they make no mention of it or reference to it in either the Spanish, Portuguese, or English editions. Given the large impact Frank's book had in Latin America between 1967 and 1969, this is perhaps a bit surprising or at least notable.

The evidence does not support some of the claims that were noted. Cardoso continued to support "stagnationist theses" in the first chapter of his book with Faletto first published in 1969 (and again in the 1979 English edition); rejection of those theses came only in chapters 6 and 7 of their book (for details, see Chapter 4 below). Cardoso's statement that "The draft version [of the 1967 ILPES manuscript] was circulated in Santiago in 1965" is contradicted by his own statements, noted earlier, that he and Faletto wrote the book "between 1966 and 1967" (Spanish edition). Similarly, although, as noted, Cardoso claimed in 1979 that his 1965 ILPES report was "the first version of dependency studies in connection with development," he himself has pointed out that this 1965 report, entitled "El Proceso de Desarrollo en América Latina," did not use the concept of dependency and did not present a typology of dependency. As he says, "The concept of this typology [of dependency] was only produced later in my collaborative work with Enzo Faletto, 'Dependencia y Desarrollo en América Latina,' published [*sic*] by ILPES in 1967" (Cardoso, 1972, p. 9). Cardoso's statement also contradicts Kahl's contention that Cardoso wrote the first paper using the term "dependency" in 1965. No evidence supports the claim that Gunder Frank was an "interpreter" of the works of Cardoso, Sunkel, dos Santos, and others. The proposition that Frank is regarded as the founder of the dependency school only "because of the language 'barrier'" is not historically grounded.

Questions of priority are important in intellectual work. They are critical aspects of the prestige system of the social sciences (Merton, 1973; Cole and Cole, 1973). Therefore the intense concern among dependency writers and their supporters about priority should not be surprising. Moreover, in this case interest is heightened by a specific feature. The dependency perspective is widely regarded as a Latin American invention. For example, it is said to be "a Third World product" (Evans, 1979, p. 25), "a native construction" (Caporaso, 1980, p. 613), a perspective on development "not original to the United States or Western Europe but to countries of the Third World" (Portes, 1976, p. 74). It is, in short, exported, imported, and consumed as if it were a Latin American contribution to world culture. Obviously this is a point of pride with the exporters and others—and an extremely sensitive point were it to be challenged. What if its founding father were a Berlin-born citizen of Germany trained at the University of Chicago? What if this late-twentieth-century, Third World product were in fact the application and adaptation on the periphery of the mid-nineteenth-century ideas of a German writing in England mainly about Europe?

We return to these last two questions in Chapter 10. In the meantime, the following conclusions are warranted. First, Frank's book was published a full two years before Cardoso and Faletto's. Second, Frank wrote his book before Cardoso and Faletto wrote theirs. Third, Faletto saw Frank's manuscript at least six months before he and Cardoso finished their manuscript. Fourth, it is plausible, though not demonstrated, that Frank's book on dependency influenced Cardoso and Faletto's book. Fifth, it is not plausible that Cardoso and Faletto's book on dependency influenced Frank's book.

"The" Dependency Perspective?

Do dependency writers agree among themselves? The proper answer to this question is, "yes and no." "Yes," in the sense that they share a basic perspective. The agreement on the essential features of this basic perspective is remarkable. "No," in the sense that they differ among themselves, often sharply, on a number of points, in their intellectual styles, in how they elaborate the perspective, and in other ways.

First, the common ground. Can one speak of "*the* dependency perspective"? Many dependency writers and commentators have complained that other people lump dependency writers together and that this is inappropriate because in fact their views differ. Thus Cardoso (1977a, p. 8) protests that the whole idea of a dependency "school" or "perspective" is an abstraction invented by North American "consumers." Domínguez states (1978a, pp. 88–89) that "there is more variety . . . than is often recognized. The awareness of variety should avoid premature pigeonholing of scholars and scholarship—there is often confusion when scholars are lumped together at a very high level of aggregation as if they all agreed—this has happened particularly to writers on dependency." Fagen writes (1977, p. 7), "For those familiar with the literature, it hardly needs to be emphasized that many of the persons so cavalierly grouped together on the common turf of dependency bibliographies could scrcely bear to sit together in the same conference room, so profound are the differences in their several ways of knowing the current realities and possible futures of Latin America." T. dos Santos (1980, pp. 357–359) refers scathingly to "various critical works" which he says "tried to lump together as one 'theory' an entire current of ideas where there are enormous internal differences," and which involve "an incredible and dishonest garbling of texts, ideas and opinions among different authors, and thus produce a repugnant intellectual promiscuity."

The frequency and intensity of these complaints compel us to pay attention to them. But immediately we must note as well that *in every case those who make these charges themselves refer repeatedly to the dependency perspective in precisely the fashion of those against whom they lodge their criticisms.* Thus in the same article in which he says the term makes him "shudder" when others use it, Cardoso himself refers at least three times, always approvingly, to "the dependentistas": "The 'vulgar' current was predominant in [certain flawed] analyses . . . The dependentistas put the question the other way around [in a more satisfactory way]." "The dependentistas showed that a kind of industrialization was occurring under the control of the multinationals, and they drew certain conclusions from it." "I shall limit myself to one question that has served to divide the dependentistas." (Cardoso, 1977a, pp. 8, 12–13, 18, 19) In a subsequent essay, Cardoso again refers repeatedly (1979b, pp. 62, 69, 71) to "los dependentistas" without shuddering and indeed quite comfortably as a descriptive term along with "los cepalinos", "los desarrollistas," and "los teóricos del desarrollo alternativo" [followers of ECLA doctrines, developmentalists, and alternative-development theorists]. In this usage he is indistinguishable from those he criticizes. In this case, instead of defending them Cardoso attacks "los dependentistas" in precisely the fashion and for precisely the reasons others have given: their utopianism and failure to specify the paths to socialism which they propose as the only acceptable solution. In doing this, moreover, Cardoso refers to "los dependentistas" as a single group without differentiating among writers and without acknowledging either his own place in the pantheon of dependency writers or his attacks on those who referred to a single dependency school.

Having criticized "premature pigeonholing of scholars and scholarship," Domínguez (1978a) constructs a grid crossing eight "perspectives on inter-American affairs" with sixteen analytic features (autonomy of the state, time horizon, ethical utility, and so on). This produces a grid of 128 cells. Domínguez fills every cell with a notation or score (high, medium, low, short, long, and so on); there are no questionmarks, "don't know," or "insufficient information" entries in the entire 128-cell table. Domínguez also had excoriated those who allegedly lump scholars together. So he "disaggregates" by dividing dependency writers into "orthodox dependency" (Gunder Frank and others) and "unorthodox dependency" (Cardoso, others). Thus Domínguez puts Cardoso, Jaguaribe, and occasionally others like Quijano and Kaplan in the same pigeonholes on all of his sixteen features.

Having protested "cavalier" but unnamed groupings-together of persons with "profound" differences, Fagen writes (1977, pp. 7–8): "Nevertheless, for our purposes—and speaking quite abstractly—a common core to the dependency way of framing the question of underdevelopment can be detected. Risking oversimplification, I would select the following assertions (presented as descriptive hypotheses) as central to and widely shared by those working within the dependency framework." It is this statement rather than the one quoted earlier that is operative in Fagen's article.

In the same book in which he says that those who write about a single dependency perspective are "dishonest" and "promiscuous," T. dos Santos (1980, pp. 355–359) lists some forty studies that deal with "*the* theory" and "*the* theme" of dependency in ways that he thinks are appropriate.

Having condemned others for being abstract, Valenzuela and Valenzuela (1978, p. 536) divide all scholarly theoretical work on development and underdevelopment into just two categories, "modernization" and "dependency," whose properties they claim to describe and evaluate in a twenty-two page article. They treat the two perspectives "as 'ideal types,' accentuating important characteristics of each framework in a manner not found in any particular author."

The foregoing survey of complaints, and contradictions by the complainers of their own complaints, suggests two conclusions which will be strongly confirmed by evidence to be presented in subsequent chapters of this book. First, dependency writers disagree about some things but agree about others. Their disagreements occur within the framework of certain agreed-upon assumptions and affirmations. Within these assumptions and affirmations, disagreements are frequent, permissible, and often intense; challenges to the assumptions, however, are infrequent, inadmissible, and subject—as we shall see—to severe sanctions. The agreement of dependency writers on the basic features of the perspective are at least as great as, and arguably greater than, the agreement of liberal writers on the development and modernization perspectives. As with the liberal perpective, so with the dependency perspective: viewed from within, the differences among individual writers often seem great; viewed from without, they seem much smaller. As the Spanish sociologist Juan Francisco Marsal (1979, p. 219) states with respect to dependency writers, "That the most distinguished authors of a theoretical perspective should themselves deny its very existence is not so unusual; it is not the first time that the trees have been unable to see the forest they created."

Second, for commentators on dependency ideas the recurring pattern is to insist loudly that dependency authors should not be lumped together; to accuse loudly other commentators of lumping them together in an illegitimate manner; and then quietly to lump them together in their own analyses. In this recurring sequence there is manifestly more symbolic, ritualistic value in stressing differences than in stressing similarities, and that is what the commentators do. At the same time, there is manifestly also a powerful (indeed, inexorable) substantive imperative to write about the similarities in the "common dependency problematica," so the commentators do that too, but quietly.

What then are the main assumptions and affirmations of dependency writers? In other words what is the "core" that they share? And what are the principal lines of variation within that common perspective?

Common Elements of the Dependency Perspective

The Fundamental Premises: Marxism and Nationalism

At the most general level of abstraction, dependency ideas attempt to marry Marxism and nationalism. For all but a minority of dependency writers, however, Marxism is the dominant partner. This dominance has important implications. In the first place, it means that "The idea of dependency is defined in the theoretical field of the Marxist theory of capitalism. Once this is established, there is no need to deny the existence of a theoretical field of dependency itself; but this latter theoretical field is one limited by and subordinated to the Marxist theory of capitalism, into which dependency analyses are inserted" (Cardoso, 1972, p. 17; Cardoso, 1980, p. 72; Cardoso and Faletto, 1979, pp. ix–xxiv).

The order of priority also means that the basic conceptual and methodological apparatus of the dependency perspective is Marxist. This is why, for example, Cardoso and Faletto affirm (1979, pp. ix, xiii) that their "methodological approach" is one "which found its highest expression in Marx" and that "without the concept of capital as the result of exploitation of one class by another it is not possible to explain the movement of capitalist society." From Marx they derive—well or badly, for good or ill—most of their fundamental methodological, conceptual, and theoretical tools, including the notions of material forces of production as primary categories, social relations of production, dialectical reasoning, surplus value, exploitation, accumulation, subjective and objective interests, class struggle, the state as the pact of class domination, and so on. These concepts, and the overall Marxist framework of which they are a part, are the essential starting points for holistic dependency writers. It is from these concepts that they begin, and it is to them that they must always return (Cardoso, 1977a, pp. 9–12, 22; Cardoso and Faletto, 1979; Cardoso, 1962, 1964, 1970, 1971a, 1974, 1980; Palma, 1978).

As Cardoso's use of phrases such as "the critical component" and "the permanent struggle" suggests, dependency ideas, like Marxist ideas more generally, combine practical and theoretical concerns, make practice the final arbiter of truth, and mix scientific and ethical, even quasi-religious, concerns. They participate with other schools of thought and practice in the running battle of quotations and of other instruments of warfare over the central issue in the Marxist tradition: "Who is the true guardian of the heritage of Marx and its 'creative developer,' who the unfaithful heir and 'revisionist,' the heretic, the betrayer?" (Wolfe, 1965, p. xxii).

For most authors dependency ideas are Marxism on the periphery, or, more specifically, the application, adaptation, elaboration, and reformulation of Marxist perspectives in dependent, peripheral units, especially nations. A minority of authors regards nationalism as a value and analytic category on a par with or even prior to Marxist socialism and Marxist analytic categories. These are not, however, the prevailing views among dependency writers. They mostly regard such views as "vulgar" notions that deserve severe criticism and sanctions. Given the axioms of Marxism, class must always, in the long if not in the short run, be prior to and more basic than nation as an analytic category and theoretical reality. This is regarded as true by definition. It is not debatable. To be sure, since nationalism is a powerful force in peripheral countries and since in practical terms it is also a value widely honored by dependency writers, there are often tensions and conflicts in this marriage between nationalism and Marxist socialism. In terms of the theory and principles which guide most of the dependency writers, however, there is no doubt that these practical tensions and conflicts must be resolved, and usually are resolved, in terms of the priority of the Marxist class categories and values over the national categories and values.

The foregoing are points of agreement at the level of the most abstract, general premises of the holistic dependency perspective. It is composed of two main approaches: orthodox dependency and unorthodox dependency, four central features of which are substantive holism, utopianism, epistemological holism (nonfalsificationism), and the premise of politicized scholarship.

Generic Features of Holistic Dependency

The basic ideas of holistic dependency or *dependencia* may be summarized in terms of the following four features:

Substantive Holism. Substantive holism is the idea that a number of attributes—dependency, development, underdevelopment, domination, exploitation, inequality, cultural distortions, authoritarianism, "formal" but inauthentic democracy, and the like—necessarily "hang together" in countries and other units on the capitalist periphery. Nations, classes, class "fractions," groups, regions, and other units of analysis are constrained and conditioned by the international capitalist system in ways that have either created underdevelopment (the "orthodox" or "extreme" version) or brought about distorted, inappropriate development (the "unorthodox" or "moderate" version). In this view, Latin America is more constrained in its efforts to develop than were the parts of the world that developed earlier. Accordingly, theoretical frameworks inspired by the experiences of the earlier-industrialized "center" (usually meaning England, Western Europe, and the United States) have limited relevance at best for dependent units. What they need are theoretical perspectives that begin from the premise of dependency, formulate hypotheses in light of this special circumstance, and evaluate system performance and policy options accordingly. In holistic dependency, this means they need socialism.

Utopianism. The highest value in holistic dependency is Marxist socialism. But socialism is not only a value or constellation of values; even more it is a symbol and a utopian goal. Socialism is vaguely defined at best. Broad verbal formulas, nonexistent future states, or idealized versions of extant systems usually substitute for empirical analysis of socialist cases. To the extent holistic dependency authors do empirical research it is about cases of underdevelopment or distorted development, not about socialism. The result is that holistic dependency compares real-world cases of capitalism, which are flawed, to ideal-world cases of socialism, which are flawless.

Epistemological holism (nonfalsificationism). The premises and hypotheses of holistic dependency are unfalsifiable. The approach rejects in principle the idea of specifying or implying the types of situations or outcomes that would disconfirm its hypotheses. The fundamental claims of the dependency perspective may be applied to concrete cases and used to interpret data, but they can never be tested against evidence. In other words, one may use empirical data to support the dependency perspective but never to question its fundamental claims, which it postulates to be true by definition.

The premise of politicized scholarship. In the context of holistic dependency social science is not an enterprise to be distinguished from political struggle; it is an instrument in that struggle. Scholarship and politics occur in different arenas and at different levels, but they are not fundamentally separate enterprises or "vocations," as in the Weberian or classical liberal conceptions. Rather, holistic dependency, propelled by the imperatives of its Marxist assumptions, sees scholarship as an agent of struggle. Scholarship and struggle are fused. Studies are seen as true or false insofar as they help to reduce domination and exploitation as these concepts are defined in holistic dependency.

Authors vary in the degree to which they subscribe to these features. The authors we call holistic dependency writers—which includes both "orthodox" and "unorthodox" dependency as those terms are used in the literature—differ on a number of points, but they all affirm all of these four features. Holistic dependency is the core of the dependency approach; the other approaches modify or challenge this core in various ways. We turn now to these variations.

A Typology of Dependency Writers

Certainly, dependency writers differ and are said to differ about a number of questions. Do they analyze dependency only within capitalism or within both capitalism and socialism? Do they see solutions to problems of dependency exclusively in either/or terms or as questions of degree as well? Do they stress abstract theory and global laws or concrete, specific situations? Are they mechanical and deterministic or interactive and probabilistic? Do they take a rigid class approach or use a more differentiated approach involving groups and class fractions as well as classes? Do they treat the state as purely reflexive of economic interests or as having its own separate interests? Is their approach ahistorical or historical? Do they see history as closed or open-ended? Do they see solutions only under socialism or under both socialism and capitalism? Is their theoretical orientation holistic or analytical? Is their way of knowing closed and unfalsifiable or open and falsifiable? Do they see scholarship as fundamentally an aspect of political struggle or as an enterprise fundamentally separate from political struggle?

Which writers give which answers? At one level of analysis, there are as many groups of dependency authors as authors. No two writers are completely alike in the ways they see the issues and answer these questions. Every author is unique.

At the same time, however, classifications are possible, useful, and pervasive in the literature. The distinction made most often is between Andre Gunder Frank and those who share his views, and Fernando Henrique Cardoso and those who share his views. Frank is said to take the "orthodox" dependency view, Cardoso the "unorthodox" view (Domínguez, 1978a). Orthodox dependency is perceived as tending to answer the questions in the preceding paragraph in terms of the first options listed; unorthodox dependency is perceived as tending to answer the questions in terms of the second set of options listed. In the United States unorthodox dependency is usually perceived as more subtle and sophisticated than orthodox dependency. This has also been the case, though to a lesser extent, in Latin American countries. In both regions the main exception to this assessment has been among the adherents to certain strains of Marxist thought and practice that have regarded "unorthodox" dependency as excessively eclectic and revisionist (for example, Weffort, 1970; *Latin American Perspectives,* 1974; Cueva, 1976; Castaneda and Hett, 1979; also, from a different angle of vision, Wallerstein, 1974, 1980, and Chase-Dunn, 1982).

In this book we retain the labels "orthodox dependency" and "unorthodox dependency" even though they can be misleading or just plain wrong. For one thing, Frank has been criticized much more than Cardoso, especially in the United States. Marxist theorists have often treated him "like some sort of country bumpkin who has marched into the living room without removing his muddy galoshes" (Binder, 1986, p. 20). Biersteker (1987, p. 49) summed up the prevailing view: "Like everyone else, I have little positive to say about the vulgar dependentistas." In U.S. social science, harsh criticism of Frank is virtually an obligatory ritual for almost everyone, whereas criticism of Cardoso is virtually a taboo except for others working in the Marxist tradition. In this sense—which is by no means trivial—Cardoso has been far more orthodox than Frank.

Furthermore, orthodox and unorthodox dependency differ less in the basic theoretical and conceptual positions they take than in the degree of ambiguity, contradiction, and eclecticism they display in advancing those positions. Therefore in this study orthodox dependency and unorthodox dependency are treated as two expressions of an overall approach that we call holistic dependency. Most previous commentators have tended to minimize the similarities and stress the differences. Here equal attention will be given to the similarities and the differences.

A final important difference between conventional classifications and the present one is the addition of other categories to the conventional orthodox/unorthodox typology. Heretical dependency, while embracing some of holistic dependency's substantive arguments, is more cautious about its way of arriving at answers. Analytic dependency is willing to consider any of the substantive questions raised by holistic dependency but rejects its utopianism, nonfalsificationism, and politicization. Bargaining studies address a few of the external concerns of holistic dependency but say little or nothing about the internal aspects. World-systems, pure-class, and modes-of-production approaches share much with holistic dependency but criticize it, often sharply, "from the left," that is, from Marxist premises.

2 Generic Features of Holistic Dependency

The most important things to know about holistic dependency are its substantive holism, utopianism, epistemological holism, and premise of politicized scholarship.

Many dependency authors and analysts of their ideas have registered objections to the very idea of characterizing the generic features of the holistic dependency approach. One objection is that different authors say different things. This concern and the reponses to it are addressed in detail in chapters 1, 3, 4, and 5; no more need be said here. Another objection hinges on the claim that dependency writings are not theoretical but focused on the analysis of "concrete situations." This argument is also addressed in subsequent chapters, but two points should be made briefly and forcefully here. First, powerful, sweeping theoretical affirmations are pervasive in dependency writings. The claim that they do not exist or are rare in these writings is false. Second, even if such explicit theoretical affirmations did not exist (and they do), it is still impossible to write about concrete situations in a theoretical vacuum. Only "vulgar" or "barefoot" empiricists think otherwise. That being the case, what is the implicit theoretical content of the descriptions of concrete situations? The generic features analyzed in this chapter and elsewhere in this book deal with both the explicit and the implicit theoretical perspectives and assumptions of dependency writings.

A third sort of objection frequently made in this context is that it is illegitimate for scholars working within one scholarly tradition to analyze and criticize the premises and hypotheses of another scholarly tradition. According to this argument, different scholarly traditions have different languages or "scripts"; valid communication and criticism can occur within these languages or scripts but not across them (Duvall, 1978, passim; Caporaso, 1978, p. 7). From this perspective, "the only valid criticism . . . is self criticism" (Cardoso, 1980, p. 65).

This view has been very influential in the dependency debate, but it is rejected here. Precisely the opposite view is equally plausible: "Self-criticism is an art not many are qualified to practice . . . We are all in the position of King Lear, who, holding absolute authority over his kingdom, 'but slenderly knew himself'" (Oates, 1987, p. 1). A third position, to which we subscribe, is that either type of criticism may be wrong or right, but each is legitimate. The issue ought to be the substance of the criticism, not who makes it. The idea that only self-criticism is valid is a solipsism, antithetical to scholarship. It closes off scholarly debates that have been fruitful in other contexts and could be fruitful regarding dependency ideas absent this prohibition. Liberals, Marxists, statists, social democrats, rational choice theorists, and others have engaged each other in scholarly debates in many other fields. There is no valid reason such debates should not also engage dependency ideas.

Those who make the argument against outsider analyses of dependency ideas use a double standard. Virtually every dependency work begins with a critique, from an outsider perspective, of modernization and development theory. The word "theory" is routinely used to describe modernization and development writings, but is largely proscribed for application to dependency writings. Indeed, for many defenders of holistic dependency, this "counter-paradigmatic" feature with respect to modernization and development thought is a major *defining* characteristic of the dependency approach. In this effort there were no restrictions on outsider critiques because of different scripts, language communities, and so on. Nor were there many complaints that dependency authors inaccurately and unfairly generalized to the entire body of modernization and development literature without differentiating among authors, even though this happened a great deal.

Why deny to nondependency outsiders the right to enter the debate that was so willingly and freely conceded to dependencia authors as outsiders? The answers that have been given in various ways to that question reveal much about the nature of holistic dependency. Rooted in the conception of scholarship as an instrument of political struggle, those answers are acceptable, indeed imperative, within holistic dependency, but not in the present work.

In sum, the arguments against identifying and analyzing the generic features of holistic dependency are familiar but unpersuasive. In the remainder of this chapter we spell out those features. In chapters 3 through 5 we examine specific manifestations of them, as well as other approaches, and provide further documentation.

Substantive Holism

Dependency ideas represent an effort to wed Marxism and nationalism, but this marriage is volatile, unstable, contradictory. Marxists are not comfortable with national units. For them, the fundamental realities are modes of production and classes. Nations often embrace values and activities at odds with Marxist premises and affirmations.

World-systems thinkers, modes-of-production analysts, and pure-class analysts avoid these problems by eliminating nationalism as a primary category. Their solution is intellectually and politically pure, although not congruent with many empirical realities of nationalism in the world. Heretical dependency writers, on the other hand, address the issues raised by this uneasy marriage in what seems to be a balanced way: they make Marxism and nationalism equal partners. And they really stick to this solution, letting the facts about concrete trends, structures, and situations tell them how to balance the two forces. While this solves some problems, it raises others, the most notable being that it makes them vulnerable to attack from "pure" Marxists. They are seen as heretics.

Holistic dependency takes still another course. Like heretical dependency, it tries to maintain the union. But like the pure-class, modes-of-production and world-system theorists—and more so than heretical dependency authors—holistic dependency writers honor the claims of the Marxist tradition and the Marxist critiques of nationalism. They are therefore back to the inherent tensions and contradictions of the uneasy marriage. They try to live with these tensions, pretend they do not exist, and disguise them in various ways. But when this is not possible intellectually or politically, their solution is to say, in effect, that Marxism and nationalism are *not* equal partners and that Marxism is the dominant intellectual and political element. At that point they uphold class values and categories, join in the denunciations of heretical nationalism, and affirm the linkage between the scholarly enterprise and political struggle.

One of the intellectual mechanisms that facilitates this solution is substantive holism—the idea that a number of features necessarily "hang together" holistically in dependent capitalist countries (Sunkel, 1971; Stein and Stein, 1970; Sunkel and Paz, 1970; Duvall, 1978; Caporaso, 1978; Fagen, 1978a). For example, Cardoso (1977a, p. 17) says that when one speaks about "dependent capitalist development," one speaks "necessarily and simultaneously of socioeconomic exploitation, unequal distribution of income, the private appropriation of the means of income, and the subordination of some economies to others." Sunkel (1971, pp. 574, 615, emphases added) puts it this way:

> The approach taken here takes the characteristics of underdevelopment as *a set of normal features inherent in the functioning of a given system* [that is, dependent capitalism]. In other words, *the structure of the system defines the manner in which it functions, and therefore the results which it produces.* These results are well known in the case of underdeveloped countries: low income and slow growth, regional disequilibria, instability, inequality, unemployment, dependence on foreign countries, specialization in the production of raw materials and primary crops, economic, social, political, and cultural marginality, etc . . . development, underdevelopment, dependence, marginality, and spacial imbalances . . . are not only interrelated, but . . . *different manifestions of a single global process, which is simultaneously a process of transnational integration and national disintegration.*

As these statements illustrate, the specific features listed by different authors differ slightly but overlap massively. The areas of overlap—and the key ideas of substantive holism—are well summarized by Fagen (1978a, p. 291, emphases in the original):

> Dependency perspectives, if fully developed—and the larger Marxist literature from which they derive and to which they return—argue that *although peripheral capitalism may, under certain circumstances, be relatively successful in accumulating capital, it cannot solve the linked problems of national disintegration, widening socio-economic gaps, relative and even absolute poverty, and the continuing pentetration and distortion of national economies and societies.* In short, the dependency way of framing the question of development leads one to ask not only why and in what fashion the global capitalist system disadvantages the economies of the periphery in their dealings with the center, but why and in what fashion peripheral capitalism, as a system of production and distribution, makes difficult to the point of impossibility the resolution of critical economic-social problems that are everywhere evident in the less-developed world.

Notice that Fagen anchors these writings in Marxism; stresses the linked and unsolvable (as the Marxists see it) nature of the problems, both empirically and definitionally, under capitalism; and inquires "why" and "in what fashion"—but never whether and to what extent—these disadvantageous relations occur. These questions are answered a priori in the dependency approach. All of this faithfully represents the ideas of holistic dependency writers, both orthodox and unorthodox.

Because of this substantive holism, these writers conceptualize dependency exclusively in the context of capitalism (which they evaluate negatively) and autonomy exclusively in the context of socialism (which they evaluate positively). They rarely if ever write about dependency in the context of socialism or autonomy in the context of capitalism. Although nationalism drives them to pay some attention to these possibilities, Marxism warns them sternly against doing so and threatens sanctions if they do. Thus they tend either to ignore these possibilities or, as in an essay by Aníbal Quijano (1970, pp. 98–99), to reject them explicitly: "Whenever the dominant interests of societies of unequal power meet, the situation is conflictual and can, eventually, lead to dependency; but this situation by itself does not constitute dependency." The prevailing view is, in the words of Cardoso and Weffort (1970, p. 33), that dependency can only be understood "in the context of relations in the international capitalism system," and that autonomy is only truly possible under socialism.

Sometimes the systemic, functional, and causal relationships posited by dependency authors do occur. But not always. Socialism does not necessarily bring national autonomy or positive developmental consequences. Capitalism on the periphery is not necessarily negative in its consequences for development or chained to national dependency. These things may or may not occur. Concrete studies and judgments about particular cases, patterns, and trends are necessary.

However, although dependency authors frequently say that they are mainly interested in concrete situations and occasionally actually study them, in fact their concrete analyses are done in light of the substantive holism just described. This means their empirical analyses are almost all about cases of capitalist dependency. These may be instances of either "the development of underdevelopment" or of "associated-dependent development," but both are always evaluated negatively. Neither is ever seen as a positive instance of development. Always the only real solution is socialism—which is not described concretely but prescribed abstractly. Increases in the degree of dependency under capitalism are regarded as significant and are discussed frequently. But decreases in the degree of dependency under capitalism—no matter how large the decrease or how important the sector or area in which the decrease occurs—are rarely mentioned, and then only to be disparaged as insignificant or irrelevant and indicative of "national capitalism," which is evaluated negatively.

The term *dependency,* chosen by the authors themselves, implies that nondependency is autonomy. Since the authors apply the term to national units, and ostensibly seek to combine nationalism with Marxism, it is logical to conclude that autonomy means national autonomy. But it does not. Reduced to its essentials, the dependency perspective is really a massive prescription for socialism. National dependency or autonomy is a secondary concern; arguably it is not a concern at all. *Dependency* is a misnomer. Dependency writers are willing to use arguments about national dependency as long as the facts fit their preconceptions; but when the facts diverge, they readily jettison national autonomy as a pertinent criterion. As Fagen (1978, p. 300) says, "once the domestic political economy has been restructured, then a relatively wide range of international ties is compatible with accelerated development. This, of course, is what some conventional developmentalists have been arguing for a long time. What was always missing from the argument was an understanding of how profound that restructuring would have to be." Remarkably, despite all the noise and apparent concern about the need to escape dependency, autonomy is valued no more here than it was in the modernization school.

By far the most substantive important value—perhaps the only consistent one—in the dependency perspective is Marxist socialism. But the content of socialism is often extremely vague and open-ended before it comes into being; its content after that remains a matter of acrimonious dispute within the holistic dependency approach as well as outside it. This brings us to the next generic feature of holistic dependency, its utopianism.

Substantive Utopianism

The idea that the holistic dependency approach is utopian may be surprising to some observers. After all, they say, in dependency writings the effort is more critical than constructive—more an indication, from the point of view of these authors, of what is wrong with capitalist societies on the periphery and why, than of what would be correct for such societies and how to get there. The dependency approach began as, among other things, a critical perspective on earlier ideas—liberal, structuralist, vulgar Marxist—about development. Virtually every book and article using the dependency approach begins with criticism of other perspectives, and all of them are mainly concerned with critiques of capitalist patterns of development.

But this emphasis on criticism and dependency has a counterpart, namely, the implication of a situation that would be better—that is, of nondependency. But what is nondependency? How would one know it if one saw it? How feasible is it? How desirable is it? Is it an absolute value? If so, what about other values? If not, what are the proper trade-offs between nondependency and the other values? How does one think about and analyze such questions?

To say that nondependency means socialism gives a hint, a direction, but begs the question, what does socialism mean? Dependency authors use three intellectual strategies in their references to socialism. First, they simply articulate broad verbal formulas—"socialist political institutions," "institutions and processes that serve the interests of the people," and so on—without any attempt to provide specifics. This is the main practice followed in the literature (for example, Cardoso and Faletto, 1979, p. xxiv).

Second, they define socialism in terms of a political, economic, and social system that does not exist and never has existed but will (they claim) exist in some future state. There is no problem of assessing the strengths and weaknesses of such a system since it is defined in ways that allow no weaknesses, only strengths. Moreover, criticisms of the model by reference to flaws in existing systems are not admissible since no existing system is said to be an adequate representative of socialism. There is a congenial vision of economic, social, and political systems without conflict, hierarchy, or tough choices. An admirably clear, explicit, and relatively modest example of this type of specification is the following passage from Chilcote and Edelstein (1974, p. 28):

The dependency model does not measure development by per capita GNP or the indices of modernity. Economic development includes the establishment of economic sovereignty (which does not imply isolation) and a level of productivity and a pattern of distribution which adequately provide for the basic (culturally determined) needs of the entire population, generating a surplus for investment in continued national development. Social and political aspects of development are less clearly stated, but generally include equality, the elimination of alienation and the provision of meaningful work, and forms of social, economic and political organization which enable all members of society to determine the decisions which affect them.

Finally, dependency writers occasionally make reference to an existing system or systems but provide an idealized version of that system, again with more emphasis on the socioeconomic than the political. In Latin America, Cuba is the country that is cited most often in this regard. Thus Fagen (1978a, p. 299) writes in detail about "an impressive catalogue of achievements accomplished in less than two decades" in Cuba in such areas as nutrition, health care, literacy, wages, unemployment, and class relations. He then says, in a footnote: "For lack of space I am not attempting to deal with issues of democratic governance as they have arisen in the Cuban development scenario—or elsewhere for that matter . . . it is somewhat premature to pass judgment on issues of democratic governance in Cuba."

Dependency writers rely mainly on the first and second of these three intellectual strategies—vague verbal formulas or nonexisting future states—more than this third, more empirical one. When they use the third strategy they tend to idealize the empirical situation in socialist countries. The reason is not hard to find. Unlike ideal, nonexistent models, real systems—in the socialist as well as the capitalist world—have flaws. One can call attention to the negative as well as the positive features of the model. Cases that were once thought to be satisfactory may become suspect. Some dependency writers (Gilbert, 1974; Fagen, 1978a, 1978b) use the USSR as an example of a socialist country, but many seem unwilling to do this. China and Cuba are now thought to be less "safe" as examples of socialism than they once were. Other cases that became attractive as models, such as Nicaragua, also had flaws, but they were often excused on account of the short history of the system, the exigencies of external pressures, or other factors. In such cases, the idea was that it was "premature" to criticize and that the cases would be less flawed later.

Thus dependency authors may be empirical, concrete, specific— even in certain respects tough-mindedly analytical—in treating capitalist cases, but they are usually far from concrete and tough-minded with regard to their preferred alternative, socialism. It is a striking, somewhat curious situation. Earlier liberal, structuralist, and vulgar Marxist approaches to development have been challenged, and to a considerable extent supplanted, by a perspective that is profoundly critical of all that has come before. Yet this alternative perspective says very little, beyond elastic, ambiguous, and profoundly utopian general formulas, about what kind of development would be better.

The utopianism of holistic dependency is related to its nonfalsifiability, but it is not the only aspect of it, as we now see.

Epistemological Holism (Nonfalsificationism)

With rare exceptions, the premises and hypotheses of holistic dependency are unfalsifiable: they usually fail to specify or imply types of data that would disconfirm them. Instead of being rejectable, they usually exist in a form in which they can only be confirmed. This property is one of the most significant features, and problems, of the approach.

It is true that dependency writings are not alone in this in the social sciences. Ironically, the structural-functional theories against which dependency writings were, in part, a reaction, also tend to be unfalsifiable. However, the fact that a problem also exists elsewhere is hardly a reason to ignore it.

Even more important, it is not true, as dependency authors and supporters frequently maintain, that all social science approaches to development are equally resistant to falsificationist standards and practices. Many important social science approaches to the study of development issues are based on and adhere to the principles of falsificationism—from the works of Aristotle or Weber in earlier times to those of Lerner or Lipset in our own.

Nonfalsificationism, or epistemological holism, is much more than the notion that fallible humans, including scholars, have a tendency to try (unconsciously if not consciously) to "save the hypothesis." Epistemological holists not only see nonfalsification as a normal human propensity; they also reject the idea of trying to minimize its distorting effects. They affirm nonfalsificationism *as a principle* (Phillips, 1976). In practice holists cannot avoid using falsificationism some of the time, but this does not change their adherence to the principle of nonfalsificationism and to the use of the principle in practice when they need it. Falsificationists, on the other hand, are just the opposite: they try to minimize the negative effects of nonfalsificationism by trying to know if and when they are wrong. They try to specify potentially falsifying data even though—and precisely because—their normal human tendencies sometimes lead them in practice to fail to live up to their falsificationist principles.

All the different kinds of falsificationism share this principle. The two leading philosophers of falsificationism are probably Karl Popper and Imre Lakatos. It should be emphasized that *falsificationism is not positivism*, with which it is often confused. Indeed, it is very different (see Alker, 1978). Popper's critique of positivism is no less sharp than his critique of holism, Marxism, and Freudianism.

Nonfalsificationism in Holistic Dependency

Obviously, socioeconomic inequalities, political authoritarianism, and other social ills are widespread in Latin America. But what are the sources of these developmental outcomes? To what extent are they attributable to, and correctable through, alterations in *external* variables, relations, orientations, and manifestations. however these might be defined (including internal manifestations of external factors), and to what extent to and through *internal* variables, however they may be defined? This question is crucial.

Admittedly, there is room for debate about the appropriate criterion or criteria for distinguishing internal and external units and for assessing the relationships between them. However, whichever way one resolves those issues, it is essential to use some criterion or criteria, or else the entire notion of dependency as nonautonomy collapses. As Weffort (1971, p. 9) has well stated, "the incorporation of the external dimension is obligatory because otherwise it would make no sense to speak of the internal [class] relations as dependency relations." Once the need for some standard is granted, what shall that criterion be? Unless this question is addressed and answered in some unambiguous fashion, and unless the criterion is used with some consistency, the whole structure of the dependency perspective is merely a linguistic framework for describing the world that admits no possibility of rejection or alteration in light of evidence.

Several conceptual and methodological devices are used recurrently in holistic dependency to facilitate nonfalsification and "save the hypothesis." For instance, writers often rely on a version of systems analysis which is noncausal and nonrejectable. Rather than testing whether, and to what extent, the inequalities, exploitation, repression, and other evils in Latin American countries are attributable to external causes, they simply *assert* the existence of interconnections, as part of a systemic relationship between the evils and the external structures and processes. Here they explicitly reject "causal" thinking in favor of a systemic relationship of "reciprocal determinations" (Cardoso and Faletto, 1970, p. 21). At times Cardoso and Faletto (1969, p. 18; 1970, p. 22) dismiss as "ingenuous" the idea that "temporal sequence" is important in scientific explanation. This passage is important because it articulates the notable premise that a phenomenon can be explained by events occurring after the phenomenon itself. In such a view, if a class, group, or nation is exploited or underdeveloped, it is *assumed* that this "expresses" the dependency relationship.

A second nonfalsificationist device used in holistic dependency is tautology. An example is the hypothesis that Latin American class structures express dependency relations. There are ways to make this hypothesis testable, but only if it allows for the logical and empirical possibility that class structures may be products of national as well as transnational processes. If by definition they are seen as products exclusively of transnational processes, namely the dialectics of global capitalism, then they obviously only express dependency relations and the hypothesis is tautological. Another tautological formulation has been identified and criticized by O'Brien (1974, p. 14). He says that in dependency writings "one is given a circular argument: dependent countries are those which lack the capacity for autonomous growth and they lack this because their structures are dependent ones."

A third device for "saving the hypothesis" is the familiar "heads I win, tails you lose." If foreigners invest in agriculture, this promotes primary-product dependency via the argument of declining terms of trade. If they invest in industry, this is "the new structure of dependency." If the national bourgeoisie is small, that is because foreigners "debilitate" it; if the national bourgeoisie is large, it responds to external interests anyway as the internal agent of neocolonialism. If the economy in a Latin American country is labor-intensive, this is exploitation and maintains dependency; if it is capital-intensive, this is the newer form of dependency which fosters unemployment, marginalization, and increasing inequalities. And so on.

Sometimes any form or degree of external contact at all is seen as evidence of dependency; however, if there is no contact, dependency is still said to continue because it is "internalized." The analyst of foreign investments thus lumps "mixed" companies together with foreign companies rather than separately or with domestic companies on the uninvestigated premise that foreigners always control the mixed cases. Jaguaribe (1973, pp. 412–473) so interprets studies of foreign investment in Mexico and Brazil. If the overall level of foreign investment is low, then perhaps it looms larger in some fast-growing ("dynamic") sector, such as manufacturing exports, which is then said to be the vital one. In short, find sectors where foreign investment is high and then explain how they are more crucial for national autonomy than other sectors (Cardoso, 1973a, pp. 144–146; contrast Baer, Kerstenetsky, and Villela, 1973, pp. 23–24).

A variation of this technique is to drive the argument back or forward in time. If dependency is advantageous now, it will not be later—"ultimately" it benefits another nation. If a country is getting more autonomy now in certain respects, its history is one of dependence, and this history and the context it established are what matter. Thus Stein and Stein (1970, p. 198) arrive at the remarkable conclusion that "the [Latin American] area as a bloc does not constitute a structure of society, economy, and politics perceptibly transformed beyond what was present at the end of the nineteenth century."

A fourth way to save the hypothesis is to refuse to confront contrary cases. For instance, the United States, Canada, Australia, and New Zealand were colonies of a capitalist nation, Great Britain; how could they have escaped underdevelopment? How did the United States avoid becoming a dependent country? No dependency author begins to deal adequately with these questions. Most ignore them completely. Cardoso (1971b, p. 61) comes right up to them and then moves off rapidly in another direction, as if he looked briefly and was unable to bring himself to look further. Frank (1972, p. 17) loftily dismisses the question in half a compound sentence: "the institutions of the Protestant British colonies in the South of the United States and the Caribbean were not noticeably more progressive than those of Latin America." He is perhaps right about the South, but what about the North, East, and West? What about the other British colonies? And what about autonomy? Jaguaribe (1973, pp. 246–247, 381–382, 429–439) comes closest to facing the question—his general theoretical perspective would allow him to do this more readily than most other authors—but his remarks are few, scattered, and very partial.

Insofar as dependency authors offer or imply any defense for this disinclination to confront a contrary case, it is usually that dependency ideas are area-specific, without application outside the Latin American geographic region. But this argument is inconsistent with the stress on capitalism as the major independent variable or complex of variables in the dependency paradigm: capitalism is obviously not area-specific. It is also inconsistent with the claims dependency authors make that their ideas *are* universal and that it is only of secondary importance that the site in which they are elaborated empirically is Latin America (Sunkel, 1971, pp. 577, 615; O'Donnell, 1978, p. 54). The other line of defense is to switch the definition of dependency from national constraint to class inequality. However, this argument not only raises the possibility, discussed earlier, of potentially contradictory definitions; it also runs afoul of the facts, since the United States, Canada, Australia, and New Zealand have had significantly less class inequality than either Latin America or Great Britain.

A final intellectual device in holistic dependency's nonfalsificationism, one of the most important, is the idea of "the anti-nation inside the nation" and, more specifically, the concept of *interest* on which it is based.

The Concept of Interest in Holistic Dependency

The concept of interest—of groups, classes, regions, or nations, sometimes several or all of these—is a crucial one in the holistic dependency literature. It is, among other things, integral to the idea of domestic appendages of external forces within dependent countries. Every holistic dependency writer, and most heretical dependency writers as well (Galtung, 1971, 1972; Jaguaribe, 1973, pp. 381–382, 411, 536), whatever his or her views on other matters, argues that dependency is maintained not just by external actors and institutions influencing the dependent country but also by internal representatives of foreign interests. There is no exception. However much Quijano and Ianni and Jaguaribe and Sunkel and Cardoso, or Chilcote and Gunder Frank and Bodenheimer and Evans and Fagen, and others, may disagree about a number of issues, they all agree on this point. The phrase, "The anti-nation . . . inside the 'nation,' so to speak" is from Cardoso (1973c, p. 200), but the concept which the phrase embodies is used by every dependency writer. Much of the content of dependency ideas turns, therefore, on the meaning that is poured into this concept, and much of their scientific utility turns on its reliability. Therein lie some problems.

An interest is aptly defined as "a goal that an actor does or should pursue" (Van Dyke, 1962, p. 576). The goals that actors *do* pursue are perceived interests and can be studied empirically. Dependency authors reject this way to identify interests. Actors can, and often do, misperceive their interests, through "false consciousness" and in other ways. Some actors intentionally do not reveal the interests they are really pursuing. Holistic dependency authors give great weight to these facts. They are confident that they can identify the interests of other actors, however, by identifying the goals they should pursue whether they pursue them or not. They assume that they will not misjudge or misstate the interests of other actors the way the actors themselves often do.

The goals actors *should* pursue are basically of two types, following Van Dyke: normative interests and instrumental interests. The normative are defined as good for their own sake. The instrumental are means to other goals, either normative or other, higher-order instrumental interests. With respect to normative goals, different analysts see these goals differently, and scholarly tools by themselves are rarely if ever able to resolve the differences. It is possible to be more scholarly and objective and/or social-scientific in identifying instrumental interests. However, instrumental interests are always means to some goal that is normatively defined. Beyond this, in the social universe the relationship of means to ends is almost always complex, uncertain, and debatable. Not only do judgments differ; they also can change quickly, and often do.

Thus the ideas of Raúl Prebisch and ECLA about industrialization and controlled foreign capital were once seen as guides to greater autonomy in Latin America; later they were seen as precisely the forms of false consciousness that produced the "new structures of dependency." Relatively developed regions were once seen as "growth poles"; then they became exploitive agents of "internal colonialism." Politicians and intellectuals who at one point were seen as progressive and autonomy-oriented were later denounced—as fashions, ideological purity tests, generations, and other variables changed—as tools of imperialism; more recently, the very analyses, policies, and behaviors that were denounced as expressions of internal dependency have once again become permissible. Since interest is such a protean concept, changes in its concrete meaning are always possible, and the direction of the change is always uncertain. A side effect of this—what might be called the Lin Piao phenomenon—is that one never knows where the lightning will strike next: a defender of the people today is an enemy of the people tomorrow, and vice-versa.

These ambiguities in the concept of interest, defined either normatively or instrumentally, are a problem in social scientific terms. Such ambiguities are inherent in the concept. It is often said that some interests, such as physical well-being, are unambiguous or objective. These are "basic needs": food, clothing, housing. Such needs seem self-evident. But important questions remain. For example, as Sidney Hook (quoted in "Reflections," 1989–90, p. 22) has stated: "It is better to be a live jackal than a dead lion—for jackals not men. Men who have the moral courage to fight intelligently for freedom have the best prospects of avoiding the fate of both live jackals and dead lions. Survival is not the be-all and end-all of a life worthy of man. Sometimes the worst thing we can know about a man is that he survived. Those who say life is worth living at any cost have already written for themselves an epitaph of infamy, for there is no cause and no person they will not betray to stay alive." The social means to achieve basic goals are even less certain. The farther one moves from the most basic physical and biological needs (or interests) to broader economic, social, and political needs (or interests), the more ambiguous and debatable the concept becomes (for a good overall discussion see Springborg, 1981). Unfortunately, it is precisely the latter types of interests that tend to be most important for social scientists and most often identified, without much logical or empirical justification and with a great deal of arbitrariness, in the dependency literature.

Since the concept of interest is ambiguous, it also can be elastic and arbitrary. It expands and contracts to meet the needs of the moment. If the analyst agrees with the values, goals, or policies of whatever group, institution, or process is under discussion, they are said to be in the interests of socialism and the people. If the analyst does not agree, they are said to be in the interests of capitalism and the enemies of the people; they are revisionist and bourgeois; they are "the anti-nation inside the nation," the "infrastructure of dependency," and the like. The elasticity of the concept of interest limits the utility of this concept not only for those who may, inadvertently or otherwise, use it to maintain the validity of their theoretical view, but also for those who may try to employ the concept rigorously as a social-scientific instrument.

The concept of interest is useful and perhaps indispensable for normative, policy, and political purposes. For these purposes, judgments about interests have to be made, even though they are inherently risky and uncertain. For social-scientific purposes, however, the inherent ambiguity of the concept of interest is a liability. If the concepts of interest, "anti-nation inside the nation," infrastructure of dependency, and so on, are to be used in social science, their content has to be identified and justified far more concretely and systematically than it is in the literature.

Since dependency writers have a broadly common outlook, conflicts do not often arise over the use of the concept of interest in abstract discourse. However, as soon as there are specific applications, disputes are pervasive and often bitter—not only between dependency writers and their critics, but also within the ranks of dependency writers themselves. This would not be a serious problem for the approach if judgments about interests were not so central to it. But these judgments are the very foundation of what purports to be a social-scientific way of coming to grips with social realities. The dependency writers claim they can identify objective interests, but the interests they characterize as objective are in fact mainly or exclusively the subjective judgments of the dependency analysts. Thus the entire dependency edifice is based on a foundation of subjective judgments of analysts who do not, and who cannot in the nature of things, agree on what these allegedly "objective" interests are. This leads inexorably to the politicization of scholarship.

The Premise of Politicized Scholarship

Theoretical perspectives that are unfalsifiable empirically need other criteria by which to decide between truth and falsity. In the case of holistic dependency, the final criterion is political struggle, that is, power. This feature is perhaps the most important single characteristic of holistic dependency, and one of the least understood.

Holistic dependency follows the line of interpretation of Marx's thought that regards as "vulgar" the idea that theories should be shown to be true or false by empirical observation (McLellan, 1976,

p. 61; Elster, 1986, pp. 12–17). In this interpretation the real and appropriate arbiter of truth or falsity is political power. Social life is struggle between incompatible interests (Balbus, 1971, esp. pp. 170–171). Intellectual work is part of this struggle. The line between scholarship and politics is blurred or nonexistent and *ought to be.* Even the ideal—to say nothing of the reality—of a relatively independent social science, in some measure protected from social forces, is alien to these premises. So is the ideal of a community of scholars with different ideologies and conceptions of interest.

In this view social science is always an instrument, tool, or agent of one or another of the opposing interests, values, groups, classes, actors, and nations postulated by the approach (Cardoso, 1977a, pp. 15–16; Cardoso and Faletto, 1979, pp. ix–xxv; Frank, 1967, pp. vii–xv). Holistic dependency places its social science in the service of socialism. Those who do not share the basic political views and allegiances of holistic dependency are, by definition, agents of capitalism. They are not just proponents of other scholarly approaches; they are also tools for imperialist domination and capitalist exploitation. Holistic dependency provides a way not only to analyze countries and classes on the periphery but also to discredit and delegitimize alternative theories and theorists. Although in scholarly practice there may be exceptions based on other criteria, such as personal ties, the principles and logic involved are these.

The premise of politicized scholarship does not stand alone, independent of the other three major features of holistic dependency. To the contrary, all the features are intimately linked to each other. Holism obtains not only within the generic features but also in their relationships to each other. Just as substantive holism pits capitalism against socialism, and epistemological holism sets falsificationism against nonfalsificationism, so the premise of politicized scholarship divides social science into one camp for and one against domination. At their different levels each of these features is an analogue, or counterpart, of the other.

The premise of politicized scholarship is by no means simply the idea that scholars should care about current affairs, take political stands, and participate in politics. It is not just the hope that their scholarship will affect events. Nor is it merely the notion that all scholarship has political premises and implications. All these propositions are true, but none is distinctive to holistic dependency: Weberians, Popperian falsificationists, and many others also affirm them.

What is specific to holistic dependency's premise is the fusion of scholarship and politics. Whereas Weber (1958, pp. 77–156) saw scholarship and politics as partially overlapping but nevertheless fundamentally separate enterprises or vocations, in holistic dependency they are merely two facets of the same process of struggle against capitalist domination. Whereas falsificationists like Popper or Mannheim use empirical tests as devices to protect against the errors into which they know their political and cultural biases can lead them, holistic dependency authors reject the principle of falsificationism and empirical tests and rely instead on struggle and political power to provide criteria for truth. Whereas outside holistic dependency a scholarly community cutting across political and ideological lines can be a fundamental premise and commitment, within holistic dependency such a community is impossible, meaningless, or pernicious. Within holistic dependency the fundamental commitment is the political struggle. All other activities including scholarship can only be understood in terms of that commitment.

It follows from this premise and these characteristics that holistic dependency is inherently polemical. The dependency movement was "guerrilla-intellectual work," an "ambush" of conventional scholarship (P. Smith, 1983, p. 2). As the use of words such as *struggle, domination, guerrilla,* and *ambush* implies, the politics fused to scholarship in holistic dependency is a special kind. It is not the politics of negotiation, civility, mutual respect, and tolerance, but the politics of total conflict, mutual disdain, and no compromise. This nonpolitical politics is a zero-sum game: dominate or be dominated. It is war—guerrilla, struggle, ambush—by other means.

In holistic dependency, the idea of the academy as a marketplace of ideas is thus displaced by the idea of the academy as a locus of struggle. Holistic dependency establishes the boundaries of permissible debate. Arguments outside those boundaries, no matter how properly put, are illegitimate by definition, and thus are appropriate targets for vilification. Those who make such arguments are perceived and portrayed not merely as scientifically wrong but as politically regressive. This is justified by claims to justice and other political and social virtues. Always the criteria are political as well as scholarly.

It is in this light also that one needs to understand the holistic dependency view of criticism. Given the premise of politicized scholarship, critics are not regarded as fellow members of a scholarly community raising scholarly issues; they are agents of opposing forces in the historical struggle. Criticisms are perceived and treated not as scholarly points to be answered in scholarly terms but as political attacks to be answered politically. Criticisms are permissible within the perspective (that is, limited criticisms from those who accept the fundamental claims uncritically) but not from without it (that is, fundamental criticisms from those who may question the fundamental claims). The parallel to the political dictum, "Within the Revolution, anything; without the Revolution, nothing" is obvious and instructive. Although it is considered legitimate—indeed, imperative—for dependency writers to attack nondependency writings on any level (substantive, epistemological, or political), it is not considered legitimate for nondependency writers even to analyze, let alone criticize, dependency writings on any level. It is legitimate only to express agreement with them. While from nondependency premises this is a blatant, intolerable double standard, it is not a contradiction from the perspective of the dependency premises just described. Rather, within these premises it is a logical and coherent response and indeed an ethical obligation.

Double standards are in fact pervasive in holistic dependency writings, as are other polemical devices, such as the use of strawmen, ambiguous words and constructions, false opposites, and the like. Double standards flow consistently from the premise of politicized scholarship and are often used skillfully by holistic dependency authors and proponents. For example, holistic dependency defines all scholarship in terms of its place in the historical struggle; treats all criticism as by definition an hostile political act; and then condemns any criticism, no matter how nonpolemical and accurate, for being politically motivated, silently invoking the nondependency proscription against politicization which in other contexts they disdain (P. O'Brien, 1985, pp. 43–44; Petras, 1988a, 1988b). The result, consistent with the premise of politicized scholarship, is to define a situation in which potential dissenters must either remain silent or be politically vulnerable. There literally is no other possibility; any other response by definition merely confirms the original charge.

Competing claims about the relation of scholarship to justice and other virtues are not admissible, let alone weighed. Holistic dependency writers have no doubt that they can identify the "objective interests" of participants in the historical drama; but social scientists who claim only to strive for a measure of objectivity, never to attain it, are treated in this perspective not only as idealists, formalists, and "positivists" but also as agents of antipopular forces. Authoritarianism and violations of human rights are criticized only when they are present in capitalist, not socialist, systems. In analyzing capitalism, it is permissible to assess the costs but not the benefits; in analyzing socialism, it is permissible to assess the benefits but not the costs. "Contradictions" can be analyzed in capitalism but not in socialism.

The premise of politicized scholarship applies within holistic dependency and among Marxist approaches as well as from them to non-Marxists. Authors in the dependency tradition who stray from the norms, the social system, and the sacred texts of Marxism are subject to sanctions. They may be ostracized or otherwise punished. These sanctions and the networks and values they are based upon are powerful enough that they have created a dilemma for those dependency writers who have incorporated ideas from other intellectual traditions into their work. Some have drawn on Latin American non-Marxist traditions, theoretical writings of Weber, Durkheim, Dilthey, and other non-Marxist Europeans, and have experimented with North American ideas and techniques for gathering data. This kind of theoretical, conceptual, epistemological, and methodological eclecticism has been well received among non-Marxist academics but has had a very different reception in Marxist circles (Weffort, 1971; Fernández and Ocampo, 1974; Cueva, 1976; Castañeda and Hett, 1979; Cammack, 1987; Petras, 1988a; Nef, 1988). A dependency writer who becomes enamored of non-Marxist approaches has very soon to demonstrate that he has not lost his Marxist foundations. He has to answer charges of scientific error and of being an ideological and political deviationist. In holistic dependency the concept of the autonomous scholar insulated from political pressures does not exist.

Conclusion

To understand holistic dependency it is essential to pay attention not only to its substantive propositions but also to its nonfalsificationist epistemology and its premise of politicized scholarship. At the substantive level, holistic dependency raises some interesting questions. It offers suggestive insights and a number of plausible propositions. The other features of holistic dependency, however, are more problematic. The prescriptions for socialism are utopian. Although some of the propositions about capitalist dependency, taken as falsifiable hypotheses, may be true, others may not. There must be some scholarly way to decide which are which. There must be some scholarly way to choose between holistic dependency ideas and other plausible interpretations. In other words, there must be some way to test dependency ideas by scholarly criteria. But holistic dependency rejects the principle of empirical tests and the Weberian premise of a fundamental separation of the scholarly and political vocations. The resistance to falsification is worrisome; the premise of politicized scholarship is even more disturbing.

Most previous scholarly commentators on dependency writings have had a different view of these matters from the one expressed in this book. Often they have addressed only the substantive level, ignoring the other levels. Or they have attempted to justify the approach. Very frequently they have maintained that the features just described may apply to "coarse and mechanistic" dependency writings (Bennett, 1984) but not to sophisticated dependency works. Accordingly, we turn in the next chapters to a more detailed examination of concrete expressions of dependency writings, especially the most sophisticated, least coarse and mechanistic ones.

3 Unorthodox Dependency: Myths and Realities

To what extent do the general characterizations and analyses of holistic dependency fit the works of specific authors? In particular, how well do they characterize the most sophisticated writings? Many scholars argue that such analyses may fit the orthodox dependency writings, but not the more subtle unorthodox dependency works. The main reference texts of the former are the works of Andre Gunder Frank; of the latter, the works of Fernando Henrique Cardoso. Below and in Chapters 4 and 5 we address these arguments.

In studying Cardoso's work we address the dependency approach at what is regarded almost universally as its strongest point. Any appraisal of the approach that did not deal in depth with it would be judged a failure. There would be little point in focusing mainly on orthodox dependency, since nearly everyone is critical of it—perhaps excessively so. Unorthodox dependency, however, has received little criticism except from other Marxists. Particularly in the United States and Europe, Cardoso is an almost revered figure whose writings are widely praised and rarely criticized seriously. Therefore, if there are weaknesses in unorthodox dependency, they will presumably also occur in the same or greater degree in less sophisticated versions of holistic dependency thinking, whereas the same would not be said about orthodox dependency.

Here one anomaly must be noted. Although most scholars insist on the absolute necessity to focus on Cardoso's work, when (very rarely) his writings are examined in depth, many of the same scholars—especially in the United States—say that such attention is unnecessary and inappropriate. In short, for many scholars it is unacceptable not to study Cardoso's writings in depth and even more unacceptable to study them in depth. I reject this sort of contradiction. (It is, however, an important datum relevant to the discussion of the consumption of dependency ideas in the United States in Chapter 10 below.)

Cardoso has written extensively on dependency. There is much repetition and many contradictory and ambiguous statements in these writings. Therefore it is important to have a comprehensive view of his works and to compare and contrast what he says in this passage with what he says in that passage and with the weight and logic of his work as a whole. While focusing on certain key works, we also examine less well-known writings. We pay more attention to Cardoso's extensive writings in Portuguese and Spanish than most previous scholars have.

The work Cardoso wrote with the Chilean Enzo Faletto, *Dependencia y Desarrollo en América Latina* (*Dependency and Development in Latin America*) is widely regarded as the *locus classicus* of dependency writings. The original work was published in 1969. A revised and expanded version was published in 1979. The book has been frequently reprinted and translated. Of all the versions presently available none states Cardoso's approach in such a comprehensive, considered, up-to-date fashion as the 1979 English edition. The 1969 version is an ambiguous work that can easily mislead the unwary reader, especially when read in isolation from Cardoso's other writings. In the 1979 edition, the text has been greatly revised and supplemented. In addition, a lengthy new Preface (18 pp.) and Post Scriptum (39 pp.) have been added. These changes and additions repeat the ambiguities and contradictions inherent in Cardoso's approach, but they also clarify the ambiguities and resolve the inconsistencies in a way the 1969 version does not. The format—the book was published by a North American university press—suggests that the work is intended for an academic readership rather than popular consumption.

For these reasons the 1979 edition is used extensively as a source in chapters 3 and 4. All page references that have no other identification are to Cardoso and Faletto (1979). At the same time comparisons among the 1979 edition, the 1969 edition, and Cardoso's other writings in Portuguese, Spanish, and English enable us to explore the elements of continuity and change, consistency and contradiction, and clarity and ambiguity in Cardoso's approach that are essential to understand it. (A detailed comparison of the 1969 and 1979 texts appears in Packenham [1982]).

In this book I use the terms "Cardoso" and "Cardoso and Faletto" interchangeably. This follows Cardoso's own practice. Parts of his joint work with Faletto have appeared under Cardoso's name only.

For example, Cardoso's contribution to Martins (1977, pp. 205–220) is identical to pp. 199–216 of the English edition, but Faletto is not named as co-author in the Martins collection.

One crucial caution: beware the "everybody knows" syndrome. Very often the only warrant given or implied for a claim attributed to Cardoso is that "everybody knows" he made it. Many of the claims thus derived flatly contradict one another; it is logically impossible for all of them to be true. Yet many people, including many scholars, are prepared to endorse or dismiss out of hand arguments about Cardoso's work without even considering the evidence, on the grounds that everybody knows he did or did not make this or that argument. Cardoso himself often uses this technique to defend his work and attack the work of others. In this kind of situation the best course is to pay close attention to the evidence of what actually has been said and to be skeptical of claims that are not supported by citations and evidence. Therefore I have provided extensive citations to and quotations from the works of Cardoso and others. Following these principles of investigation, our study reveals a series of massive gaps between the claims made about unorthodox dependency and the writings themselves.

The Myth of Inferences from Concrete Situations

Inferences from or Applications to?

The first issue is whether Cardoso's approach is mainly to make inferences *from* concrete situations of dependency (or underdevelopment), or mainly to advance an abstract theory of dependency for application *to* concrete cases.

In 1970 Cardoso wrote an influential paper whose title in English is "'Theory of Dependency,' or Concrete Analyses of Situations of Dependency?" The paper was a reply to a critique by Weffort of his book with Faletto. Cardoso posed the question in the title rhetorically. As he wrote (1971a, p. 29), he favored "a type of analysis which recaptures the political significance of economic processes and which . . . insists on the possibility of explaining social, political, and economic processes in terms of specific, concrete situations of dependency." In the Preface to the English edition Cardoso and Faletto again state emphatically and repeatedly that their approach is not to present a "theory of dependency" but "rather" to stress diversity, specificity, and "concrete situations" as ways to understand and explain events in Latin America. They write (pp. xii–xiii, xiv, xx, xxiii):

> The basic methodological steps in dialectical analyses require an effort to specify each new situation in the search for differences and diversity . . . For our historical-structural analysis the crucial methodological question was to delineate moments of significant structural change in countries characterized by different situations of dependency . . . Dialectical methods . . . demand an attempt at concreteness with regard to the abstract forms of "capital expansion." So we must analyze the diversity of classes, fractions of classes, groups, organizations, and political and ideological movements which form, in a lively and dynamic way, the history of capitalistic expansion in Latin America . . . To avoid misinterpretations, we refer to "situations of dependency" rather than to the "category" or to the "theory" of dependency.

Almost all commentators on Cardoso's work have accepted such claims as accurate. For example, Fagen argues that the dependency literature has "low theoretical as opposed to conceptual-descriptive content" (1977, pp. 7, 25). Duvall says it is inappropriate to refer to dependency writings and their "knowledge claims" as either "theory" or even as "concepts in theory" (1978, pp. 55, 57, 68). Palma (1978, pp. 909–912) states that dependency is not a theory because theories are "formal," "mechanical," "static," "unhistorical" schemes "unable to explain the specificity of economic development and political domination in Latin America." Dependency à la Cardoso and Faletto, by contrast, is in Palma's view "a methodology adequate for the study of concrete situations of dependency, from which concrete concepts and theories can be developed and from which strategies of development can be set up in terms of specific situations of each society."

Claims such as these are pervasive in writings about unorthodox dependency and central to defenses of the approach (see also Caporaso, 1978b, p. 20; Cardoso, 1977a, pp. 12, 22; Kahl, 1976, pp. 187, 195, 201; Mamalakis, 1987, p. 205; Seers, 1981b, p. 18; Valenzuela and Valenzuela, 1978, pp. 543, 546, 551, 552). But that does not make them valid. In fact they are untenable.

In the first place, at the same time that Cardoso denies his work is theoretical, he himself also says it *is* theoretical. This contradiction could be considered merely a semantic confusion not worth mentioning if Cardoso did not constantly criticize others for saying about his work nothing different from what he himself says repeatedly. Cardoso wrote in 1977 (1977a, p. 15) that "I was always reluctant to use the expression 'theory of dependency'." This passage has been widely cited as gospel. It is manifestly inaccurate. Consider the following passage: "The idea of dependency is defined within the broader framework of the Marxist theory of capitalism. As long as one is clear about that, there is no reason to deny a theoretical field of its own for dependency analysis and no need to put quotation marks around the term theoretical. In that context it is clearly permissible to think of the theory of dependency." This sounds like exactly the kind of statement Cardoso rejects. In fact, it comes from Cardoso himself in an essay published originally in 1972 and republished in a collection essays in 1980 (Cardoso, 1972, p. 17; 1980, p. 72).

In this essay Cardoso refers repeatedly to "the theory of dependency" without putting quotation marks around the expression (Cardoso, 1980, pp. 66, 73). The original Spanish and Portuguese versions of Cardoso and Faletto (1969, pp. 161–162; 1970, p. 139) refer to "the concept of dependency as a theoretical instrument"; this passage is deleted from the English edition (p. 172). The section of the Preface of the English edition in which Cardoso and Faletto say they deal with concrete situations "rather than" the "theory" of dependency is itself entitled "Theory of Dependency and Capitalistic Development" (p. xx). In his article entitled "The Consumption of Dependency Theory [*sic*] in the United States," where Cardoso says he avoided the expression "theory of dependency," he himself uses that expression, approvingly, at least four times: "On balance, the effect of dependency theories on the sociological imagination seems to me to have been positive. Thanks to these theories . . . I do not agree with the idea that to improve the quality of analysis, the theory of dependency should be formalized . . . I do not want to endorse the ingenuous expectation that theories about dependency explain everything" (1977a, pp. 19, 21).

Moreover, most of the book by Cardoso and Faletto is powerfully shaped and informed by the most sweeping theoretical perspectives and generalizations. Most of these generalizations have no empirical base in the book at all; none has more than very thin empirical support. None of the patches of descriptive history in the book—

many more in the English edition than in the Spanish edition—even attempts to justify the sweeping theoretical generalizations.

Far from denying, as Palma (1978, pp. 909–912) asserts he does, "that there are any 'general categories' within Marxism," Cardoso (1971b, p. 18) affirms that "to get to the concrete, Marx begins precisely with the abstract." Cardoso (1974, p. 69) summarizes the main features of his book with Faletto as follows: "The dependency perspective is used as a theoretical effort to synthesize the political-economic aspects of [the] whole process [of accumulation, surplus value, developed and underdeveloped economies, and so on], showing that imperialism generates asymmetric relations between National States and that imperialist exploitation, using these national states, articulates politically the local class domination with the international domination by multinational corporations." For Cardoso (1972, p. 5, and 1980, p. 59), "The first issues are the methodological question and the theoretical question. Criticism of dependency analyses, and the interpretation of their scope, must therefore be centered on the theory and the methodology which inform it."

Within this broad overall perspective, some of the sweeping theoretical generalizations made by Cardoso and Faletto are "historical-structural," such as:

> the situation of underdevelopment came about when commercial capitalism and then industrial capitalism expanded and linked to the world market nonindustrial economies that went on to occupy different positions in the overall structure of the capitalist system . . . some [economies] produce industrial goods; others, raw material. This requires a definite structure of relations of domination . . . It is necessary to analyze how the underdeveloped economies were linked historically to the world market and how internal social groups defined the outward-directed relations implicit in underdevelopment. Dependence on the socio-political level also began historically with the expansion of the economies of the early capitalist countries. (p. 17. See also pp. 77, 81)

Like most such passages throughout the book, this one has no "historical grounding" or documentation whatsoever.

Other theoretical statements are cross-national. These are statements applied to all the countries or to some large subset of the countries in Latin America at some historical "moment." For Cardoso and Faletto a historical "moment" can refer to a few days, a

few years, or many decades, but either way their cross-national generalizations refer to several countries at that "moment" rather than
to over-time processes. Here are a few examples:

> The distinctive feature of the transition period in Latin America in
> the relations among social groups and classes was the growing
> participation of the urban middle classes and of the industrial and
> commercial bourgeoisie in the system of domination (p. 127).
> The masses were generally oriented toward participation and social
> and economic distributivism (130).
> The masses, already important in this period, were needed for the
> process of industrialization, as a labor force but also as a part of
> the consumer market . . . The industrial bourgeoisie, whether in an
> enclave economy or where production was controlled by national
> groups, typically appeared in the different countries in one of the
> following ways (132).
> Participation of the masses . . . depends on how much the public
> sector of the economy developed in the earlier phase and, above
> all, on how much control the state exercised over the modern
> monopolistic sectors (165).
> The weakness of the attempts to transform the status quo through
> mobilization of the unincorporated masses is due in part to the lack
> of structure of these masses and to their poverty and low level of
> expectations. In part it is also due to the divisions among the wage-
> earnings sectors created by the new bases of development and
> dependence (169).

There are dozens of such cross-national theoretical generalizations
in *Dependency and Development*. Most of them are, like these examples, flat, unqualified declarations. Most of them have no more
concreteness and specificity as they appear in context in the book
than they have as they appear here. They are almost never documented or even illustrated. Many of them claim to describe all of
Latin America for the particular "moment" being discussed. Cardoso
(see 1977a, p. 21) has criticized others (sometimes with justification,
often without it) for precisely these kinds of middle-range, cross-
national generalizations, even if they are documented, on the grounds
that they are "formal," "abstract," "general," wrenched-from-con-
text, and so on. Why is it permissible for Cardoso to make sweeping
generalizations without any documentation but impermissible for
others to make generalizations even if they do have documentation?

It is doubtful that the answer to this question lies within the scholarly sphere alone.

Furthermore, the very scope and structure of the book require a schematic, theoretical approach. This fundamental point has been insufficiently noted by commentators, who have followed uncritically Cardoso's concrete-situations-rather-than-theory-of-dependency claims. This short book deals with all Latin American countries since 1810. It places all of these cases into one or another of only three basic categories or "situations" of dependency. As if they were not enough, a great deal of space—in the Spanish edition, well over half the text—is taken up with lengthy theoretical, methodological, and conceptual discussions; chapters 1 and 2 and 5 through 7, plus the new preface, are all mainly schematic, conceptual, theoretical, and methodological. In the Spanish edition so also is Chapter 3. The new chapters 3 and 4 and the new Post Scriptum are all more descriptive but still necessarily brief historical sketches.

It is crucial to emphasize, however—this is the last point—that although a "mainly descriptive" approach is obviously impossible within such a structure, the emphasis on theory compared to description is not simply a function of space limitations, the needs of addressing a large topic, and other practical considerations. Nor are the theoretical emphasis and content of their work simply heuristic aids to analyses of concrete situations in different contexts, as Cardoso and Faletto (see p. xxiii) sometimes claim them to be: "Of course, analyses of situations of dependency imply theories and require the use of methodologies. But . . . we refer to 'situations of dependency' rather than to the 'category' or to the 'theory' of dependency." The theory in unorthodox dependency is not inferred from concrete historical cases; to the contrary, it is is a sweeping, universal, abstract theory which is applied to concrete cases—as Sunkel (1971, p. 577), and in his contradictory fashion Cardoso himself (1971b, p. 18; 1972, pp. 5, 13, 19), have suggested. At such times Cardoso's view is not vastly different from that of Wallerstein (1979, p. 6) when he wrote that "to be historically specific is not to fail to be analytically universal." Case materials and other data are used to illustrate the sweeping theoretical propositions Cardoso works with, not to generate or test them. If his approach is a "methodology for the analysis of concrete situations," then that methodology and the concepts and epistemology embedded in it are also profoundly, sweepingly, and rigidly theoretical.

The Meanings of "Situation"

The use by Cardoso and Faletto of terms such as "situation," "concrete," and "specificity" creates an impression which is extremely misleading. Consider "situation." The authors write (pp. xii–xiii) that "The basic methodological steps in dialectical analyses require an effort to specify each new situation in the search for differences and diversity, and to relate them to the old forms of dependency, stressing, when necessary, even its contradictory aspects and effects." Do they implement such claims? What does "situation" mean for them?

Cardoso and Faletto use the term "situation" in at least three quite different senses in their book. First, they use it to refer to three fundamental analytical and historical categories that organize the entire book. These three "basic situations" are "enclave" dependency, "nationally-controlled" dependency, and the "new dependency" of "internationally-dynamized" and "internationally-controlled" production for the internal market (see esp. pp. xvii–xx). According to Cardoso and Faletto, the most important features of the histories of every country in Latin America from 1810 to 1979 fit into one of these three categories. Accordingly, they cover the first two "basic situations" in fifteen pages in the Spanish edition (1969, pp. 39–53), thirteen pages in the Portuguese edition (1970, pp. 39–51), and forty-five pages in the "expanded and emended" English edition (pp. 29–73). They cover the "new situation" of dependency in thirty-one pages in the Spanish edition (1969, pp. 130–160), twenty-five pages in the Portuguese edition (1970, pp. 114–138), and sixty-two pages in the expanded English edition (pp. 149–171, 177–216). (In all the editions, chapters 4 and 5 are about the "moment of transition" from the first two "basic situations" to the "new dependency.")

These few pages are the complete basis for the claim by Cardoso and Faletto (p. xxii) that "Characterization of contemporary forms of dependent development could be perhaps the most significant contribution by 'dependentistas' to the theory of capitalist societies. If there is any novelty in this essay, it consists, together with the characterization of past forms of dependency, in the attempt to delineate what has been called 'the new dependency.'" These pages are also the complete basis for their claims (p. 173) that "We stress the specificity of installations of capitalist production in dependent societies . . . it is necessary to determine the way in which state, class,

and production are related in each basic situation of dependence . . .
In one case, we point to the specificity of the enclave economies; in
the other, to national control of the export system." Notwithstanding
these claims, there is little concreteness or specificity when "situation"
is used in these ways and when Cardoso and Faletto write (p. 17)
that "the situation of underdevelopment [*sic*] came about when commercial capitalism and then industrial capitalism expanded and
linked to the world market nonindustrial economies that went on to
occupy different positions in the overall structure of the capitalist
system."

The second meaning of "situation" is a series of elaborate complexes of abstract variables which Cardoso and Faletto say are inte-
grally related to the three basic situations of dependency and will be
used to carry on their concrete analyses, but which in fact bear no
logical relation to the situations and little relation to the few patches
of concrete analysis that appear now and then in the book. Thus a
passage (p. xx) that follows immediately upon their identification of
the three "basic situations" of dependency continues: "So, the forms
adopted by dependency may vary considerably. This variation in form
is expressed in the socio-political context through the size and type
of the working class as well as of the bourgeoisie, the size and type
of 'middle class,' the weight of bureaucracies, the role of the armies,
forms of state, the ideologies underlying social movements, and so
forth."

In this passage Cardoso and Faletto attempt to link the discussion
immediately preceding, about the three basic situations, to the idea
that "the forms of dependency may vary considerably." But this is a
non sequitur: obviously, in a typology of only the three basic situations to characterize all of Latin America since 1810, room for
variation barely exists. Cardoso and Faletto assert a logical connection between the three "basic situations" and the long string of
variables (like "size and type of working class") which allegedly
"express" a "considerable variation" in the forms of dependency.
But the three situations are based on completely different criteria
from the string of variables, and there is no indication nor any a
priori reason why the variables should flow logically from the situations. Moreover, the gap between these variables, which they say
they use to analyze concrete situations, and their actual "analysis"
of those concrete situations, is Grand Canyonesque, as we shall see
in a moment.

But before describing that gap, it is crucial to note that even if they *were* to use these lists of variables to analyze concrete cases, as they claim to do but do not, their statement still poses a major contradiction and unanswered question. It clashes head-on with Cardoso's claim (1977a, p. 16) that "in the struggle that takes place among the components of a structure there are no 'dimensions' of 'variables' at stake, but tensions between interests, values, appropriations of nature and society, all of which are unequal and in opposition." What are "size and type of the working class as well as of the bourgeoisie, the size and type of 'middle class,' the weight of bureaucracies," and so on, if not "dimensions of variables"? Cardoso and Faletto insist (p. xii) that the identification of abstract dimensions and variables is a senseless procedure in which "the very basic characteristic of dependency studies—the emphasis on global analysis—disappears." If that is so, then how can they provide these lists of variables and dimensions as guides to concrete analyses?

As a third variant, the term "situation" also refers to descriptive historical sketches, usually quite brief, of major patterns and trends of events in single countries or clusters of countries. When Cardoso and Faletto use "situation" in this sense they stress the distinctive, unrepeatable, noncomparable qualities of each country and each historical moment. Each situation is unique. When writing in this fashion, they deny or come close to denying the utility or validity of any comparative or analytic statements whatsoever. In these passages the lists of variables the authors say are essential to guide their concrete analyses are sometimes used, sometimes ignored, while other categories and explanatory factors enter and exit in ad hoc, unsystematic ways, like strollers in a park on a pleasant summer day.

In their historical sketches Cardoso and Faletto come closer than anywhere else in their work to living up to their claims about dealing with concrete situations. However, to the extent that they do this, their empirical work is either entirely cut off from the theoretical and conceptual methodology which they say guides their analysis of concrete situations, or it is interpreted strictly in terms of the theory and used to illustrate the theory. In the former case (for instance, Chapter 3 of their book) the sketches of concrete cases sit like undigested lumps within the capacious boundaries of the three "basic situations," with no reciprocity between theory and cases. In the latter case (as in the Post-Scriptum) the concrete cases may be spelled out in some detail, but they are always interpreted in terms of the sweeping theoretical generalizations that inform the entire study. In neither case are the analyses of concrete cases allowed to affect the main arguments they make.

Summing up, then, the operative meaning of their statement that "The basic methodological steps in dialectical analyses require an effort to specify each new situation in the search for differences and diversity" appears to be the following: first, the three "basic situations of dependency" that characterize all of Latin American history since 1810 (enclave dependency, nationally controlled dependency, and the new dependency of internationally dynamized and controlled production for the internal market); second, a series of sketches of main events and trends in various countries whose histories are, within the bounds of the three "basic situations" (*and* within the fundamental theoretical position which informs the book) utterly unique, distinctive, and noncomparable; and third, a series of complexes of abstract variables that are not related systematically either to the three basic situations or to the historical materials. The historical materials do not significantly affect the main theoretical position of the book; at most they illustrate it. What *really* matters for the main substantive arguments in the book are neither the concrete materials, nor the three basic situations, nor the complexes of variables, but rather the theoretical position from which they start and to which they always return.

We shall say more presently about the nature of this theoretical position. Before that, however, there is one other extremely important feature—the fifth—of Cardoso and Faletto's approach to the question of concrete situations and theory that must be mentioned here. Consider the following passages (p. 165, emphases added): "Participation of the masses, especially in the economy, depends on [various factors] . . . . In a country *like Mexico* [certain things happen] . . . . On the other hand, in countries *like Argentina and Brazil,* [the patterns are different] . . . ." A country "like Mexico"? Countries "like Argentina and Brazil"? In the name of concrete situations, how many countries "like Mexico" are there in Latin America—or anywhere else in the world—especially after one eliminates countries "like Argentina and Brazil" because they also represent a different "model" of dependent country? The passage quoted is no slip of the pen; we are also told about countries "like Chile" and "like Mexico and Venezuela" and "industrialized countries of Latin America like Mexico and Brazil" (pp. 124, 125, and 163). Nor did Cardoso and Faletto change their minds after ten years; the 1979 Post Scriptum refers to "countries like Brazil, Chile, Colombia, Peru, Mexico, and Venezuela" (p. 203). Indeed, most of the lengthy Post Scriptum, and much of the rest of Cardoso's writing on dependency, are written precisely in these terms.

Thus his many disclaimers to the contrary notwithstanding, Cardoso makes pervasive use of specific, concrete cases as abstract models in precisely the fashion he says he deplores and condemns when others do it. The statement that concludes Cardoso and Faletto's text—"We do not try to place theoretical limits on the probable course of future events" (p. 176)—is false. It is flatly contradicted not only by innumerable explicit statements, such as that "this interpretation proposes that there are necessary structural limitations on a nationally controlled industrial development within which the various social forces operate . . . Within the framework of the structural possibilities engendered by earlier social practices, certain courses are indicated and other alternatives are excluded" (p. 154), but also by the structure and argument of the book as a whole, and indeed the entire corpus of Cardoso's dependency writings.

The idea that unorthodox dependency is inductive, concrete, and specific—rather than deductive, theoretical, and universal—is a myth. Let us now examine another myth—this one about "historical-structural analysis."

The Myth of Historical-Structural Analysis

Cardoso frequently affirms that his analysis is "historical-structural" (see pp. ix–xx). Such analysis is supposed to "illuminate the basic trends through which capital expansion occurs and finds its limits as a socio-political process" (xx). It is also supposed to enable "general platitudes and reaffirmations about the role of capitalist modes of production [to] turn into a lively knowledge of real processes" (xviii). Finally, and most importantly, it is supposed to show how the structural features of earlier situations of dependency limit and shape subsequent situations (pp. xiii, 173–174).

Of the three claims, the first and second are met minimally with the schematic and selective historical materials presented in chapters 3 through 6 of their book. In meeting those two claims Cardoso engages in a one-sided analysis of change; what he calls "general platitudes and reaffirmations" are sweeping Marxist theoretical generalizations that are in fact very debatable. Within the dependency perspective, based on Marxism, they may be platitudes; seen in a broader context, they are far from platitudinous.

The third claim is not met at all. There is a huge gap between the claim to provide "historical-structural" explanations and the ahistorical quality of the analyses actually given. Cardoso's analysis is structural—in the sense of a theoretical perspective based on classes and interests—but not historical. He includes historical facts but not historical explanation. Although Cardoso claims to use history to explain events, his explanations ignore both the history that he himself has presented and other historical explanations; his actual explanations are in terms of abstract, ahistorical, theoretical constructs.

Consider the evidence. In the 1979 edition Cardoso and Faletto state in Chapter 3 (p. 30, emphasis added) that "the present [meaning late twentieth-century] situations of dependency *cannot be understood* without an analysis, however brief, of the historical situations [in the nineteenth and early twentieth centuries] that explain how Latin American nations fit into the world system of power and the periphery of the international economy." They then present material on "concrete historical situations" between 1810 and the early twentieth century (pp. 30–66). In the 1969 version of their book, however, the authors *also* claimed to understand the present situations; yet the original edition contains *none* of the concrete analyses of "historical situations" that are presented for the first time on pp. 30–66 of the 1979 edition. To the contrary, this new material, which they say is essential to understand the present situations, in fact draws heavily on sources that became available only after they formulated their original arguments and indeed after their book was originally published. Manifestly, then, their analysis of the new dependent situations in the twentieth century is not founded, as they claim, on analyses of "historical situations."

The new material thus provides some belated, though still very slight, measure of support for the repeated claims of Cardoso and Faletto that they place great stress on concreteness and specificity; but it has no substantive effect. Even if the authors already had some of the concrete material presented on pp. 30–66 of the 1979 edition when they wrote the 1969 version, but simply did not report it at that time, it still could not be said that they show, as they claim to show, how the "enclave" and "nationally-controlled" situations "limited" and "controlled" the new situations.

In Chapter 4 the authors make a limited effort actually to use the concepts of "enclave" economy and nationally-controlled economy to analyze concrete cases. When they do this, however, they report as many cases disconfirming their classifications as confirming them, even though they themselves take no notice of such disconfirmation. For example, Cardoso and Faletto write as follows (pp. 124–125): "Because of the weakness of their bourgeois sector, countries dominated by an enclave economy had a rudimentary domestic market. Within the range of possible variants in this type of economy, there were only two cases of policies concerned with expansion of such a market, that is, with industrialization. The first case included countries like Chile . . . . The second case included countries like Mexico and Venezuela" This says, first, that a "rudimentary domestic market" is a characteristic of an enclave economy. Then it says there were two types of exceptions to this, and lists three countries (Chile, Mexico, and Venezuela) as examples of the exceptions. Recall, however, that there were only six examples of the enclave economy to start with—Mexico, Bolivia, Venezuela, Chile, Peru, and Central America. Thus there are as many cases of the exceptions to the general pattern as cases of the general pattern itself.

Throughout their chapters 1 through 3 and part of 4, Chile was classified and analyzed as an enclave economy. In Chapter 4, however, the reader is suddenly told that "In Chile, control of the state and therefore of the profits generated by the enclave was in the hands of the local oligarchy and of a [local] mercantile-financial bourgeoisie" (p. 112), and again, that in Chile "the external sector imposed itself where there already existed an important [local] mercantile-financial sector and therefore a middle class capable of creating the national bases for economic expansion" (p. 125). If the local oligarchy and bourgeoisie "controlled" the profits of the enclave, and if there was "a middle class capable of creating the national bases for economic expansion," then how can Chile be called an enclave in the first place?

Cardoso and Faletto write that in countries "like" Mexico and Venezuela "by revolution [*sic*] the middle sectors entered the state apparatus and used it to create a national economy. In all cases the domestic economy developed through pressure from middle groups allied with the existing bourgeois capitalist sector, or with the worker peasant sector, or with both" (p. 125). These cases are clearly not enclaves at all as the term was originally defined (pp. xviii–xx, 69–73) or for that matter by any definition one can think of. Indeed, in another essay Cardoso (1973b, p. 9) himself classifies Chile, right along with the standard cases Argentina, Brazil, Uruguay and Colombia, as a nationally controlled economy, and the source he gives for this classification is his book with Faletto! He is not deterred in this by the fact that throughout most of chapters 1 through 4 of Cardoso and Faletto, Chile is classified with Mexico, Bolivia, Venezuela, Peru, and Central American countries as *the* enclave economies in contrast to Argentina, Brazil, Uruguay and Colombia, which are classified as *the* nationally controlled economies.

Despite these problems, in Chapter 4 there is an effort to work with the concepts of enclave and nationally controlled economies, as the authors promise. After Chapter 4, there is no longer even an effort. Chapter 5 begins with a number of sweeping cross-national generalizations to all of Latin America (pp. 127–133) in which the enclave/nationally-controlled distinction is irrelevant. At times the authors are explicit about this: "The industrial bourgeoisie, whether in an enclave economy or where production was controlled by the national groups, typically appeared in the different countries in one of the following ways: [they list the three ways] . . . . In all cases, the problem of industrialization consisted in knowing which groups could take investment and market decisions and channel investment into the domestic market" (p. 132). After describing the third way Cardoso and Faletto do add (p. 132) the sentence, "This case appeared more often in the enclave situation." They do not elaborate. This is the only hint among all the cross-national generalizations on pp. 127–133 that the enclave/nationally controlled distinction still has any significance.

In the remainder of their Chapter 5 (pp. 133–148), the authors describe four countries (Argentina, Brazil, Mexico, Chile) in order to illustrate these generalizations. The overwhelming emphasis of the chapter is on the *similarities* among the cases. It is true that, once they have presented their generalizations, the authors first describe Argentina and Brazil, which earlier were said to be economies of the nationally controlled type, and then they describe Mexico and Chile, which earlier were said to be economies of the enclave type. But these are organizational, presentational devices. The authors do not use these cases to illustrate the analytic types. In this chapter the enclave/nationally controlled distinction is not used analytically. The differences between the two cases *within* each category are just as great as the differences between cases in different categories. There is no indication that in the "phase of consolidating the domestic market" it matters at all whether the previous pattern was one of a nationally controlled economy or an enclave economy. There is no effort to make such a demonstration. Therefore there is no reason to believe that the previous discussion of these two categories, which the authors say is crucial to their historical-structural analysis, is in any meaningful way a necessary background to the discussion in their Chapter 5.

But it is in the final chapters of the book—chapters 6 and 7 and the new Post Scriptum—that one sees most clearly the hollowness of the claims of "historical-structural analysis." These chapters deal with the topics for which their work is best known—the "new situation of dependency" based upon the "dynamism" and "control" of multinational corporations which produce increasingly for an internal market. In these chapters the earlier historical-structural situations and categories disappear completely. The authors make no attempt to demonstrate that they are relevant. Indeed, *they do not even mention them.* The supposedly crucial historical-structural categories for differentiating and explaining cases—enclave and nationally controlled economies—are quietly abandoned.

In Chapter 6, the main distinction is entirely new; it is that between "industrial-periphery economies" and "agro-export economies" (p. 159). These categories are not dissimilar to the categories used in earlier theories of modernization and development that Cardoso says he rejects. These terms are not defined precisely. The main examples of "industrial-periphery economies" are the three largest, most populous, most industrialized, and in some ways most "modern" and "developed" Latin American countries—Argentina, Brazil, *and Mexico.* Earlier these countries had been treated as analytically distinct. Argentina and Brazil were examples of nationally controlled economies (and also, as we saw, of economic "failure"); Mexico was an example of an enclave economy (and the one example of economic "success"). Now they are treated as analytically similar cases of "industrial-periphery economies" in contradistinction to "agro-export economies," and also as the major cases to illustrate the idea that dependency and development are not contradictory. What other countries fit into the "industrial-periphery economies" category, and which countries belong in the "agro-export economies" category, are questions that are not answered in chapters 6 and 7. The authors give few specific, concrete examples of the second type.

In the Post Scriptum, none of the supposedly essential historical-structural categories is used or even mentioned. The Post Scriptum deals with changes in the international order and in Latin America during the preceding decade. On the one hand, the Post Scriptum is the most detailed discussion of specific situations in the entire book. On the other hand, it interprets all of these specific situations in terms of a holistic, universalistic, Marxist theoretical perspective. Within that perspective the authors make a number of middle-range generalizations and generate various middle-range typologies, but there is no indication that in any of these formulations the enclave and nationally controlled categories and histories have any relevance whatever. For instance, the authors write that "In countries like Brazil, Chile, Colombia, Peru, Mexico, and Venezuela, the public sector" plays a certain role (p. 203). This middle-range generalization mixes together cases that were enclave and nationally controlled economies, and possibly also "agro-export" as well as "industrial-periphery" economies, but no attempt is made to relate the new categories to any of the old ones. The same is true for the distinction made now (p. 211) between "the Brazilian or Peruvian military-bureaucratic-authoritarian model" on the one hand and the cases of Venezuela, Colombia, and Argentina, on the other. *The old distinctions are irrelevant to the new ones, and there is no indication how the new analyses flow in any sense from the old analysis, or why they could not stand (or fall) completely alone, without any reference to the earlier discussion.*

Cardoso might argue at this point that these changes in categories are simply illustrations of his stress on change and the ways in which some things are transformed into others. He might argue, in other words, that this is simply his "dialectical," "change-oriented" methodology at work. Such an argument, however, suffers from the following very serious weaknesses.

First, it does not address Cardoso's own claims (pp. xii–xiii) that in his "historical-structural" analysis "the basic methodological steps . . . require an effort to specify each new situation . . . and to relate them to the old forms of dependency." Nor does it address his claims (p. 174) to describe "the form and effects of [the new] type of dependence on classes and the state with reference to past situations" or to "show how the different structural possibilities of an enclave situation and of a situation in which the export system is nationally controlled affect the social, political, and economic changes that take place in the countries under consideration."

Second, if this is Cardoso's response, it means that historical-structural "analysis," when it is not merely a slogan, is really just descriptive history for its own sake. It also means that there is no historical continuity in the approach. All is change. The old forms and situations do not influence the new ones; they change into something completely different. If this is his defense against the legitimate charge that he does not show how the old forms and situations of dependency influence the new ones, then there would have to be predictive power in the assertions about change. Otherwise his approach would have no utility—not even theoretical utility, to say nothing of the practical utility he claims for it. Otherwise Cardoso would not be offering a dynamic theory of change; he would merely be pinning labels on past processes now completely irrelevant. In other words, if Cardoso wishes to argue that he focuses on change rather than on continuity, then he needs to show that he really does have the capacity to deal with change, not merely to describe it and attach labels to it after it happens.

Cardoso also makes a number of other claims which he does not carry out, and which in fact are often precisely contrary to the approach he actually uses. Thus he says that essential features of his methodology are that it is dialectical and change-oriented; that it proposes ("pinpoints") alternatives; and that it is able to predict events.

The Myth of Change-Oriented and Dialectical Analysis

Cardoso states repeatedly that his approach is fundamentally change-oriented and dialectical (pp. ix–x, xiv; Cardoso 1971a, pp. 30, 36, 44; Cardoso 1977a, pp. 14–17, 21; Kahl 1976, p. 180). What does this claim mean?

Throughout Cardoso's writings there are two and only two fundamental kinds of change. One is the transformation to socialism; the other is the transformation from one to another kind, type, situation, form, or moment of dependency. These are, for Cardoso, the only two fundamental kinds of change that have occurred in Latin America or that he conceptualizes for the future. Other changes he describes he immediately dismisses as superficial, illusory, or otherwise irrelevant (see pp. 199–200). Cardoso's scant treatment of what socialism is and how to get there is discussed in other parts of this book. Here let us focus on the other kind of change he says he cares about.

Cardoso's concern is, almost exclusively, to theorize about, delineate categories for, and—to a limited degree—describe and analyze dependent situations under capitalism. In that context he devotes a certain amount of attention to change processes, but they are by no means his only emphasis; he also devotes a great deal of space to the description of static phenomena. To the degree he does focus on change, his analysis is strangely limited. Describing his method (1977a, p. 16, emphases in original) Cardoso says that "what interests me is pointing out contradictions and formulating relationships in which *the same* thing is transformed into *the other* by means of a process which takes place in time and which brings certain classes or fragments of classes into relation with others through struggle and opposes them to rival blocs—for example, how one and *the same* 'national' bourgeoisie is internationalized into *something else*, or how 'public servants' are transformed into the 'state bourgeoisie' by redefining the allied and enemy camps." The examples Cardoso uses are instructive. A "national" bourgeoisie (in quotation marks) becomes an internationalized bourgeoisie (without quotation marks); "public servants" become "the state bourgeoisie." Neither here nor elsewhere, however, does Cardoso ever refer to an "internationalized" bourgeoisie becoming *national,* or to a "state bourgeoisie" becoming *public servants* (or even "public servants").

What is notable is that Cardoso's analyses of "change" are focused almost exclusively on new forms of dependency, domination, and exploitation. Cardoso states (1977a, p. 14; also Kahl, pp. 180–81) that "dialectical analysis should above all be analysis of contradictions, of the reproduction of forms of domination, and, at the same time, of the transformation and expansion of a given economic form or type of society." He says much about the "reproduction" and "expansion" of domination under capitalism but very little about changes ("transformations") away from dependency and its alleged concomitants. This brings us to Cardoso's claim to use a dialectical approach. Again the question is, does he really use it or merely say he uses it?

Contradictions abound in Cardoso's writings. But these are inconsistencies in his writings, not analyses of social contradictions in the sense of opportunities for change and improvement. Cardoso claims that the contradictions in his writings are part of a dialectical approach, but this claim is also open to the most serious question.

In a genuinely dialectical approach, there is a tension between thesis and antithesis which is identified, addressed, and resolved creatively in terms of a new thesis or synthesis. This is not at all what happens in Cardoso's writings. Far from identifying and addressing the tensions, Cardoso tends to obscure them. To the extent tensions are obscured and avoided in this fashion, creative resolution in terms of a new thesis or synthesis cannot and does not occur. The contradictions simply persist unidentified, unattended, and unresolved. This is the main pattern in Cardoso's work. It can be extremely useful to win support for whatever view he is arguing at the time; Cardoso has used it brilliantly in that way. But it has little to do with a genuinely dialectical approach.

In those instances where Cardoso does identify such tensions or inconsistencies, there is no resolution in terms of a creative synthesis; rather, he does one of two things. One response is to state that the world is contradictory; therefore analytic contradictions are to be expected; therefore there is no need—and he makes no effort—to resolve or even to address the contradiction. A good example of this is the following passage (Cardoso, 1972, p. 12), a polemic against Marxist critics: "There will not be any lack, of course, of frantic and superficial critics complaining that 'there's a contradiction' between the (general) idea of dependency and the result one reaches in analyzing dependency in the monopoly and international phase of capitalism. How shocking! Poor dialecticians who are afraid of the dialectic! They have no imagination. They think that concepts are 'immutable truths,' ever-present essences, and therefore they do not perceive that concepts have a movement, an history, a limited theoretical-practical reach."

That is all he has to say about the contradiction. In such a passage, as elsewhere (see Cardoso, 1977a, pp. 15, 21), Cardoso assumes that social scientists who are concerned about inconsistencies and ambiguities in scholarship are necessarily oblivious or disdainful of inconsistencies and ambiguities in social processes. In fact, this assumption does not follow logically; in fact, it is false. It is possible to have a rich appreciation of social contradictions and ambiguities while simultaneously believing that clarity, consistency, and orderly thinking can be useful ways to grasp a part of social reality and that obscurantism and contradiction can be obstacles to that end.

When he says that some representations are oversimplified, Cardoso implies that other representations—more contradictory and ambiguous—might not be. Indeed, Cardoso often conveys the idea that by being ambiguous, contradictory, and obscure one can "keep up" with complex reality better than by being clear and consistent. But again, this is not so. *All* representations are simplifications—including dialectical ones. No analyst can "keep up" with all the contradictions, ambiguities, and complexities of the world. Not even novelists or poets can do that. Nor is that a valid test of their value. The insights of the ablest poet, novelist, or social scientist are valid insofar as they capture some important piece of reality, imperfectly, not because they capture it all. No one ever has captured it all, and no one ever will.

A second response is simply to assert the primacy of one rather than the other side of the contradiction. When this happens, there is no dynamic confrontation between the two parts of the contradiction and no creative resolution in terms of a fresh synthesis. There is simply a backing off one part of the contradiction and a reaffirmation of the other part. Examples of this type of response are given in the first section of Chapter 4 below.

In failing to deal adequately with contradictions, Cardoso seems to be following Hegel and Marx where they are least coherent: "Hegel apparently believed, at least some of the time, that our views about the world have to be contradictory because the world itself contains contradictions. This view is hardly intelligible . . . Sometimes [Marx] seems to espouse the doctrine of [Hegel's] *Logic,* that the world is contradictory in the sense that two mutually inconsistent statements can both be true. This view, frankly, is nonsense" (Elster, 1986, pp. 34, 194). Unfortunately, these are Cardoso's main ways of dealing with contradictions. They are very far indeed from the genuinely dialectical analysis Marx himself sometimes used to illuminate contradictions and paradoxes in capitalism (see Elster, 1986, p. 194).

The Myth of Alternatives to Dependency

Especially in his later dependency writings, Cardoso insists that a basic feature of his approach is the identification of alternatives to dependency and ways to achieve them. Thus in the 1979 edition Cardoso and Faletto say how important it is "to identify the structural possibilities for change, pin-pointing the alternatives to dependency existing at any given historical moment. In other words, our approach should bring to the forefront both aspects of social structures: the mechanisms of self-perpetuation and the possibilities for change" (pp. x–xi; also see pp. xiii, xiv, xvi, xviii, xix, 171). Cardoso (1977a, pp. 17, 18) states that "when speaking of 'dependent capitalist development,'" one "necessarily" explores not only the existing features but also "the conditions under which this order of affairs is negated." In such an approach, he says, the following question is fundamental: "Does the theoretical representation of the dynamic of [the] process proposed by dependency studies permit us to comprehend the forms of capitalist expansion on the periphery and realistically to make out the alternatives to it?"

As the preceding statement suggests, Cardoso also maintains that the alternatives he offers are realistic, specific, practical, nonutopian. He says his approach is fundamentally concerned with "practical policies," "practical circumstances and political issues," and "the political nerve center" (quoted in Kahl, 1976, pp. 183, 137). "We must not fool ourselves that slogans are enough or clever tactics are enough. I've never been a utopian; ideas don't count unless they express some real force, some power in society . . . I am not interested in a new pseudotheory or mythology, a new scholasticism. It only makes sense if you can combine theory, research, the historical moment, and practice . . . Behind my thought stands the shadow of Marx. Or better, the force of Marx: the link between them is through practice" (Cardoso as quoted in Kahl, 1976, pp. 139, 178, 188).

Cardoso insists further that a fundamental aspect of his approach is to specify the means by which to achieve these alternative ends. He states (quoted in Kahl, 1976, pp. 180–181) that "what really interest me are the new forms of dependency—the emerging forces, the dialectic of what is developing against the current situation, hidden within it, like those forces that erupted when I was in France [in 1968]. If we understood them we might learn how to transform society without starting from the state." Properly understood, he says (1977a, p. 11), the dependency approach must pose the question, "How and under what conditions is it possible to overcome a given situation of dependency?" This question "ought to be asked in terms of 'What are the classes and groups which, in the struggle for control or for the reformulation of the existing order (through parties, movements, ideologies, the state, etc.), are making a given structure of domination historically viable or are transforming it?'" In other words, "Do the studies enable us to define the classes and groups that give life to dependent structures through their political struggles?

Do they make it possible to go beyond the structural frame of reference in order to clarify the relations between ideologies and social and political movements in specific political conjunctures, so as to assist action to transform reality?" (Cardoso, 1977a, pp. 16, 18)

Given the frequency of these claims, one would suppose that the discussion of alternatives and how to achieve them would be central aspects of Cardoso's approach. But in fact Cardoso's delivery on the claims is almost nonexistent. This nondelivery is a constant feature of unorthodox dependency writings, no less true of the later works than the earliest ones.

Consider the text itself of Cardoso and Faletto's classic work. In both the 1969 edition and the revised and expanded 1979 edition it contains only two passages on alternatives to dependency. They are, in their entirety, the following:

A national society can achieve a certain autonomy of decision without thereby having a production system and an income distribution comparable to those in the central developed countries or even in some peripheral developing countries. This can occur, for example, when a country breaks its ties with a given system of domination without incorporating itself totally into another (Yugoslavia, China, Algiers, Egypt, Cuba, and even Revolutionary Mexico) (1969, p. 25; 1979, pp. 18–19).

There are examples of underdeveloped nations that have tried, sometimes successfully, to reorient the production system while preserving a reasonable degree of autonomy. When development and autonomy are achieved simultaneously, resources and economic and organizational creativity located within the nation have been mobilized. Political conditions have made this possible. In the cases of the Soviet Union and China, there was a period of relative economic isolation through a partial closing of the market, which blocked pressures to expand consumption of the goods and services typical of mass industrial societies. In general, there was a broadening of state control over the production system as well as a channeling of new investment toward sectors considered strategic to national development. Such sectors were those of infrastructure or advanced technology, or even those connected with national defense. All this required a corresponding reorganization of the social system, a relatively authoritarian discipline (even in cases like Japan where a capitalist regime was maintained), and a revolution in national goals, including the priorities of education.

This was not the course followed by Latin America as it attempted to enter the era of modern industrial production. (1969, pp. 148–149; 1979, p. 162)

These statements leave unanswered a number of important questions. Cardoso mentions countries as diverse as the Soviet Union, China, Japan, Yugoslavia, Algeria, Egypt, Cuba, and "even Revolutionary Mexico" as models of autonomous development. Is not autonomy (self-steering capacity) confused, or at least conflated, with autarky ("In the cases of the Soviet Union and China there was a period of relative economic isolation")? If, as Cardoso claims so often, the only acceptable alternative is socialism, then how can he offer cases like Japan or "even Revolutionary Mexico" as examples? Is the Soviet Union representative of the socialist idea or tradition? Is China? Is Cuba? If analyzing degrees of autonomy and dependency is a "senseless" enterprise, as they claim elsewhere, then how can Cardoso and Faletto speak of "preserving a reasonable degree of autonomy" in these countries? If national autonomy is not "their concern" and is not "at issue" because the real focus of dependency analysis is classes and class alliances, then why speak of national autonomy as an alternative to dependency? These questions are not addressed.

The new Preface and Post Scriptum in the 1979 edition are not helpful either. In them Cardoso insists that the only desirable or acceptable alternative is socialism. He says virtually nothing about the nature of socialism either abstractly or concretely. Abstractly he says only that it is more "just" and "egalitarian" than capitalism (p. xxiii). As the Brazilian political scientist Simon Schwartzman has correctly pointed out (1977, p. 167), when other writers use such terms Cardoso vilifies them for allegedly being "formal," "abstract," and so on. Cardoso mentions Cuba as a socialist case (once in the 1969 edition, thirteen times in the 1979 edition), but he never analyzes Cuba or any other concrete socialist case. Thus there is never any indication by him either in abstract or concrete terms what socialism looks like or how one would know it if one saw it.

Cardoso's specification of alternatives, in short, is mostly rhetorical, symbolic, and polemical. There are more statements claiming that the specification of alternatives is integral to his approach than statements actually saying something specific about what those alternatives are or how to achieve them. The failure to specify or say anything at all about "how to get there" (to socialism) is particularly notable. Cardoso claims to have provided a method for identifying groups and classes, tactics and strategies, that "in specific political conjunctures" can "assist action to transform reality." But in fact he has done nothing of the kind. For example, nothing in the 1979 edition—or anything else Cardoso has written—identifies the groups, classes, strategies, or tactics that were the "emerging forces . . . developing against the current situation, hidden within it" in Nicaragua, Jamaica, Grenada, or other parts of Central America or the Caribbean where "socialist" forces "struggled" in the late 1970s and the 1980s. Nor is there any guidance in Cardoso's writings for such groups and classes in other countries where socialist forces were less influential. Not only has he failed to identify conditions that facilitate transformations to socialism; he has failed even to make the effort. His claims in this regard are entirely empty.

The Myth of Predictive Capacity

Cardoso claims that his dialectical, change-oriented, historical-structural analysis enables him to predict "unanticipated" trends and processes and "unforeseen" situations in Latin America. For example, in the 1979 edition Cardoso and Faletto write (pp. xiv, xxii): "Significant data are those that illuminate trends of change and emerging processes of history in unanticipated ways . . . By means of this analysis it was foreseen how a general trend (industrial capitalism) creates concrete situations of dependency with features distinct from those of advanced capitalist societies." Elsewhere Cardoso says (quoted in Kahl, 1976, p. 181) that "Lots of journalists have good intuitions, but cannot predict anything, or give a real explanation."

The expected ability to predict events is completely unrealized. In the first place, Cardoso did not "foresee" the new dependency. By his own account, as well as that of many others, this new form of dependency took shape in the fifties and he did not even begin writing about it until the mid-sixties. Along with many others Cardoso noticed the new pattern of foreign investment in manufacturing partly for domestic consumption in Latin America, theorized about it, described a bit of it, and attached a catchy label ("associated-dependent development") to it. In no sense did he predict it.

In the second place, Cardoso has not "illuminated trends of change and emerging processes of history in unanticipated ways." On the few occasions when he has made specific predictions that can be tested, he has tended to be wrong. Thus the first chapter of Cardoso and Faletto predicted industrial stagnation for Argentina and Brazil; that prediction was shown to be false before the book was even finished (although the authors left it in the book in both the 1969 and 1979 editions). In the same book they also predicted increasing national dependence for Latin American countries in the 1970s (pp. 162, 174). Yet two authorities in the field concluded just the opposite about the decade for which Cardoso predicted an increase in national dependency in Latin America: "As the 1970s draw to a close, it is becoming increasingly evident . . . that the presence and influence of the United States in Latin America and the Caribbean are declining, that several Latin American nations are becoming significant actors in international affairs in their own right, and that an increasingly competitive relationship between the United States and Latin America has evolved" (Lowenthal and Fishlow, 1979, pp. 3–4. Also see Packenham, 1976, and Lowenthal, 1986, 1987).

In the Post Scriptum to the 1979 edition Cardoso acknowledges these facts but not that they refute his earlier prediction. Instead, he now denies that he was ever interested in the question of national autonomy or degrees of national autonomy/dependency, switches to a class definition of dependency, and insists that such national autonomy as exists still "expresses" foreign and capitalist "interests." He also continues to affirm his predictive capacities by ignoring the earlier predictions he did make, and claiming that the events of the 1970s lie "within what we perceived as possible ten years ago" (p. 205).

This latter claim brings us to a third point. Many of Cardoso's "predictions" are so vacuous or elastic that they encompass virtually any imaginable outcome. For instance, Cardoso and Faletto predicted (pp. xiv, xxii, xxiv) that the 1980s in Latin America would bring either more dependent capitalism (in one form or another) or a change to socialism. This perhaps appears to be an interesting, genuine prediction until one recalls their frame of reference. For them dependent capitalism and socialism are the only two fundamental categories of analysis for Latin America. They are exhaustive and mutually exclusive for this universe of cases. "Dependent" is not a discriminating adjective in this context since in their parlance capitalist countries in Latin America are dependent by definition, even if they acquire "formal" autonomy. Their statements are true but unhelpful, since any imaginable events fit the predictions.

It may be said that (a) predictive capacity is an excessively de-
manding standard in these (macrotheoretical) parts of the social
sciences, and (b) to hold Cardoso to such a standard is unfair. There
is a case for proposition (a), and also a case against it. We shall not
discuss the matter here. There is, however, no case whatsoever for
proposition (b), because it is Cardoso himself who has claimed to be
able to "illuminate" trends and processes in "unanticipated" ways,
to have "foreseen" how situations were going to evolve, and to have
"perceived as possible ten years ago" the patterns that came into
being in the late 1970s and the 1980s.

A fourth and final point should be noted. Even as he claims the
capacity to foresee events, Cardoso also denies that social scientists
have such a capacity and disdains efforts to make predictions. Thus
he and Faletto state that the "probable course" of future events will
depend "not on academic predictions, but on collective action guided
by political wills that make work what is structurally barely possible"
(p. 176). "Luckily," Cardoso (1977a, p. 21) writes, "as much as
social scientists strive to enclose the structural possibilities of history
in their own constructs, history continually makes us *dupes de nous-
mêmes,* and astonishes us with unexpected revelations." This pattern
of taking two sides of an argument, arguing against himself without
making the contradiction apparent, is pervasive in Cardoso's writings.

4 Specific Features of Unorthodox Dependency

To determine whether unorthodox dependency fits the four generic features of holistic dependency specified in Chapter 2, it is necessary to note several points that are relevant to all of them before taking up these features individually.

Unorthodox dependency is full of contradictions on a variety of levels and sublevels, about both secondary issues and fundamental questions. These contradictions are consistently resolved in particular ways. The contradictions are facilitated and complemented by a series of devices—ambiguous words and phrases, nonparallel constructions, false opposites, nonsequiturs, polemical appeals, and so forth—that obscure the contradictions and deflect attention onto other issues. The contradictions and devices are pervasive, inherent, and important characteristics of unorthodox dependency; unless one understands them it is impossible to understand the approach.

Cardoso is intellectually eclectic. He mixes elements of the social science of Max Weber and other non-Marxists with the Marxist thought (on classes) and the Leninist thought (on imperialism) that are the main foundations of his approach. Many other authors have also influenced Cardoso's thought. Cardoso himself has named Dilthey, Durkheim, Mannheim, Radcliffe-Brown, Malinowski, Merton, Parsons, Redfield, Pierson, Bastide, Willems, Azevedo, Fernandes, Touraine, Echavarría, Sartre, Lukács, and Gramsci, among others, as writers or teachers who have influenced his thinking (Kahl, 1976, pp. 129–136; Cardoso, 1977a, p. 10).

Cardoso's eclecticism has been noted by both supporters and critics of work. For example, Kahl (1976, p. 129), who is basically supportive, says that Marx and Weber have been Cardoso's "main models." Cueva (1976, p. 13), a critic ideologically to Cardoso's left, describes the 1969 edition of Cardoso and Faletto as "a book whose main points are difficult to organize and discuss because it utilizes two theoretical frameworks, Marxist and 'desarrollista,' and it lends itself to two interpretations depending on what you emphasize and what specific meaning you attribute to the concepts used."

Although supporters and critics alike have noticed such contradictions, few have perceived correctly how they are resolved. Cueva (1976, pp. 14–15) says that "In general, it is the analysis of classes and class conflict which is the Achilles heel of dependency theory . . . [Cardoso and Faletto] fall into the error of studying the state without reference to the class structure." This interpretation was dubious before the English edition appeared (see Cardoso, 1971a, 1974, 1977a); it is explicitly and totally rejected in the English edition. Cueva might have worried less. Supporters of Cardoso's work, who are much more numerous than critics, have also failed to perceive that although Cardoso is eclectic, ambiguous, and contradictory, he is much more faithful to Marxist postulates and criteria than to non-Marxist ideas. These supportive authors, usually eclectics or non-Marxists themselves, have often read their own ideas into Cardoso's work (see Chapter 10 below). From their perspectives, they might have worried more.

In this chapter, as in Chapter 3 and for the same reasons, we draw heavily on the 1979 English edition of Cardoso and Faletto; all page numbers given without further citation refer to that book.

Substantive Holism: Contradictions and Their Resolution

Definitions of Dependency

Scholarly commentators frequently cite one or another of Cardoso's definitions of dependency and proceed as if it were the one he actually used consistently in his work. But Cardoso does not stick to one definition. He even says that his definitions are not to be treated "formally." Why then are they given at all? How are they used?

Contradictory definitions of dependency (and other key concepts) are important manifestations of the substantive holism of unorthodox dependency. Each definition reflects an aspect or facet of the constellation of phenomena that allegedly go together holistically in the approach. The possibility that these facets might not go together, which exists in the real world, is either excluded by definition in holistic dependency or treated as insignificant and irrelevant. However, when the facets do go together in the real world, that is regarded as significant and relevant.

When Cardoso gives a definition he insists that it is the correct one and disparages other definitions. Although each set of disparaging comments could logically be applied to the other definitions he himself offers, Cardoso never does this; instead, he ignores his earlier and later disparagements and defenses of the other definitions. This illustrates the political use of substantive holism and more broadly how holistic dependency's features are interrelated.

Let us examine the evidence. Cardoso and Faletto give at least four different, mutually exclusive definitions. They say that dependency is mainly external; mainly internal; mainly the interaction of external and internal; neither external, nor internal, nor the interaction of the two, but capitalism on the periphery.

According to the first definition, the main characteristic of dependency studies is the emphasis on external analysis. The authors state flatly that "From the economic point of view a system is dependent when the accumulation and expansion of capital cannot find its [*sic*] essential dynamic component inside the system . . . Capitalism is a world system" (pp. xx–xxi). Dependent situations "have their main features determined by the phases and trend of expansion of capital on a world scale" (p. xxiii). In this view development within Latin America "derives from capitalist expansion and the strengthening of imperialism . . . We seek a global and dynamic understanding of social structures instead of looking only at specific dimensions of the social process" (ix). They refer to "the emphasis on global analysis" as "the very basic characteristic of dependency studies" (xii).

In such passages, the insistence on the primacy of global analysis is unmistakable. Multinational corporations "are obligatory points of reference for the analysis. The very existence of an economic 'periphery' cannot be understood without reference to the economic drive of advanced capitalist economies" (xvii). Further, "the history of central capitalism is, at the same time, the history of peripheral capitalism . . . Latin American countries depended on various countries that acted as centers and whose economic structures influenced the nature of the dependence" (pp. 23–24). In the new dependency of the post-populist period in Latin America, "levels of development may seem very high. But both capital flow and economic decisions are controlled from abroad. Even when production and marketing are carried out within the dependent economy, earnings go to swell capital funds available to the central economies" (160–161). This is "capitalist development originating in the dominant centers of international capitalism" (170).

No matter how much the writers may add to or subtract from these passages—and they do a lot of both—there is no question that in them they are claiming that dependency studies are fundamentally about the impact of external forces on internal developments in Latin America. (For additional passages making the same argument, among many that could be cited, see pp. xvii, 15, 21, 180; Cardoso, 1974.)

Conversely, according to the second definition the main characteristic of dependency studies is the emphasis on internal aspects of dependency. Although on pages 3–4 the authors disparage "the belief, common among economists, that development depended mainly on the ability of each country to take the policy decisions that its economic situation might require," on page 6 they argue that it was the "balance" and the "play" of political and social forces *within* Brazil and *within* Mexico that explained development in those countries. On p. 22 they elaborate the point: "Dependence should no longer be considered an 'external variable'; its analysis should be based on the relations between the different social classes within the dependent nations themselves."

Throughout the work they make similar statements. For example:

> The concept of dependence tries to give meaning to a series of events and situations that occur together, and to make empirical situations understandable in terms of the way internal and external structural components are linked. In this approach, the external is also expressed as a particular type of relation between social groups and classes within the underdeveloped nations. For this reason, it is worth focusing the analysis of dependence on its internal manifestations . . . Through the actions of groups, classes, organizations, and social movements in the dependent countries, these links are perpetuated, modified, or broken. Therefore, there is an internal dynamic that explains the course of events and thereby makes possible a political analysis. (pp. 15, 174)

Thus while Cardoso and Faletto note the links to "hegemonic countries" and the importance of global context, they state flatly that the main emphasis is internal.

The contradiction between the first two definitions is not resolved: instead, there is a third definition. It is that the main characteristic of dependency studies is the emphasis on the interplay between external and enternal forces. What their approach seeks to explain, they say, is "the interrelationship of classes and nation-states at the level of the international scene as well as at the level internal to each country . . . how internal and external processes of political domination relate one to the other . . . The real question lies in the interrelationship at both levels" (xvii; also pp. 177–178). Or again: "by definition, links of economic dependency imply a relationship between local and external classes, states, and enterprises . . . what happens 'internally' in a dependent country cannot be fully explained without taking into consideration the links that internal social groups have with external ones" (pp. 21–22).

When Cardoso and Faletto use this third definition, they "conceive the relationship between external and internal forces as forming a complex whole whose structural links are not based on mere external forms of exploitation and coercion, but are rooted in coincidences of interests between local dominant classes and international ones" (xvi). In stating that the main emphasis of dependency analysis is the interplay between external and internal, Cardoso and Faletto assume, as they do also in definitions one and two, that a distinction exists between internal and external; otherwise they could not refer to interplay, interrelationships, and links between them as they repeatedly do. Moreover, in his famous article on "The Consumption of Dependency Theory," Cardoso (1977a, p. 20) wrote that his approach "leaves no doubt about the distinction between central and dependent economies."

Yet there is a fourth definition which denies precisely this distinction. It says that dependency is not mainly about external factors, nor internal factors, nor the interaction between them; those distinctions are irrelevant or of secondary importance. Thus in both the 1969 edition (p. 162) and the 1979 edition (p. 173), Cardoso and Faletto wrote as follows: "We return to the tradition of political thought that there is no metaphysical relation of dependence between one nation and another, between one state and another." Similarly, in an essay first published in 1970, Cardoso wrote that he denied any "metaphysical distinction" between "external factors and internal effects," and that he "reject[ed] every type of analysis of dependency based on this perspective" (1971a, p. 30).

How can Cardoso deny the external-internal distinction and the very existence of either "physical" or "metaphysical" dependency between nations and states when he himself writes so often about dependency as the "objective economic subordination" (p. 21) of nations and states? How can he say this while he also maintains that his approach is fundamentally concerned with "the effects" of the reorganization of the world economy, and especially of multinational corporations, on the national economies of Latin America—the nature of such effects, their historical and structural features, changing forms over time, concrete expressions, consequences, and so on (for example, pp. 149–171, 180, 188–199)? These latter topics would seem to be central to dependency studies, and the term "dependencia" is the one Cardoso elected to use.

The main answers to these questions lie in the Marxist fundamentals of the approach and the theoretical and political imperatives they infuse into it. More specifically, it is that for Cardoso and others the real question is not about dependency versus autonomy but about capitalism versus socialism. Fundamentally, in this literature, the most accurate definition of dependency is capitalism on the periphery; the most accurate definition of escape from dependency is not national autonomy, and even less national autarky, but socialism. We shall not take up this theme in detail here, since we deal with it in other parts of the book, including the next section. We have been focusing on definitions; now we turn to substantive propositions.

Major Substantive Propositions

The holism of unorthodox dependency may also be seen by examining contradictions and ambiguities in three sets of major substantive issues and they ways they are resolved.

For most scholars one of the principal defining characteristic of unorthodox dependency is the rejection of the idea of "the development of underdevelopment" in favor of the idea of "associated-dependent development." But to characterize the approach in this way says nothing about what it accepts or favors in normative terms. In unorthodox dependency, is "associated-dependent development" under capitalism regarded as desirable development? Is it even regarded as acceptable development? Or is it regarded as neither desirable nor acceptable? If it is the former, the difference between orthodox and unorthodox dependency is great. If it is the latter, the difference is much smaller.

By frequently attacking the thesis that "associated-dependent development" is impossible, Cardoso has deflected attention away from these questions. At times he has even stated or implied possibilities for genuine reform and progress under capitalism, as when he cites

Hirschman approvingly on "possibilism" (p. xi), or refers to the unpredictibility of future events, or says that "*to some extent* the interests of the foreign corporations become compatible with the internal prosperity of the dependent countries. In this sense, they promote development" (1973a, p. 149, emphases in original). This last statement particularly seems to have influenced a lot of readers. When he makes these kinds of statements, Cardoso can be read as arguing that "associated-dependent development" under capitalism might be desirable or at least acceptable.

In the English edition, however, Cardoso and Faletto unambiguously reject such arguments. In this most definitive statement of their views they write, "It is not realistic to imagine that capitalist development will solve basic problems for the majority of the population. In the end, what has to be discussed as an alternative is not the consolidation of the state and the fulfillment of 'autonomous capitalism,' but how to supersede them. The important question, then, is how to construct paths toward socialism" (p. xxiv). Nor was this a new argument for Cardoso; he had made the same claims many times before (see Cardoso, 1973a, pp. 162–163; 1974, p. 69 and *passim;* 1977a, p. 17). The answers to the first pair of questions are now clear. Dependent development under capitalism is neither desirable nor acceptable. These points, which have received little attention, are far more fundamental than the point that dependent development is possible, which has received much attention.

The second set of questions is: Does the dependency perspective include national dependency? Is it possible within that perspective to analyze degrees of national dependency? On the one hand, Cardoso and Faletto use the term "dependency" to refer to the alleged concomitants of capitalism on the periphery: relations of social domination, socioeconomic inequalities, the state as a pact of class domination, capital as the result of the exploitation of one class by another, and so on. On the other hand, they also use it in a narrower, less holistic way to refer to constraints on national units. The former usage is much broader than ordinary language; it is the holistic usage. The latter usage is closer to ordinary language; it might be called national dependency.

That some such distinction as this exists in the literature is manifest. There have been ambiguities and contradictions, however, about whether Cardoso's approach includes national dependency and admits the analysis of degrees of national dependency. At times he seems to answer both questions in the affirmative. For instance, often he considers national dependency as part of holistic dependency. Thus he counts "the subordination of some economies to others" as one of the "necessary and simultaneous" features of "dependent capitalist development" along with socioeconomic exploitation, unequal distribution of income, and other attributes (1977a, p. 17). He states flatly (p. 162) that the industrialization in Latin America in recent decades has been achieved "at the expense of the autonomy of the national economic system and of policy decisions for development." In many passages (for example, pp. xx–xxiv, 22–24, 160–161, 170), Cardoso explicitly includes national dependency as a central aspect of holistic dependency.

At times, moreover, Cardoso has also stated or implied that he favors analyzing degrees of national dependency. Thus he writes that "it ought to be possible to measure the continuum that goes from 'dependency' to 'independence' and to characterize variable degrees of dependency," and he refers approvingly to "contributions towards evaluating the performance of states and economies in terms of degrees of independence" (1977a, pp. 15, 23). Further, statements such as the one just noted, that Latin American industrialization was achieved "at the expense of the autonomy of the national economic system," while cast in dichotomous terms, have to mean an increase in the degree of national dependency since these countries were already dependent before the "new dependency" of "associated-dependent" industrialization. Indeed, this is Cardoso's argument (1973a, pp. 142, 144, 149, 161) about Brazil after 1964.

But Cardoso has also answered both questions in the negative. He does so again in the English edition. There is an initial indication of his view in the Preface: "Characterizing dependency is like characterizing 'capitalism,' 'slavery,' or 'colonialism.' It would make no sense to compare slavery in the United States with slavery in the Antilles or in Brazil only in order to assess 'degrees of slavery' varying from minus to plus . . . Similarly, there would be little sense in attempting to measure 'degrees of dependency,' making formal comparisons of dependent situations" (p. xii). Consistent with his overall approach, even as he answers in the negative Cardoso also maintains a measure of ambiguity by using qualifying words and phrases, not-quite-parallel constructions, and so on. For instance, after saying it would make "no sense" to compare degrees of slavery, he says that "similarly, there would be little sense" to compare degrees of dependency: "similarly" closes the door, but using "little" rather than "no" leaves the door open just a bit. So does "only." Nevertheless, the thrust of the passage is clearly opposed to the inclusion of national dependency as a central aspect of holistic dependency, and it implies that it may not be a part of it at all.

But the clearest statement and resolution of this contradiction come in the new Post Scriptum. Cardoso and Faletto first present a detailed account of changes in the international system that reduced national dependency, defined in terms of "power" (their word, p. 198), in Latin American countries between the late 1960s and late 1970s. In presenting this information, they usually avoid saying explicitly that these trends were indicators of reduced national dependency; instead, they couch most of their discussion in terms of "attempts" and "tries" without saying explicitly how the "attempts" came out (see pp. 196, 198). This reluctance to concede that national dependency declined, despite the evidence they themselves present, also comes out when they emphasize that "the more significant changes in the foreign policy of Latin America would be unthinkable but for the prevailing conditions in the world scene, which have disrupted the previous balance and opened opportunities for new national policies" (p. 197). Yet again the thrust of their argument is clear: they are describing in some detail reductions in degrees of national dependency in Latin American countries in the last decade; they are answering both questions posed earlier in the affirmative.

No sooner do they complete their affirmative answer, however, than they give a negative answer, which turns out to be definitive. In a remarkable passage, they finally take the plunge of saying explicitly, rather than in the language of "tries" and "attempts," what their survey clearly suggests, namely, that national dependency has declined; then they immediately take it back, saying that the information they have presented in the preceding twenty pages is irrelevant to their approach! They write (p. 201): "*Strictu sensu*, the capacity for action of various Latin American states has increased. In this sense, one might consider that they are 'less dependent.' Our concern is not, however, to measure degrees of dependency in those terms—which fail to ask, 'less for whom? For which classes and groups?' Which classes have become more sovereign? Which alliances and class interests within each country and at the international level lead the historical process of economic development?" Just so there is no doubt, they repeat the same points a few pages further on (p. 212):

"There may have been a redefinition of the 'forms of dependency,' in certain Latin American countries there may be 'less dependency,' and the state in these countries may be capable of exercising a greater degree of sovereignty. But for us, what is at issue is the nature of class conflicts and alliances which the dependency situation encompasses." And the remainder of their discussion until the end of the book continues along these same lines.

The mystery—or at least the confusion—that has surrounded this issue is now dispelled. Unorthodox dependency includes national dependency and can be analyzed as a question of degrees as long as the national dependency increases (or stays the same). Under these circumstances, Cardoso and Faletto say a very great deal indeed about national dependency. If national dependency decreases, however, then they say it is irrelevant. It is not their "concern"; it is not "at issue." From the point of view of substantive holism and its conceptual accoutrements, this procedure is eminently justifiable. From other points of view it is a classic example of switching definitions in order to "save the hypothesis" no matter what the data show. Cardoso has argued that such a criticism is rooted in a capitalist North American mentality impaired by intellectual "necrophilia" (Cardoso 1977b). However, sophisticated Marxists in Brazil and England (Weffort, 1971, pp. 7–14; Warren, 1980) have made identical criticisms of Cardoso.

Unorthodox dependency's substantive holism is also evident in the treatment of a third pair of questions. Is the state an expression of class interests, or is it at least partially independent of them? Are the claims of Cardoso and Faletto in this regard context-specific or universal? Cardoso and Faletto handle these issues the same way as the previous ones: first they give one answer, then they take it back; first they challenge holistic dependency, then they reaffirm it. By the end they leave no doubt that the contradictions and ambiguities must always be resolved in the latter direction.

Thus when they analyze trends in world capitalism in the last decade, Cardoso and Faletto refer (pp. 185–186) to three theories or models (their terms) for "considering the relationship between the state and the multinationals": "the liberal theory," "the 'dependence' model," and "the mercantile model." They say they favor "an approach combining the last two models." Since their mercantile model (which also fits other definitions of the mercantile concept) "underlines the importance of the nation-state as a reorienting principle of world order," they are clearly implying that they consider the role of the state to be in some measure independent of social forces. This implication is supported further on, when they write "Not always and not necessarily do Latin American embassies respond only to the interests and pressures of the United States and the multinationals" (p. 198); when they cite approvingly (p. 214) Alfred Stepan's book *The State and Society* (1978b), whose main thesis is that state organizations are often relatively autonomous of social forces; and when they describe case after case in which "the state has expanded and fortified itself" (p. 201) during the last ten years in Latin America.

However, just as they abandoned the national definition of dependency in the face of facts inconvenient to their substantive holism, so also they abandon the mercantilist definition of state-society relations. "*If* the state has expanded and fortified itself," they write, having just filled fifteen pages with examples of precisely that trend, "it has done so as the expression of a class situation . . . Under these conditions, the state and the nation have become completely separated: all that is authentically popular . . . has come under suspicion, is considered subversive, and encounters a repressive response . . . the state has become a strategic element, functioning as a hinge that permits the opening of the portals through which capitalism passes into industrializing peripheral economies . . . The generalization of this model, in Brazil, in Mexico, in Peru, in Venezuela . . . married foreign interests with the local bourgeoisie, and in [Brazil, Mexico, Venezuela] with the interests of local states" (201–203, emphasis added).

So much for the mercantilist model! So much for the idea of the "relative autonomy" of the state, the "independence" of Latin American embassies, and the increase in "political" options! So much for the notion that in unorthodox dependency there are no "generalized models"! What Cardoso and Faletto now assert is the idea of "the state as the agent of capitalist enterprise." They state flatly that "the state expresses the imposition of one class or alliance of classes over others . . . any state, through bureaucratic and productive organizations, expresses a relationship of class domination (and consequently has social bases), assumes an ideology as if in the common interest, develops and implements policies that respond to the fundamental pact of domination, but also claims to attend to the aspirations of dominated groups" (pp. 208–209). These statements are not inductions from historical cases. They are certainly not "descriptive statements whose validity is contingent on particular context," as Duvall (1978, p. 55), citing Cardoso as authority, contends. They are precisely what Duvall (p. 55) and others say they are not, that is, "universal" claims to knowledge "intended to be general formulations applicable to a wide range of situations and contexts."

Having established the theoretical baseline in these universalistic terms, Cardoso and Faletto move on to the "specificity" and the "concreteness" of Latin America, as follows: "In the industrialized countries of Latin America which we are considering, the state embodies an alliance between the interests of the internationalized sector of the bourgeoisie and those of public and entrepreneurial bureaucracies. The local bourgeoisie links itself to these sectors" (pp. 209–210). This is an example of "specificity" and "concreteness" in Cardoso and Faletto's analysis. "Certainly," they assure the reader, "inversions" of these relations between classes and states can occur: for example, "The military bureaucracy may predominate in the control of the state." "But in the end," they hasten to add, "long term policies must be compatible with the social bases of the state . . . The nature of the dominant state relationship develops through the strengthening of the alliance between the local entrepreneurial sector, associated with the multinational foreign enterprises, and the state productive sector" (p. 210). Cardoso and Faletto maintain this position throughout the rest of the book.

What about specifically Latin American institutional, ideological, and cultural expressions? What about Latin American forms of corporatism, for example? "These formal aspects of the juncture between the state and civil society should not obscure the characteristics of the state in contemporary Latin America which we have already pointed out. The state is the expression of the dynamism of business enterprises and of the classes that control them" (p. 215). For Cardoso and Faletto, "corporativist forms . . . express the pact of domination among classes trying to implant capitalist development." Any other conception of corporatism is dismissed summarily. They oppose the analysis of the "historical roots of corporativism" on the grounds that the topic is not "important." They oppose studying the "cultural dimension" of corporatism and state-society relations on the ground that to consider culture to be a pertinent topic necessarily involves treating it as "immutable." They conclude with the argument that the only realistic options in Latin America are two: "technocratic elitism" under capitalism, or "a democratic society" under socialism (pp. 215–216).

In this fashion Cardoso and Faletto are able simultaneously to include numerous qualifications and hedges that can make their position on state-class relations seem subtle and unorthodox, and also to defend, as the Brazilian political scientist Simon Schwartzman has noted (1977, pp. 169–170), an "orthodox class position, the explanation in the most conventional Marxist terms of all politics by the confrontation of groups and classes without reference to the problematic of the state." On this third set of issues as on the first two, whenever Cardoso and Faletto resolve such contradictions it is always in the latter direction rather than the former.

The substantive holism of unorthodox dependency is complemented and facilitated by another of its four major features, utopianism.

Utopianism

Cardoso's writings make a fundamental division of the world into "the two great contemporary socio-economic systems, capitalism and socialism" (p. 178). He tells us what he thinks about capitalism, but how does he see socialism in concrete, specific terms? His characterization is vague and ambiguous. Leninism and Stalinism are denounced, but Mao's cultural revolution, the Chinese case generally, and Fidel's Cuba are used repeatedly as examples of participatory democracy, substantive democracy, and authentic socialism. A dictatorship of the proletariat is rejected, but the idea that socialism has no room in the long run for the bourgeoisie is maintained. Cardoso is equally hard to pin down on the subject of how to get from capitalism to socialism. Bloody revolutions are not necessarily prescribed, but the possibility that they may be required is maintained.

Concrete cases of socialism are never compared to concrete cases of capitalism. Rather, concrete cases of capitalism (which have flaws) are compared to idealized versions of socialism (which are flawless). The superiority of the socialist state is assumed. It is not a debatable subject. The socialist state, an idealized, abstract, nonspecific concept, is a utopian vision rather than a concrete category.

One of the most important manifestations of Cardoso's utopianism is his definition of the state as "the basic pact of domination that exists among social classes or fractions of dominant classes and the norms which guarantee their dominance over the subordinate strata" (Cardoso, 1979a, p. 38). Since this is a definition, it is not amenable to alteration in light of evidence; it is taken to be true axiomatically. It rejects flatly any notion of the state as a social contract.

Cardoso makes a distinction between state and "regime," which he defines as the "formal rules that link the main political institutions (legislature to the executive, executive to the judiciary, and party system to them all), as well as the issue of the political nature of the ties between citizens and rulers (democratic, oligarchic, totalitarian, or whatever)" (Cardoso, 1979a, p. 38). By making the distinction between state and regime primary and the distinction among "democratic, oligarchic, totalitarian, or whatever" regimes secondary, Cardoso is saying that any capitalist state is a pact of domination of one class over another; no matter whether it is a relatively good capitalist state or a relatively bad one, it must be replaced by a socialist state.

In such an approach, democratic England might have better "formal rules" than bureaucratic-authoritarian regimes in Latin America, or Mussolini's Italy, Franco's Spain, or Nazi Germany, but still they are all capitalist states in which one class dominates another, and that is the more important distinction. By this line of reasoning, the state in formal capitalist democracies such as Venezuela, Colombia, or Costa Rica still rests on a pact of domination, and the only acceptable solution is socialism (pp. 199–216). If a country such as Brazil were to continue its processes of liberalization and democratization to the point where a multiparty system or two-party system with regular competitive elections were firmly established, civil liberties were widely respected, and other features of a political democracy were in place, so long as capitalism persisted the state would still represent a pact of class domination, the democracy would still be only formal, and socialism would still be the only acceptable solution. While progress of a second order might have been achieved, first-order progress would await a transformation to socialism.

Since 1978 Cardoso has been deeply involved in Brazilian politics. He became an important legislative and party leader. For a time during the mid-1980s he was discussed as a possible candidate for president. Cardoso the politician has eschewed the utopianism of Cardoso the dependency writer (see Chapter 9 below). But this suspension occurred in spite of—in flat contradiction to—his dependency writings, not because of them. As a politician he was logically vulnerable to criticisms he made in his dependency writings of political actors and institutions in capitalist states.

Epistemological Holism (Nonfalsificationism)

Much evidence of the nonfalsificationist epistemology of unorthodox dependency has already been presented in chapters 1–3 and earlier in this chapter, and there is no need to repeat it here. It is more useful to discuss contradictory themes in the epistemology of unorthodox dependency and to identify a neglected but central manifestation of its nonfalsificationism.

Cardoso's Survey Study

Unorthodox dependency writings are also contradictory and eclectic on epistemological questions, although less than on substantive issues. Consider, for example, Cardoso's survey-based study (1971b) of the ideologies of industrial entrepreneurs in Argentina and Brazil. This book is not simply a report of post hoc inductions. Rather, it is designed as an empirical test of hypotheses deduced from the general dependency approach as elaborated by Cardoso and his collaborators. The theoretical perspective specifies that the international capitalist system drives a wedge into various groups and classes within Latin American societies, which then divide into factions that differ ideologically in predictable ways. Cardoso studies one of these groups—industrialists—in two structurally similar countries, Argentina and Brazil. He hypothesizes that industrialists with greater ties to the international market will be less open to alliances with workers, less likely to perceive common interests with the rural sector, and less inclined to favor expansion of mass markets, than those with fewer international ties. Cardoso finds that the survey data confirm the hypotheses to a remarkable extent. Faria (1971), analyzing the same data, tends to agree (but see also Kahl, 1976, pp. 174–176, for a number of well-considered cautions about Cardoso's concepts, measures, data base, and other features).

Should one conclude from the evidence of this survey study that unorthodox dependency embraces falsificationism? I think not. If it were the epistemology Cardoso used consistently, defended explicitly, and stressed in the way he practices, champions, and emphasizes epistemological holism, then one could conclude that he really supported it. But that is scarcely the case. In the main he practices and champions nonfalsificationism and attacks falsificationism. He seldom if ever defends falsificationism explicitly. In almost none of his other dependency writings does he emphasize the epistemology of his survey study of entrepreneurs at all; to the contrary, he downplays it in contrast to the repeated emphasis he gives to a nonfalsificationist epistemology. In 1973 he wrote to Kahl: "At certain times I may have tried to force empirical tests of general theory in the book on the Argentine and Brazilian entrepreneurs, but it it not my basic desire to formalize the theory. Indeed, in subsequent writings I have issued a polemic against formalization. I know that some younger scholars are attempting to turn the theory of dependency into a logico-deductive model in order to generate specific hypotheses for test. But that is not the procedure that I refer to when I insist on the necessity of linking theories with facts" (Cardoso letter quoted by Kahl, 1976, p. 188). Cardoso's subsequent dependency writings are strongly in the same direction (for example, Cardoso, 1977a; Cardoso and Faletto, 1979).

As Phillips (1976, p. 123) points out, falsificationism (which he calls "the analytic method") "is such a moderate and reasonable position that no scientist, not even a holist, can avoid putting it into practice" some of the time. Therefore to cite an example of falsificationism in practice in unorthodox dependency is easy, but it proves nothing about the epistemology of the approach qua approach. The important questions are, which epistemologies are defended and which are attacked in principle? Which ones are used in practice most of the time? Among these, which are defended and praised explicitly and which are seldom if ever defended explicitly? What is the weight, logic, and structure of the overall position? What is the attitude of mind that informs and guides the researcher? On these questions the evidence is clear. Cardoso has opted overwhelmingly for a nonfalsificationist brand of dialectics rather than any form of falsificationism, which he conflates with positivism and rejects.

Another piece of evidence, besides the survey study of entrepreneurs, that is occasionally used by commentators who attribute falsificationism to unorthodox dependency is Cardoso's rejection of the "development of underdevelopment" thesis in favor of the idea of "associated-dependent development." This shows, they argue, that Cardoso is a falsificationist. Such an argument is misspecified and overdrawn. It exaggerates the differences between these two theses. It also fails to understand what is central to nonfalsificationism.

Obviously much of Latin America had industrialized well before either Frank or Cardoso wrote. It was impossible for Cardoso, or Frank, to fail to notice that fact, and neither of them did (on Frank, see Chapter 5 below). Does the analyst deal with inconvenient facts by shifting to another level of argumentation in order to save the basic hypothesis no matter what the facts? Or does he remain open to the possibility that even basic hypotheses may be challenged by such facts and therefore alternative hypotheses must be considered? Is the attitude of mind, in other words, one of considering the possibility of facts refuting hypotheses, or one of constantly finding a way to save the hypotheses? Let us examine that question, using as evidence exactly the example offered by those who say unorthodox dependency embraces falsificationism. It will be seen that while it is true that unorthodox dependency recognizes "associated-dependent development" rather than just "the development of underdevelopment," the conclusions about epistemology that are sometimes drawn from this hardly follow.

Saving the Hypothesis Through Ideological Escalation

One of the most fascinating, illuminating, and neglected facts about *Dependency and Development in Latin America* is the massive change between the beginning and end of the volume (specifically, between Chapter 1 and chapters 6 and 7) in regard to the central empirical premise of the book, and the central empirical/theoretical question which is supposedly being addressed. In discovering these changes we learn much about the theory, method, and epistemology which inform Cardoso's work.

The theme of Chapter 1 is the disappointment of those whose expectations about economic dynamism in Latin America after the mid-1950s were not fulfilled. Writing in the late 1960s, Cardoso and Faletto state unambiguously that the point of the inquiry is to try to account for this alleged "stagnation," "lack of requisite economic vitality," and "slowdown" in economic growth. This theme continues in the 1979 English edition, where the same phrases are used (pp. 5, 6, 7). Cardoso and Faletto cite ECLA sources and Celso Furtado to assert that, except for Mexico, Latin American countries, particularly Argentina and Brazil, were recurrently subject to stagnation, low economic vitality, and slow economic growth; that this is the central problem to be explained in the book; and that in order to understand this problem one had to look outside the nation-state to the global international system.

In other words, at the beginning the central issue is very similar to the central issue of the orthodox dependency approach. In Chapter 1 the theme of "associated-dependent development," for which unorthodox dependency is famous, is nowhere to be seen. "Everybody knows" this cannot be so; but it is so. The only way to know it, however, is to read the text rather than to rely on what everybody knows.

The criteria of "development" and "stagnation" used by Cardoso and Faletto in Chapter 1 are utterly conventional: low (or negative) rates of growth in gross national product (pp. 5, 7, also p. 10). "Of the three most industrially advanced countries," they write, "only Mexico has managed to maintain a high rate of growth for a longer period (than the decade of the fifties) . . . Mexico's economic structure differentiates it from other countries of Latin America" (p. 5). In other words, the problem they say they are trying to understand is why countries like Argentina and Brazil are "failures" in these terms and why Mexico is a "success." In spite of its inequalities and foreign dependence, which they acknowledge (pp. 5–6), they see Mexico as successful because it maintained high growth rates. At this point they are saying that capitalist development is fine; the problem is how to get more of it. There is nothing in Chapter 1 about the inherent incapacity of capitalism to serve human needs and the necessity for socialism. The authors explain the "success" of Mexico as follows: "Mexico, after a difficult period of readjustment and profound transformations brought about by a nationalist policy, would seem to have realized its possibilities for expansion largely thanks to its integration into the world market through foreign investment and the diversification of its foreign trade, in which tourism plays an important role" (p. 6).

Having thus explained Mexico's "success" as a product of (1) its Revolution, (2) its "nationalist policies" [*sic*], (3) its "integration into the world market through foreign investment" [*sic*], (4) "tourism" [*sic*]—explanations ascribing positive results to factors which, in most of their work, they judge to be profoundly negative—it remains for them to explain the contrasting "failures" of countries like Argentina and Brazil. "In view of the above, it is possible to generalize the question of why national economies as promising as Argentina's lacked the requisite vitality" (p. 6). In the original Spanish edition the final paragraph of Chapter 1 ends with the sentence, "What is needed is an analysis that makes possible a broader and more sophisticated answer to the general question of how development or stagnation is possible in Latin American countries" (Cardoso and Faletto, 1969, p. 10). (In the English edition, the words "or stagnation" are deleted [p. 7; also see p. 10] but the rest of the sentence is the same.) As the first chapter ends, that is the question posed for analysis in the remainder of the book.

Having stated the problem thus, Cardoso and Faletto return to it directly only in the final two chapters. In the interval they deal with methodological and theoretical matters and present a schematic history of all Latin American countries from 1810 to roughly 1950. When they finally do return to this problem in chapters 6 and 7, however, they change the terms of reference entirely. The question why most countries in Latin America, except for Mexico, "lacked the requisite vitality," a question which they said at the outset was the main purpose of the inquiry, is now quietly but completely abandoned. Implicitly the authors now reject their initial premise that sustained industrialization was not taking place; in these final chapters they appear to concede that it was possible and did occur. The new question is, what is different about the new situation of dependence, in which sustained industrialization has become possible? As they write: "Some countries of the region have managed to accelerate industrialization through the transfer of foreign capital together with advanced technology and organization for production. But they have done this at the expense of the autonomy of the national economic system and of policy decisions for development" (p. 162).

It must be emphasized that these shifts in empirical premise and focus of inquiry are never explicitly identified; they simply happen. The authors began the book studying a question based on an empirical premise that by the end of the book they evidently decided was faulty; so in the final two chapters they quietly adopt a new empirical premise and change entirely the question they say the book is meant to answer.

The point at which this subtle but crucial transition occurs is in Chapter 6. It follows directly upon a lengthy section entitled "The Structural Limits on the Process of National Industrialization." In this section the authors summarize attempts to develop through national capitalism in the fifties and sixties which, as the section title implies, "came to the dead end of the present state of capitalist development in Latin America: modernization at the cost of growing authoritarianism and continuing poverty typical of 'development with marginal population'" (p. 153). In this section the premise of Chapter 1 could, logically, still hold. Now, however, in a new section entitled "The Opening of Domestic Markets of External Control," comes the crucial passage: "The foregoing explains why attempts to maintain the rate of industrialization cannot succeed without profound political-structural changes. What has not been made clear is that foreign industrial capital was searching for new markets. This search became connected with internal interests in a way that was acceptable at least to those in power" (p. 157).

The phrase "why attempts to maintain the rate of industrialization cannot succeed" seems to maintain the premise and the purpose stated in Chapter 1. But this phrase turns out not to be the operative one. As the passage, and indeed the remainder of the book proceed from this point forward, it becomes ever clearer that the operative phrase is really "without profound political-structural changes." The second and third sentences of the passage immediately state both what those changes were and the two fundamental terms, external and internal, of the dependency framework: "foreign capital was searching for new markets," and the presence of "internal interests" to which foreign capital could "connect." Two pages later comes a section on "Dependence and Development" in which the new empirical premise is that industrialization has occurred and the new question for investigation is to identify the conditions which make industrialization at once possible and too costly to be acceptable (loss of national control, authoritarianism, socioeconomic inequalities, and so on). From then on to the end of the book the arguments are the ones about the "new situation" of dependency with which the authors are so closely identified and that have been so influential.

For present purposes the main significance of the changes is that they show how Cardoso and Faletto deal with disconfirming evidence. They began with the premise that the most important problem to be analyzed was industrial stagnation in countries "like" Argentina and Brazil. Industrial stagnation indicated "failure"; the problem was to explain and correct this failure. Even as they were finishing their book, however, events were rendering their premise invalid. As Hirschman (1971, p. 352) has noted, in 1968 the economic performance of the largest countries of Latin America "was little short of brilliant." He added that to those "imbued" with "the action-arousing gloomy vision" that "creates more gloom than action," such performance came "as a distinct embarrassment." In the face of such facts Cardoso and Faletto did not conclude that their initial view was too pessimistic. They did not reason that if industrial stagnation is used as an indicator of failure then industrial dynamism should be used as an indicator of success. Instead, when they had to face the reality of industrial dynamism in the region, they suddenly minimized its importance and shifted the focus of attention entirely to other features—socioeconomic inequalities, political authoritarianism, and national dependency—that could still be seen negatively. In this fashion they could continue to argue that the development experience is negative on balance even if it is a success in some respects, such as industrialization.

The question, then, is not only whether contrary evidence is recognized but also how it is handled. In particular, the question is whether contrary evidence is ever allowed to raise questions about hypotheses, or if some way is always found to "save the hypothesis" by repairing to aspects of the holistic model that are not falsified. Since capitalist development in the real world always has flaws, there is and always will be some way to save the hypothesis. Since the alternative offered in unorthodox dependency, socialism, is nonexistent, it is never flawed and there is no way to reject the proposition that it is a better alternative.

These features of Cardoso and Faletto's analysis lend strong support to Hirschman's (1979, pp. 81–87) hypotheses about "ideological escalation" among Latin American social scientists. Hirschman praises the creativity of these analysts, but he also suggests that a "counterpart" to these achievements has been a continuous process of "ideological escalation" in which "new, more difficult tasks were continuously presented to the state and society whether or not the previous task had been successfully disposed of." Hirschman's hypothesis that the most recent "escalation" proclaimed in the literature is one in which "Latin America must solve its problems by redistributing wealth and income domestically and by overcoming 'dependence'" fits extremely well the evidence of unorthodox dependency writings. In the specific instance of Cardoso and Faletto's influential book the only way in which fit is lacking is that, remarkably, a process that Hirschman perceives as occurring over a period of years happens between chapter 1 and chapters 6 and 7 of a single text.

The Premise of Politicized Scholarship

Cardoso's premises about the relationship between scholarship and politics are sustained by his reading of the Marxist tradition. He says that dependency analyses "are considered more 'true' because they assume that, by discerning which are the historical agents capable of propelling a process of transformation and by providing those agents with theoretical and methodological tools for their struggles, these analyses thus grasp the meaning of historical movement and help to negate a given order of domination. They are therefore explanatory because they are critical" (1977a, p. 16; see also Cardoso and Faletto, 1979, pp. ix–xxiv). In such a formulation ideas are not true or false; they are "true" or "false." They are "tools" serving "historical agents" engaged in "struggle." They are "discerning" only if they "help to negate a given order of domination." They have "explanatory" power "because they are critical."

In explicating the Marxist character of holistic dependency, its repudiation of the notion of "a corpus of formal and testable propositions," and its divergence from analytic dependency and other Weberian approaches, Cardoso (1977a, pp. 15–16) writes as follows: "The divergence is not merely methodological-formal. It is, rather, at the very heart of studies of [holistic] dependency. If these studies do in fact have any power of attraction at all, it is not merely because they propose a methodology to substitute for a previously existing paradigm or because they open up a new set of themes. It is because they do so from a radically critical viewpoint." Thus Cardoso refers succinctly but explicitly to all the main features of holistic dependency (substantive, epistemological, political); to their interrelatedness; and to the centrality of the politicized-scholarship premise.

As the foregoing remarks suggest, unorthodox dependency has much in common with critical theory. Like critical theory, unorthodox dependency draws heavily on an eclectic mix of Marx and Weber (and others) and has a view of the relation between social science and society different from either positivism or falsificationism. An illuminating analysis of critical theory (also called dialectical hermeneutics) and its relation to other approaches, with extensive citations, may be found in Alker (1978). He analyzes systematically four major approaches regarding (among other things) issues of scientific autonomy, insulation, and value neutrality. He summarizes that analysis as follows (Alker, 1978, Table I, pp. 53–54):

Positivism (Russell, Vienna circle, Carnap): "The logical systems ideal of science seeks autonomy by minimizing value relevance and insulating all stages of theory development."

Falsificationism (Popper, Lakatos): "Falsificationism does not deny societal inputs, but tries to correct for them through rational social criticism."

Revolutionary hermeneutics/methodological anarchism (Kuhn, Feyerabend): "Kuhn usually defends insulation of science, but recognizes cosmological overlaps with social philosophies; Feyerabend defends some violations of autonomy."

Critical theory/dialectical hermeneutics (Adorno, Habermas): "Science is seen as subordinate to organized practical interests; autonomy/neutrality claims are criticized in the light of social structures preventing genuine consensus and making autonomy less than it could be. Theory and practice are internally related."

Alker's analysis of critical theory provides a valuable perspective on the premises of unorthodox dependency. In unorthodox dependency, perhaps even more than in critical theory, scholarship is fused to politics and struggle. Thus even as Cardoso insists on the politicized character of the scholarly enterprise, he also insists that scientific explanation is possible and that he (and Faletto) offer scientific explanations. The argument, in other words, is that social science is possible; their work is social scientific; all social science work, including their own and that of their critics, is necessarily and simultaneously an "agent" of forces in historical struggle; in this struggle some social science is progressive (for socialism) and other social science is regressive (not necessarily committed to socialism); the idea of a social-scientific community across those divisions is a mystification serving antipopular interests.

The politicization of scholarship helps to explain many features of unorthodox (as well as orthodox) dependency writings. For example, it makes it legitimate to examine tensions and trends that increase national dependency and internal inequality, but not those that increase national autonomy and internal equality. It is legitimate to move back and forth among different, often conflicting definitions of key concepts in order to preserve major hypotheses in the face of inconvenient facts. It helps to explain why the contradictions and ambiguities in unorthodox dependency writings occur so pervasively and are resolved in the directions they are rather than others. Where social science is conceived as an agent of struggle, it is necessary to build support and attack opponents.

Devices to Obscure Contradictions

Contradictions and ambiguities are useful for political purposes. They are also pervasive in Cardoso's dependency writings, enabling him to come down, or more accurately appear to come down, on two or more sides of virtually any issue. For instance, having noted that both "local socio-political process" and "local economic organization" are "reproduced" by "the general features of capitalism as it exists on a world scale," Cardoso and Faletto still say that "it is the diversity within unity that explains historical process." Statements about global capitalism are first valued as "obligatory points of reference for the analysis," then disparaged as "general platitudes" (pp. xvii–xviii). First (pp. xii–xiii) they vigorously reject the view that "all forms of dependency had common features" and the idea of a "a general . . . form of dependency that permeates all types of situations." Later, however, they say that there are indeed "common factors in capitalism which affect all economies under consideration" (p. xvii).

The contradictions of unorthodox dependency are complemented and facilitated by a variety of devices—ambiguous words and phrases, nonsequiturs, nonparallel constructions, polemical appeals, strawmen, and like devices—that obscure the contradictions and deflect attention onto side issues. For example, Cardoso and Faletto write that "Political and economic processes appear . . . as if they were the expression of a struggle between nation-states, but they also involve conflicts between social groups and classes" (p. 178). "As if" implies the struggle is not a national struggle, but "they also" implies that it is.

In a similar vein they write: "In this book, we do not pretend to derive mechanically significant phases of dependent societies only from the 'logic of capitalist accumulation.' We do not see dependency and imperialism as external and internal sides of a single coin, with the internal aspects reduced to the condition of 'epiphenomenal.'" (p. xv). The first sentence appears to reject the idea that phases of dependency are linked to the logic of capitalist accumulation, and the second sentence appears to reject the idea that dependency and imperialism are two sides of the same coin. But by using the qualifying words "mechanically" and "only" in the first sentence, and a clause ("with the internal aspects reduced to the condition of 'epiphenomenal'") which is either a qualification or a nonsequitur in the second sentence, Cardoso and Faletto leave open the possibility that the two ideas they appear to be rejecting might actually be supportable absent the qualifying words and clause. That possibility is precisely what they do affirm at various points elsewhere in the text, for example: "Of course, imperialist penetration is a result of external social forces (multinational enterprises, foreign technology, international financial systems, embassies, foreign states and armies, etc.). What we affirm simply means that the system of domination reappears as an 'internal' force, through the social practices of local groups and classes which try to enforce foreign interests, not precisely because they are foreign, but because they may coincide with values and interests that these groups pretend are their own" (p. xvi; also pp. xvi–xvii).

Other devices are polemical attacks and the construction and demolition of strawman targets. Cardoso criticizes "the simplistic reductionism so common among the present-day butterfly collectors who abound in the social sciences and who stroll through history classifying types of dependency, modes of production, and laws of development" (1977a, p. 21). He gives no examples or documentation to support his point. It fits rather well the basic structure of his book with Faletto, which classifies the history of every country in Latin America from 1810 to the present into three and only three "basic situations of dependency," but he does not cite it, either. Cardoso and Faletto attack the view, which they attribute to unnamed vulgar dependency writers, that "considerations of external factors or foreign domination [are] enough to explain the dynamic of societies" (p. xviii). In fact, no dependency writer takes this position. Certainly Andre Gunder Frank (1967, pp. vii, xi, 106–115, 145–150) does not; he always has included the internal aspect of dependency as well as the external, even when he has stressed the latter. Cardoso and Faletto's uncited target is a strawman.

One could go on listing examples almost indefinitely, but there is no need. The central point is that while unorthodox dependency has overall coherence, it also has many contradictions and ambiguities which deflect attention onto side issues. In politics, the ability to maintain ambiguity and contradiction is a vital skill. In social science, clarity and consistency are more highly valued; the heart of the enterprise is to understand social reality, to learn the nature of things, and to follow wherever facts, logic, and reason lead. Of course, to the extent politics and scholarship are fused, the political skills of ambiguity and contradiction become as valuable in the scholarly arena as they are in politics.

Cardoso's statements have often confused scholarly commentators, and no wonder, for taken in isolation many of them can certainly be misleading. This is why it is essential to make a comprehensive analysis of of his contradictory statements rather than to base interpretations on pieces of the argument and one or another side of its contradictions. These features, incidentally, are not artifacts of the English translation; they are equally pervasive in Cardoso's writings in Portuguese and Spanish. (This is my own conclusion; for similar conclusions about Cardoso's work in articles published in Latin America, see Weffort, 1970, 1971; Schwartzman, 1977; Prowess, 1978.)

Another ostensibly social-scientific device that is used politically, this one emphasizing conflict, is the concept of interest.

Interest as a Polemical Device

"Interest" is a key word and concept in unorthodox dependency. So are closely related words and concepts such as "link," "bind," and "alliance," which in this discourse have the same properties. The concept of interest has the same substantive, epistemological, and political functions in unorthodox dependency as in holistic dependency generally.

Although "interest" connotes tough-mindedness, factualness, rigor, and objectivity, in fact its content is usually provided by the arbitrary, unsupported, subjective judgment of the analyst. When Cardoso and Faletto write (p. xvi) that "the system of domination reappears as an 'internal' force, through the social practices of local groups and classes which try to enforce foreign interests," their affirmation is not inferred from evidence. Nor is it tested against evidence. It is a judgment and an accusation. Similarly, when they refer to interests that local groups "pretend are their own" or "claim to attend to" (pp. xvi, 209), it is they who decide that local groups really represent external interests. The fact that such groups believe they represent internal interests and may actually do so is irrelevant in unorthodox dependency.

The concept of interest is a powerful polemical tool. There is no end to the internal, local, or national groups, classes, class fractions, institutions, goals, values, ideas, policies, leaders, and processes that can be designated to be expressions of external interests. If the analyst dispproves, he simply says they express capitalist and external interests. They are the "anti-Nation . . . inside the 'nation,' so to speak" (Cardoso, 1973c, p. 200). This can mean not only the usual suspects, such as employees of multinational corporations, but also ostensibly nationalist elements such as local capitalists and entrepreneurs, technocrats, bureaucrats, the military, "elements of the rising middle class," various working-class groups and class fractions, certain intellectuals, and state enterprises and state bureaucracies (pp. 27–28, 175, 213; Cardoso, 1973a, pp. 160–163, 172–176). Nothing is immune. The only requirement is that the analyst disapprove at the moment of what the agent is doing, saying, representing, or "expressing." For instance, traditional groups such as large landlords "are often the main sustaining force for foreign interests" (p. 27).

In similar fashion, any group, actor, or policy of which the analyst approves at a "specific moment" can be said to express socialist interests and thereby to manifest "authentic," "genuinely popular," and "truly national" forces, values, and patterns of behavior. Thus just as "external," "dependent," and "capitalist" are synonyms in Cardoso's writings, so also are "internal," "autonomous," and "socialist." But Cardoso is much less concrete regarding what groups, policies, and actors express the socialist interests than in specifying those that express capitalist interests. He refers abstractly to the category of "an authentically national pattern" of development (1973a, p. 157) but he says next to nothing regarding the nature of that pattern. He says what "authentic" national development is not but very little regarding what it is.

In practice the criterion used by Cardoso to identify the groups, actors, and policies that advance the cause of "genuine" development is whether Cardoso approves of them or not. If he does, they express internal interests, advance the cause of socialism, and are authentically national. If he does not, they express external interests, advance the cause of capitalism, and represent the "anti-nation inside the nation." In the overwhelming majority of cases, if not all of them, Cardoso's criteria boil down to this. There are few if any lines in the entire corpus of Cardoso's writings on dependency in which he identifies as authentically national any phenomenon of which he disapproves. Virtually all such phenomena are said to be internal manifestations of external, which is to say capitalist, interests.

Conclusion

Most commentators have contended that the generic features of holistic dependency elaborated in Chapter 2 do not fit unorthodox dependency. This chapter has shown that such contentions are false. The generic features of holistic dependency fit unorthodox dependency quite well.

It is far from clear, however, that scholarship can now affect the perceptions and evaluations of unorthodox dependency that dominate writings about Latin America and the Third World. These perceptions and evaluations have attained the status of myths. These myths are firmly established. "Everybody knows" they are correct. For many people the factual basis for them may no longer be relevant; as a practical matter the myths may no longer be amenable to correction. Unorthodox dependency has become a symbol to invoke and a rich supply of contradictory ideas from which to choose whichever idea seems appropriate at the moment.

Nevertheless, whether or not dominant perceptions and evaluations can be changed, the enterprise of scholarship as an activity separate from politics and theatre ought to go on. It is inherently worth doing: it is what scholars ought to do. And eventually it may even alter the dominant but erroneous mythology about unorthodox dependency. For both reasons it has been necessary to establish what unorthodox dependency says in a comprehensive, documented fashion rather than selectively or on the basis of what "everybody knows." It is also important—now that we have identified and documented what unorthodox dependency says—to locate that approach in a spectrum of dependency approaches. Therefore in the next chapter we deal more with the boundaries of holistic dependency and the varieties of dependency and dependency-related analyses.

5   Varieties of Dependency Thinking

In the current typologies of dependency writings the main distinction is between orthodox and unorthodox dependency. Many commentators also separate unorthodox dependency from Marxism and emphasize variations over time within the same approach. Although such typologies and distinctions are valid up to a point, they have major defects. They do not say enough about other types of dependency and dependency-related analyses in the literature. Their focus on orthodox and unorthodox dependency has impeded the perception and exploration of other ways to analyze dependency hypotheses, particularly those here called the heretical and analytical approaches. Moreover, they are often inaccurate about the characteristics of orthodox and unorthodox dependency, their relations to Marxism, and the trends over time in these two approaches.

Six major types of dependency and dependency-related approaches can be identified: (1) pure-class approaches (including world-systems theories, modes-of-production analyses, and the like); (2) orthodox dependency; (3) unorthodox dependency; (4) heretical dependency; (5) analytic dependency; and (6) bargaining studies (see Table 5.1). We shall first describe briefly the pure-class and bargaining approaches, which are "dependency-related." This means that neither is strictly speaking a dependency approach, although each for different reasons is often characterized in that way. By fixing these two approaches clearly in mind we can perceive more accurately how to locate the other four dependency approaches.

Pure-Class, World-Systems, and Modes-of-Production Approaches

As noted earlier, holistic dependency attempts to bring Marxism and nationalism together. The union is not equal: Marxism is the dominant partner over nationalism. Pure-class and bargaining approaches,

Table 5.1 Varieties of dependency and dependency-related approaches

Name of approach	Examples	Nature of approach
World-systems, pure-class, modes-of-production	Wallerstein, Weffort, Laclau	Rejects/minimizes national premise of SH; affirms Utop; differing views on EH and PS
Orthodox dependency	A. G. Frank	Affirms SH, Utop, EH, PS; "extreme" version
Unorthodox dependency	F. H. Cardoso	Affirms SH, Utop, EH, PS; "moderate" version
Heretical dependency	Galtung, Jaguaribe	Affirms much of SH; cautious about or rejects Utop, EH, PS
Analytic dependency	(See Chapters 6 and 7)	Open to all substantive propositions but rejects Utop, EH, PS
Bargaining dependency	Moran, Tugwell	Focuses on a few aspects of national dependency, esp. state/MNC relations; ignores/ neglects internal aspects of dependency

Abbreviations: SH (Substantive Holism); Utop (Utopianism); EH (Epistemological Holism); PS (Premise of Politicized Scholarship); MNC (Multinational Corporation)

by contrast, make no attempt at unification. The exclusive or over-whelmingly dominant mode of analysis is one or the other—class in the first case, nation-state in the second.

In pure-class theories the categories nation and nationalism are theoretically unimportant or nonexistent. One of the first scholars to articulate the pure-class position specifically in relation to dependency ideas was the Brazilian political scientist Francisco Weffort. In an early critique of Cardoso and Faletto's book he noted that "the idea of dependency seems to suffer from an inevitable theoretical ambiguity," because the dependency writers "try to elaborate two different concepts: external dependency, denoting the relations of the Nation with 'center countries,' and structural dependency, a more complex notion which denotes at the same time external relations and their internal structural effects on classes and modes of production . . .

The imprecision of the notion of dependency . . . is in its oscillation, in a theoretically untenable fashion, between a national approach and a class approach" (Weffort, 1971, pp. 7, 10).

Weffort diagnosed the problem brilliantly. The solution he proposed is more problematic. It was to focus entirely on class and to ignore the category of nation. As he put it, "the Class-Nation ambiguity . . . ought to be resolved in terms of a class perspective, for which there is neither a 'national question' in general nor dependency in general. Nor is the Nation conceived as an explanatory theoretical principle" (Weffort, 1971, pp. 13–14). Weffort's solution has the virtue of logical consistency. But by eliminating the nation as a category of analysis except as a reflection of events in the economic sphere, it ignores much empirical reality. Weffort reports no empirical research employing this perspective.

Another critique of dependency ideas within the Marxist tradition comes from the "modes-of-production" approach. One of its earliest and most influential exponents was the Argentinian political scientist Ernesto Laclau (1971, as reprinted in Klarén and Bossert, 1986, pp. 166–188). His basic idea was that dependency analysis—by which he meant mainly the writings of Gunder Frank—used the concept of capitalism too broadly and indiscriminately. Frank had argued against the dualistic idea of both feudalism and capitalism in Latin America; his view was that when Europeans reached Latin America, it became capitalist. Laclau argued that this interpretation was too sweeping. He charged that Frank had failed to distinguish "the capitalist mode of production" from "participation in a world capitalist system" (Laclau in Klarén and Bossert, 1986, p. 186). Laclau took the view that various modes of production—including feudal and slave modes—were intermixed with capitalist modes, which were not all the same in any case.

Laclau's work has been influential in Marxist circles. It gave rise to a vigorous debate between "circulationists and productionists" and also helped to stimulate other work (for summaries and examples, see Higgott, 1983, pp. 58–65; Chilcote, 1984, chs. 5 and 6; Randall and Theobald, 1985, pp. 122–134; Taylor, 1979). The important point for present purposes is that the terrain of Laclau's argument was entirely Marxist. National units were secondary or nonexistent. The real questions—production, distribution, and exchange—did not require attention to nations and nationalism.

Another manifestation of the class perspective is the world-systems approach, whose most influential expositor is Immanuel Wallerstein (1974, 1979, 1980). Wallerstein projects an integrated class vision onto the entire world. Capitalism is a world economic system that emerged in the sixteenth century and is with us still. In the capitalist world economy there is one world system of exchange and one world division of labor. National units and class divisions within them exist but can be understood properly only in the context of this world system. There are core, periphery, and semi-periphery states, which frequently contend with one another, but such conflicts by themselves do not alter the fact of the world system as such. The only way such conflicts can alter the world system is "via the intervening variable" of the "world-wide class consciousness of the proletariat" (Wallerstein, 1979, p. 293).

In this view the concepts of core, semi-periphery, and periphery states are "intellectual tool[s] to help analyze the multiple forms of class conflict in the capitalist world economy" (Wallerstein, 1979, p. 293). This applies to both capitalist and socialist states. "There are today no socialist systems in the world economy because there is only one world system. It is a world-economy and it is by definition capitalist in form. Socialism involves the creation of a new kind of world-system, neither a redistributive world-empire nor a capitalist world-economy but a socialist world-government." This seems utopian but not to Wallerstein: "I don't see this projection as being in the least utopian but I also don't feel its institution is imminent" (Wallerstein, 1979, p. 35).

World-systems theory is in the spirit of holistic dependency and shares much with it but rejects its national premise. In our terms it is holistic dependency without nationalism. Thus Wallerstein says (1979, pp. 35–36) that socialist world-government "will be the outcome of a long struggle . . . in all areas of the world economy (Mao's continual 'class struggle') . . . states as such are neither progressive nor reactionary. It is movements and forces that deserve such evaluative judgments." Like holistic dependency, world-systems theory is substantively holistic, utopian, and unfalsifiable.

Bargaining Studies

If in pure-class and world-systems theories the most theoretically significant units are classes within and across national boundaries, in bargaining studies the most theoretically significant units are nation-states and the actors with whom they deal. If in the former approaches the fundamental issue is exploitation of popular classes by capitalist classes, in the latter the basic issue is power relations among nation-states and other actors.

A classic example of the genre is Hirschman's study of Germany's use of foreign trade as an instrument of national power in the twenties and thirties. Hirschman used the term dependence, which he defined strictly in terms of power or influence, long before it became fashionable (1980 [original version 1945], pp. 13–26, 29–35, 45–48). In the contemporary literature the two pioneering bargaining studies are books by Moran (1974) on Chilean copper and Tugwell (1975) on Venezuelan oil. They describe and analyze the ways in which over time a Latin American state gained control of the central economic resource of its society that had previously been owned and controlled by foreign private actors. Other empirical studies using the bargaining approach include Krasner's (1973a, 1973b) articles on Brazilian coffee policy, Grieco's (1984) book on India's experience with the international computer industry, and, more ambiguously, Bennett and Sharpe's (1985) analyses of bargaining encounters between the Mexican state and the international automobile industry.

Bargaining studies have tended to focus on relations between multinational corporations and the state in the host countries (Moran, 1974; Tugwell, 1975; Grieco, 1984; Bennett and Sharpe, 1985). Often they have been informed by the notion of the "obsolescing bargain." This is the idea that the bargaining position of a multinational enterprise vis-a-vis host governments tends to weaken over time as (a) the enterprise commits more resources to the host country and thus becomes more of a hostage to it; (b) the host government and local firms learn more about how to operate the enterprise; and (c) the legitimacy of the foreign enterprise is eroded by nationalist ideology and the logic of host-country politics. The obsolescing bargain has enabled host governments to gain ownership and control in most of the extractive industries and public utilities in Latin America during the last two or three decades (for a thorough review with citations, see Sigmund, 1980).

Although interesting and important from various scholarly and policy perspectives, bargaining studies do not address the main concerns of holistic dependency. The conceptual frameworks, foci of empirical inquiry, and central intellectual and political preoccupations of bargaining studies and holistic dependency are quite different. In bargaining studies, changes in degrees of national power and influence are significant, whereas in holistic dependency they are analogous to degrees of slavery and insignificant. In bargaining studies conflicts between Third World states and foreign private enterprises within capitalism are the main subject if not the only one; in holistic dependency such conflicts are of no more than secondary importance—family quarrels within capitalism.

Most important, bargaining studies give little or no attention to the internal aspects of development that are central in holistic dependency. Hirschman's main topic is Germany's use of its foreign trade to enhance its national power; he is not much interested in the structure of politics and society within Southeastern Europe. When Moran writes (p. 121) that Chile "moved once and for all to end the condition of *dependencia*," he is referring to the nationalization of the Anaconda and Kennecott copper mines, not to Chile's internal social, economic, and political arrangements. Although Tugwell, Grieco, Krasner, and Bennett and Sharpe may touch on internal aspects of dependency, these are not their central concerns. For holistic dependency authors, by contrast, internal aspects are the heart of the matter.

A Comparison of Orthodox and Unorthodox Dependency

In most of the scholarly literature great stress is placed on such questions as "the development of underdevelopment" versus "associated-dependent development," the weight to be placed on "external" versus "internal" aspects of dependency, and on "formal," "abstract" modes of analysis versus the "dialectical" analysis of "interests" in "concrete situations," as ways to distinguish "subtle and sophisticated" unorthodox dependency from "vulgar and mechanical" orthodox dependency (for example, Cardoso, 1977a; Domínguez, 1978a, 1978b; Palma, 1978; Valenzuela and Valenzuela, 1978; Seers, 1981; Gereffi, 1983; Evans, 1985a, 1987; T. Smith, 1985a; Klarén and Bossert, 1985; Bennett and Sharpe, 1985; Walton, 1987; Biersteker, 1987; Stern, 1988a). Some of these distinctions are invalid; others are valid up to a point; few are as important as the literature says they are.

It is true that Frank has often taken extreme positions. In abstract terms (not the only way he argues, although many say otherwise) one of his main theses has been the idea that both underdevelopment and development are "inevitable" products of capitalism (Frank, 1975, p. 104; subsequent page citations are to this work). Development and underdevelopment are not clearly defined; Frank uses various indicators which sometimes are inconsistent. Capitalism is everything that has happened in the nonsocialist world for at least the last four centuries; it is "a single world-wide economic and social system" that includes not only capitalist "traits" (market relations, proletarianization, and so on) but also "feudalism, mercantilism, colonialism, etc." (pp. 44–45). Among the other extreme arguments—some definitional, some empirical, some prescriptive—that Frank makes are the following: "underdevelopment and colonialism are perfectly correlated in both directions" (p. 7); "internal colonialism" is the intranational expression of international imperialism; stratification systems are multiple but classes are always dichotomous; "the proletariat . . . most certainly includes the peasants, 'subsistence' peasants included" (p. 94); "only the proletariat—and those already liberated by socialism"—can "liberate underdeveloped countries" (p. 105); in only one country—the Soviet Union—have "imperialism-colonialism and underdevelopment, both of the USSR and of its regions and peoples . . . by general agreement been eliminated" (p. 103); "if rivers of blood are necessary for liberation from capitalism and underdevelopment now, oceans of blood may be necessary" in the future (p. 110).

In certain respects, Cardoso's arguments are less extreme than Frank's. Cardoso seldom if ever uses the word "inevitable." He uses the phrase "the development of underdevelopment" less often than Frank—although Cardoso also has used it, as we shall see. Cardoso has stressed the internal aspects of dependency and the possibilities for a certain form of development under dependency more than Frank. Cardoso has given less emphasis than Frank to the penetration of world capitalism into "feudal" social relations, to the centrality of the proletariat in the "liberation" of "underdeveloped" countries, and to the USSR as an exemplar of socialist development. At no time has Cardoso seen violent revolution to be inevitable, as Frank does, although Cardoso has not rejected it under some circumstances. Cardoso's writings are more eclectic, contradictory, and ambiguous on a wide range of issues. These features in turn create an impression—only partly correct—of greater moderation in Cardoso's dependency writings than in Frank's.

But by no means all of the supposed differences between orthodox dependency and unorthodox dependency exist in fact. In a number of ways one is just as extreme as the other. It is not true that Cardoso rejects entirely the idea of "the development of underdevelopment." To the contrary, he employs it frequently ("the situation of underdevelopment came about when . . . "), as do other authors identified with unorthodox dependency (Cardoso and Faletto, 1979, pp. 17, 77, 81; Valenzuela and Valenzuela, 1978; Palma, 1978; Sunkel, 1973; Sunkel and Paz, 1970). Frank defines development and underdevelopment vaguely or with contradictory indicators; so does Cardoso. Frank sees internal exploitation as an "expression" of "external" capitalism; so does Cardoso. Frank sees stratification systems as multiple but classes as dichotomous; so does Cardoso, who makes repeated references to the dominant, bourgeois, capitalist class or classes, on the one hand, and the "popular classes," on the other. Frank includes the proletariat as part of the peasantry. Cardoso generally avoids the use of the term "proletariat," and he never includes peasants as part of the proletariat; but his pervasive use of the concept of the "popular classes" does the same thing with less extreme-sounding terminology. Thus not only most urban workers and peasants, but also other strata are lumped together in Cardoso's concept of "popular classes."

Frank (1967, pp. xi–xiii) rejects emphatically the notion that national capitalism based upon the autonomous development of a national bourgeoisie is a desirable or acceptable "way out" for Latin America. So does Cardoso. Frank (1967, pp. xii–xiii) argues that in Latin America and elsewhere the way to progress must involve "the masses of the people" together with "those who would honestly and realistically serve the progress of the people," such as certain right-thinking intellectuals, but not the bourgeoisie. Cardoso makes exactly the same argument: the only solution involves "truly popular forces, capable of seeking socialist forms for the social organization of the future" (Cardoso and Faletto, 1979, p. 216) together with "the intellectuals in Latin America . . . because they are the voices of those who cannot speak for themselves" (Cardoso as quoted in Kahl, 1976, epigraph).

In parallel fashion, orthodox dependency is just as moderate as unorthodox dependency in a number of ways. Does Frank deny possibilities for development under dependency? If one read only commentaries on his work rather than the work itself, one would certainly think so (see Domínguez, 1978, p. 107). Yet evidence of

Frank's attention to possibilities for development is abundant. For example, in the preface to his classic work (1967, p. xi) he writes that capitalist development is "contradictory development which generates at once economic development and underdevelopment on international, national, local, and sectoral levels." This passage is prominently placed yet few commentators have said anything about it. Is it because the ideas in it are identical to those of unorthodox dependency?

Frank applies this perspective to Chile and Brazil. In the Chilean case study (Frank, 1967, pp. 1–120) he does write exclusively about "the development of underdevelopment." Even here, however, the evidence is contradictory and semantics are part of the problem. For example, Frank writes that "Because of capitalism, Chile's economy was already underdeveloping throughout the three centuries before independence" (p. 6). This sounds like a statement of the most extreme orthodox dependency. However, one sentence later he also writes that "dependent and underdeveloped development toward the outside has been ingrained in the Chilean economy since the conquest itself." This is the same as unorthodox dependency, and it suggests that Frank's term "underdevelopment" in the first sentence refers to distorted, unequal development as well as underdevelopment per se. Such a usage of the term would be identical to that of Cardoso, Sunkel, Valenzuela and Valenzuela, Palma, and others.

In the Brazilian case study Frank writes extensively about both "the development of underdevelopment" and "the underdevelopment of development." The second emphasis is almost never acknowledged by commentators. Yet in the Brazilian study he devotes more attention to the latter (pp. 167–213) than to the former (pp. 150–167). In discussing "the underdevelopment of development," Frank takes up the topics of unorthodox dependency: industrialization; class, regional, and rural-urban inequalities; foreign investment; the alliance of foreign and national capital; technological dependency; the relationship between "external dependency" and "internal colonialism;" and political authoritarianism (pp. 167–213). When he writes about "the development of underdevelopment" in Brazil, Frank writes mainly about the North, Northeast, and Central interior regions of the country in the sixteenth, seventeenth, and eighteenth centuries (pp. 150–167). When he writes about "the underdevelopment of development," he writes mainly about the Center-South and South in the nineteenth and twentieth centuries (pp. 167–213). These are essentially the same arguments that Cardoso makes, except that

Cardoso wrote less about the North and Northeast and dates the advent of development in the South and Center-South somewhat later than Frank.

Another issue where the differences between Cardoso and Frank are exaggerated is that of the importance of external or internal aspects of dependency. It is not true that Frank ignores the internal features or that Cardoso ignores the external features of dependency. To the contrary, each author deals at length with both aspects. The opening sentence of Frank's seminal book (1967, p. vii) reads, "I believe, with Paul Baran, that it is capitalism, both world and national, which produced underdevelopment in the past and which still generates underdevelopment in the present." The phrase "capitalism, both world and national" makes clear right from the start that Frank conceived of dependency as a condition or situation having internal aspects as well as global and international features. So does his statement that capitalist development generates at once development and underdevelopment "on international, national, local, and sectoral levels" (p. xi). Frank elaborates these ideas consistently throughout the book and indeed all his dependency writings (for example, Frank, 1967, p. xi; 1969, pp. xxi–xxiii). He frequently puts the words "external" and "internal" between quotation marks to indicate that each is part of the other, that they are part of an interacting whole, and that the class distinction is more fundamental than the national distinction (pp. 99–115). Throughout his work Cardoso does the same and for the same reasons.

The alleged differences are either much smaller than claimed or nonexistent regarding other issues. When Cardoso and Faletto (1979, p. xv) write that "Latin American societies have been built as a consequence of the expansion of European and American capitalism," they say nothing about variations within the center or between the Latin and non-Latin parts of the periphery. They acknowledge diversity within Latin American situations of dependent capitalism, but they never acknowledge that capitalism coming out of imperial Spain or Portugal was different in important respects (political, social, cultural) from capitalism coming out of imperial England, France, or Holland. Nor is there any expression of awareness that the sociopolitical and cultural consequences of the spread of capitalism in Latin America were different from its consequences in the United States, Australia, Canada, and New Zealand. In these respects the arguments of orthodox dependency are the same as Cardoso's.

The disparity between the characterizations made by commenta-

tors about Frank's work and the reality of what Frank has written
justify the complaint of Wallerstein (quoted on jacket of Frank, 1979)
that Frank's work is "widely discussed, passionately debated, and
hastily read . . . He warrants careful, not sloppy, reading." The
writings of unorthodox writers have also not been read with the care
they deserve. In the case of Cardoso, if one reads his work selectively,
it is possible to see him as unorthodox, or quite orthodox, or even
as a liberal completely outside the dependency perspective. But if one
reads his work comprehensively one becomes aware of the contradictions and the ways they are resolved.

Dependency and Marxism

A number of commentators have put dependency and Marxist writings in separate categories. In particular, they have argued that while
orthodox dependency may or may not be Marxist, unorthodox dependency is definitely not Marxist (Myer, 1975, pp. 41, 45, passim;
Harding, 1976, p. 7; Domínguez, 1978b, pp. 513–514; Seers, 1979,
p. 13; Francis, 1980, pp. 47–51; Sigmund, 1980a, p. 345, and 1980b,
pp. 30–32; Hewlett, 1980, pp. 138–139; Horowitz, 1982, p. 81;
Chilcote, 1984, pp. 40–47; Hall, 1984, p. 45). These arguments are
hard to sustain. True, dependency ideas do represent an effort to
strengthen the relatively weak Marxist treatment of nationalism, and
they may be said to represent a blending or marriage of Marxism
and nationalism. But this does not necessarily put them outside the
Marxist tradition. That tradition is broad and flexible; it sustains an
enormous variety of regimes and bodies of thought. Committed democrats and brutal dictators alike have cast themselves as Marxists.

The fundamental ideas and logic of unorthodox dependency no
less than orthodox dependency are Marxist. Among these are the
priority of class over nation as an analytic category; the idea that
capitalism is exploitative by definition and that the only solution to
this exploitation is socialism; the holistic mode of analysis; the claim
of dialectical reasoning; the centrality of the concept of interest; the
insistence on dichotomous rather than continuous modes of analysis;
the focus of concrete empirical research on capitalism and the paucity
or absence of concrete empirical research on socialist systems; the
use of concepts such as accumulation, surplus value, modes of production, material forces of production, and social relations of production. All these ideas and others index the massive overlap and

essential linkage between Marxist and unorthodox dependency modes of analysis. Much evidence on these points has been presented earlier in this book. What follows supplements that discussion with respect to a few points.

When critics within the Marxist tradition have charged that unorthodox dependency writers have been unfaithful to Marxist tenets, the accused have been indignant, affirming in the strongest terms their fidelity to those tenets and charging that it is not they but the critics who misunderstand Marxism. A classic illustration is a debate, rather well known in Latin American Marxist circles, between Weffort (1971) and Cardoso (1971) in Santiago in 1970. Weffort said that Cardoso erroneously treated class and nation as concepts of theoretically equal status and tried to use a nation-oriented theory of dependency to displace Marx's theory of capitalist classes and Lenin's theory of imperialism. Cardoso denied the charges; claimed that Weffort's rendition of the thought of Marx and Lenin was "formal," "univocal," and "superficial"; and argued that it was he not Weffort who was correctly interpreting Marx's and Lenin's ideas as well as constructively elaborating and refining them. In response to similar charges in 1974, this time by Fernández and Ocampo (1974), Cardoso (1974, p. 71; see also p. 69) replied, with evident heat, as follows:

> I did not try to deny Lenin's characterization . . . of imperialism. I reject vehemently the insinuation that my work is "a new form of imperialist apologetic." Nor do I believe that this kind of silly insinuation [*insinuação boba*] is a valid criticism of Frank. Finally, no one that I know among the "dependentistas" has considered "the struggle against imperialism as secondary to the class struggle and the battle against capitalism" . . . It is easy to create a paper enemy and then destroy it. What is difficult is to discuss arguments at the level at which they are presented. But only the second way is intellectually honest.

The claim that unorthodox dependency is inconsistent with Marxism and Leninism is often based on misperceptions of the ideas of Marx and Lenin. Mandle (1979, p. 178) writes that Evans's book on Brazil is "the Left's first systematic recognition that a path of capitalist economic development remains feasible for at least some contemporary underdeveloped countries . . . This view stands in marked contrast to most Marxist and radical views which hypothesize that only the adoption of socialism can propel poor nations toward economic advance." Sigmund (1980b, pp. 31–33) divides dependency writings into two types, Marxist and non-Marxist, and associates the Marxist type exclusively with the idea of the "development of underdevelopment" under capitalism and not at all with the idea of dependent development. Even Cardoso (1973a, p. 149) himself says that "In many Latin American intellectual circles the idea that associated dependent development is in some important sense dynamic will be considered a controversial, revisionist assertion." Stepan (1973b, p. ix) agrees with him, stating that Cardoso's "associated-dependent development" thesis "calls for a theoretical reformulation of the impact of economic imperialism."

Contrary to the foregoing claims, however, the idea that development can be compatible with or facilitated by dependent capitalism was not an innovation of unorthodox dependency writers; it was advanced by Marx as early as 1853 and by Lenin no later than 1921. They both anticipated the idea of associated-dependent development and were even more aware of its positive implications than unorthodox dependency authors have been.

Marx's views on these matters are stated most fully in his essay "The Future Results of British Rule in India" (1853), where he wrote that "England has to fulfill a double mission in India: one destructive, the other regenerating—the annihilation of old Asiatic society, and the laying of the material foundations of Western society in Asia." Marx reasoned that the railroads introduced by the British would break down the isolation of traditional villages and thereby cause a "social revolution." Railroads would create needs for coal, iron, and other materials which would in their turn generate—by a process we might today call "backward linkages"—the development of modern industry: "You cannot maintain a net of railways over an immense country without introducing all those industrial processes necessary to meet the immediate and current wants of railway locomotion, and out of which there must grow the application of machinery to those branches of industry not immediately connected with railways. The railway-system will therefore become, in India, truly the forerunner of modern industry" (Marx, 1972, pp. 583, 586).

Lenin shared Marx's view of the revolutionary effects of railroads on peripheral countries. With them, he wrote in his pamphlet "Imperialism" (1917), "the elementary conditions for industrial development have been created." Moreover, "The export of capital greatly affects and accelerates the development of capitalism in those countries to which it is exported. While, therefore, the export of capital may tend to a certain extent to arrest development in the countries exporting capital, it can only do so by expanding and deepening the further development of capitalism throughout the world" (Lenin as quoted in Warren, 1980, p. 81). For Lenin as for Marx, "Socialism is better than capitalism, but capitalism is better than medievalism, small production, and a bureaucracy connected with the dispersed character of the small producers" (Lenin as quoted in Lipset, 1981b, p. 31).

Of course, none of the foregoing means that Marx and Lenin thought that capitalism was acceptable, desirable, or feasible in the long run. Rather, theirs was a double criticism. It was directed on one hand against the naive view that capitalism's effects on the periphery were only negative—against, in other words, an exclusive "development of underdevelopment" perspective. On the other hand, it rejected unequivocally any perspective which did not assume and demonstrate that capitalism anywhere, by its very nature, was on balance exploitative and dominating and would need to be replaced by socialism. On each of these fundamental features the parallels between the views of Marx and Lenin and unorthodox dependency could not be more complete.

Like other Marxists, orthodox and unorthodox dependency writers differ among themselves about many things, including (very often) how to read Marx. But this does not mean they are necessarily separate from Marxism.

Variations and Continuities over Time

The scholarly literature contains many assertions about variations in dependency ideas over time. In particular, it is argued that the early writings were less moderate and more rigidly Marxist than the later ones, both in general and within the work of the same author (Portes, 1976, p. 78; Sigmund, 1980a, p. 345; Hirschman, 1980, pp. 45, 49–50; Chilcote, 1982, p. x; Evans, 1987, p. 320). Such claims are partly accurate but on the whole misleading regarding the dynamic of dependency ideas over time.

It is true that Frank's "development of underdevelopment" idea (1967) preceded, and was superseded by, Cardoso's notion of "associated-dependent development" (Cardoso and Faletto, 1969; Cardoso, 1973a). However, the differences between orthodox and unorthodox dependency on this point are much smaller, as we have just seen, than the two phrases would suggest. Moreover, this change took place very early. The dominance of Frank's ideas compared to Cardoso's lasted only two or three years, if that long. Almost as soon as it appeared Cardoso and Faletto's book (1969) stole the thunder from Frank's 1967 book among the majority of the most influential scholars in the United States and Latin America (Halperín-Donghi, 1982, pp. 116–117). The change from Frank's orthodox dependency version to Cardoso's unorthodox version was much less substantial than it is usually understood to be and occurred very early on. It has no bearing on changes since then or variations in the thinking of individual authors.

If we look at these latter questions, the allegations about trends are inaccurate. Take for instance the claim (Sigmund, 1980a, p. 345) that Cardoso's position in the 1969 version of *Dependencia y Desarrollo en América Latina* was more "radical" than his position in his 1973 article on "Associated-Dependent Development". In fact, the 1969 edition was less radical, less anticapitalist, and more eclectic than Cardoso's subsequent dependency writings. The 1973 article attacked reformism within the capitalist system. It argued that "insertion" into "the circuit of international capitalism" (Cardoso, 1973a, p. 163) meant both dependency and distorted development. As the 1970s wore on, these arguments became even more forceful and strident (Cardoso, 1974, 1977a; Cardoso and Faletto, 1979).

Cardoso did not become more "possibilist" in his dependency writings in the middle and late 1970s, as Hirschman (1978; 1980, pp. 45, 49–50) suggests. Although there are elements of possibilism at all stages in Cardoso's thought, especially if one counts rhetorical admonitions, authentic (more than rhetorical) possibilism was if anything weaker in his later dependency writings than in the early ones. Thus no sooner did Hirschman's (1978) essay praising Cardoso for adopting a more possibilist approach to dependency issues first appear, than the revised and expanded edition of Cardoso and Faletto's book was published in 1979. In it Cardoso attempted to annihilate nearly every major aspect of Hirschman's approach: a power definition of dependency, disaggregation of dependency into component parts, emphasis on degrees of freedom and autonomy, partial solutions under capitalism, *ceteris paribus* assumptions as analytic tools, and so on. To be sure, Cardoso did not name Hirschman as an object of his criticism; quite the contrary, he invoked Hirschman and the rhetoric of possibilism in support of his own approach. But these invocations have little to do with the substance and method actually used and prescribed by Cardoso and Hirschman, respectively. The 1969 edition was not very possibilist, either, but of the two the 1979 edition was less so.

The claim (Chilcote, 1982, p. x) that Cardoso "dismissed altogether the theory of dependency" in the seventies, or later for that matter, is at the least overstated and misspecified. Cardoso repeatedly dismissed the dependency ideas of Frank, Rui Mauro Marini, and others but never his own. To the contrary, he consistently defended them against all critics: Weberians, positivists, orthodox dependency writers, and other Marxists. Cardoso often protested alleged distortions of his ideas by others but never rejected them himself the way, for example, Frank (1974) rejected some of his own earlier ideas.

The best way to see the real continuities and changes is to review the whole period beginning with Cardoso's earliest writings on dependency in the late sixties until he stopped writing about it in the late seventies and early eighties. Such a review shows no evidence of change from a radical to a more moderate, less Marxist view. To the extent there is change it goes in the opposite direction. But the bulk of the evidence shows no major change either way; it shows instead, as Cardoso himself and others have argued, a firm foundation in the Marxist fundamentals from beginning to end (Cardoso, 1971a, 1974, 1977a, 1980; Cardoso and Faletto, 1979; Palma, 1978; Packenham, 1982). This conclusion is strengthened even more by examining Cardoso's writings in the early sixties (see Chapter 1 above).

Cardoso is less a "permanent heretic" (Domínguez, 1978a) than the opposite, that is, one who defines the permissible outer boundaries of innovation, contradiction, and ambiguity within the Marxist tradition without becoming a heretic. Those outer boundaries move around depending on concrete circumstances of the specific "conjuncture" or "moment" and other contingent factors in the historical struggle. They have to be defined by a combination of political and intellectual considerations. Cardoso has played an important role in this. He has always claimed to be within the Marxist tradition; despite criticisms, he mostly fits those terms.

If, as we have seen, Cardoso's dependency ideas are not heresy, whose are?

Heretical Dependency

In terms of the generic features of holistic dependency the real heretics are Johan Galtung, Helio Jaguaribe, and in a more complex and contradictory way, Guillermo O'Donnell. They have written in the dependency vein up to a point but also have differed from it. Although each of them has addressed both internal and external aspects of dependency, none has defined dependency in the framework of Marx's theory of capitalism. This is heresy.

In Galtung's view, "The world consists of Center and Periphery nations; and each nation, in turn, has its center and periphery." This scheme yields four main categories: The center of the Center (cC); the center of the Periphery (cP); the periphery of the Center (pC); and the periphery of the Periphery (pP). This is identical to, although stated in more formal terms than, holistic dependency. So is Galtung's heavy reliance on the concept of interest. Thus "imperialism is a system that splits up collectivities and relates some of the parts to each other in relations of harmony of interest, and other parts in relations of disharmony of interest, or conflict of interest." How are these harmonies and disharmonies of interest determined? Galtung gives a clear answer: "[They] are stipulated by an outsider as the 'true' interests of the parties, disregarding wholly or completely what the parties themselves say explicitly are the values they pursue." Galtung's reasons for using this method are the same as Cardoso's and are explained very clearly: "One reason for this is the rejection of the dogma of unlimited rationality: actors do not necessarily know, or they are unable to express, what their interest is. Another, more important reason is that rationality is unevenly distributed, that some may dominate the minds of others, and that this may lead to 'false consciousness.' Thus, learning to suppress one's own true interests may be a major part of socialization in general and education in particular" (Galtung, 1972, pp. 93–94).

In other respects, however, Galtung is sharply at odds with holistic dependency. He defines dependency relationships as "a species in a genus of dominance and power relationships." His argument "is not reductionist in the traditional sense pursued in Marxist-Leninist theory, which conceived of imperialism as an economic relationship under private capitalism . . . According to this view, imperialism and dominance will fall like dominoes when the capitalistic conditions for economic imperialism no longer obtain. According to the view we develop here, imperialism is a more general structural relationship between two collectivities, and has to be understood at a general level in order to be understood and counteracted in its more specific manifestations" (Galtung, 1972, p. 94). By denying a necessary and exclusive linkage between capitalism and dependency Galtung opens up possibilities for reformist capitalism and criticism of socialist dependency that are taboo within the dependencia tradition. It is why Fagen (1977, p. 24; 1978a, p. 296) accuses Galtung of "cold warriorism," excessive abstraction, ahistoricism, and attempting "to analyze [socialist] asymmetries and dynamics as if there were no differences in center/periphery relations under capitalism and socialism." In fact Galtung never argues that there are no differences; he is just open to the possibility that there might be similarities. But that is enough to constitute heresy within holistic dependency.

Similar challenges to holistic dependency appear in the extensive writings of Helio Jaguaribe (1969, 1973, 1974, 1978, 1986a, 1986b). Like Galtung, he subscribes to part of holistic dependency's substantive agenda but tends to be skeptical of its utopianism, nonfalsificationism, and politicization. Unlike Galtung, whose writings are rather abstract, Jaguaribe has combined theory with an empirical focus on Latin America. He is the only dependency writer who has devoted as much attention to autonomy as to dependency. He describes two ways to reduce dependency and increase autonomy, one revolutionary, the other reformist. His reformist alternative occurs through what he calls "national developmentalism" based on "varying combinations of national capitalism and state capitalism." Like Galtung, Jaguaribe challenges sharply the view that socialism is necessarily associated with national autonomy. Almost alone among dependency writers Jaguaribe has repeatedly emphasized "national viability" as a precondition for national development and national autonomy. He argues that certain small Central American, Caribbean, and South American nation-states are simply not viable as independent national units. Their only hope, in his view, is some form of integration with larger states or other small states (Jaguaribe, 1973, pp. 536, 333–347, 399–402, 456–469).

Jaguaribe's views also have been sharply criticized by holistic dependency authors (Cardoso, 1973a, pp. 143, 150–164; Frank, 1972, pp. 138–145; Vasconi and T. dos Santos in Jaguaribe et al., 1970, pp. 260–263, 274–278; Jaguaribe replies in Jaguaribe et al., 1970, pp. 264–272, 284–293). They see his ideas as expressions of national capitalism, a double epithet and sure sign of intellectual and political deviationism in the Marxist tradition. Some of these criticisms are inaccurate and even bizarre—for example, the charge (Cardoso, 1973a, p. 150) that Jaguaribe is an "economic determinist." Despite criticisms, Jaguaribe's standing remained high and many of his ideas have been vindicated.

A more contradictory but still very significant challenge to holistic dependency comes from Guillermo O'Donnell. It appears not in his well-known works on bureaucratic authoritarianism but in an interesting book he and Delfina Linck published in 1973, *Dependencia y Autonomía,* which unfortunately has received relatively little attention. O'Donnell wrote all of it except for its third chapter (O'Donnell and Linck, 1973, p. 9).

In *Dependencia y Autonomía* O'Donnell begins (pp. 15–16) by defining dependency in power terms, as "the reverse of domination, power, and influence." In a significant passage he writes that "studies about political power can be of great help in clarifying the dependency theme and in making it more precise." By "studies on political power" he means works by Dahl, Lasswell, Kaplan, and other non-Marxists as well as the Marxists Poulantzas and Miliband. By "the dependency theme" he means works by a long list of Latin American and North American authors: Bambirra, Baran, Bodenheimer, Caputo, Cardoso, dos Santos, Furtado, Ianni, Marini, Pizarro, Schmitter, Vasconi. Curiously, although he cites every other well-known dependency writer, as well as the power theorists, nowhere does he mention the name or work of Andre Gunder Frank.

O'Donnell's definition of dependency in terms of power leads him to explore in the first two chapters a number of ideas that holistic dependency repeatedly attacks. Thus he disaggregates dependency into various issue areas, domains, and "dimensions." He distinguishes power resources, the utilization of those resources, and actual power exercised. He discusses degrees of dependency and autonomy. Most important, he compares dependency under different dominant actors, both capitalist and socialist. Thus he notes that just as the United States replaced England in dominating Argentina and other Latin American countries in the nineteenth century, so also in this century Cuba, after its "liberation" from the United States, "fell into military, economic, and technical dependence on the Soviet Union . . . Although the dominant actor and the form of the dependency changed, the central point remains that Cuba has continued to be dependent" (O'Donnell and Linck, 1973, pp. 35, 46).

Not even Galtung or Jaguaribe draws as much as O'Donnell does on the writings of non-Marxist "power" theorists such as Dahl and Lasswell. In this respect O'Donnell work was vulnerable to charges of heresy and such charges were made: he notes that his argument "that the dependency problem must be tackled as a phenomenon that is by no means exclusive to the contemporary capitalist system . . . has already originated some fire from my most 'orthodox' Marxist friends and colleagues" (O'Donnell, 1974). In general, however, he was not attacked by holistic authors nearly as much as Galtung and Jaguaribe were and he logically might have been.

One reason for his escaping major attacks is that in the second part of the book (chapters 3 through 5) O'Donnell abandons the "power" approach in favor of a thoroughly holistic approach. Although he documents transnational class ties, he ignores the ways Argentina's size, wealth, population, diplomatic and political skills, and nationalism, among other factors, protect a measure of autonomy for her. By dichotomizing dependency/autonomy relations— rather than treating them as phenomena with contradictions and degrees of dependency, as he did in his chapters 1 and 2—he finds only dependency, no autonomy; sees national and class dependency as inextricably linked rather than partly independent processes; and views capitalism by definition as hopeless and socialism by definition as the only solution. Although O'Donnell does not refer specifically to the contradiction between the two parts of his argument, he does state that "from a strictly academic point of view, this book is a premature product" (O'Donnell and Linck, 1973, p. 9), and later adds that "even though this book has academic work as its background, it is more, and very unabashedly so, a 'political writing' in the Latin and European tradition, in the sense that it is pointed to a politicized and not only an academic public and purports to have a 'message' more immediately relevant to present politics than is usually true of academic writings" (O'Donnell, 1974).

A second reason for his lenient treatment is that after this book O'Donnell wrote little in an explicit dependency vein. None of his subsequent publications used the word dependency in the title. He cited a few dependency authors, particularly Cardoso, frequently and positively but made little further use of *Dependencia y Autonomía,* especially those first two chapters. He did not make a point to identify himself as a dependency writer, and readers did not, either. This low identification and visibility may have impeded criticisms that could have been made of his analysis of dependency in terms of power.

Further, although O'Donnell's extensive writings on bureaucratic authoritarianism have some similarities to dependency ideas, they are also quite different. Their historical and substantive scope is much more focused: whereas dependency is about all aspects of Latin American development in all countries since at least 1810 and in many versions since 1500, bureaucratic authoritarianism is about political regimes in Southern Cone countries in the late twentieth century "post-populist" period. Also, O'Donnell's ideas about bureaucratic authoritarianism are much less resistant to falsificationist criteria—both in practice and in principle—than are those of holistic dependency.

6   Analytic Dependency and a Capitalist Situation (Brazil)

To explore holistic dependency's substantive research program and set its assumptions and methods into sharper relief, we focus here and in the next chapter on two concrete situations of dependency, one capitalist (Brazil), the other socialist (Cuba). These cases are carefully chosen. In the holistic dependency literature the paradigm case of sacrificing democracy, social justice, and national autonomy on the altar of dependent capitalist development is post-1964 Brazil. To the extent there is such a thing as a paradigm case of the socialist alternative, post-1959 Cuba is it. No cases are nearly as crucial theoretically and methodologically in the dependency literature as these two. Although volumes could be written about each of them—and also about analytic dependency in abstract terms—a chapter on each is sufficient for present purposes.

Basic Principles of Analytic Dependency

Analytic dependency is similar to holistic dependency in the scope of its substantive concerns: issues of national political, economic, and social development in an international context. Both holistic dependency and analytic dependency have, therefore, a much broader substantive focus than bargaining dependency. Analytic dependency is closer to heretical dependency than to any other approach. However, it is even more cautious about holistic dependency's substantive holism, more firmly opposed to its other features, and, in general, more inclined to emphasize systematic and documented empirical research than is heretical dependency.

Analytic dependency differs from holistic dependency in four major ways. First, it is open to the possibility that the features linked by definition in holistic dependency may be either linked or not linked in the empirical world. Second, it rejects substantive utopianism in favor of substantive realism: that is, it compares real-world capitalism to real-world socialism rather than to ideal-world socialism as does holistic dependency. Third, its epistemology is falsificationist rather than nonfalsificationist. Fourth, it rejects the premise of politicized scholarship in favor of the premise that scholarship and politics are fundamentally different vocations.

Holistic Dependency	*Analytic Dependency*
Substantive holism	Possibility of delinking substantive holism
Utopianism	Realism
Nonfalsificationism	Falsificationism
Fuses scholarly and political vocations	Separates scholarly and political vocations

The fundamental principles upon which analytic dependency is based are well known and widely accepted in many areas of scholarship outside holistic dependency. The classic formulation of the differences between scholarly and political vocations is Weber (1958, pp. 77–156; original publication in 1919). The principles of falsificationism as an alternative to both holism and positivism have been formulated by Popper (1957, 1959, 1963, 1976) and Lakatos (1970). The basic principles underlying analytic dependency are the traditional conventions of scholarship in the social sciences. They are at work whenever scholars resist political pressures, reject ad hominem arguments, and use facts to test hypotheses. Since they are well known, a lengthy description of these principles in abstract terms is unnecessary here. What is needed is to show how they relate to the substantive issues raised by holistic dependency and how they operate in the analysis of concrete cases.

Delinking Substantive Holism

In holistic dependency, as we have seen, one speaks "necessarily and simultaneously" of the domination of some classes and nations by others, of the exploitation of classes and nations, and of a host of alleged "concomitants" of these processes of domination and exploitation, such as socioeconomic inequalities, the state as a "pact of domination," and so on. Analytic dependency does not deny that these processes ever exist or that these alleged concomitants are ever present; sometimes they do exist and are present. It seeks, however, to answer the questions with data rather than by definition. It insists that concepts considered fair and legitimate when data are supportive must also be considered fair and legitimate when data are not supportive. Holistic dependency assumes that under capitalism all power disparities (among nations, classes, or any other units) are necessarily exploitative, and that under socialism—"true" socialism—there is neither power disparity nor exploitation. Analytic dependency, recognizing that such associations may exist, allows facts and judgments about different situations, cases, and relationships to determine whether the postulated associations exist or whether other types of relationships, inconceivable under the premises of holistic dependency, obtain in fact.

Analytic dependency therefore defines national dependency itself strictly in terms of power rather than simultaneously in terms of power, exploitation, and capitalism. Exploitation and capitalism (or socialism) may be associated with dependency, but it is best to keep them out of the definition itself. The difference between holistic dependency and analytic dependency is parallel to the difference between Karl Marx and the contemporary North American economist Richard Cooper (1979, p. 344):

> Like Lewis Carroll's Humpty Dumpty, we are, of course, free to define words the way we choose. Marx defined "exploitation" as the excess, if any, of market value over labor value embodied in a good. On this standard, virtually all economic transactions involve exploitation . . . The difficulty with this definition is twofold: it uses a word that has pejorative connotations to describe a universal phenomenon, and it fails to make distinctions among different types of 'exploitation' so defined that may be crucial in dealing with the question of rectification.

In analytic dependency, to be dependent is to be (relatively) weak; to be nondependent or autonomous is to be (relatively) strong, powerful, or influential. (For present purposes, these latter three terms are synonyms.) Autonomous nations, classes, groups, regions or individuals are relatively strong, dominant, or powerful; dependent nations, classes, groups, regions or individuals are relatively weak or dominated. Notice that in this approach the attribute in question, dependency, is distinguished analytically from the unit to which it is applied (nation, class, and so on). Rates, types, and directions of influence can vary either independently or together between and among these different units.

Defining dependency in terms of power is not a panacea. Power is itself a complex, difficult, elusive phenomenon. There is no complete consensus on its dimensions or how to analyze it. To recommend that the literature on power be drawn upon to study dependency relations does not necessarily imply incorporating the theoretical baggage of balance-of-power approaches to international relations (a good discussion of this issue is Baldwin, 1980). Nevertheless, the literature on power can be extremely useful to anyone interested in the analytic dependency approach. Since that literature is well established it is a mistake to ignore it or waste resources reinventing it independently.

It teaches, for instance, that power has numerous sources, not just wealth, force, knowledge, technology, or any other single resource; that it is not static; that it can be used efficiently or inefficiently, for good or for ill. Power can be increased or depleted; it can be described in terms of its magnitude, distribution, scope, and domain, and very often the only way to avoid hopeless ambiguities or oversimplifications is to make just these kinds of distinctions. A single actor's power may vary in different issue areas at different times in different domains over different persons or groups; many competing explanations—for example, resources, skills, motives, costs—are offered for different types and patterns of power relations; and power relations may usefully, though not exclusively, be seen as a subset of causal relations. Finally, although serious, disciplined analysis of power is extraordinarily difficult and complex, human beings and societies probably cannot do without the study of power (Dahl, 1968). If one substitutes "dependency" for "power" in the above, one sees how valuable and fertile the literature on power can be for analyzing constraints and opportunities in national (or other) units.

The Brazilian Case

Analytic dependency will help us to explore holistic dependency hypotheses about Brazilian development. Following Cardoso and Evans, we focus on the period from the late fifties, especially from 1964, to the mid-1970s. They are the years in which the "historical-structural specificities" of the model are said to apply most strongly (although both authors also contend that their model applies more generally to "countries like Argentina and Mexico as well as Brazil" [Cardoso, 1973a, p. 156; Evans, 1979, ch. 6]).

We begin with the assumption that Brazil, like all Latin American countries, is a dependent country in the sense that compared to a powerful country like the United States, it is relatively highly constrained by the international environment on many issues. At the same time Brazil, again like all Latin American countries, is not totally helpless. Within the context of its dependence there is room for maneuver. Indeed, in most respects Brazil, by virtue of its size, resources, distance from the United States, and other factors, is less constrained by the international environment than any other Latin American country. We also assume that dependency and its logical opposite (autonomy) can be defined as a continuous variable as well as a dichotomous variable. In other words, we can think of dependency not only in either/or terms (is Brazil dependent or autonomous?) but also in terms of degrees and trends (is Brazil more dependent than the United States? Was Brazil more or less dependent before 1964 than after 1964? Did Brazil have less power or more power to guide its own external and internal affairs after 1964 than before?).

Holistic dependency makes claims about both external and internal aspects of Brazil's dependent situation. To examine these claims from an analytic dependency perspective means using falsificationist criteria. Specifically, the claims of the model are noted; falsifiable criteria are established; operational indicators are given; relevant data are sought. If the data are supportive, that is reported and the hypotheses are sustained for this case. If the data are not supportive, that also is reported and analysts (and readers) must make a judgment about what it means. The analytic method does not mean the rigid, mechanical abandoning of a research program because of any single disconfirming fact; no research program is sustainable by that standard. It means that some indication of the kinds of facts that would cast doubt on or reject the hypothesis must be given and taken seriously by the analyst. The falsificationist epistemology of analytic dependency is an attitude of mind toward evidence, not a rigid formula, but it is a serious attitude. It says: if the data show a pattern refuting my conjectures, I need to rethink my conjectures. I cannot just complain about the data or explain them away, saving the hypothesis no matter what.

In order to show that analytic dependency could have been used at the same time that holistic analyses were originally done, we draw heavily on sources available in the mid-1970s. Some later sources are also used to bring the analysis up to date and emphasize certain points.

Authoritarian Brazil: External Dependency

Chilcote (1974) has characterized Brazil's post-1964 relationship to the United States as a "subservient, dependent" one. According to Moreira Alves (1973, p. 162) the Brazilian economy had become "totally dependent on foreign powers and their investments." Jaguaribe (1974, p. 72) saw Brazilian dependency as "rising, and becoming increasingly irreversible." He warned (1973, p. 462) that unless these tendencies were corrected within certain "historical deadlines" ranging from one to at most three decades hence, the chances of Brazil and other Latin American countries "ever obtaining an autonomous development will sharply decrease and will finally disappear altogether." For Cardoso (1973a, pp. 146–149) the "moving force" in the model of associated-dependent development was the multinational corporation. As a result of the multinationals' operations, "The dynamic basis of the productive system has changed . . . groups expressing the basic interests and modes of organization of international capitalism have gained disproportionate influence." In his view (p. 163) the post-1964 system "pushed the local bourgeoisie to adapt to the beat of international capitalist development, thereby establishing an effective subordination of the national economy to modern forms of economic domination."

Holistic dependency authors refer to both the magnitude and the qualitative features of the alleged subordination. Note that their hypotheses refer repeatedly to increasing degrees of dependency as well as to changes in the form of dependency. For instance, Cardoso refers to changes that "became significant in the late 1950s and are now [post-1964] occurring at an even more rapid rate" (1973a, p. 142; also pp. 144, 149, 161).

Magnitude of External Penetration

One of the major elements in the view that Brazil's overall dependence increased after 1964 is the hypothesis that there was an increase in the magnitude of external penetration of Brazilian resources and productive capacity through increases in foreign loans, direct investments, and exposure to international markets. This is certainly a plausible hypothesis: in general, all other things being equal, the more a nation's economy is penetrated by loans, investments, aid, and reliance on external trade, the more dependent the nation is.

In fact, most of the evidence supports this hypothesis; some of it counters the hypothesis; and some of the evidence is incomplete or ambiguous.

In several significant ways external penetration of Brazil's economy increased dramatically after 1964. The most dramatic indicator of this was the foreign debt. In the years 1960–64 the yearly average of the foreign debt was less than $3 billion. In 1972 the figure reached $10 billion. By the end of 1975 it was over $22 billion, and climbing (Baer, 1976, p. 49; Cline, 1976, p. 71).

Another indicator is foreign trade. The more foreign trade, the more reliance on the external economy—that is, the more external national dependence. In 1964 total exports amounted to $1.43 billion; in 1974, they were $7.97 billion. In 1964 total imports were $1.09 billion; in 1972 they were $4.2 billion; in 1974, after a fourfold increase in the national oil bill and other increases, they were $12.5 billion (Robock, 1975, p. 113; also Baer, 1976, p. 49; Cline, 1976, p. 66).

Still another instrument of increased external economic penetration is multinational organizations like the World Bank and the International Monetary Fund. In general their impact on Brazil increased: for instance, Brazil replaced India as the recipient of the largest loans from the World Bank.

Foreign investment also increased dramatically. This trend was more pronounced in portfolio investment (loans, finance capital) than in direct private investment (equity capital). Thus net foreign loans to Brazil increased from a yearly average of $350 million in 1960–64 to a yearly average of $5.12 billion in 1972–74. Net foreign direct investment increased from a yearly average of $70 million in 1960–64 to a yearly average of $770 million in 1972–74 (Baer, 1976, p. 49). This is an increase by a factor of nineteen in the annual amount of net foreign lending and an increase by a factor of eleven in the annual amount of net foreign direct investment during this period. Notice also that the absolute figures are much larger for loans than for direct investment.

Moreover, the increase in the foreign penetration of Brazil's economy according to the foregoing indicators was significantly greater than the growth of the Brazilian economy as a whole. In 1964, Brazil's gross domestic product (GDP) was in the neighborhood of $21 billion, and per capita income about $270. By 1974, GDP was estimated to be about $56 billion and per capita GDP to be about $540. This means that gross domestic product increased roughly three times and per capita product increased roughly two times from 1964 to 1975 (calculated from data in Ruddle and Barrows, 1974, pp. 432–433, and Baer, 1976, p. 47). The national debt, however, increased about seven times during this same span of years, imports about eleven to twelve times, exports six to seven times, annual loans about nineteen times, and annual direct investment about eleven times. To put the same point another way, if one takes each of the foregoing indicators of external economic penetration of Brazil as a percentage of gross domestic product, first in 1964 and then in 1974, one finds that in each case the foreign share increased during the period. As a share of annual gross domestic product from 1964 to 1974, the foreign debt thus rose from 14 percent to 38 percent, imports from 5 percent to 21 percent, exports from 7 percent to 14 percent, annual foreign loans from 2 percent to 9 percent, and annual direct investment from 0.3 percent to 1.3 percent (calculated from data in Baer, 1976, pp. 47, 49; Cline, 1976, p. 71; Robock, 1975, p. 113; Ruddle and Barrows, 1974, pp. 432–433).

All this indicated increased dependence for Brazil. There were a few relevant countertrends, however. The most important relates to the role the government in general and state enterprises in particular played in the Brazilian economy. The quantitative role of the state in the Brazilian economy had been growing fairly steadily since 1930, including growth in the years after 1964. According to one informed estimate, the government sector accounted for over 60 percent of Brazil's fixed investment in 1969 (Baer, Kerstenetzky, and Villela, 1973, pp. 30–31). This trend did not subside in the 1970s or 1980s.

It is difficult to say whether this expansion in the state's role fully balanced the increase in the role of the multinational corporations and in the importance of other foreign economic forces. Clearly, however, it was a massive and dramatic expansion which countered the multinational and foreign increases to a considerable extent.

The big loser in this three-player game, it appears, was the Brazilian private sector. The private sector's loss has been one reason for the frequent tactical marriage of convenience in Brazilian domestic politics between domestic Brazilian capitalist entrepreneurs protesting both multinational corporations and Brazilian statism, and Brazilian socialists opposing capitalist imperialism and the Brazilian state. The entrepreneurs even accused the military regime of leftist tendencies; one article by J. C. de Macedo Soares Guimarães was published in 1975 with the disarming title, "Communism and Its New Name: State Capitalism" (cited in Souza Barros, 1976). Obviously the basis of the on-again/off-again alliance between such entrepreneurs and Brazilian socialists was not always ideological.

Another countertrend may be found in the area of bilateral aid from the United States. Brazil was a major recipient of U.S. economic and technical assistance in the immediate aftermath of the 1964 revolution. After 1970, however, the flow of U.S. bilateral aid slowed to a trickle and had practically no significance. From the point of view of U.S. economic influence on Brazil, the real action was in the private sector and the multinational agencies.

Overall, the picture was mixed. On balance, however, the magnitude of external penetration almost certainly increased because of the weight of the first set of trends described. In contrast to the "closing" of the economy that characterized import-substituting growth from the 1930s through most of the 1950s, Brazil's economy from 1964 to the mid-1970s "opened up" and this meant more dependence in quantitative terms.

Qualitative Nature of External Penetration

But the dependencistas' argument that Brazil's dependence increased is based on much more than the magnitude of the foreign penetration of the Brazilian economy. A large part of their argument is also based on the qualitative structural features of that penetration. In particular, one needs to look at foreign penetration of the most dynamic sectors of the economy, that is, the sectors that were growing at the fastest rate. Thus Moreira Alves (1973, pp. 163–164) argued that

> official figures, published to reassure Brazilians, state that only 6 percent of our national capital is foreign-owned. This already frightening percentage is misleading . . . Six percent is an enormous

amount of foreign dominance, especially if, as is the case, it is strategically placed in the most dynamic industries. Hitler's armies probably never controlled directly more than six percent of the economies of France, Poland, and the other occupied lands. This does not mean, however, that they could not master the total economic potential of these countries in order to strengthen Germany's war effort.

Nearly all writers on dependency, including the most sophisticated ones, made a similar point, although usually without the overblown Hitlerian analogies. For instance, Cardoso (1973a, p. 144; also pp. 149, 161) argued that "in Brazil the level of foreign private investment in the dynamic industrial sectors has been so high and so sustained that the state sector and national entrepreneurs clearly no longer play a dominant role in such key decision-making centers as the capital goods and durable consumer goods industries." Clearly the qualitative nature of the external penetration is an important aspect of dependency in holistic dependency writings. It is also notable that such writings identify single dimensions or variables—dynamic industrial sectors, the state sector, national entrepreneurs—for specific, ceteris paribus analyses; characterize trends over time on these dimensions; assume that the state and the national entrepreneurs once played dominant roles but do not any longer; and evaluate negatively the trends described. In all these respects holistic dependency employs the same conceptual tools as analytic dependency, but always to index increases in dependency, never to index decreases.

As the evidence shows, holistic dependency authors are correct that some of the particularly dynamic sectors of the economy were penetrated disproportionately (that is, more than in the economy overall) by foreign actors and influences. However, the qualitative nature of external penetration has several aspects, not all of which indicate increasing dependency. In fact, if one considers a wide array of qualitative features of external penetration and domestic control, there is a strong case that Brazil's overall dependence qualitatively decreased rather than increased after 1964.

Dynamic Sectors. Among the sectors disproportionately penetrated by foreign capital were trucks and automobiles, tractors, industrial machinery, pharmaceuticals, tobacco, office machinery, rubber products, perfume, and plastics (Robock, 1975, pp. 61–65; Baer, 1976,

p. 48). (All of these sectors were foreign-dominated; most but not all of them were dynamic.) It is not true that all the most dynamic sectors were highly penetrated: shoes, sugar, and soybeans were among the particularly dynamic sectors where domestic control was high. Nor was it only the dynamic sectors where foreign control was high: Morley and Smith (1973, pp. 136–137) calculated that "about 60 percent of foreign investment profits come from the nondynamic or vegetative part of manufacturing." Even so, the argument that foreign capital—especially new foreign capital—was concentrated in the faster-growing sectors of the economy appears to be largely correct.

Diversification. Another important qualitative feature of external dependency is diversification. How diversified was the Brazilian economy? How diversified were Brazil's trade partners and sources of loans, investment, aid, and technology? In particular, did this diversification increase or decrease after 1964? In general, all other things being equal, the greater the diversification, for any level of aggregate penetration, the less will be Brazil's dependency, since more diversification gives Brazil more options and less dependence on any one sector, partner, or source of capital.

According to virtually every one of the indicators of diversification just cited, Brazil reduced its dependence after 1964. There was a definite, very strong trend toward diversification in sources of foreign investment in Brazil. The United States remained the largest single foreign investor, but its share in total external investment went down from a high of nearly 50 percent of total foreign investment in the middle and late 1960s to 34 percent in 1974. Between 1969 and 1973 France, Japan, Switzerland, the United Kingdom, West Germany, and Canada all expanded their investments in Brazil at a faster rate than the United States (Robock, 1975, p. 67). To the extent such diversification in sources of foreign investment in Brazil may have been offset by coordination through multinational enterprises, it has less meaning in reducing dependence. This is an issue that deserves further study. Still, it is unlikely that such coordination, if it occurred, completely neutralized the effects of the diversification.

Similar trends toward greater diversification were evident on nearly every other indicator of external economic penetration, and in some instances the changes were dramatic. For example, Brazil's commodity export structure diversified markedly. Coffee constituted 42 percent of total exports during the period from 1965 through 1969 but only 12.6 percent in 1974. During this period, however, manufactures increased from 7.2 to 27.7 percent, and sugar from 5.0 to 15.8 percent. Soybeans did not exist as part of the export structure in 1965–69 but represented 7.4 percent of it in 1974 (Baer, 1976, p. 50).

Brazil's trading patterns also changed. The United States' share of Brazilian trade in 1967–68 was 33.2 percent; in 1974, it was only 21.5 percent. The only countries besides the United States whose share of Brazilian trade was less in 1974 than in 1967–68 were the seven countries of the Soviet bloc, whose share fell from 6.2 to 4.1 percent, and the five countries in the European Free Trade Area, where the proportion dropped from 5.3 to 3.7 percent. During this same span of time, however, the share of the European Community (nine countries) increased from 32.6 to 34.2 percent, that of the Latin American Free Trade Area (ten countries including the Andean bloc) from 9.8 to 11.9 percent, Japan from 3.3 to 5.7 percent, and Asia (excluding Japan), Oceania, Spain, Africa, the Middle East, and the rest of the world, from 14.9 to 18.9 percent (Robock, 1975, p. 115). Foreign sources of loans and technology also diversified during this period. Again, the significance of all these trends is reduced only marginally, if at all, as a result of transnational coordination by the multinationals.

On top of everything else, of course, Brazil's overall economy diversified very substantially. This also was an extremely important indicator of reduced dependence. Once an agricultural monoculture in sugar, and later coffee, by the 1970s Brazil had become an industrial power producing everything from plastics and footwear to airplanes and automobiles to ships and tanks. Its agricultural economy itself diversified enormously. All of this reduced its dependence.

For a long time it was argued that Brazil's heavy reliance on one country (the United Kingdom or the United States) as a trade partner and source of investment and technology, and on one commodity (sugar or coffee, for example) as the prop of the overall economy and/or the base for exports, restricted its options and made it highly dependent on the international environment. This was a legitimate, plausible, and influential line of argument for Brazil for many years; it is still made regarding a number of countries in Latin America, especially in the Caribbean and Central America.

To the extent such an argument had or has force, it follows logically that diversification in sources of capital, export structure, trade partners, technology, and internal economic activities reduces dependence. And that is what happened in Brazil after 1964.

Holistic dependency writers do not concede this point, however. For the most part they ignore the trends toward diversification. If they acknowledge these trends at all they regard them as merely aspects of a new form of dependency with greater differentiation and complexity (Evans, 1979, pp. 81–83). In this interpretation, either monoculture or diversification indexes dependence: no matter what happens, dependence is said to remain constant or increase but never to decrease. Although this argument contradicts falsificationist logic, within the premises of holistic dependency it is coherent and necessary.

Vital Sectors. A third qualitative aspect of foreign penetration, besides the degree of penetration of dynamic sectors and diversification, is penetration of the most vital sectors of the national economy. By most vital sectors I mean those that are crucial for the economic infrastructure of the country (sectors that are bases for the rest of the economy to grow and function), and for national security militarily, strategically, diplomatically, and economically. The more these vital sectors are penetrated by foreign actors, the more dependent Brazil will be; the less they are penetrated, the less dependent.

The trend after 1964 was overwhelmingly toward greater Brazilian control of the economy's most vital sectors. The major agent of this increasing national control was, of course, the state. After 1964, continuing a trend that began at least as far back as 1930, the state took increasing control over vital national economic sectors. It became the principal controlling agent in the following industries and sectors: oil, steel, electric power generation, railroads, ocean transport, harbors, banking, iron ore, telecommunications, atomic energy, and highways. In addition, the state had powerful fiscal and monetary tools through its control of the Central Bank, the Bank of Brazil, the National Development Bank, the National Housing Bank, and the National Price Control Council (Baer, Kerstenetzky, and Villela, 1973, pp. 23–24). Each of these sectors and industries, including banking, is vital to national security and the economic vitality of the country.

From an analytic dependency point of view, control over oil, steel, electric power, railroads, ocean transport, harbors, banking, iron ore, telecommunications, atomic energy, and highways is more crucial for Brazilian autonomy than control over the other sectors. If they are not all more vital than trucks, automobiles, and capital goods, most of them are much more significant than pharmaceuticals and light manufacturing, where foreign capital was controlling. But from the point of view of holistic dependency the picture is different. For Cardoso (1973a, p. 163), national control over the vital sectors indexes important changes in the form but not important reductions in the degree of dependence. For Moreira Alves (1973, pp. 164–165), "The state occupies barren unprofitable economic space, as in the case of the railroads we bought back from the British, or that of the steel industry, which demands heavy investments for mediocre profits." According to him, what really matters is "everything that we consume in our daily lives," such as Coca-Cola, toothpaste, and aspirin.

Technology. One other area that must be mentioned in this context (the quality of foreign penetration) is technology dependency. Brazil's dependence on foreign technology is massive. Informed Brazilians have estimated that 97 percent of Brazil's productive capacity in the industrial sectors in the 1960s and 1970s was dependent on foreign technology (Packenham, 1976, p. 101). Whatever the correct figures may have been—systematic data on the subject are lacking—clearly the absolute level of technology dependence was extremely high. However, our question here is not the absolute level but the trend after 1964, and in this period the sources of technology, like other economic resources, diversified. The level of dependence in 1964 was already so high that any increase would be minute, while small steps were in fact taken to find ways to reduce technological dependence (Baer, Kerstenetzky, and Villela, 1973, p. 30; Adler, 1987; Seward, forthcoming). Both these moves, however, were in early stages. Hence, while the trend in technology was toward slightly less dependence, the magnitude of the change was not great.

Summing up the qualitative nature of external penetration, we can say that after 1964 Brazil's dependence increased substantially in dynamic sectors but decreased significantly because of diversification and in the vital sectors, and diminished marginally in technology.

Authoritarian Brazil: Internal Dependency

The external aspects are not, of course, the only important parts of the holistic dependency perspective. Internal aspects are equally important. Thus Cardoso (1973a, p. 146) says that his fundamental concern is the "consequences" of the "new trends in international capitalism" for "the development policies of the countries located at the periphery of the international capitalist system." He wants to explain how patterns of dependence "condition, or set constraints and limits to" the development process. Such an argument poses two questions: What were the main features of the development process or model, and what were the influences of the external environment on that model compared to the previous one?

The main features of Brazilian development from 1964 to the mid-1970s are well known: after an early phase of stabilization to 1967, very high rates of growth in aggregate terms, especially 1968–1974; a reliance on the market and on material incentives with substantial governmental intervention in key areas; high and increasing class, regional, and urban-rural social and economic inequalities; political authoritarianism and repression.

For our purposes the significant question is the degree to which this developmental model was a product of internal or external causes. Specifically, did external influences—the "consequences" of "the new trends in international capitalism" for the development model—increase after 1964, as holistic authors contend? Or, on balance, did such external influences on the development model decrease after 1964? In other words, did dependence "condition and constrain" development more after 1964, or was it the influence of national values, goals, and traditions that increased? To answer these questions, we need to look at both the direction and the magnitude of influences on the post-1964 development model.

Direction of Influences

Economic Aspects. The holistic dependency view seems to find its strongest support in the economic aspects of the model. It is true that the post-1964 economic model was essentially capitalist. But this was hardly outside the tradition of Brazilian nationalism: Brazil had long been a capitalist country. Moreover, within its historical experience there had long been a tendency toward significant state involvement in economic matters. The post-1964 regime did not reverse that state involvement in the economy; to the contrary, it maintained and expanded upon those tendencies. If, as is certainly true, the post-1964 regime in Brazil was not socialist in the holistic dependency sense of a Chinese or Cuban type economy, neither was any of the regimes that preceded it. Therefore, even when we look at the economic model, there are reasons to challenge or qualify the argument that external influence increased significantly after 1964.

Political Aspects. The holistic dependency view is that the post-1964 authoritarianism and repression were required by the model of dependent development. Cardoso's (1973a, pp. 146–147) "main hypothesis . . . is that the accumulation process required that the instruments of pressure and defense available to the popular classes be dismantled." The hypothesis that repression was not necessary he rejects as "a purely formal," "idyllic," "naive, static view of an historical process." Evans (1979, p. 48) follows the same line of reasoning: "In the context of dependent development, the need for repression is great while the need for democracy is small."

Although these arguments are widely accepted, they are open to severe challenge. In the first place, dependent development continued into the 1980s while political authoritarianism and repression declined and eventually disappeared. Second, the most powerful traditions in Brazilian politics were neither liberal nor radical (although they contained significant, rapidly growing elements of the former and minor, less rapidly growing elements of the latter) but patrimonial, hierarchical, paternalistic, clientelistic, and corporatist (Faoro, 1958; Skidmore, 1973; da Matta, 1978, 1987; Schwartzman, 1982; W. G. dos Santos, 1984; Roett, 1984). It is equally plausible to perceive the post-1964 authoritarian regime as a reaffirmation of traditional Brazilian political models as to see in it any indication of expanded foreign influence.

Third, although the United States supported the military coup and, in general, supported the regime during the early years, this by itself does not necessarily mean the political model reflected expanded foreign influence. It is essential to make a distinction between the direction of foreign influence and the magnitude of that influence. U.S. policy until 1968 was pro-regime, but U.S. influence was not very great compared to the influence of domestic forces. After 1968 the United States became much more critical of Brazil's military regime; again its influence was limited. Finally, various studies (Ste-

pan, 1978a; W. G. dos Santos, 1986) raise grave doubts about the
"historical necessity" or "inevitability" of the coup.

Social Aspects. Doubts about the holistic dependency propositions
as explanations for the Brazilian development model are strongest in
respect to the social aspects of the model. Before 1964 social and
economic inequalities in Brazil were already among the highest in
the world. After 1964 they became even more pronounced. This was
one of the most disturbing features in the entire developmental
model: while political repression was abhorrent but affected directly
only a small proportion of the population, the social problems affected the majority of the population.

But what feature could be more Brazilian than socioeconomic
inequality? What were the powerful egalitarian elements in the Brazilian tradition that were being smothered by foreign pressures?
Where in the external environment was there anything to compare
with the elitism, the tolerance for massive socioeconomic disparities,
the preference for social harmony, and the distaste for social conflict
that are powerful components of Brazil's national traditions? (See da
Matta, 1978, 1987; Schwartzman, 1982; W. G. dos Santos, 1979,
1984.)

The holistic dependency argument that increasing inequalities in
Brazil reflected increasing foreign influence on the developmental
model also states that most of this external influence came from the
United States. In this view the impact of the United States on Brazil's
social model after 1964 is seen to be mainly or exclusively anti-
egalitarian. It is of course true and important to note that capitalism,
by definition, requires and generates socioeconomic inequalities; that
U.S. cold war anticommunism opposed radical revolutionary movements; and that liberal U.S. developmentalism favored incremental-
ism and tended to abhor genuine social revolution. But the degree of
social and economic inequality varies enormously among capitalist
societies. Whether capitalist economic growth, in societies like Brazil
that are already highly inegalitarian, requires increasing those inequalities, is an extremely debatable question (an excellent review of
the literature on this issue is Cline, 1975).

Moreover, the overwhelming thrust of Brazilian nationalism has
always been at least as anti-Communist and antiradical as U.S. policy,
and much *more* socially elitist. Where in the North American tradition, for example, is there anything to compare with the landlord in
Brazil's Northeast who told his tenants who wanted to organize a

peasant league: "Everything has been ordained by God. He knows what He is doing. If He gives land to me and not to you, to reject this is to rebel against God. Such a rebellion is a mortal sin . . . You have to accept poverty on earth in order to gain eternal life in heaven. The poor live in God's grace. The rich don't. In this way you are more fortunate than I, since you are closer to heaven" (quoted in Page, 1972, p. 43).

Not even the most conservative Republican or southern Democrat in the United States could support such a philosophy. Very few U.S. citizens, to take another example, would be comfortable with the social distinctions and hierarchies involved in relationships with *empregadas domésticas, porteiros,* and *babás* (domestic servants, custodians, and nannies) which most Brazilians have known all their lives, take entirely for granted, and rarely see as the contradictions to liberal or radical ideological principles that they manifestly are (da Matta, 1978).

North American liberal doctrines and practices are conservative when compared to radical doctrines and practices, but they are progressive when compared to social conservatism. Brazil's national tradition is one of the most conservative in Latin America and without question far more conservative than North America's. The liberal-conservative distinction was neglected in the period of disenchantment with liberalism (roughly, mid-sixties to early-eighties). But it remains significant and still deserves attention. It presents important challenges to the prevailing holistic dependency argument.

Clearly there is a strong case for the view that changes in Brazil's developmental model tended to reaffirm rather than counter authentic social, political, and economic traditions in Brazil. One response to such a view is to acknowledge Brazil's powerful elitist, authoritarian, and capitalist heritages but to argue that these traditions would have changed in a socialist, democratic, egalitarian direction were it not for the coup/revolution of 1964. On some such grounds as these one might argue that the effect of the external environment on Brazil's development model after 1964 increased rather than decreased.

The substantive merit of this line of reasoning is debatable, however, and in our view dubious. Our interpretation rests on the record of Brazil's history for nearly five centuries. It stresses what has happened; it pays less attention to what might have happened in the past. The other interpretation does the reverse, underplaying what has happened and emphasizing what might have happened. Nevertheless, each approach has its strengths and weaknesses; the reader can take his pick and assess the argument that is constructed on each approach.

So far our assessments of the thesis of increasing foreign influence on the development model after 1964 have been related to the directions of the foreign and national influences on the model. We have been noticing that the changes have tended to reaffirm as well as to counter Brazil's economic, political, and social traditions. We turn next to changes in the magnitude of Brazil's capacity for setting its own developmental course before and after 1964.

Magnitude of Influences

In addition to the facets of Brazil's national power discussed earlier in this chapter, three other topics are pertinent here: the magnitude of Brazil's resources and productive capacity, the technical skills and capacities of its government officials and private-sector leaders, and nationalism.

National Resources and Productive Capacity. All other things being equal, the more resources and productive capacity a nation has, the more power it has (the less dependent it is). Brazil, Mexico, and Argentina are less dependent than Panama because they have many more resources and productive capacity. That is to say, they are much more powerful than Panama on most issues most of the time. How does the Brazil of "associated-dependent development" compare with the earlier Brazil on this facet of internal dependency?

By most measures of the total magnitude of national resources and productive capacity, Brazil became less dependent after 1964. Whether one looks at gross national product, gross national product per capita, industrial output, total population, or nearly any other conventional measure of aggregate resource and production growth, Brazil's record during this period (mid-sixties to mid-seventies) was notable (Baer, 1976, p. 47; W. G. dos Santos, 1985, p. 312; Barros de Castro and Pires de Souza, 1985). Even human resources, an area of long-standing Brazilian weakness, while retaining enormous deficiencies and problems, also received a number of improvements (Skidmore, 1988, p. 284). Some scholars compare the vast scale of the changes in Brazil's economy to those of Meiji Japan or the Soviet Union in its first two decades (W. G. dos Santos, 1985, p. 232; Lamounier, 1989, p. 130). These analogies refer to the scale of the transformation and not to its content, especially as regards the issue of socioeconomic equality, but it still contributed to societal pressures to end military authoritarianism. Even if such analogies are misplaced, the fact that serious analysts make them itself says something important about the changes and their implications.

Since the resources and productive capacity of most other countries were not growing as fast, Brazil's record indicates a reduction in this facet of its dependence during these years. Again, such data by themselves say nothing about how the wealth was distributed internally any more than data on distribution by themselves say anything about what there was to distribute.

In the seventies a few analysts noted the significance of Brazil's growth for reductions in dependency. At that time, however, the negative associations with the military regime were so strong, and the appeal of holistic dependency ideas was so great, that such arguments could have little impact (Hirschman, 1987, p. 21). A decade later these trends and their implications for dependency were more widely recognized: "Until a generation ago . . . Brazil was not really powerful . . . All that has been changing . . . Few nations have grown so much, so quickly and on such a grand scale as has Brazil in the last 25 years. Even with its current problems, Brazil is a nation to be reckoned with . . . Brazil is still quite vulnerable to international economic reverses but it also has more power to affect the world economy" (Lowenthal, 1986, pp. 8, 13).

Technical Skills of Officials. Other things being equal (as always), the more technically skillful leaders in the public and private sectors are in using the resources they have to work with, the less dependent is the country. What has been the trend in recent decades? The indicators here are "soft" and precise data are scarce. Still, some generalizations can be made.

The skills of Brazilian government officials and private-sector actors in dealing with the international business community improved markedly. Brazilians and foreigners alike reported that these officials and businessmen tended to drive harder bargains in international economic negotiations after the early 1960s than during most of the previous years. The terms of joint ventures involving foreigners stiffened to Brazil's benefit. When the Brazilian government pushed exports as a leading sector in the economic boom, foreign firms were told to export whether they wanted to or not. Brazil paid close attention to agreements on patents, licenses, and royalty payments for foreign technology, and it enforced those agreements. The provisions were tightened and royalty payments were reduced. Laws on remittance of profits were looser than those prevailing in the period 1961–64 (when they were very tight indeed) but tighter than the legislation on the books between 1953 and 1961. Brazilian diplomats further enhanced their reputation as the most able corps in Latin America (Baer, Kerstenetzky, and Villela, 1973, p. 30; Robock, 1975, pp. 66, 68).

The continuing evolution of the Brazilian state gave it greater capacity to cope with the international and national environments. Brazil's economic dynamism made it more attractive to foreign investors and lenders and thus enabled Brazilians to drive harder bargains. The level of competence and sophistication in technical discourse rose significantly because of the dramatic increase in the pool of trained economists and other technocrats.

In the 1970s scholars who drew attention to these phenomena were attacked by partisans of holistic dependency for (so the argument went) legitimizing authoritarianism, dependency, and capitalist exploitation (Cardoso, 1977b). The issue then was less whether the statements were true than what their political effect was thought to be. By the mid-1980s, however, the phenomena had become so important that even holistic dependency authors denied them no longer. Thus Evans (1985b, pp. 38–39) acknowledges that "the development of the people and skills necessary to take an intiative in the computer industry had been going on for at least a decade before the intiatives were taken [in 1973–74]. Equally important was the prior development of organizational capacities . . . within the state apparatus which made it possible for the state to serve as a base for those willing to make the attempt . . . without a small number of committed individuals able to link their particular cause to very general and powerful nationalist themes, an indigenously controlled [computer] hardware industry would not exist in Brazil."

Nationalism. Brazil's capacity to steer its own developmental course also increased because an earlier trend toward a more powerful Brazilian nationalism (a trend beginning at least by 1930) continued unabated during the post-1964 period.

This point is not sufficiently appreciated. It is frequently argued that the post-1964 regime's willingness to participate in the international capitalist system implied a decrease or abandonment of Brazilian nationalism. Thus Cardoso (1973a, p. 163) claimed that "we will soon be unable to understand, in the light of the pre-1964 experience, what is now meant by nationalism." None of the several myths about post-1964 Brazil is more pervasive and more profoundly in error than this one. The strategy, tactics, and style of post-1964 Brazilian nationalism differed from those used before 1964, but no one can doubt that nationalism continued.

Consider, for example, the incidence of major diplomatic conflicts and their outcomes. Although many aspects of U.S.-Brazilian diplomatic relations were positive after 1964, there was also an increasing number of points of tension and conflict on which Brazil prevailed. Among these were Brazil's claims for new territorial rights two hundred miles beyond its shores, population-control diplomacy in Stockholm, Brazil's pro-Arab policy in general and its anti-Zionism vote in the United Nations in particular, Brazil's support for the MPLA in Angola, and, perhaps most significantly, the Brazil-West Germany accord on nuclear reactors (Gall, 1976; Pang, 1975). By any reasonable standard these were central issues of foreign policy, not marginal ones. They showed an intensification of Brazilian nationalism and a decline in Brazilian dependence.

The following statement by the late J. A. de Araújo Castro (1972, p. 30), a career diplomat who for many years was Brazil's ambassador in Washington, illustrates the kind of ideology that lay behind these diplomatic maneuvers, and indeed behind the entire posture of the post-1964 regime toward the international environment: "No country can escape its destiny and, fortunately, or unfortunately, Brazil is condemned to greatness . . . Small, mediocre solutions are neither appropriate nor interesting to Brazil . . . We have to think big and plan on a grand scale . . . the primordial objective of the Foreign Policy of Brazil is the neutralization of all external factors which might limit its National Power. This policy could be neither more authentic nor more Brazilian. Nationalism is not, for us, an attitude of isolation, of prevention, or of hostility. It is, on the contrary, a strong impulse toward international participation."

As this statement makes clear, the aims of Brazil's leaders in promoting international cooperation, participation, and "insertion into the international capitalist system" were not to abandon Brazilian nationalism but to enhance it. They aimed to play the international game and come out ahead. Their course was risky and uncertain. To set objectives is not necessarily to achieve them; in fact, this policy of *grandeza,* as it came to be known, was excessively ambitious, as subsequent events made clear. Moreover, one may evaluate the internal development model they chose to accompany international *grandeza* as gravely flawed. But that is a different issue. Brazilian nationalism did not decline after 1964, and this fact is another reason to doubt the claims of expanding foreign control over the developmental model.

In sum, regarding the internal aspects of the model of dependent development in authoritarian Brazil, there are many reasons to doubt that Brazil's dependency increased after 1964. The likelihood is that it decreased. Between 1964 and the mid-1970s Brazil extended and intensified long-standing national predilections for capitalism, political authoritarianism, and profound socioeconomic inequalities. Increases in its resources and productive capacities, the enhanced technical skills of its officials, and the continuing power of nationalism gave Brazil greater capacity to achieve the goals of whatever development model it followed. In all these ways Brazil reduced its national dependency. The widely accepted empirical premise of the model of associated-dependent development—that the model meant increased national dependency—may be seriously questioned.

"Abertura" and the New Republic

Following holistic dependency authors, we have emphasized the period from the late 1950s, particularly after 1964, to the middle 1970s. From the mid-1970s to the end of the 1980s, some of the trends just described continued and others changed. In what follows we sketch very briefly the main features of those trends; statements in this section not otherwise documented are supported in Lowenthal (1986), a source that updates various topics addressed in the preceding sections.

The magnitude of external penetration of Brazil's national economy continued to be high after the mid-1970s. Brazil's external debt continued to soar and contributed to a protracted economic crisis in the 1980s. The huge size of the debt constrained Brazil both externally and internally. But its very size also had the opposite effects. The debt was so large, and Brazil's role in the worldwide debt situation was so important, that, paradoxically, Brazil's international influence was enhanced as well as constrained. Trade dependency continued to be very high. Direct foreign investment fell off but remained substantial until the mid-1980s.

The qualitative features of the external penetration also displayed many continuities from the earlier period. Foreign investment in dynamic sectors remained high, though at lower levels than before. The trend toward diversification—of the Brazilian economy, sources of loans, investments, trade partners, and technology—also continued, although in some years at lower levels than before (Hirst, 1984). Throughout the 1980s the debate over *estatização* ("statization," or expanding state control of the economy) continued, while the long-term trend toward national control of the vital sectors, whether in public or private hands (still mostly the former), was maintained and in some areas expanded (Barros de Castro and Pires Souza, 1985). Even technology dependency, traditionally one of the most difficult areas of dependency to change, continued to decrease in important areas such as the computer industry (Adler, 1987; Westman, 1985; Evans, 1985b). However, a different phase appears to have begun in 1990, when the newly elected democratic government of Fernando Collor de Mello began a program of dramatic economic-liberalization policies. It is too early to know how extensive, successful, and enduring they will be.

In the internal aspects of dependency some changes were greater than in the external areas, but many continuities also were visible. The high level of economic dynamism of the "miracle" years 1968–1974 did not continue. Some of the economic shakiness, especially in the 1980s, was attributable to international influences. On the other hand, in part because of the diversification, increased bargaining power, reductions in technological dependence, and other changes noted above Brazil did not suffer the same degree of economic decline that most Latin American countries did after 1982.

Continuity was greatest in the social model, where enormous inequalities persisted (W. G. dos Santos, 1985; Jaguaribe et al., 1986; Lamounier, 1989). This continues to be the most disturbing feature of modern Brazil and the one with the greatest potential to challenge the system in fundamental ways. As before, however, the heart of the problem is much more internal than external.

Brazilian foreign policy continued to express nationalism, frequent conflicts with U.S. positions, and various kinds of links with Third World blocs and ideologies as well as traditional pro-U.S., pro-capitalist, and pro-Western impulses (Hirst, 1984; Wesson, 1981).

The biggest change was in the political model, where a new liberal-democratic republic replaced military authoritarianism (Selcher, 1986; Skidmore, 1988; Lamounier, 1989; Stepan, 1989). The path to the new order was mainly elitist, gradual, and nonviolent. Such a path was both quintessentially Brazilian and well designed to optimize the chances of a successful transition away from authoritarianism (Dahl, 1971; Huntington, 1984; O'Donnell and Schmitter, 1986). But even though the transition was due overwhelmingly to internal influences, it was also consistent with and supported by international trends such as the overall decline of military regimes, the rise of liberal democracies in Latin America, and the transformations in Marxism in other parts of the world. As for the specific influence of the United States, if it endorsed the coup in 1964, it also welcomed the political liberalization of the seventies and eighties.

By the criteria of analytic dependency, the transition from authoritarian rule and the installation of a democratic republic in Brazil, though obviously flawed and incomplete in many ways, were worthwhile events of considerable political and theoretical significance. From the holistic dependency point of view, by contrast, these events were not very important. They did not change the capitalist state; they only changed the regime. Although a liberal regime could "provide a forum for the resolution of differences among the bourgeoisie" (Evans, 1979, p. 48), it could not provide "real" democracy. Thus holistic dependency neither predicted *abertura* (political liberalization) and the New Republic nor gave them much significance once they occurred.

However, holistic dependency was easily able to deal with the fact of Brazil's precarious new democracy once it occurred. The notion that dependencia was a "temporary theory," designed to apply only to the period of military authoritarianism in the sixties and seventies and to be forgotten thereafter, has no basis in dependency writings themselves. A theoretical perspective broad enough to incorporate all of Latin American history from 1810 (or 1500) to the present, and which confidently predicts and makes prescriptions for the indefinite future, scarcely can be said to stop at the 1980s. The issue is not whether holistic dependency is able to incorporate recent and future political events into its capacious framework, but what theoretical and policy significance it attaches to such events and what validity its claims have.

The evidence for the period from the mid-seventies through the eighties shows that some of the trends were consistent with holistic dependency hypotheses, but many were not. The hypothesis that "there has been a basic change in the main axis of the power system" (Cardoso, 1973a, p. 146) remains plausible—but not necessarily in the direction postulated. The more recent events continue to support two major conclusions: first, not only increases but also decreases in dependency are significant; second, holistic dependency exaggerates the negative consequences of Brazil's insertion into the international capitalist system.

Conclusion

This chapter has suggested some ways to address the questions raised by holistic dependency authors about capitalist dependency, without necessarily accepting their answers.

Using the analytic dependency approach to study the concrete case of Brazil documents not only constraints on autonomy and development but also opportunities for autonomy and development. It shows that as Brazil became more dependent in some ways it became less dependent in others. It raises doubts about the hypotheses of holistic dependency writers, which have been widely accepted for years, that the "new industrialization" of "associated-dependent development" in Latin America increased and intensified national dependency. It shows that such hypotheses are at best partial and one-sided. It also suggests that some of the alleged "internal manifestations of external dependency" were in fact not that at all. Some negative features of the Brazilian model were less characteristic of "the anti-nation within the nation" than of Brazil's complex national traditions in their contemporary manifestations.

The reactions of holistic dependency writers and their supporters to analytic dependency have been intensely negative. Cardoso and Faletto (1979, p. xii) reject the idea of studying degrees of dependency, saying it is like comparing degrees of slavery. According to Cardoso and Faletto (1979, pp. ix–xiv; Cardoso, 1977a, pp. 15, 21), analytic dependency is static, ahistorical, nonstructural, nondialectical, unidimensional, univocal, positivist, abstract, formal, and structural-functional. Duvall (1978, pp. 55, 60) claims that "dependency is a label for a general frame of reference, rather than a term which applies to a particular conceptual referent within the frame" and that therefore to use the analytic dependency approach to address holistic dependency's claims is "misdirected and a nonsensical enterprise" if it is used as a way to "reflect on dependencia theory." Caporaso (1978b, p. 19) says that disaggregating the concept of dependency and using *ceteris paribus* assumptions are practices that reflect "an empiricist orientation" of "American political and social science" which is inappropriate for examining holistic dependency hypotheses. The Valenzuelas (1978, p. 556) state that to study dependency in terms of power disparities "misses the point completely."

Some of these criticisms may be germane or even valid with respect to various quantitative studies of dependency ideas based on cross-national aggregate data, but none is germane or valid with respect to analytic dependency. Analytic dependency is historical, structural, and concrete. Far from being static, it analyzes continuities and changes over time. It is not positivist but falsificationist. It is not unidimensional but multidimensional. It does not isolate power dimensions from economic dimensions; it is centrally concerned with economic aspects of dependency. It does not ignore internal aspects of dependency; to the contrary, it puts the internal aspects at center stage. But it refuses to accept uncritically holistic dependency claims that social ills in Latin America are always internal "expressions" or "manifestations" of dependency; rather, it insists on evidence and allows for the possibility that such claims may be false as well as true—that internal ills may be "authentic national expressions" as well as aspects of dependency.

Moreover, we have seen that although holistic dependency is obviously not defined only in terms of power, it is always defined partly in power terms. Despite claims to the contrary (Cardoso and Faletto, 1979, pp. 201, 212), constraints on national units and changes in the amount or extent or degree of such constraints are indeed "concerns" that are "at issue" in holistic dependency. Holistic dependency authors have been extensively and intensively concerned with constraints on national units—so long as such constraints increase or stay the same or change from one form to another. It is only when such constraints decrease that attention to them is said to "modify the field of study" (Cardoso, 1977a, p. 15) or "miss the point" (Valenzuela and Valenzuela, 1978, p. 556) or be "nonsensical" (Duvall, 1978, p. 60).

In fact, many of the holistic dependency criticisms of analytic dependency better apply to holistic dependency itself. Holistic dependency writings have been far less concrete and specific, far less concerned with the ways history does and does not affect the present, and far less sensitive to contradictions that dialectically open the way to change, than analytic dependency. Holistic dependency's reliance on elastic, unfalsifiable concepts is much closer in its epistemology and methodology to structural functionalism than anything in analytic dependency which employs a falsificationist epistemology.

Holistic dependency can be useful insofar as it draws attention to the ways national and international factors may interact with one another regarding development on the periphery. But substantive holism keeps moving the fundamental focus of attention away from such questions to the question of capitalism versus socialism. The unfalsifiable epistemology and politicized-scholarship premises of holistic dependency deny scholarly criteria for determining whether some of its key ideas may be wrong. And its theoretical and policy alternatives tend to be utopian and insufficiently contextual. They lack realism and practical applicability in most concrete situations. In these respects and others there is much to be said for analytic dependency as an alternative.

7 Analytic Dependency and a Socialist Situation (Cuba)

Does socialism eliminate or reduce dependency and its alleged concomitants? In the holistic dependency view, the answer is yes. Indeed, socialism would be the only desirable or acceptable way to address the problems of dependent capitalism. In holistic dependency the truth or falsity of this claim is not a matter to be tested empirically. It is not a question amenable to resolution by reference to historical experience. Rather, the analyst using this perspective first assumes it to be true and then demonstrates that it is true by citing data that support it (Cardoso and Faletto, 1979, p. x).

Analytic dependency addresses the question differently, refering to historical experience to test the claims of holistic dependency. In analytic dependency, comparative analyses of capitalist and socialist cases are indispensable. Broadly speaking, two kinds of comparisons immediately suggest themselves: cross-sectional comparisons and longitudinal comparisons. When one does cross-sectional comparisons, one typically compares, say, the situation of Eastern European countries vis-à-vis the USSR with the situation of Latin American countries vis-à-vis the United States. When one does longitudinal analysis, one can compare the situation of the same country before and after the advent of socialism: say, Cuba before and after 1959, Chile before and after 1970, Nicaragua before and after 1979, Grenada before and after 1979. In this chapter the longitudinal method is used and the case selected for analysis is Cuba.

The longitudinal method normally enables the analyst to hold variables constant better than one can when studying two different countries. Language, historical tradition and memory, cultural baselines, basic geographic and material circumstances, and population are all factors that are more or less constant whenever one studies a particular case over time. When some profound event, like the Cuban Revolution, occurs in one country, the relative constancy of these factors permits the analyst to make reasonable inferences about the degree and form of changes in the country that may have been brought about (or not) by that profound event. Of course, in fact other variables do change; it is not true that the profound event is the only alteration. So the method is not airtight, to say the least. No method is airtight. However, longitudinal analysis—comparing different systems within the same country over time—clearly has natural strengths that deserve to be exploited. Comparative analysis can be done by comparing different systems over time within the same country as well as by comparing different countries to one another.

Within Latin America Cuba is by far the best case available if one wants to make systematic longitudinal comparisons of capitalism with socialism. Its experience with socialism is now more than three decades old. By contrast the socialist experiments in Chile and Grenada were very short-lived—Allende's socialist experiment lasted only three years, the New Jewel regime only four. The Sandinista regime in Nicaragua lasted eleven years—longer than the Chilean and Grenadian regimes, but much less than the Cuban regime. Moreover, as an experiment in socialism Nicaragua was a more ambiguous case than Cuba, and the scholarly literature about it is more often tinged with emotionalism, politicization, and theatricality. Although these characteristics have by no means disappeared in scholarly work about Cuba, they are less pervasive than they once were.

This chapter does not take up the phase that began with the post-1986 Gorbachev reforms. For one thing, as we write the situation is so fluid and uncertain that it is nearly impossible to analyze it accurately and systematically. Additionally, while these reforms and the Cuban responses have major implications for Cuban-Soviet relations and Cuban development (Purcell, 1990), they also seem to be moving the USSR away from socialism. This uncertainty renders the post-1986 experience less pertinent to our analytic purposes than the previous phase. For these reasons we focus on the socialist period up to about 1986 and the comparisons between it and the earlier capitalist dependency.

Structural Economic Dependence Before and After 1959

Basic to the dependent condition is structural dependence: monoculture, reliance on exports, trade-partner concentration, capital dependence, technological dependence, and the like. Cuba's leaders and many others outside Cuba predicted that Cuba's structural economic dependence would change significantly under socialism. What has happened?

History has not been kind to those predictions. Drawing on earlier studies (Domínguez, 1978b; LeoGrande, 1979; Blasier, 1983; and especially Mesa-Lago, 1981), I made a survey of the main aspects of structural economic dependence in socialist Cuba compared to capitalist Cuba (Packenham, 1986a, pp. 61–66). My finding are summarized as follows:

Aspect of economic dependence	Change/No change after 1959
Monoculture of national production	No change
Overall trade dependence	No change
Monoculture of exports	No change
Trade-partner concentration: USA/Comecon countries	No change
Trade-partner concentration: USA/USSR	Less dependence
Capital dependence	No change
Debt dependence	More dependence
Energy dependence	More dependence
Technological dependence	No change

Clearly, Cuba's structural economic dependence since 1959 has been neither eliminated nor significantly reduced in terms of those indicators. Moreover, these general conclusions are confirmed and extended in a comprehensive recent study by Mesa-Lago and Gil (1989).

Interpretations of Socialist Dependence

Despite the foregoing data, many analysts continue to reject or minimize the degree and significance of Cuba's post-1959 dependence. One way is to reject a priori the possibility of any analogies, parallels, or comparisons between the influences of the two superpowers on smaller countries. Thus Kaufman (1976, pp. 14–15) has noted that many policymakers and partisans of communism as well as capitalism "reach the point of absurdity by denying the possibility of a comparison, on the grounds that the policies of the superpowers are not identical and are therefore incomparable." But comparisons are possible and necessary. The claim in holistic dependency that socialism is superior to capitalism implies the possibility and necessity of comparisons. Analytic dependency uses comparison as a way to test that claim.

A second way is simply to ignore the subject. Thus Cardoso (1973d, p. 2 and passim) affirms that the Cuban revolution proved that "dependency can be broken." He does this by referring in detail to Cuba's relationship with the United States while remaining silent on the subject of Cuba's relationship with the Soviet Union.

A third way is to reject or minimize the evidence that has just been noted about Cuba's economic dependence after 1959 and to argue that even in terms of those indicators Cuba's dependence has declined. The most important analysis of this sort is LeoGrande (1979). He compared Cuban structural-economic dependence before and after 1959 and found that out of 28 indicators six showed no significant change in dependence, while sixteen showed improvement.

Although LeoGrande's work is serious and useful in some respects, it has major methodological flaws. As Mesa-Lago (1981, p. 229) points out, "of those sixteen indicators, ten were used to measure one variable (trade-partner concentration in which a significant reduction in dependence was registered) while in another variable (that is, the foreign debt that showed a significant increase in dependence) only one indicator was used." LeoGrande also defines dependency in terms of capitalist characteristics such as profit remittances and income inequalities, and then points to the absence or reduction of those characteristics under socialism as proof that dependency is eliminated or reduced because of socialism. This is tautological. Further, when dependency declines on some indicator, he attributes it to socialism; when it does not decline, he says it is a legacy of capitalism. In short: heads socialism wins, tails capitalism loses. Even so, LeoGrande concludes that structural economic dependency has not been eliminated, only (in his view) reduced. While LeoGrande's work is interesting it does not effectively challenge the idea that structural economic dependency under socialism remains very high.

A fourth approach has perhaps been the most subtle and influential way of dealing with the evidence of continued structural economic dependence under socialism. In this approach, it is conceded that the transition to socialism has not eliminated or massively reduced dependency measured in the foregoing structural-economic terms. The proposition some holistic dependency analysts put forward, however, is that although dependency in those terms—"conventional" dependence—has continued since 1959, the exploitation that characterized capitalist dependency has been eliminated or at least massively reduced under socialism. The USSR is defined as a socialist country whose relationship to Cuba is nonexploitative. As Fidel Castro himself has put it, "How can the Soviet Union be labeled imperialist? Where are its monopoly corporations? Where is its participation in the multinational companies? What factories, what mines, what oil fields does it own in the underdeveloped world? What worker is exploited in any country of Asia, Africa, or Latin America by Soviet capital?" (as quoted in Fagen, 1978b, p. 74).

In this view, the Cuban regime and its foreign and domestic policies are fundamentally "Cuban, un-Soviet and independent" of Soviet influence except in ways that have helped Cuba (Fagen, 1978b). The argument is also that "even though structurally Cuba's international ties and situation still imply a significant level of vulnerability, these ties and situation have not in the main conditioned the Cuban economy in negative ways as far as achieving the primary goal of directing development toward human well-being and more equitable distribution" (Fagen, 1978a, p. 300). In this view, Cuban foreign policies too have been nationalistic, autonomous, and "authentically Cuban" rather than influenced by the USSR. Great stress is laid on an alleged "convergence of interests" between Cuba and the USSR (Erisman, 1985; Duncan, 1985). In the domestic sphere, the transformation to socialism has met the "real needs" of the "vast majority" of the Cuban people. Whereas dependency on capitalism is said to have been malign in its consequences for the Cuban population, ties of "conventional" dependency to the Soviet Union, characterized as a socialist country, are said to be benign or "benevolent" in their consequences for the Cuban people (Fagen 1978a, 1978b; Brundenius, 1984; Halebsky and Kirk, 1985).

Proponents of this approach have advanced their claims at two levels which are empirically interrelated and intertwined but analytically separable. On the abstract plane, they argue that the mechanisms of capitalist exploitation are eliminated under socialism and replaced by nonexploitative socialist mechanisms. Concretely, they argue that specific features—both internal and external—of Cuba's dependency under socialism have been much more benign and less exploitative than those of capitalist dependency.

Most of the evidence does not support these arguments. Although the mechanisms and specific features of Cuban dependency under socialism are somewhat different from those under capitalism, in the Cuban case after 1959 various socialist mechanisms and processes of domination and exploitation have been at work. These mechanisms and processes have not been discussed or even noted in the holistic dependency literature. Although in some ways they may be more benign than their capitalist counterparts, in most ways they are more malign, repressive, and exploitative. In the following section we sketch the main mechanisms of influence and exploitation in analytical terms. The section after that will provide a more detailed discussion of the way they have operated in concrete terms in Cuba since 1959.

Generic Mechanisms of Socialist Domination and Exploitation

One of the main mechanisms by which the Soviet Union influenced Cuban domestic and foreign policies and institutions is through the leverage established by Cuba's structural economic dependence on the Soviet Union. In other words, the structural economic characteristics described in the first part of this chapter are "fungible," or translatable, into influences on specific policies and institutions within Cuba. A Russian embassy official, Rudolf Shliapnikov, told the Cuban Communist party official Aníbal Escalante in 1967 that "We have only to say that repairs are being held up at Baku for three weeks and that's that" (from a speech by Raúl Castro as quoted in Thomas, 1977, p. 701). Baku is the Soviet Union's port for shipping oil to Cuba.

If one multiplies that chilling comment across the broad spectrum of the USSR's points of economic leverage, one begins to appreciate the magnitude of Soviet influence on Cuba affairs. Mesa-Lago (1981, p. 187) sketches some of these points of leverage as follows:

> The USSR has the capacity to cut the supply to the island of virtually all oil, most capital, foodstuffs, and raw materials, about one-third of basic capital and intermediate goods, and probably all weaponry. Additionally, loss of Soviet markets would mean an end to their buying about half of Cuban sugar at three times the price of the market as well as purchase of substantial amounts of nickel also at a subsidized price. The USSR could also exert powerful influence over such COMECON countries as the GDR, Czechoslovakia, and

Bulgaria, which are particularly the key ones in trade with Cuba, to stop economic relations with Cuba. Finally the USSR could stick to the 1972 agreements and ask Cuba to start repaying in 1986 the debt owed the Soviets. These are not hypothetical scenarios because in 1968 the USSR used the oil stick and in the 1970s the economic-aid carrot to influence crucial shifts in Cuban foreign and domestic policies.

LeoGrande (1979, p. 26), who in general sees Cuba as less constrained by the USSR then Mesa-Lago does, writes in a similar vein as follows:

> Cuba is highly vulnerable to a conscious policy of politico-economic coercion on the part of the Soviet Union. Most analysts of Cuban-Soviet relations are convinced that the USSR took advantage of this vulnerability in late 1967 and early 1968 by delaying petroleum shipments to Cuba and by moving very slowly in the 1968 annual trade agreement negotiations. Shortly thereafter Cuban foreign policy moved more into line with Soviet policy; e.g., Cuba toned down its denunciations of pro-Soviet communist parties in Latin America, retreated from its active support of guerrilla forces in the continent, and in August 1968 gave qualified support to the Soviet intervention in Czechoslovakia.

This first mechanism is much more potent in the case of dependency on the Soviet Union than it ever was under capitalist dependency. The reason is that the Soviet state controls and coordinates the instruments of economic leverage to a far greater degree than the U.S. state ever controlled this country's economic activities in Cuba. Indeed, the failure of the U.S. government to guide its private investment and trade policies in directions conducive to U.S. public interests in the 1950s has been identified (Johnson, 1965) as a major flaw in its policy, which contributed to difficulties with Cuba and eventually to the collapse of the relationship between the two countries.

A second mechanism—really a large, complex set of mechanisms—is organizational. Many organizations provided institutionalized linkages between the Soviet Union and Cuba. It has been suggested (Blasier, 1983, p. 68) that "Studying Soviet relations with Latin America without studying the relations between the Communist Party of the Soviet Union (CPSU) and the Latin American parties would be as unrealistic as ignoring multinational corporations in examining

U.S. policies toward the area." This point certainly holds for Cuba. Yet many holistic dependency analyses of Cuba that are greatly concerned about multinational corporations before 1959 are silent on the subject of the CPSU after 1959.

Domínguez (1978b, p. 159) has concluded, on the basis of a detailed study by Andrés Suárez, that in the first half of the 1960s "Prime Minister Fidel Castro acquiesced in the formation and development of a revolutionary party, and eventually a Communist party, first as an effort to obtain further support from the Soviet Union, then as a condition of continued Soviet support . . . As the disastrous year of 1970 came to an end, the Soviet Union once again rescued Cuba, but this time on condition that a major reorganization of the Cuban government, under Soviet guidance, be undertaken." Thus not only the Cuban Communist Party but the entire Cuban bureaucratic apparatus was reshaped in significant measure by the Soviet Union.

The main instrument for this reshaping was the Cuban-Soviet Commission for Economic, Scientific, and Technical Collaboration, established in 1970. According to Domínguez (1978b, pp. 159–160), the details of this agreement "made evident how vast and decisive Soviet influence would become within the Cuban government." The Commission henceforth coordinated the efforts of the Cuban Ministries of Foreign Trade, Merchant Marine and Ports, Basic Industries, and Mining and Metallurgy. It also coordinated the activities of the Agency for Agricultural Development, the Agricultural Mechanization Agency, the Institutes of Fishing and of Civil Aeronautics, and the Electric Power Enterprise. The Cuban-Soviet Commission itself became a new agency which pushed the Cuban government toward further bureaucratization and centralization of power. The Commission met "frequently and regularly." All the agencies it coordinated were required to have "systematic, formal bureaucratic procedures under the guidance of Soviet technicians (whose numbers in Cuba consequently increased vastly in the early 1970s) in order to make effective use of Soviet assistance." In addition, the Cuban Ministry of Interior and its espionage branch, the DGI (General Directorate of Intelligence), worked closely with the Soviet KGB (Talbott, 1978b, p. 39).

In 1972 Cuba joined the Council for Mutual Economic Assistance (CMEA, or COMECON). From the mid-1970s on the Cuban five-year plans (themselves a conceptual device borrowed from the USSR) were fully coordinated with Soviet five-year plans. Even the Cuban system of national accounting was reshaped along Soviet lines (Mesa-Lago, 1981, pp. 199–202; Domínguez, 1978b, pp. 159–60). In short, the Soviets were deeply involved in guiding and reshaping every sector of Cuba's economy and most government ministries. In no country in Latin America was U.S. involvement as great as the USSR's in Cuba. If it had been, enormous protests in both Latin America and the United States would have been inevitable. But the USSR's involvement in reshaping Cuban institutions was scarcely noticed let alone protested.

A third mechanism is the common interests that Fidel Castro and the Cuban leadership share with the Soviet leaders. This commonality of interests was not total by any means, but it was high by any standard and very high indeed compared to the area of common interests between either of them, on the one hand, and the interests of the Cuban people, on the other.

What were the major interests of Fidel Castro and the Cuban ruling elite? As Thomas, Fauriol, and Weiss (1984, p. 5) have recently pointed out, these interests or priorities remained unchanged over the life of the regime since 1959. They are, in order of importance, (1) maintaining undiluted power for Castro; (2) making Cuba a "world-class" actor with major international influence; and (3) transforming Cuban society. Castro has had considerable success in achieving these goals, and the degree of success has been directly related to the order of priority. This success owes a very great deal to the Soviet Union. Soviet support was indispensable economically and militarily for the survival of the Castro regime. It enabled Castro to play an international role he otherwise could never have played, and it helped him greatly in his efforts to reshape Cuban society.

What were the main interests of the USSR in Cuba? At least until the late 1980s Cuba was in Blasier's (1983, pp. 99–128) appraisal an "economic liability" for the USSR but a "political asset":

> Cuba may be the Soviet Union's most important political windfall since World War II . . . Cuba has played a unique role in bolstering the authority and appeal of Soviet doctrine, the universal claims of which require intermittent validation. Communist Cuba has helped make the Soviet contention that communism is the wave of the future more believable. Thus the Marxist-Leninist regime in Cuba has strengthened Soviet influence, most particularly in the Third

World. But Cuba has had more than a demonstration effect; Castro has sought to mobilize revolutionary forces around the world and supported, where it suited him, Soviet political objectives. Soviet leaders have been particularly pleased that Cuba introduced the first Communist state in the Western Hemisphere, and it has been a useful ally in political competition with the United States. (p. 99)

In addition, Cuba was able to do in Africa, the Middle East, the Caribbean and Central America things that the Russians could not do as well or at all. It represented Soviet positions in the "nonaligned" movement. It supported unpopular Soviet actions in Czechoslovakia, Afghanistan, and Poland. It established a Soviet-type model as against the Chinese model.

Thus although the interests of Fidel Castro and the Soviets were not identical by any means, they were relatively congenial. Each was useful to the other and both sides knew it. With respect to these two sets of actors, therefore, the widely held thesis of "convergence of interests" had much validity.

However, it is essential to distinguish the interests of the Cuban ruling elite from those of the Cuban population as a whole. What domestic interests are served by supporting Soviet invasions of Czechoslovakia and Afghanistan and Soviet sponsorship of military suppression in Poland? These policies make no sense in terms of the interests of the Cuban people. They make great sense, however, in terms of the interests of Fidel Castro. As Blasier (1983, p. 109) has written, "Castro has his own reasons for approving Soviet military support for faltering socialist governments in Czechoslovakia, Afghanistan and Poland. He would hope to have such support if the Cuban government were similarly threatened . . . The main justification for Soviet military suppression is that socialist regimes are being threatened with 'foreign intervention' by 'imperialist' nations . . . if Castro is counting on the USSR to protect him from 'imperialism' (or local forces linked to 'imperialism'), he must necessarily approve the Soviet defense of 'socialism' elsewhere."

What this example suggests, and the next section documents in a more detailed and systematic way, is that most policies in Cuba do not serve the interests of the Cuban population nearly so much as they serve the interests of the Cuban ruling elite and its Soviet sponsors. If, as holistic dependency writers (Cardoso, 1973a; Evans, 1979; Cardoso and Faletto, 1979) claim, there is a *tri-pé* alliance of multinational, state, and local capital in countries on the periphery of capitalism that exploits the population of these countries, there is also a *bi-pé* alliance of Soviet and Cuban elites which exploits the Cuban population in ways and to a degree never experienced in pre-1959 Cuba or most other peripheral capitalist countries. Whereas the *tri-pé* alliance in capitalist cases is comprised of foreign private capital, national private capital, and national public or state capital, the *bi-pé* alliance in socialist cases is comprised of foreign state elites and national state elites.

Unfortunately, this sort of analysis is never made by holistic dependency authors or other partisans of Cuban socialism. They reject or ignore even the possibility of conflicting interests between the Cuban elite and the Cuban population. They claim or assume that what has been good for the Cuban and Soviet elites has also been good for the Cuban people. Yet if the standards they use to analyze critically such peripheral capitalist countries as, say, Brazil or Cuba before 1959 are applied to Cuba after 1959, then it becomes clear that the Castro elite, whose interests are dialectically and intimately intertwined with those of the Soviet government, is systematically dominating and exploiting the Cuban people.

Specific Features of Socialist Domination and Exploitation

Holistic dependency authors have offered a number of hypotheses about the concrete processes, institutions, and policies they believe have characterized socialist dependency in Cuba. First, they say, socialism has made possible changes in Cuba's internal social structure which were impossible under capitalism and which are more just and equitable than the pre-1959 capitalist social system. Second, under socialism there is no capitalist investment and therefore no profit repatriation from Cuba to the USSR. Hence socialist economic dependency is not exploitative. Third, socialism has made possible a true, "substantive" democracy in the place of authoritarianism or the merely "formal," procedural political democracy that obtained before 1959. Fourth, socialism has broken the pattern of dependency on imported U.S. culture and replaced it with authentically national cultural expressions. Finally, since 1959 Cuba's foreign diplomatic and military activities have been autonomous, independent, authentically national policies in the Cuban national interest, whereas before

1959 these activities and policies were subordinated to and exploited by the interests of the United States (Fagen, 1978a, 1978b; Leo-Grande, 1979; Brundenius, 1984; Skidmore and Smith, 1984, 1989; Halebsky and Kirk, 1985).

These hypotheses stress the internal aspects of post-1959 Cuban development as much as—if not more than—the external aspects. This is consistent with holistic dependency's stress, in its analysis of of peripheral capitalist countries, on the internal "expressions" of dependency. Let us examine specific features of Cuba's socialist policies and institutions to see how these hypotheses stand up.

Social and Economic Aspects

The Revolution's accomplishments in the social sphere have often been called magnificent. Economic problems are noted but blamed on the U.S. economic embargo. They are not taken very seriously or given much weight as a commentary on the Revolution. While this picture has its elements of truth, it makes two kinds of errors. It is one-sided and incomplete in its assessment of the social gains. It also misperceives and underestimates the economic failings.

We begin with the Revolution's proudest achievements—the social sphere. Post-1959 accomplishments—many real, some imagined—in the areas of literacy, educational opportunity, rural development, land reform, housing, health care, nutritional standards, employment, class relations, "moral reforms" (against prostitution, gambling, coruption, and homosexuality), and racial and sexual equality are widely noted and have been described in detail by many authors. There is no need to repeat those accounts here. However, even in this sphere of greatest accomplishment, the record is by no means universally positive or nonexploitative. Nor is all this social progress related to the Revolution, socialism, and Soviet support; much of it has roots in the capitalist period.

In the first place, in comparison with other Latin American countries, Cuba before 1959 was not only relatively well-off in per capita income but also quite progressive in terms of such social indicators as literacy, educational opportunity, and per capita levels of energy consumption, daily newspaper circulation, radios, television sets, and physicians. Indeed, on these indicators Cuba was on a par with many European countries. If it is true that these patterns refer to aggregate statistics of resources concentrated in the cities, it is also true that in

1959 most Cubans (56 percent) were urbanites. This point is not sufficiently noted. In addition the Cuban population was 75 percent literate and 99 percent Spanish-speaking. How many radios did the rich listen to compared to the poor? Nutritional levels were higher and infant mortality rates were substantially lower in Cuba than in most of Latin America. And there was never the phenomenon of boat people, even under Batista (Fagen, 1969, pp. 22–23; González, 1974, pp. 14–19).

Second, some of the accomplishments in the social sphere are more apparent than real. Much employment is still disguised unemployment. Rural-urban disparties persist. The political elite, which is ipso facto also the economic and social elite, is still overwhelmingly male and white. In these respects and others the unequal and exploitative features attributed to capitalism continue under socialism—sometimes in lesser degree, sometimes in the same or even greater degree. The political power of Cuban women is no greater today than it was in 1959. Persecution of homosexuals is far greater under Cuban socialism than it ever was under capitalism, in part because it is now backed by the force of Fidel Castro's personality and the Cuban state apparatus as well as cultural predilections. Access to the political elite for blacks and mulattoes (Batista himself was mulatto) has remained about the same (del Aguila, 1984, p. 172; Domínguez, 1978b, pp. 224–227, 494–504).

Third, during the course of the Revolution there have been dramatic worsening trends in many areas of early apparent achievement. The first impulses toward social equality have been replaced by powerful trends toward social elitism—not the old capitalist forms but the new socialist forms. Thus the initial opposition to *sociolismo*— buddyism or cronyism—has given way to a "new class" of party functionaries and state bureaucrats with privileged housing, department stores, vacation villas, access to hard currencies and luxury goods. As in the Soviet Union, rates of divorce increased dramatically after 1959 and in the 1980s stood at very high levels on a world scale (González, 1974, p. 10; Domínguez, 1978b, pp. 232, 501; Maidique, 1983, pp. 30, 32).

Fourth, given the nature of the Cuban state and of state-society relations since the Revolution, most of these social benefits have very high political costs directly and necessarily associated with them. The government apparatus that provides food, housing, health care, and educational opportunity, at the same time as it provides these benefits and for that very reason, also has enormous power over individuals and groups in Cuban society. Every Cuban knows this, and such knowledge, together with the other political mechanisms of the Cuban state, makes significant dissent by Cuban citizens virtually unthinkable except by those few—very few—who are willing to accept the most severe risks and costs. A state that has the power to deny food to political nonconformists, and that is willing to use that power, has unique instruments for maintaining "popular support."

Finally, the argument that a socialist transformation, a profoundly undemocratic political system, and massive economic decline were necessary in order to make social changes is dubious. Costa Rica has had a comparably progressive socioeconomic profile—low unemployment, high health standards, low illiteracy—at the same time that it has retained a pluralistic, democratic political system. It also enjoys a higher standard of living and much greater economic dynamism than Cuba.

In light of these considerations, the social achievements look less compelling than many analyses would suggest. Undoubtedly some of the achievements were easier to bring about under socialist dependency, but it was not the only way to achieve them, and they come with a dark exploitative side which we have just begun to describe.

There is also, of course, the enormous economic price that has been paid and is still being paid. Before 1959 Cuba had one of the most impressive socioeconomic profiles of any country in Latin America. In 1952 it ranked third among all Latin American countries in gross national product per capita. Since 1959, Cuba has been transformed into one of the least productive countries in the region. In 1981 it ranked fifteenth in a list of twenty countries in gross national product per capita. No other country dropped in ranking from 1952 to 1981 by more than three places; Cuba dropped twelve places (Thomas, Fauriol, and Weiss, 1984, p. 29). The Cuban Revolution, in short, has performed extremely poorly in terms of productivity and creating new wealth (as distinguished from dividing up wealth that already had been created).

It is of course true that there have been no capitalist investments, and thus no profit remittances, by the Soviet Union. Socialist systems do not make capitalist investments or remit capitalist profits. Moreover, since in Marxist economic terms profit is by definition exploitative, it follows that a system without profit is in that respect nonexploitative. These points are true by definition.

However, to anyone not bound by Marxist definitions it is manifest that capitalist investment and the profit system can be features of a generative, productive, positive-sum process. Such a notion is unacceptable to Marxists—including "sophisticated" Marxists—but outside the Marxist view it is nothing more than elementary economics. Critics of capitalist investment often cite examples where profits exceeded total investment to illustrate the exploitative effects of capitalism. Such arguments are fallacies for several reasons. They ignore the multiplier effects of the capital invested. They also ignore cases where investments were unproductive and the investor lost his investment; the risk of such losses is one of the factors that entitles an investor to profits. Finally, they ignore the fact that the Cubans themselves at the practical level frequently rejected their theoretical premises about the exploitative effects of capital when they appealed for direct private investment, commercial loans, and hard capitalist currencies. The intellectual and policy fallacies of the Marxist theory are also shown in relation to protests against the economic embargo on Cuba at the same time that free trade and investment are said to be exploitative. If trade is exploitative, as they claim, the embargo—pejoratively but inaccurately called a blockade—logically has to be a plus for Cuba. Yet, illogically, they claim it hurts them. If that is so, then obviously trade—and its inevitable concomitant, economic dependency—must also be positive in its effects.

Increasingly it looks as if the social gains of the Revolution came largely from simply dismantling the productive mechanisms of capitalist dependency without replacing them in effective ways. A once productive island has thus been transformed into a massive economic liability. Its problems have a variety of sources, including the frequent arbitrary and ill-informed interventions of Fidel Castro himself. The U.S. economic embargo is also cited as a reason. The most fundamental problems, however, are not random, personal, or inspired by capitalism; they are inherent in the character of Cuba's associated-dependent socialist situation. The economy's main weaknesses, in other words, are structural.

As Leontiev (1971, pp. 19, 21) pointed out two decades ago, these problems are "fundamentally the same as those that plagued the Soviet Union and other socialist countries," namely, "the characteristically low productivity of labor, rooted in the basic differences between a socialistic and an individualistic society." Leontiev went on to argue that the productivity of labor "seems to be lower now than it was before the revolution. With the same equipment and under otherwise identical physical conditions the same worker, or the same group of workers, seem to produce in all branches of industry and agriculture smaller amounts of goods, or goods of lower quality, or both, than would have been produced before the revolution. The so-called moral incentives . . . seem ineffective as a means of inducing laborers, white-collar workers, managerial and supervisory personnel to perform their respective jobs as well as they did before the revolution."

Subsequent events have confirmed this analysis. While the Cubans have made some adjustments, given their ideological and political commitments they cannot really correct these structural defects, which are inherent in the Cuban model, without changing the model itself. Once socialist Cuba divided up—fairly rapidly—the fruits of earlier capitalist development, the economic and other costs have become more evident. Some observers say these economic and social costs exist only for the Cuban upper and middle classes. But this argument is no longer plausible. Most of the approximately 125,000 Cuban boat people in 1980 were working and poor people. To date a full tenth of the Cuban population has fled the island. Many more— between one and two million more according to various estimates (Skidmore and Smith, 1984, p. 284; Domínguez as quoted in Maidique, 1983, p. 31)—would leave if they could. Nothing remotely resembling these phenomena existed before 1959, not even during the worst days of Batista.

Political Aspects

But if there are problems and costs in the social and economic areas, even more profound modes of domination and exploitation under socialist dependency occur in the political, cultural, and military-diplomatic areas. Again, they affect not only the affluent but also the middle class, working class, and poor people of Cuba directly and intensely.

In Cuba there is not even a pretense of democratic rule in the sense of citizens controlling governmental officials. To the contrary, the logic of the Revolution both publicly and within the ruling circles is the reverse: leaders guide, direct, and control citizens in the ways of revolutionary truth and virtue. The idea of citizens controlling leaders is characterized by the leaders as bourgeois, reactionary, and counterrevolutionary. In Cuba, "the Revolution and its leaders legitimate the constitution, the courts, the administration, the party, the mass organizations, and the elections—and not vice-versa" (Domínguez, 1978b, p. 261)

Accordingly, within Cuba itself power centers first and foremost on Fidel Castro, and second on the people closest to him. Fidel Castro has been the "socialist caudillo" of Cuba for more than three decades—most of his adult life and the entire duration of the post-1959 system. It is a remarkable achievement with few parallels on a world scale. Castro has well met his first priority of maintaining undiluted power for himself during this period.

Especially in the seventies and eighties, the Cuban Communist Party, the civilian bureaucracy, and the military have grown in numbers, organizational capacity and complexity, and influence—although all of them remain systematically subordinate to Fidel Castro and the PCC. At the next level down the hierarchy of power are the mass organizations: the Committees for the Defense of the Revolution (CDRs), the Federation of Cuban Women (FMC), labor unions, youth organizations. Finally there are elected legislative bodies (assemblies) and judicial structures at national, provincial, and local level. However, except in strictly limited and sharply controlled ways, these bodies do not have the functions associated with them in political democracies.

These political mechanisms are used for various domestic and foreign policy objectives set by the political elite. One of the main stated objectives is to create new socialist citizens who will be free of the values and characteristics that are glorified and practiced in politically liberal, capitalist societies. The regime is explicitly and resolutely antiliberal. Liberal societies place a high value on individualism, competition, pluralism, the basic freedoms, and group autonomy. From the point of view of the Cuban system, these values and practices are egotistical, alienating, atomizing, divisive, and undisciplined. The aim of the Revolution is, and must be, to get rid of them. Cuba's leaders have argued that because capitalism was in place for hundreds of years in Cuba, these values and practices are deeply ingrained. To get rid of them, therefore, it is necessary to have a vanguard of enlightened teachers and leaders who will assist the unenlighted masses to realize their true needs and interests.

Thus the Cuban political system is explicitly and comprehensively elitist and hierarchical both in the principles which underlay and legitimize it and in its political institutions and processes. The principles and institutions are enormously powerful devices for controlling and exploiting Cuban citizens. Under these principles literally no sphere of human activity is immune from the possibility of state supervision and control. In other words, there are no moral or ethical constraints on state action vis-a-vis the individual except the "needs of the Revolution" as determined by the top leadership. Any degree of state penetration of any area of individual and group life is legitimate. The elaborate and powerful organizational structures of the Cuban state, the legitimating myths of the Revolution, Fidel Castro's charisma, and other factors all assure that in practical terms the actual degree of that penetration is enormous.

In these circumstances, civil liberties have no meaning either conceptually or practically. Neither does the idea of the autonomy of individuals and groups from state power. In Cuba, the idea of a "legitimate opposition" is totally foreign and subversive. The operative principle is, "Within the Revolution, anything; outside the Revolution, nothing." This standard is very elastic. It means whatever the state chooses it to mean.

In Cuba the communications media are totally controlled by the political elite. Criticisms of the regime and its leaders—even (especially?) jokes about them—are rigorously prohibited. According to Hugh Thomas (1971, p. 1463), "Compared with the Cuban press, that of Spain [under Franco] might be considered sparkling." Lee Lockwood (1970, p. 18) notes that the media in Cuba are not only dull, dogmatic, repetitious, and sycophantic but also uninformative. "In fact," he writes, "the Cuban press is so mediocre that even Fidel can't stand it; I had personally witnessed how every morning at breakfast, he read the AP and UPI wire service reports first (and carefully) before skimming idly through *Granma*." Castro has railed at the U.S. media because of their alleged elitism, monopoly power, and subservience to government policies, yet these charges fit his own system infinitely more accurately than the U.S. system. Clearly such control of the media—both print and electronic—affords Castro a powerful instrument for controlling and exploiting the Cuban population. Just to give one concrete example, the Cuban government controls entirely information about the human and material costs of Cuba's military activities in Africa. It is inconceivable that the government would (or could) tolerate investigative reporting or a pluralistic, free press.

The political elite have several mass organizations to enforce loyalty to the regime and its objectives and to supervise and punish possible counterrevolutionaries. Of these the most important are the Committees for the Defense of the Revolution (CDRs). They were founded in 1960 with a membership of about 800,000 persons; by 1983 there were more than 5 million members, or more than half the entire population (and about 80 percent of the adult population). The specific goals have been many and somewhat varied over time: vigilance, local government, public health, civil defense. However, the major continuing theme has been vigilance. CDRs exist primarily to ensure that Cubans are "integrated" into the Revolution. Being integrated is in effect "a requirement for normal life in Cuba, whatever one's feelings toward revolutionary rule and policies." Thus "even former members of the prerevolutionary upper class, still living in Cuba in mansions with domestic servants, have been reported belonging to a committee, because being a member makes life easier" (Domínguez, 1978b, p. 264). By contrast, "nonintegration" is more than inconvenient; it is dangerous. Nonintegrated persons are publicly vilified. CDR militants hold "repudiation meetings" to "chastise, browbeat, and humiliate" those who want to leave Cuba. Merely not belonging to the CDRs is a political act. In a society that insists on revolutionary militancy those who stand on the sidelines are vulnerable (Domínguez, 1978b, pp. 260–267; del Aguila, 1984, pp. 154–156).

Under such circumstances the regime does not need to use much physical violence or imprison many people in order to operate a totalitarian system. Of course, politically motivated violence, imprisonment, and torture have been used by the regime on thousands of Cubans. However, the circumstances just described, plus the U.S. "escape hatch," have kept at relatively low levels the amount of overt physical violence and imprisonment in Cuba compared to such cases as the USSR, the People's Republic of China, or Cambodia. But the system is no less totalitarian for all that. Moreover, there are other effective forms of violence besides political murder and physical torture and imprisonment. This is a point that is made frequently against capitalist culture but seldom against Cuba, where it applies with even greater force.

Culture and Education

Nowhere are the influences of the Soviet model of development in Cuba more evident, and more contrary to "human well being," than in the cultural and educational spheres. Intellectual work at all levels is intensely politicized. All cultural, artistic, and educational activity is evaluated and rewarded exclusively in terms of its contribution to the Revolution, as judged by the political elite. Intellectual independence and criticism of the regime are met with official contempt, mass humiliation, and various forms of psychological and physical repression. The most notorious examples are those of the poets Heberto Padilla and Armando Valladares and the dramatist Anton Arrufat, but they are only the tip of the iceberg (Ripoll, 1982).

Today the vast majority—one estimate is 95 percent—of Cuban writers and creative artists are in exile. Most of them are not ex-Batistianos. Most opposed Batista. Many were actively involved in the fight against his regime and some even had positions in the Castro government in the early years. But the cultural regimentation and dogmatism were intolerable to them and they left. Many of these exiles have made and are now making distinguished contributions in the cultural sphere. One has only to mention, for example, the works of a Carlos Franqui, a Cabrera Infante, or a dozen distinguished social scientists. On the island itself, however, the picture is very different. As Thomas, Fauriol, and Weiss (1984, pp. 42–43) report:

> In 1964, in a famous interview in Paris, novelist Alejo Carpentier was asked why he had not written a novel about the Cuban Revolution. He answered that unfortunately he had been raised and educated long before the Revolution and the burden of creating new revolutionary novels would have to fall on the shoulders of a younger generation. "Twenty years from now," he affirmed, "we will be able to read the literary production of the new Cuba." Those 20 years have elapsed. Tragically, the Cuban revolution cannot offer a single notable novelist, a famous poet, a penetrating essayist, not even a fresh contribution to Marxist analysis . . . Censorship and fear have smothered creativity in Cuba. What is left on the island is merely the incessant voice of official propaganda.

The situation would seem to be better at the level of mass education. However, as is often the case, impressive figures regarding aggregate gains in educational opportunity are misleading. For one thing, "despite claims to the contrary, higher education remains elitist in Cuba" (Thomas, Fauriol, and Weiss, 1984, p. 41). Tests of political loyalty and political achievement are applied at all levels of the

educational system to determine who has access to the best facilities
and training.

Moreover, the quality of education has not kept pace with the
increases in the overall quantity of educational opportunity—which,
as noted earlier, were already relatively great before 1959. To the
contrary, the dogmatic and politicized character of education has
impoverished its quality. The quality is now much inferior to what
it was before 1959 and is today in democratic countries such as
Costa Rica. For example, when U.S. liberal Congressman Stephen
Solarz of New York visited Cuba in 1978, he met with a group of
sixteen students at the University of Havana. According to journalist
Strobe Talbott (1978a), the students were impressive in delivering
"set pieces" consistent with current government policy, but "on subjects where the government's line was not yet clearly defined, students
and teachers alike were intellectually incapacitated. At the end . . .
Solarz thanked [his hosts] for a revealing demonstration of 'democratic centralism' at work. The students seemed unaware of his
irony."

Scholarly analyses of Cuban education confirm this journalistic
impression. According to a very sympathetic study (Pérez, 1985, p. 4)
of historical studies in socialist Cuba:

> Appreciation of the present, together with a recognition of the
> achievements of the Revolution, require awareness of a certain
> version of the past. It is this central task that Cuban historiography
> is given. It is with the old past that the new present is compared, a
> comparison that seeks to underscore the vices of capitalism and the
> virtues of socialism. The recent literature has examined the nature
> of capitalism in prerevolutionary Cuba, an inquiry that begins with
> the Spanish conquest and emphasizes exploitation, corruption, and
> oppression in the old regime—in short, a chronicle of how truly
> bad the old days were. The achievements of the Revolution, by
> implication, are thereby set off in relief—accomplishments never to
> be taken for granted.

At the level of secondary education Cuban officials themselves have
conceded publicly numerous shortcomings in quality: shoddy construction and durability of school buildings and facilities, rising drop-
out rates, more cheating on the part of students and teachers
(Thomas, Fauriol, and Weiss, 1984, p. 42).

The Militarization of Cuban Society

The regimentation and politicization of education and culture have parallels in the militarization of society, which has both internal and external aspects.

The militarization of Cuban society is partly rooted in the guerrilla experience that defeated Batista. The concepts and habits forged during those years continue to affect Cuba and are now reinforced and supplemented by the penetration into Cuban political organizations and processes of numerous aspects of the Soviet model. For example, in 1980 thirteen out of sixteen members of the Political Bureau of the PCC had been early guerrilla followers of Fidel and Raúl Castro (Thomas, Fauriol, and Weiss, 1984, p. 15). The regular armed forces of Cuba are the largest in all of Latin America with the possible exception of Brazil, a country with thirteen times as many inhabitants and 74 times as much territory. Even if Cuba's defense needs are greater, this huge disparity is still notable. Cuba's regular armed forces number between 200,000 and 375,000 members. In addition, there are another 100,000 to 500,000 men and women in the militia, several thousand border guards, 10–15,000 state security police, a "Youth Labor Army" of 100,000, and several hundred thousand members of the military reserves (del Aguila, 1985, pp. 160–161; Thomas, Fauriol, and Weiss, 1984, p. 57; Domínguez 1978b, pp. 346–350; Fagen 1978a, p. 77). If one adds the paramilitary aspects of the CDRs and other mass organizations, one sees that virtually the entire population is militarized in one way or another. Indeed, Castro has stated that instead of a vote for every citizen, he would offer them a gun, and he has said many times that he had created an armed camp in his nation (Thomas, Fauriol, Weiss, 1984, p. 57). All this is a far cry indeed from the 47,812 (Domínguez, 1978b, pp. 346–347) poorly trained, ineffective troops of Batista's army, navy, and reserve forces at their greatest strength. It is such facts that led Thomas (1987, p. 726) to say that in Cuba "the emphasis on war and weapons, on the importance of fighting, borders on the psychopathic."

Foreign and Military Policies

The subject of Cuban foreign policy before 1959 is complex. On the one hand, U.S. government influence was enormous at times, as the history of the Platt Amendment and many aspects of the relations with the governments of Grau San Martín and Fulgencio Batista attest. U.S. private interests also were very influential in Cuba. In these respects among others Cuban politics was heavily influenced by the United States. On the other hand, the pluralistic character of U.S. government institutions and of its public-private relations diluted and complicated these influences and provided some political and economic "space" both within Cuba and for Cuba's foreign policy. The character of Soviet institutions, and therefore of its influences on Cuba, is very different. Today Cuba is much more tightly tied in its foreign and domestic policies to Moscow than it ever was to Washington. In fact, the major constraint on Soviet influence is its physical distance from Cuba. Ironically, physical distance is one of the factors holistic dependency rejects as irrelevant because it is not an aspect of its touchstone distinction between capitalism and socialism.

Soviet influence was not significant at the beginning of the Revolution. It became important only about a year and a half after Castro came to power in Janaury 1959 (Blasier, 1983, pp. 100–103). Through most of the sixties the relationship grew but there were also major differences between the Soviet and Cuban governments on domestic and foreign policies. The Cubans veered from one extreme to another in their economic policies and favored insurrectionary violence against established governments in Latin American countries. The Soviets opposed both these tendencies. In the 1970s, however, conflicts between the Cuban government and the Soviet decreased in both domestic and foreign policy. After 1968 the Cuban government accepted the Soviet government as its "senior partner" in foreign policy. Thus Cuba supported Soviet policy in Czechoslovakia (1968), Afghanistan (1979), Poland (1981), Angola (1979), Ethiopia (1979), Nicaragua (1979), and El Salvador (1979). The Cubans were an effective sponsor for Soviet policies in Africa and Central America and in regard to the so-called nonaligned movement of Third World countries. They sided with the USSR against the People's Republic of China.

From the late 1960s to the mid-1980s there was no important foreign policy question on which the Cubans publicly challenged the Soviet Union. On the contrary, the Cubans have followed the Soviet lead as loyally as any Eastern European country (perhaps more loyally than most) even on distasteful issues such as Czechoslovakia,

Afghanistan, and Poland. If private disagreements or qualifications existed they were not expressed publicly.

The scale and scope of Cuban involvement with Soviet foreign and military policies were astonishing for a country of ten million people which never imagined, let alone implemented, such levels of military activity in the context of capitalist dependency. Cuban military operations in Africa and the Middle East exploded in magnitude in during the collaborative phase of Cuban-Soviet relations that began in the late sixties. The highest total number of Cuban troops and military advisers in those regions at any time in the sixties was an estimated 750–1,000 in 1966. In 1976 it has increased to an estimated 16–19,000 and by 1978 to an estimated 38–39,000 (Blasier, 1983, p. 112). "Cuban forces abroad in the late 1970s accounted for two-thirds of the military and technical personnel stationed by all Communist states in the Third World—exceeding Soviet troops in Afghanistan and Vietnamese forces in Southeast Asia. In addition to troops, Cuba dispatched technicians, advisers, and constructions workers to Algeria, Iraq, Jamaica, Libya, Mozambique, Nicaragua, Vietnam, and Grenada in the late 1970s and early 1980s" (Thomas, Fauriol, and Weiss, 1984, p. 12; also see Mesa-Lago, 1981, pp. 50–53, and del Aguila, 1984, p. 125).

In 1978 Cuba had not only about 35,000 military troops and advisers in Angola and Ethiopia, but 200 in Libya, 300–400 in South Yemen, 100–150 in Guinea-Bissau, 50 in Tanzania, 20 in Iraq, and 15–60 in Zambia (Blasier, 1983, p. 112). In 1981–83 Cuba's overseas military presence continued at the same levels in most of the foregoing countries (except for Guinea-Bissau, where it dropped to 50) but increased to 3,000 in Libya, 2,200 in Iraq, and 800 in South Yemen. In addition there were 170 Cuban military personnel in Algeria and 2–4,000 in Nicaragua. Another 22–25,000 economic technicians were operating in these countries (del Aguila, 1984, p. 125). According to Fidel Castro, more than 100,000 members of the Cuban armed forces had served in Africa by the end of 1980. In 1982 Cuba had about 70,000 military troops, military advisers, and civilian advisers in 23 countries around the world (Thomas, Fauriol, and Weiss, 1984, p. 12).

Not only military personnel but weapons capabilities increased very rapidly during this period. In 1981 there were about 2,400 Soviet military advisers in Cuba to provide training and support for the military equipment that had flowed into Cuba since 1975. (There were also several thousand Soviet civilian advisors.) Cuba's ground and air forces, nearly all provided by the Soviets, included 200 MIG fighters and 50 other kinds of combat aircraft; 38 combat helicopters; 650 tanks; 1,500 anti-aircraft guns; and dozen of military transport aircraft, including at least seven long-range jets each capable of carrying 150 to 200 combat equipped troops (Cirincione and Hunter, 1984, p. 175).

In short, the military has been by far the most "dynamic" sector of the Cuban economy for at least a decade. The Soviets have paid most of the economic costs in this sector. One of the main arguments of holistic dependency is that foreign capital is concentrated in the most dynamic sectors of the associated-dependent countries, and that therefore foreign capital is more influential than mere aggregate investments would suggest. By this logic of "dynamic-sector analysis" the Soviet role in Cuba is greater than U.S. capital ever was in Cuba.

Many commentators maintain that Cuba's foreign policy reflects Cuba's own interests. However, it is not plausible that a country of Cuba's size, location, and precarious economy would, in its own interests, send 70,000 troops and military advisers beyond its borders—most of them to Africa and the Middle East, where the troops are Cuban but the officers and the uniforms are Russian. It is also argued that this foreign military involvement is "popular" in Cuba. But what does "popular" mean in a country where dissent is "counterrevolutionary" and "antinational," where the media and the means of production are state-controlled, and where a massive, powerful apparatus of political mobilization and "vigilance" is in place? If it is popular, and in Cuba's interests, why are casualties unreported in Cuba, the dead buried outside Cuba, and the wounded kept out of public exposure (Leiken, 1981, p. 100; Pastor, 1983, p. 191)? Why, despite intense political pressures and safeguards against release of information on the subject, was there evidence of resistance to the African wars among the managerial elite; of "insubordination among some troops"; and of "widespread unhappiness among the Cuban people concerning compulsory military service" (Domínguez, 1978b, p. 355)?

Conclusion

This chapter has not established—nor has it sought to establish— that Cuban revolutionary institutions and policies are a total, mechanical replication of Soviet models and preferences. Even less was pre-1959 Cuba a mechanical response to influences from the United States. My argument does reject, however, the proposition that Cuba's domestic development and foreign relations under socialism have been autonomous and nonexploitative. I make an analytical and empirical case for a very different hypothesis, namely, that under socialism a *bi-pé* alliance of Cuban and Soviet elites systematically dominated and exploited the Cuban people for its own ends.

These conclusions are sharply at odds with the claims of holistic dependency authors about the character and consequences of socialist dependency. These authors have frequently called for studies of "concrete situations" of capitalist dependency, and occasionally they have done such studies. But they have never done studies of concrete situations of socialist dependency. It is hoped that this examination of the specific features and the mechanisms of a socialist situation will contribute to the comparative analysis of capitalist and socialist dependency.

The barriers to such comparative analysis are many. They include not only the intellectual strictures of Marxism but also numerous and complex sociological, historical, and political obstacles. Because of these barriers, it is difficult for most scholars writing about Latin America even to think of analyzing socialist cases in anything like the same critical spirit one routinely uses to analyze capitalist cases. Critical analyses of capitalist cases are not necessarily perceived as inherently critical of capitalism; even if they are, that is regarded as permissible. Studies that are critical of socialist cases, by contrast, are perceived as inherently antisocialist, which is not permissible, even if they are merely trying to find out what is going on.

These kinds of sociological, historical, and political barriers go back to the Vietnam War and to taboos generated during the era of Joseph McCarthy in the United States. But the roots extend even deeper and more broadly. In the 1930s George Orwell discovered to his immense sorrow that the intelligentsia "could not conceive of directing upon Russia anything like the same stringency of criticism they used on their own nation." In Catalonia Orwell learned that while the Communist-controlled government was filling up the jails with "the most devoted fighters for Spanish freedom, men who had given up everything for the cause," the intelligentsia that controlled the Western press did not know and refused to know, because "they were committed not to the fact but to the abstraction" (Trilling, 1952, pp. xvii, xxii).

In thinking about socialist dependency it is time to consider not the abstraction but the fact. If real-world cases of capitalism are compared to ideal-world cases of socialism, the socialist cases look better, and always will. That comparison is bogus. A genuine comparison will not, and should not, necessarily lead to any particular set of conclusions and opinions about the relative merits of the two kinds of dependent situations. But it does allow the debate to become realistic and serious and thus more conducive to human well-being in dependent countries.

8   The Consumption of Dependency Ideas in Latin America

The next four chapters—two each on Latin America and the United States—deal with the effects and implications of dependency ideas and the reasons for their appeal. The structure of each pair of chapters is the same. The first one makes a survey of the nature and size of the impact and an assessment of the overall significance of the dependency movement in the region/country. The second chapter of each pair explores a particularly salient feature of the dependency movement and its legacy in that region/country in greater detail. Thus Chapter 9 shows how in Latin America a dynamic trend toward intellectual autonomy emerged from the cultural and psychological dependency discussed in Chapter 8. Chapter 11 shows how in the United States the dependency movement politicized scholarship at the institutional level as well as at the individual level discussed in Chapter 10.

Dependency Ideas in Latin America and the United States

In gauging the impact and significance of dependency ideas it is important to separate the discussions of Latin America and the United States. For example, dependency ideas were less influential among intellectuals and scholars in Latin America than in the United States. This proposition may surprise many people in the United States, but I do not believe that most informed Latin Americans, or a number of informed North American students of the two regions, would disagree with it.

For one thing, in Latin America broadly similar ideas had already been very influential before the dependency perspective as such even existed. Since Latin American intellectuals had been familiar with such ideas longer than their North American counterparts, they were in a relative sense less influenced by the more recent stimulus.

In addition, in Latin America the reception to dependency ideas was not conditioned as it was in the United States by the traumas of the Kennedy assassination, Vietnam, urban and racial tensions, and Watergate. These events and their aftermaths profoundly affected North American society. Among intellectuals they shattered confidence, inspired pessimism, and instilled a deep sense of guilt. When, as part of this process, liberal perspectives on modernization and development collapsed, dependency ideas moved rapidly into the vacuum. These events also coincided with an explosion in the numbers of U.S. scholars studying Latin America. They were mostly younger scholars who were especially receptive to the multifaceted appeals of dependency thinking. None of these features existed in the same forms or to the same degrees in Latin American countries, where Vietnam did not weigh nearly so heavily, liberal theories had never been so popular, dependency ideas were not as new, and the generational phenomenon was less pronounced and took a very different form.

Although powerful faddish factors led to the embrace of these ideas in both places, in Latin America the fad passed more quickly than it did in the United States. Among leading Latin American intellectuals the high point of dependency influence was the early seventies. Thereafter, ambivalence about these ideas grew and was increasingly resolved in the direction not so much of denouncing dependency thinking as ignoring it. This was especially so among unorthodox dependency authors and supporters. The point is symbolized by the titles of the North American and Brazilian editions, respectively, of a noted book by Peter Evans (1979, 1980): the texts are the same, but in the U.S. it is called *Dependent Development;* in Brazil, it is called *A Tríplice Aliança* [The Triple Alliance].

Moreover, in Latin America during the seventies and eighties the most innovative and important scholars were largely indifferent to the dependency "craze," as Pike (1973, p. 157) has called it. They were a new generation of social scientists whose influence and importance became very substantial indeed. This fact was not fully appreciated at the time even in Latin America, and it is still not widely known in the United States; but it is critical to understanding the meaning of the dependency movement. In the United States, by contrast, most scholarly specialists on Latin America and the Third World continued to champion the dependency perspective throughout the seventies and, in many cases, well into the eighties.

Nevertheless, it would be a great mistake to ignore or minimize the influences of dependency ideas in Latin America. They "had an immediate and decisive influence, not only on the reading public, but—perhaps more importantly—on the collective effort to define the issues and themes around which a new view of Latin America was to be built" (Halperín-Donghi, 1982, p. 115). To record and document the range, depth, and signficance of those influences is the important scholarly task to which we now turn.

The Magnitude of the Influences in Latin America

Influences on Social Scientists

A Chilean economist (Palma, 1978, p. 881) wrote that "in one way or another the dependency perspective has so dominated work in the social sciences in Latin America and elsewhere in recent years that it would be literally impossible to review the overwhelming mass of writing that has appeared." A Spanish sociologist and Latin Americanist (Marsal, 1979, p. 219) wrote after an extensive survey that "dependency theory has been the predominant sociological theory of recent decades in Latin America . . . at the peak of its influence it was thought capable of replacing all previous sociological theory." An Argentine political scientist (Cavarozzi, 1982, p. 152), said that the book by Cardoso and Faletto published in 1969 was "without any doubt . . . the analysis of Latin American political and social processes that has had the largest impact in academic and intellectual circles in the Latin American region of any work in the last fifteen years." Other informed scholars have made similar judgments (Balán, 1982; Halperín-Donghi, 1982).

There are, in addition, a number of quantitative indicators of the influence of dependency ideas. As early as 1979 the classic work by Cardoso and Faletto had been through sixteen printings in Spanish and an undetermined number of printings in Portuguese and it was still going strong in both languages. (It had also been translated into English, French, German, and Italian.) Sunkel and Paz's *El Subdesarrollo Latinoamericano y la Teoría del Desarrollo* (1970) had been through fourteen printings as of 1980. A book by the North American historians Stanley and Barbara Stein, *The Colonial Heritage of Latin America* (1970), written quite self-consciously from a dependencia point of view, had a Spanish edition published in Mexico that went through twelve printings between 1970 and 1980. These levels of demand are unusual by the standards of Latin American publishing of any kind and for academic publications they are extraordinary.

Another relevant indicator is the number of monographic studies spawned by dependency thinkers and written by Latin Americans within the framework of their ideas. Dependency authors have compiled detailed lists of such studies. Cardoso (1972, p. 19–20; 1980, p. 74) cites specific analyses by Latin American authors of states, local bourgeois groups, unions, workers, social movements, ideologies, urbanization, marginalization, and other phenomena which "in one way or another were inspired by the dependency perspective." Although the quality of these analyses, "like that of any other area of scientific work," was in his view "highly variable," Cardoso concluded that they produced an "indisputable enrichment" of knowledge about Latin American societies. T. dos Santos (1980, pp. 355–359) listed more than a hundred empirical, theoretical, and critical dependency studies by authors from all over the world but mostly from Latin America. Still another long list with many Latin Americans is given by Frank (1974, pp. 102–106).

So far we have looked at the aggregate picture. But the influences of dependency ideas also varied by time period, country, and type of intellectuals within countries. In the earliest days—the late sixties—Andre Gunder Frank's ideas were popular in almost all countries and among a wide range of scholars, including many who later opted for unorthodox dependency. As the Argentinian historian Tulio Halperín-Donghi (1982, pp. 117–118) put it, throughout Latin America Frank's work initially "gained vast and enthusiastic favor, and not only among the misinformed. The reason . . . was that it was perfectly attuned to the mood of the times." For a time, Frank's writings were "not only attractive to [the] left-leaning public . . . He also had something to offer those who looked at Latin America's predicament from a perspective less concerned with immediate revolutionary prospects, but still with an open mind."

But Frank's work was "a dazzling, fleeting comet whose . . . success was both resounding and comparatively short-lived" (Halperín-Donghi, 1982, pp. 116–117). After the publication of Cardoso and Faletto's work in 1969, Latin American intellectuals tended to divide rather sharply. One group (not a formal group but a categorical group) immediately denounced orthodox dependency and endorsed unorthodox dependency. For such persons, many of whom had initially shared the exhilaration that accompanied the appearance of Frank's book, orthodox dependency became less a subject of serious study than an object of joyful ridicule. This view is well summarized by—and expressed in—Halperín-Donghi (1982). The other group continued to support orthodox dependency (although not necessarily the works of Andre Gunder Frank). Perhaps its most widely known representative was Theotonio dos Santos, a thoughtful analyst, powerful writer, and one of the founders of the dependency approach. Others included Aníbal Quijano, Rui Mauro Marini, Franz Hinkelhammert, Armand Mattelhart, Tomás Vasconi, Orlando Caputo, Roberto Pizarro, and Vania Bambirra.

It is unclear which of these two groups was larger. In the late sixties and early seventies both were significant in size and influence in all the larger and more developed countries of the region and in some of the smaller and poorer countries as well. During the rest of the seventies and the eighties the strength of the different dependency currents diversified. Those whose support for orthodox dependency survived the arrival of unorthodox dependency tended to continue to support it. It is often assumed that orthodox dependency was mainly influential in the United States and unorthodox dependency in Latin America (Cardoso, 1977a). In fact many Latin American intellectuals supported orthodox dependency. In Latin America support for orthodox dependency has been more stable than support for unorthodox dependency. In the United States the reverse is true.

Among those in Latin America who supported unorthodox dependency the situation evolved differently. For many there was a gradual, subtle, indirect, partial drifting-away toward other interpretations. This change was ambiguous, inconclusive, and nondefinitive. Dependency terminology and themes were less often rejected than neglected. Bridges were not burned. The possibility of returning to dependency perspectives was held open.

Influences on the Church, Higher Education, and the NIEO

The "progressive" wing of the Roman Catholic church, including leading liberation theologians such as the Peruvian Gustavo Gutiérrez (1973, pp. 81–99) and the Brazilian Leonardo Boff (1978, pp. 264–295), was influenced by dependency ideas. Gutiérrez draws explicitly on many dependency authors, especially Cardoso, dos Santos, and Sunkel but also Hinkelhammert, Pizarro, and others. For Gutiérrez (p. 81), "Dependence and liberation are correlative terms. An analysis of the situation of dependency leads one to attempt to escape from it." His arguments are a "state of the art" version of dependency thinking as it stood at the time he wrote. In some respects his synthesis even anticipates subsequent clarifications and trends. For example, Gutiérrez is not ambiguous, as dependency writers often were, about the primacy of class over nation. Moreover, he cites, as they seldom did, the writings of Mariátegui that foreshadowed various dependency themes (pp. 87, 90–92). Gutiérrez and Boff both explicitly regarded dependencia ideas as a scientific advance which enabled them and others to read the scriptures with greater understanding. As Silva Gotay (1981, p. 220) argues, while dependency ideas did not "produce" liberation theology they did provide the "scientific" concepts and methodology which enabled them, they thought, to "decipher . . . the liberating character of the gospels."

Another area affected profoundly by dependency ideas was higher education (by which I mean institutional aspects of the educational system, such as curriculum). Elguea (1984, p. 3) examined syllabi for graduate programs (two masters and three doctoral) in the sociology of development in four leading Mexican universities. His data "cover the whole span of the sociology of development as an academic discipline in Mexico, from the early seventies to 1984, and all the existing graduate programs dedicated to this subject in that country." He counted "all required texts that deal with the sociological aspects of economic growth, i.e., the sociology of development." As Table 8.1 shows, dependency readings were either on a par with modernization readings or ahead of them. This was already the pattern in the period 1970–75 and it was even stronger in the period 1976–81 (except at the Universidad Iberoamericana). When individual writers are examined dependency authors again do very well (see Table 8.2). By all measures (most-cited author, share of top three or four or five, share of total) dependency authors are more frequently cited than modernization authors. Clearly the ideas of the periphery were more pervasive in these curricula than those of the center. In this sense at least the earlier intellectual dependency had been reduced.

A third policy area influenced by dependency ideas was the movement for a New International Economic Order (NIEO). It sought to change the basic rules of the game and institutions of the international

Table 8.1 Theoretical orientation of textbooks and required readings in development courses in Mexican graduate programs in sociology, 1970–1981 (percentages and number assigned)

Educational institution	1970–1975			1976–1981		
	Modernization	Dependency	N	Modernization	Dependency	N
El Colegio de México	45% (18)	55% (22)	40	26% (21)	74% (61)	82
Universidad Nacional Autónoma de México (UNAM)	59% (44)	41% (30)	74	23% (22)	77% (73)	95
Facultad Latinoamericana de Ciencias Sociales (FLACSO)	—	—		36% (35)	64% (61)	96
Universidad Iberoamericana	—	—		52% (26)	48% (24)	50
Totals	54% (62)	46% (52)	114	32% (104)	68% (219)	323

Source: Elguea, 1984, p. 4.

Table 8.2 Most quoted authors of textbooks and required readings used in development courses in Mexican graduate programs in sociology (UNAM not included), 1970–1981 (approach and frequency)

Author	Approach	Number of times quoted
Cardoso, F. H.	Dependency	40
Germani, G.	Modernization	20
Stavenhagen, R.	Dependency	14
Marini, M.	Dependency	13
Weber, M.	Modernization	11
Dos Santos, T.	Dependency	10
González Casanova, P.	Dependency	9
Medina Echavarría, J.	Modernization	8
Prebisch, R.	Dependency	8
Eisenstadt, S. N.	Modernization	7
Frank, A. G.	Dependency	7
Furtado, C.	Dependency	7
Rogers, E.	Modernization	7
Sunkel, O., and P. Paz	Dependency	5
Lerner, D.	Modernization	3
Amin, S.	Dependency	3

Source: Javier A. Elguea, unpublished paper, based on survey reported in Table 8.1. The classification of approaches as either modernization or dependency is Elguea's; see also Elguea, 1989.

capitalist economic order. NIEO proponents came not only from Latin America but also from much of the rest of the Third World (and even parts of the First World). The NIEO was a powerful force in North/South relations in the 1970s. NIEO ideas and dependency ideas are not identical: NIEO ideology said little or nothing about class struggles within developing countries and did not speak out against the elites of Third World countries. But they agree in challenging the ideal of global economic liberalism associated with the North and in affirming that the interests of the South and the North are fundamentally in conflict. Holistic dependency gave intellectual coherence and legitimacy to the NIEO's policy proposals. It provided a broader framework for NIEO thinking. It thus helped to unify a very disparate group of Third World countries around a more or less coherent set of policies (Murphy, 1984, pp. 105–112; Krasner, 1985, pp. 42–44, 82–86, 94).

Influences on Governments

Last but not least, dependency ideas informed the outlooks and behaviors of various Latin American governments. Sometimes they actually had a direct influence on government policy. More often they helped to legitimate, popularize, or justify specific government policies. While they were usually part of a field of influences rather than the only one or the most important one, they were significant. Policies seldom are the product of just one influence.

In Chile both the "maximalist" left and the more moderate "gradualist" left during the Allende period (1970–73) based their ideologies, strategies, and policies on various forms of dependency thinking. The maximalists drew on orthodox dependency, the gradualists on unorthodox dependency (Ayres, 1972; Allende, 1973; Valenzuela and Valenzuela, 1975). The Revolutionary Government of the Armed Forces of Peru during the Velasco years (1968–75) had strong utopian, moralistic, antimarket, redistributionist features which dependency thinking contributed to, made more coherent, and helped to legitimize (Thorp and Bertram, 1978, pp. 294–295; North, 1983; Sheahan, 1983). Dependency ideas, both orthodox and unorthodox, turned up prominently in the governments of Luis Echeverría (1970–76) in Mexico, Michael Manley in Jamaica (1972–80), and Maurice Bishop in Grenada (1979–83).

One of the governments whose policies were most strongly influenced by dependency ideas was the Sandinista government in Nicaragua after 1979. Sandinista leaders who studied in Chile during 1970–73 "returned with new 'dependency' theories suggesting that a total break with capitalism was necessary for development to occur in the Third World periphery." Rui Mauro Marini, Theotonio dos Santos, Vania Bambirra, and Andre Gunder Frank are said to be among the writers who were influential (Cruz Sequeira, 1984, pp. 101, 108). Radical intellectuals from Europe, Latin America, and the United States used Nicaragua as a laboratory "where they could experiment with theories they could not test at home" (Gleijeses, 1984, p. 130).

Dependency ideas also supported and legitimized Sandinista political arrangements. Henry Ruíz, one of the nine members of the ruling national directorate, stated in June 1982, after the Sandinistas had firm control of the army and the police, that "the revolution's honeymoon is coming to an end. By this I mean the romantic idea among those who believed that the Sandinista peoples' revolution was an idyllic revolution in which the interests of a group of traitors and the interests of real working people could be fused; a shortsighted point of view from which our revolutionary directorate never suffered" (Ruíz as quoted in Nolan, 1984, p. 126). President Daniel Ortega characterized Nicaraguans who criticized his visits to the USSR and other Communist countries as "people who were born in Nicaragua by accident but who think like foreigners occupying our country" (Kinzer, 1985a). When Sandinista officials formally suspended all remaining civil liberties in Nicaragua, they said it was necessary to defend the nation against the "internal allies and agents of imperialism" (Kinzer, 1985b). These are all text-book examples of the use of the holistic dependency concept of the "anti-nation inside the nation" as a political smear to stifle dissent.

Nonleftist military governments such as Brazil from 1964 to 1985, Argentina from 1966 to 1973 and 1976 to 1983, and Peru from 1975 to 1980 also drew on the terminology, if not necessarily the precise concepts, of dependency analysis. Brazilian officials—from President João Figueiredo to Coronel Edison Dytz, who headed the Special Informatics Secretariat (SEI), a key administrative unit—made high-profile statements incorporating dependency themes (Seward, forthcoming). The Office of the President in Argentina in 1973 produced a report entitled *Política Económica y Social: Ruptura de la Dependencia* [Economic and Social Policy: Breaking Dependency] (Ayres, 1976, p. 475). Like the Sandinista and Fidelista regimes, right-wing military governments also used the idea of the "anti-nation inside the nation" to justify political authoritarianism and repression.

So far we have mainly been concerned to describe and document the magnitude of the influence of dependency ideas. We turn next to interpretations of those influences.

Interpreting the Effects of Dependency Ideas on Culture and Policy

Assessments of the dependency movement and its consequences have been positive and negative. Positive assessments are numerous (Cardoso, 1972, 1977a, 1980; Palma, 1978; T. dos Santos, 1980; Bresser Pereira, 1982; Cavarrozzi, 1982; Halperín-Donghi, 1982). Among the many specific achievements credited to the dependency movement by Latin Americans, and also North Americans (for citations, see Chapter 10), are:

fruitful criticisms of development and modernization theories produced largely (though not exclusively) by scholars in the United States in the fifties and early sixties;

successful criticisms of structuralist theories of development produced by Latin American economists at ECLA and other institutions also during the fifties and early sixties;

the refinement and revitalization of Latin American Marxism;

fruitful criticisms of the ideologies of Latin American Communist parties which were doctrinaire, antiquated, and overly committed to a rigid view of the role of the proletarian class in history;

the further disabling of an already weakened Alliance for Progress and other aspects of U.S. foreign policy, thus helping to reduce U.S. hegemony in the region;

the elaboration of an intellectual and ideological basis for resisting political authoritarianism in Brazil, Argentina, Chile, Uruguay, and other countries in the late sixties and the seventies;

helping to provide an intellectual foundation for theories about bureaucratic authoritarianism that were extremely influential in the seventies;

helping to legitimate and support the Cuban revolution and its Marxist social system;

helping to legitimate, support, and guide other diverse experiments in the region, such as the Allende regime in Chile, the Manley governments in Jamaica, the Sandinista regime in Nicaragua, and the New Jewel regime in Grenada;

changing the hitherto dominant pattern, in which Northern or Center social science flowed to the South or Periphery, to one in which the flow was reversed;

increasing the pride and self-confidence of intellectuals in the South;

helping to provide an intellectual basis for the movement for a New International Economic Order.

Most Latin American intellectuals agreed with such assessments, especially during late sixties and early seventies.

There were also critical assessments of many different kinds. Perhaps the most frequent and well-known ones came from Marxists who complained that dependency writings are not sufficiently faithful to Marxist methodologies and substantive claims (Weffort, 1971; Laclau, 1971; Cueva, 1976; Castañeda and Hett, 1979). Dependency writers themselves often made this criticism of each other. Such a view also informs surveys of Latin American Marxism that ignore dependency writings (Aguilar, 1978; Löwy, 1982; Liss, 1984). In such surveys the implicit argument is that the eclecticism of dependency writings removes them from the Marxist tradition.

Critical assessments also came from non-Marxists of all types and points across the political spectrum (Campos, 1979; Paz, 1979; W. G. dos Santos, 1980; Véliz, 1980; Merquior, 1982, 1983; Burstin, 1985; Rangel, 1986). Some of these criticisms addressed substantive and epistemological features. An eloquent and (at the time) rather lonely example is the following passage written in 1969 by the Chilean economic historian Aníbal Pinto (as quoted in Hirschman, 1971, p. 85):

> There is now a new school of thought on Latin America which casts the whole matter into a biblical mold and amounts to transposing the doctrine of original sin onto the social terrain. Here is a summary of this thesis: Latin America, with its evil destiny, was forced into the world capitalist system by the European powers right after Columbus and the Conquest. A great many calamities derive from this historical fact, yet they are small if compared to what happens during the next stage when the Continent is fully inserted into the international order organized by the "truly" capitalist nations, with Great Britain at the helm. That stage is reached in the nineteenth centry after Independence. Subsequently, with export-led growth really taking hold, the evils become even greater and more numerous. But this is not the end of Latin America's "purgatory in life." Another phase of expiation and, in a way, of even greater degradation was yet to come. It duly arrived with "inward-looking" development and "dependent" industrialization whose adverse repercussions and insuperable limitations have been described ad infinitum.

> Such reasoning makes one wonder whether the first and foremost trouble with Latin America was not perhaps the departure of Columbus from the port of Palos . . . its basic weakness [consists in] the complete failure to understand the contradictory character of every social process.

The non-Marxist criticism was also directed at the politicization and antiscientific dogmatism of much Marxist thought in Latin America, including much dependency writing. Buarque de Holanda (1980) and Pereira and Buarque de Holanda (1980) lamented the presence of ideological vigilante groups—*patrulhas ideológicas,* or "ideological squad cars"—that enforced the orthodoxies of the left. These patrulhas sought to punish anyone in the social sciences and humanities who did not cast arguments in acceptable jargon, attack the certified enemies, and refrain from critizing the certified sacred cows such as Cuba under Castro and Nicaragua under the Sandinistas. Although new, less politicized tendencies became stronger in the late seventies and the eighties, the patrulhas remained powerful in Brazil. In the intellectual culture in Mexico, according to Fuentes (1985), "inquisitorial intolerance, lynch law and public burnings" were still operating in the 1980s. He sharply criticized these features and argued that "our ideas will only be respected if we respect the ideas of others." Although dependency writers did not necessarily support the specific acts to which Fuentes referred or the patrulhas in Brazil, their advocacy of the premise of politicized scholarship reinforced a climate which made them possible and effective.

Finally, criticisms were directed at dependency thinkers for reinforcing an old antiscience tradition in Latin American thought (Roche, 1976a, 1976b, 1977; W. G. dos Santos, 1980; Schwartzman, 1981: Hodara, 1983). Thus W. G. dos Santos (1980, p. 25) laments the sort of Marxism that

> exhausts itself in Byzantine controversies over who are the true European or American interpreters of the original gospel, Lewis or Althusser? Is Foucault really a Marxist? And Habermas? What should be done with the Frankfurt school? Meantime, the pedestrian, modest, and tiring work of patient and careful researchers is disdained, left to the "empiricists" and "functionalists," that is, all who are deficient in not having achieved an intellectual orgasm when having read . . . the verbal and mental contortions of the most recent group of Italian 'theoreticians' whose objective is to dissipate, once and for all, whatever doubt may still remain as to whether or not a Marxist theory of the State exists.

Although dos Santos is at pains to distinguish "second-class Marxism" from "good quality Marxist studies that without a doubt are also produced in Latin America," much of his critique also applies to unorthodox dependency, even though he does not so apply it. From the point of view of its consequences for scholarship, policy, and development in the region, this antiscientific component of dependency thinking had severe costs. In the words of the Venezuelan historian of science Marcel Roche (1977, p. 74), it was "a sort of luxury of intellectuals from rich and *blasé* countries which we [Latin Americans] cannot and must not accept."

As these examples suggest, some of the reservations Latin Americans had about the dependency movement are not greatly different from those expressed elsewhere in this book. For that reason we shall not go into them further here. Other lines of criticism, however, are quite different. They have been advanced by a long line of important Latin American intellectuals and a few others (Hirschman, Lévi-Strauss) of special distinction. These criticisms are consistent with the data reported in this study. They deserve attention.

Are Dependency Ideas Themselves Dependent?

Cultural dependency—the phenomenon of Latin Americans borrowing and imitating foreign ideas—is not new in Latin America. Commentators have observed and discussed it for many generations. In 1881 the Brazilian literary critic Sílvio Romero (1978, p. 18) argued sweepingly that "All our schools, in whatever realm, have generally done no more than to provide a low-key gloss of ideas taken from Europe, sometimes at second or third hand." A half century later the French anthropologist Claude Lévi-Strauss (1969, p. 107), then (in the thirties) teaching at the University of São Paulo, echoed Romero's remarks and added a key point about the importance of the latest fashion or *moda:* "Our students wanted to know everything: but only the newest theory seemed to them worth bothering with . . . Fashion dominated their interests: they valued ideas not for themselves but for the prestige that they could wring from them. That prestige vanished as soon as the idea passed from their exclusive possession . . . we were besieged by students who knew nothing at all of the past but were always a month or two ahead of us in the novelties of the day." After yet another fifty-year interval the Chilean historian Mario Góngora (1983, pp. 671–672) again recorded the proclivity for cultural dependency and devotion to fashion: "Spanish America tends to take the most recent results of European science and research, but it does not take the inner dialectic from which those results proceed . . . Spanish America picks up the results, so to speak, in a series of instant 'flashes,' and with each new flash believes that all previous results have somehow been nullified."

When making these kinds of critical observations of the region's dependence on foreign ideas, Latin American scholars and intellectuals have tended overwhelmingly to focus on liberal and conservative ideas. In an influential essay the literary critic Roberto Schwarz (1977, pp. 18, 24–25) criticizes the adaptation in Brazil of European ideas *fora do lugar*—"out of their place." Schwarz takes as his point of departure "the common-sense observation, almost a sensation," that "in Brazil ideas have been off-center [*fora do centro*] in relation to their European usage." As a result, he says, one attributes "independence to dependence, utility to caprice, universality to exceptions, merit to kinship, equality to privilege, etc." The focus of this consumption of out-of-place ideas, for Schwarz, is always nineteenth-century liberalism in its political and economic manifestations. The explanation for it is historical and involves "relations of production and parasitism in the country, our economic dependence and its companion *(par)*, the intellectual hegemony of a Europe which has been revolutionized by capital."

Although concern with intellectual dependence on non-Marxist currents is long-standing and fairly frequent, concern with dependence on Marxism is not. Historically such concern has been rare. Since capitalism and liberalism have had a greater influence on Latin America, for a longer period, than Marxism, the emphasis is perhaps not surprising, particularly in the nineteenth century. But in the twentieth century Marxist ideas have been widely and deeply dispersed in the region, and not only in the form of dependency ideas. In the social sciences and humanities, especially at the level of undergraduate education, and in many of the media, Marxism in its various forms has been hegemonic for decades. Nevertheless most of the attention to cultural and ideological dependency in the region has still concentrated on liberalism. Marxist and radical ideas are mainly interpreted as aspects not of cultural dependency but of cultural autonomy—as, for example, in most interpretations of Cuban socialism, the Allende period in Chile, the Sandinista period in Nicaragua, guerrilla movements in other parts of Central America and the Caribbean, and the dependency movement itself.

The idea that intellectual dependency expresses itself through the consumption of capitalist liberal ideas is also, of course, a prominent theme in the dependency literature. The proposition that theories originating in the center have little utility in the periphery has always been a fundamental claim of the dependency approach. As Cardoso and Faletto (1969, p. 161; 1979, p. 172) put it, "theoretical schemes concerning the formation of capitalist society in present-day developed countries are of little use in understanding the situation in Latin American countries." An extremely important, though seldom noted, feature of this proposition is that logically it applies not only to its intended targets (modernization theories, capitalist economics, and so on) but also to the very foundation of dependency thinking itself: Marxist theory. Marx's theory of capitalism clearly was concerned more than anything else with "the formation of capitalist society in present-day developed countries." Therefore to follow the injunction of Cardoso and Faletto would appear to compel the conclusion that dependency ideas, like modernization theory and capitalist economics, are themselves dependent and therefore "of little use in understanding the situation in Latin American countries."

Dependency authors draw no such conclusions. Like most others, they have focused on how *other* bodies of thought are dependent. But a few writers, humanists as well as social scientists, have perceived and stated publicly that cultural dependency applies to ideas on the left as well as to those in the center and on the right (Hodara, 1971; Paz, 1979; Véliz, 1980; Urquidi, 1982; Fuentes, 1984; Krauze, 1986; Rangel, 1986; Vargas Llosa, 1986).

Thus the Mexican novelist and diplomat Carlos Fuentes (1984, p. 34) says that Latin Americans "adopted liberalism, positivism, and then Marxism as our passports to modernity. We believe we can thus overcome our historical shortcomings. If the philosophy at hand frightens the United States, so much the better." He calls Marxism-Leninism "the latest incarnation of a Latin American penchant for what the French sociologist Gabriel Tarde called 'extralogical imitation.' This consists of adapting the latest, or prevalent, or most 'universal' philosophical mode to our national realities, whether it suits them or not." Three other prominent Mexicans, the economists Victor Urquidi, Vicente Sánchez, and Eduardo Terrazas (1982, pp. 14–15), refer to Latin American "dependence on Western culture" as a characteristic that produces "a tendency to imitate while searching for ideas and solutions . . . a certain dependent passivity exists that paralyzes creative imagination . . . [This] is clearly reflected in the political arena, where efforts are made by both the left and the right to copy virtually without modification and without taking into account the real differences [between Latin America and the dominant Western culture] in the economic, social, and political background. The natural outcome is failure, together with the emergence of spurious political forms."

Most of these commentators argued in general terms about leftist thought, or in the context of particular policy debates, on Cuba or Nicaragua, for example, rather than with specific reference to the dependency movement. But not all. An explicit analysis of the dependency movement as a manifestation of cultural dependency is given by the Chilean economic historian Claudio Véliz (1980, pp. 279–306). He begins by setting the dependency movement in the context of previous instances of cultural dependency: European liberalism which appeared in Latin America at various times since the eighteenth century; various forms of European fascism that were particularly prominent in the period of the Great Depression after 1929; earlier forms of Marxism. He then concentrates on Marxism in the last few decades: "With very few exceptions the Latin American intelligentsia continued in the sixties and seventies to tread the path of dependent orthodoxy, loyally echoing the views they found most congenial from among those current in Europe, the United States, or even the Far East . . . Latin American intellectuals of the sixties and seventies were the willing and inevitable victims of the process of cultural dependency they so forcefully impugned in their writings and utterances" (p. 293).

Although Véliz does not himself provide much supporting evidence, his characterizations of the radical intellectuals are accurate with respect to dependency authors. Véliz claims (pp. 293–297) that they relied heavily on categories imported from European, North American, and Asian Marxism; glorified the Cuban Revolution and refused to analyze and evaluate it in a balanced way; disdained the opinions and assessments of common working and middle-class people about their "true interests" in favor of their own abstract opinions and assessments about those interests; and preached violent revolution in situations where it made little sense and thus contributed to the rise of harsh military authoritarianisms. Orthodox dependency authors did all of those things. Unorthodox dependency authors did all of them except preach violent revolution, about which they were ambiguous (they did not necessarily prescribe it, but they also did not oppose it and they applauded it when it occurred).

Véliz also refers to "old habits of cultural dependence that are

hard to break," to a "dependent cultural mood," and to "the dependent attitude of the intelligentsia" (pp. 283–285). Such phrases suggest a syndrome of what has been called psychological dependency.
Véliz himself neither uses this phrase nor elaborates his observations
about dependent "moods" and so forth as a psychological phenomenon in any systematic way. But he suggests that not only are dependency ideas expressions of cultural or intellectual dependency; they
may also be part of an even broader and deeper phenomenon.

Psychological Dependency

In the social-psychological literature dependence is defined as a perception and feeling of restraints on action, and a fear of failing, that
exceed the constraints and risks of failure that actually exist. Those
writing in this literature do not deny that dependency exists in objective terms. They say, rather, that psychological dependency occurs
when perceptions and feelings of dependence are greater than the
actual constraints and when genuine opportunities and degrees of
freedom are minimized or ignored. Another feature of psychological
dependence is the perception or feeling that all dependence is de-
meaning. Positive, productive, fruitful aspects of dependence are ignored, minimized, or disparaged as mere illusion or as disguised
forms of manipulation and exploitation. Thus psychological dependence implies that it is necessary to withdraw from any form of
dependence into an autarkic situation of pure self-containment. Finally, there is in the literature the idea of counterdependence, that is,
the psychological state of altering feelings of dependence, inferiority,
and ineffectiveness. Counterdependence is a rebellion against dependence which, if successfully negotiated, can lead to greater independence or interdependence; if unsuccessful, it can cause further
dependence (Pareek, 1968, pp. 470–473; Singer, 1972, pp. 40–51).

Dependency writers themselves have said little about the psychological aspects of dependency and nothing about the ways their own
writings express them. To the contrary, they have either ignored such
ideas or vilified them. A few students of North-South relations and
of Latin American political economy, however, have explored the
connections between the subjects they study and the psychological
literature on dependence (Hirschman, 1971, pp. 85, 88–89, 271–
276, 350–354; Hodara, 1971; Mazrui, 1978, pp. 368–370; Williams, 1982).

Hirschman's Notion of "Fracasomania"

In a number of works written over a period of many years the economist Albert Hirschman (1961, 1971, 1978, 1979, 1987) has repeatedly returned to a phenomenon he calls *fracasomania,* or "the insistence on having experienced yet another failure" (1971, pp. 88–89). He argues that this phenomenon is especially likely to be found in dependent, late-developing countries. He has noted in particular its frequent appearance in Latin America (1971, pp. 328–337, 350–353; 1978, pp. 49–50; 1979; 1987). He also argues (1971, pp. 337, 335) that once it takes hold *fracasomania* itself makes an independent contribution to the conditions of dependency, distorted development and/or underdevelopment, and that that it is not only "the general public" but "even more the intellectuals [who] fail frequently to recognize that change is being achieved."

More specifically, the following tendencies, among others, are said to be associated with *fracasomania:* (a) a stress on grand dichotomies and either/or solutions; (b) a failure to perceive positive changes that have already occurred; (c) a failure to perceive concrete alternatives and opportunities for positive change that have existed in the past and that exist in the present; and (d) an emphasis on "the action-arousing gloomy vision" that "creates more gloom than action" (Hirschman, 1971, chapters 3, 13–16, esp. pp. 331–337, 350–353; the quotation is at p. 352).

Although he does not examine their writings systematically, Hirschman seems to include dependency authors such as Cardoso and Sunkel within the scope of these hypotheses. As early as 1970 he wrote (1971, p. 350) that "it must now be said that Latin American social scientists have themselves made an important contribution to this headlong rush to the all-revealing paradigm." Later (1978, pp. 45–46, 49–50) he included Cardoso and Sunkel as dependency authors to whom his criticisms about excessive concern with failure and insufficient awareness of success applied. A year later he again included under the same heading not only dependency writings but even structuralist thought of the ECLA sort; he explained this decision as follows (1979, p. 86): "It is with some reluctance that I have put forward the thoughts of the preceding pages, if only because they may offend some of my closest friends. Nevertheless, when a series of disastrous events strikes the body politic, everyone's responsibility must be looked at, including the intellectuals."

In any event, whatever he may have thought, the evidence from dependency writings clearly and overwhelmingly fits Hirschman's hypotheses about the four elements of *fracasomania:*

(a) Dependency texts repeatedly focus on grand dichotomies and either/or solutions. For them it is either capitalism or socialism, period. For them, analyzing degrees of dependency is like analyzing degrees of slavery. Marginal adjustments within capitalism are either meaningless or, worse, pernicious mystifications.

(b) Changes that have already occurred within capitalism that might be regarded as positive are either ignored or placed in a theoretical context that minimizes or rejects entirely their positive aspects. Capitalist industrialization is seen as so distorted and inextricably tied to negative concomitants (the state as a pact of capitalist domination, socioeconomic inequality, limitations on national autonomy) that any positive effects are vitiated. By definition, associated-dependent development under capitalism is unacceptable; the only acceptable solution is Marxist socialism. Increasing foreign involvement in dynamic sectors is said to index worsening dependency; but decreasing foreign involvement in vital sectors and increasing diversification of trade partners and in sources of foreign capital are ignored or rejected as indexes of lessened dependency.

(c) Concrete alternatives to dependent capitalism are seldom perceived and never emphasized. Although there is much rhetoric in the dependency literature, especially in the most recent writings, about possibilism, dialectical thinking, and contradictions that offer possibilities for change, dependency writings in fact say little or nothing about concrete alternatives to dependent capitalism. As noted in (b), concrete positive developments within capitalism are always analyzed theoretically in a fashion that minimizes their significance for genuine development. Dependency texts never analyze ways in which the internal contradictions of capitalism have been and might in the future be turned into concrete possibilities for transformations toward socialism. They analyze cases of dependent capitalism concretely and prescribe socialism abstractly, but never examine concrete cases of socialism.

(d) The "action-arousing gloomy visions" of dependency authors have created some action but more gloom. Dependency ideas have influenced a number of governments and other practical actors in Latin America. However, the consequences of those influences, when translated into public policy and regime consequences, have not on the whole been such as to brighten most of the human spirits involved. In other countries—the majority in Latin America, certainly—the influences of dependency thinking have been varied and less direct (or even more indirect) but they have not been more positive. In these countries, dependency ideas have increased hopes and expectations in important sectors of civil society without providing concrete and effective guidelines to satisfy those expectations. At best, these escalating gaps between expectations and realizations have been harmless in terms of their policy and regime consequences; at worst, they may have inadvertently contributed, along with many other factors, to the demise of pluralistic politics and to the rise of new forms of military authoritarianism. According to Hirschman (1979, pp. 85–86), countries that illustrate the point are Argentina, Brazil, Chile, and Uruguay during their periods of military rule from the late sixties to the eighties; countries more isolated from the "main currents" in Latin American social science and its "strange process of ideological escalation," such as Colombia and Venezuela, were more "resistant to the authoritarian wave."

The Irresponsibility Corollary to the Fracasomania Hypothesis

Hirschman hints at a corollary to the *fracasomania* hypothesis but does not state it explicitly. It might be called the irresponsibility corollary. It is the idea that the insistence on failure is accompanied by a refusal to accept responsibility for failure. Instead of accepting responsibility, the fracasomaniac puts it on something or somebody else outside of "authentically" national and popular forces and actors. Purcell (1984) has stated the point clearly and succinctly: "Having freed Latin Americans from a tendency toward self-denigration, dependency theory allowed them to go too far in avoiding responsibility for their actions. And neither self-denigration nor blaming others is very useful for dealing successfully with the challenges Latin American now faces."

A number of Latin American analysts have formulated hypotheses and provided evidence consistent with the irresponsibility corollary. The Mexican historian Daniel Cosío Villegas (1967, p. 9) has referred to Mexicans' "Olympian intellectual disdain toward the U.S.: they insult the U.S. and blame it for all their woes, they rejoice in its failures and wish it would disappear from the map . . . in this aspect (as well as many others), Mexicans are not as original as they think, because all Latin American countries, without exception, share this same disdain." A Brazilian journalist (Pedreira, 1983b) writes in the following ironic way about President João Figueiredo's speech to the United Nations in 1983: "The President exempts himself and his ministers from all blame. Who and what are to blame? The winds of fortune, the international economy, the unjust relationship between the powerful and the weak, the rich and the poor—not here within Brazil, but out there, in the commerce among nations. The guilty ones are therefore beyond the reach of the government, which has no means to do anything about the situation . . . To the contrary, here within Brazil, we are all innocents, we bear no responsibility for our fate."

In a related though different vein the Argentine journalist Jacobo Timerman (1982, p. 130) has referred to a "method of explaining a goal not by what one desires to obtain or accomplish but by what one desires to avoid" as being "typical of the left-wing and right-wing totalitarian mentalities whose terrorist violence broke out in Argentina." He goes on to say of those who used this method: "They could never explain what it was that they wished to construct, but they were always categorical in terms of what they wished to annihilate." Cardoso (1973a, p. 175) also has warned against such tendencies; he refers to "the tragic fact that the power elite, as well as the opposition intellectuals, are unable to formulate realistic alternatives to the basic problems . . . It is to be hoped . . . that the intellectuals will not invent other myths . . . as incapable as the present ones of producing viable policies for the participation of the popular classes in politics." But Cardoso's characterization also fits dependency writings, including his own.

It is instructive to compare and contrast the dependency perspective and the irresponsibility corollary with what the Brazilian critic Antonio Cândido (1980, pp. 18–19) calls the *cultura do contra*. The phrase literally means "counterculture" but "critical culture" is a better rendering in English. Cândido adopts it partly in a humorous vein but also "with a great deal of conviction, because in fact I think it is necessary to profoundly reconsider our way of life, our goals, our habits, our behavior, our educational system, and above all our political, social, and economic organization." Moreover, he regards the elements of the cultura do contra as "The most vital, productive, and inspiring" ones in Brazilian life.

Although there is a superficial similarity between Cândido's *cultura do contra* and the dependency perspective, basically they are quite different, especially on the crucial matter of responsibility. In Antonio Cândido's formulation, the cultura do contra is directed against not only foreign influences but also the evils within Latin American societies. His formulation, while not denying the fact of external influences, also maintains a significant measure of authentically national responsibility for internal failings. In the dependency perspective, by contrast, national evils are always redefined as internal manifestations of external interests. Responsibility is always placed on the foreign enemy—expressed either externally or internally— never on authentic national forces. In this sense holistic dependency diverges sharply from the approach of Antonio Cândido and not in a direction that is positive for Latin America.

None of the cultural and psychological effects of dependency ideas described in the preceding sections can properly be called positive. There is one major sense, however, in which the rise and spread of dependency ideas may be said to have had positive effects.

The Dependency Movement as Counterdependence?

It is plausible to hypothesize that the rise and spread of dependency ideas represented a process of counterdependence. Before dependency ideas, and even before Mariátegui, Haya de la Torre, and Prebisch and ECLA, there was a powerful literature of self-incrimination in Latin America. Writers like Bunge, Oliveira Vianna, Euclides da Cunha, and Francisco Encina stressed the ills of Latin America and blamed them on "intrinsic" defects such as racial composition, laziness, sadness, lack of initiative, lack of perseverance, inability to cooperate, and so on (Hirschman, 1961, pp. 4–9). This literature of self-incrimination was an earlier form of *fracasomania* in which the failures were blamed entirely on internal factors.

In the literature of self-incrimination the solution to Latin America's problems was to imitate advanced countries. Thus the nineteenth-century Argentinian author and statesman Domingo Sarmiento wrote, "Let us achieve the state of development of the United States. Let us be the United States." Another nineteenth-century Argentine liberal, Juan Bautista Alberdi, wrote that "In economics even more than in politics the best example for Americans to follow is America herself. In economics North America is the great model for South America" (both as quoted in Hirschman, 1971,

p. 275). For these writers, the blame for their problems was entirely internal, and the solution was to be more like external models.

Dependency ideas were a complete reversal of the literature of self-incrimination. They said that Latin Americans should blame not themselves but external actors and processes and their internal manifestations. They should not imitate foreigners; they should reject foreign (in this view, capitalist) models entirely. In dependency writings, the tendency to exculpate national actors and processes and to hold external forces responsible was carried to an extreme and became, as we have argued, counterproductive and damaging. Nevertheless, it may be that as a transitory phase and process it had a number of merits. Among other things, it may have been a vehicle for rebelling against excessive self-incrimination and dependency.

If the foregoing were true, the next important question would be whether the intellectual and psychological rebellion represented by the dependency movement has been negotiated successfully and led on to greater independence and capacity for interdependence, or whether it has led back to other forms of dependence. The full answer to that question is not yet in. There are, however, some encouraging signs. In some sectors Latin American intellectual life displays new tendencies toward greater responsibility, independence of thought, and interdependence with other intellectual traditions and communities. Those tendencies are perhaps unparalleled in the region's history; certainly they are evidence of a lessening of psychological dependency. Nowhere were these tendencies stronger in the late 1970s and the 1980s than in Brazil, where dependency thinking earlier had its strongest and largest number of influential representatives.

Several ironies abound in all this. It was in Latin America's least dependent country, Brazil, where *dependencia* ideas had their most powerful initial expression. It was precisely during the period of intellectual preoccupation with dependencia that Brazil did more to reduce its dependency than at any previous time in its post-colonial history. It was in Brazil where the most important and enduring intellectual currents had nothing to do with the dependency fashion. And it was in Brazil during the last fifteen years or so where the trend away from the dependency way of thinking has been strongest.

If dependency ideas have been a manifestation of psychological counterdependence, then that is their most important positive feature. Otherwise, their net impact on culture and policy has been negative.

Claims, widely repeated, that they represented intellectual and psychological autonomy are not sustainable. In recent years the most sophisticated, innovative, authentic social and political thinking in Latin America has come not from dependency authors but from those who either disdained the dependencia approach or abandoned it, as we shall see in the next chapter.

Although these latter trends are stronger than they have ever been in Latin America, it is much too early to say they are firmly established. It is equally premature to say that the hypothesis that the dependency movement was a manifestation of psychological counterdependence leading to greater autonomy has been fully sustained. Whatever the future may hold, however, one thing is certain. Contrary to the allegations of dependency authors and their supporters, the most serious threat to the standing of dependency ideas does not come from academic critics whom they regard as enemies in the struggle. It comes from the dependency approach itself. By far the deepest wounds suffered by dependency authors are self-inflicted.

9   Ex-Consumers and Nonconsumers in Latin America

Did the dependency movement engender, through counter-dependence, a more autonomous and responsible discourse? There is evidence that it did. In recent years important shifts have been occurring in the ways Latin American intellectuals interpret development, politics, and international affairs. Especially in countries with relatively large social-science communities, the almost complete domination of Marxist approaches has weakened, Marxist approaches themselves have changed, and a more pluralistic discourse has emerged. Contrary to some observers, we do not believe that the recent changes are necessarily permanent. We do believe, however, that they are more than superficial, fairly widespread, and of considerable significance— not only for their own sake, but also because they enhance the prospects for democratic political institutions in the region.

One of the countries where these trends have emerged strongly is Brazil. Examining the Brazilian case not only provides detail and nuance in the overall argument, but also gives a sense of the directions in which scholars throughout the region have been moving.

The Consumption of Dependency Ideas in Brazil

To perceive the changes in the discourse in Brazil since the middle and late 1970s, it is necessary first to know the earlier situation. An excellent baseline is found in a rich survey by Luís Carlos Bresser Pereira (1982) of major theoretical interpretations of Brazilian society from the 1920s through the 1970s. Bresser Pereira finds that through the 1940s conservative thought was dominant, Marxist currents were next in importance, and liberalism was the least influential mode of discourse. There was a change in the 1960s and 1970s, however: Marxist approaches, already important, became even stronger and dominated the discourse. To paraphrase a famous aphorism by the classical Jesuit scholar J. A. Antonil (1711), Brazilian intellectuals' interpretations of politics and development in these years were "A hell for liberals and a paradise for Marxists." More specifically, according to Bresser Pereira, three major interpretations of Brazilian society, economy, and polity were dominant in the 1960s and 1970s.

One interpretation was what Bresser Pereira calls "functional-capitalist." This perspective originated as a critique of the "national-bourgeoisie" interpretation that had been influential before, and was discredited by, the Revolution of 1964. The basic postulate of the functional-capitalist interpretation is that Brazil was always a capitalist country and that even its pre-capitalist elements were "functional for capitalist accumulation." Caio Prado Junior, Fernando Novais, João Manoel Cardoso de Mello, Boris Fausto, Francisco de Oliveira, Lúcio Kowarick, Manoel Berlinck, and Luciano Martins are some of those cited by Bresser Pereira (pp. 278–284) as examples of authors working in this perspective. In the terminology used in the present study, this functional-capitalist approach is an example of pre-dependency or nondependency Marxism.

Second, there was the "imperialist superexploitation" interpretation. This perspective also began as a critical response to the 1964 Revolution and also criticized imperialism as "the major cause of underdevelopment." However, according to Bresser Pereira it was "much more radical" than the functional-capitalist interpretation because it dealt not only with Brazil but with all of Latin America, not only with the exploitation of workers but their superexploitation, not only with the need for socialism but also with the need to choose between violent revolution and fascism. Andre Gunder Frank, Ruy Mauro Marini, Theotonio dos Santos, and Florestan Fernandes are the four authors cited by Bresser Pereira (pp. 284–287) as examples of this interpretation. In the terminology of the present study, this is the orthodox dependency interpretation.

The third, in Bresser Pereira's words, was the "new dependency" interpretation. This perspective shares much with the first two interpretations, although it is "less radical." The essential points about this interpretation are not only its theoretical concept of dependency—the idea of the linkage between external imperialism and internal class structures—but also its recognition of the "new fact" of the massive entry of multinational industrial enterprises into Latin America, especially Brazil, and its analysis of the "new form of dependency, developmentalist . . . but exclusionary," that is thereby generated. The most important author in this group, says Bresser

Pereira (pp. 287–294), is Fernando Henrique Cardoso, but he also lists many others, including José Serra, Maria da Conceição Tavares, Antônio Barros de Castro, Paul Singer, Celso Furtado, and himself. In the terminology of the present study, this is the unorthodox dependency interpretation.

Bresser Pereira also discusses briefly (pp. 294–298) a fourth approach, the "hegemony of industrial capital" interpretation, which began to take form in the 1970s, is still embryonic in its development, and is found mainly in recent work by himself and Luciano Martins.

Bresser Pereira argues that the three principal interpretations are all "leftist" *(interpretações de esquerda)*. He regards the "imperialist superexploitation" interpretation as the "most radical and the least plausible"; the "functional capitalist" interpretation as in the middle of the group ideologically; and the "new dependency" interpretation as the "most realistic" of the three. "The first two interpretations," he writes, "are basically Marxist. The third has strong Marxist influences but includes non-Marxist authors like Celso Furtado" (p. 298.). The fourth, embryonic, interpretation regarding the hegemony of industrial capital in the seventies is also, says Bresser Pereira, basically a Marxist interpretation. For him, therefore, all the major theoretical interpretations of the last two decades that he deals with in his essay are wholly or mainly Marxist.

Bresser Pereira's study is a valuable contribution to the analysis of development theory and ideology in Brazil. It surveys and analyzes the writings of some 85 authors and about two hundred books and articles over a fifty-year period. His categories of interpretations are interesting and useful. For the sixties and at least the first half of the seventies, his portrait of a Brazilian intellectual world dominated by Marxist perspectives of different sorts is, on the whole, accurate and useful. His study provides further documentary support for the analyses in Chapter 8 concerning the influences of dependency ideas in Latin America.

However, although the scope and depth of Bresser Pereira's important article are formidable, it is still necessary to supplement and modify the picture he paints. He himself explicitly disavows (p. 298) the idea that his coverage is comprehensive. As an economist Bresser Pereira is understandably more concerned with the economic and social aspects of development treated in these writings than with political aspects. Most important for present purposes, he underestimates the diversity of currents in the period after the mid-seventies.

In these years, there was another major shift. Theory and practice came together to produce a more pluralistic climate that challenged the earlier Marxist hegemony.

Ex-Consumers and Nonconsumers in Brazil

In the political and intellectual atmosphere of the late sixties and early seventies in Brazil, the Marxist arguments were widely accepted. Relatively few intellectuals were able to mount effective challenges to them. In the late seventies and eighties, however, the hegemony of the Marxist ideas changed qualitatively and diminished quantitatively. Many Marxists modified their earlier views; some non-Marxists now found their ideas gaining wider acceptance; new types of analysts who fit poorly into Bresser Pereira's categories appeared and occupied important intellectual space. These authors disagreed about many questions, including how to characterize the changes. Some said they rejected all categories and labels—although without specifying how communication can occur without categories or labels. Those who moved away from or broke with Marxism did not necessarily do so directly or explicitly; their move was usually more subtle or implicit than that. Still, major and important changes did occur in the thinking of most of the leading Brazilian intellectuals.

The analysis here will refer mainly to what Schwartzman (1987, pp. 12–13) has called the "high clergy" of the Brazilian intellectual and educational community, that is, those social scientists and intellectuals who have the best training, resources, and other positive conditions for scholarly work. It is not wholly applicable to what he calls the "low clergy," that is, persons with less training and resources. The former are less numerous but more influential both intellectually and politically.

The first group to examine is Marxists who amplified and modified their views.

"Marxist-Liberals" and Social Democrats

In the middle and late seventies some of the Marxists or neo-Marxists who had earlier denounced bourgeois institutions and processes began to tolerate and even support them—not only theoretically but also in their own political actions. This was a very significant change in which most of the leading thinkers of the Brazilian intellectual left participated. This is not to say that they rejected entirely their earlier views, or agreed entirely with each other. They did neither.

One expression of this change came from former members of the revolutionary left. By the mid-1970s the military government had more or less decimated the guerrilla left as a political and military force. Most of its members were dead, in prison, or (the largest number) in exile. The demonstrated capacity of the military government to deal effectively with armed insurrection led most of the survivors to question the feasibility of that approach. Their reflections on the ethical content of their revolutionary activities, their years of exile, and the context of *abertura* after 1974 were among the factors that led them also to question the desirability of that course and to view more hopefully the possibilities for democratic change. They emerged from their experiences and reflections highly critical of Marxism-Leninism as a dogmatic religion and of the bureaucratic, totalitarian character of vanguard political parties. A memoir that conveys these views is Fernando Gabeira's *O Que É Isso, Companheiro?* (1979).

A second variation in Marxist thought might be called Brazil-style Eurocommunists. The authors in this camp were not altogether happy about this label (Coutinho, 1980, pp. 13–16), but it was widely applied to them by Brazilian intellectuals. In their view socialism was to be achieved democratically, peacefully, and on the basis of the national experience, not foreign intervention. Party activity should include appeals to the middle sectors as well as the working class, and alliances with other parties were not prohibited. Internal party democracy, criticism, and dissent were also preferred over democratic centralism and the idea of party doctrine as infallible dogma. The authors in this camp were still critics of liberalism and even of social democracy as theoretical and political positions, and they still held that the only true democracy was Marxist socialism. But they were willing to work with the other political groups and insisted that Marxist socialism be democratic (Coutinho, 1980; Konder, 1980; Werneck Viana, 1981).

A third change in leftist thinking appeared among what might be called Brazilian social democrats or democratic socialists. These terms do not readily lend themselves to precise definition. However, the general idea is "a synthesis of socialism and democracy." What is implied is a political regime based on the rule of law, freedom of groups and individuals, peaceful cooperation among groups and political parties, nationalism, and a variety of reforms and state actions designed to address in an evolutionary, peaceful fashion the social and economic problems of capitalist society (Chauí, 1984, pp. 179–180). In Brazil as in Europe social democrats tend to divide into two main subgroups. Both subgroups agree on the main outlines of social democracy as just described, and they agree also that attention must be placed both on "civil society" and on political institutions. However, their emphases differ.

In Brazil the subgroup giving somewhat greater emphasis to the processes and institutions of civil society, particularly social movements, trade unions, and the like, includes such thinkers as Francisco Weffort, Marilena Chauí, José Álvaro Moisés, Lúcio Kowarick, and Eder Sader. In this subgroup one of the main theoretical and practical questions is how to respect the autonomy of social movements and at the same time get them involved in politics so they can protect their interests. This subgroup of social democrats—who also accept the term "democratic socialists"—includes some of the main thinkers (Francisco Weffort, Marilena Chauí) of the Partido dos Trabalhadores (PT) and is found largely, though not exclusively, in São Paulo, especially at the Centro de Estudos de Cultura Contemporânea (CEDEC). For some of the members of this subgroup these ideas were the elaboration and expansion of an earlier tradition, but for others (for instance, Weffort) they represented a very considerable change from the earlier Marxism which was more economicist and harsh in its criticisms of bourgeois political institutions (Chauí, 1984; Weffort, 1984).

The other subgroup also stresses the importance of both civil society and political institutions. However, it tends to give greater emphasis than the first subgroup does to the state and political institutions. In this subgroup by far the most important example is Fernando Henrique Cardoso. He ran for the federal Senate in 1978. Elected a *suplente,* or substitute, he succeeded to an active Senate seat in 1982 when his PMDB party colleague Franco Montoro was elected governor of São Paulo state. In 1985 he ran for mayor of the city of São Paulo but lost in a close race to former President Jânio Quadros. He was reelected to a full term as federal senator in 1986.

No one examplified the change in Marxist thinking in a more vivid and significant way than Cardoso. As an academic writer in the late sixties and throughout the decade of the seventies Cardoso had regarded elections, legislatures, political parties, and many other features of politics in bourgeois societies as "formal" expressions of the "pact of class domination" of the capitalist state. As a political candidate, party official, and legislative leader he participated intensively in the activities of those formal institutions. Cardoso's academic writings are full of discussions of capitalism, socialism, class structures, class exploitation, dialectics, modes of production, historical materialism, formalism, dependency, and imperialism. His political speeches and interviews have very little on those topics; they are mostly about democracy, elections, parties, participation, economic policy, the people, mass party, the social question. These themes are as close as he gets to classes, to say nothing of exploitation, capitalism, socialism, imperialism, dependency (Cardoso, 1978; 1981).

In the body of his political statements as well as in their topical headings, the same dedication to liberal notions of democracy and opposition to radical Marxist notions of democracy are again in evidence. Thus Cardoso (1978, p. 33) sounds very much like T. H. Marshall when he states "the people is the totality of its citizens, and therefore the democratic way can only be found when all citizens participate together." No class struggle there. When he says (1981, p. 37) that the expansion of political democracy will reduce social and economic inequalities even though it cannot and will not eliminate them entirely, Cardoso again reads very much like Marshall. In his academic writings he used the concept of "interest" to single out groups, individuals, or institutions of which he disapproved as "the anti-nation inside the nation" and an "internal manifestation of external capitalism." In his political speeches and interviews he defends the idea of the legitimacy of divergent interests, and, in consequence, of bargaining and negotiation.

There are repeated references to "social pacts" and "democratic pacts"; referring to his own political party at the time, the PMDB, Cardoso says (1981, p. 36; see also 1978, pp. 32–33): "we are the only party able to compose the new social pact, in which workers, salaried middle classes, liberal professions, and plundered national entrepreneurs may enter along with the enormous mass of unemployed. We are the only party that can compose this social pact, govern in accord with it, and present programs and projects which represent the combined interests of these layers of the population." Nothing there about the state as the pact of domination or the conflicting and irreconcilable interests of social groups, classes, and class fractions in situations of dependent capitalist development.

Asked his views on socialism in the Soviet Union, China, and Cuba, Cardoso (1978, p. 59) ignores Cuba but says that socialism "of the sort that is in power . . . in the USSR or even in China" reflects an "abyss between the nineteenth century ideal and the twentieth century reality."

To be sure, liberal, Weberian, and other non-Marxist categories and ideas were not totally new in Cardoso's thought. He has always been an eclectic, contradictory, ambiguous thinker drawing heavily on many non-Marxist as well as Marxist authors and concepts in his scholarly work. Moreover, throughout his career he consistently opposed authoritarian regimes of the right and consistently argued that economic development can be accomplished democratically. He has often supported liberal democratic concepts such as popular participation, multiparty elections, the rule of law, civil liberties, diversity of political parties and interest associations, and the autonomy of political parties and interest associations from the state. But these themes are much stronger and clearer in his political statements than they were in his dependency writings. Moreover, while political writing and activity were not new for Cardoso, they became a much larger part of his professional life. In the decade of the eighties, when Cardoso's political involvements deepened, his academic productivity declined and so also did the visible Marxist elements in his writings.

Because of his prominence as a "man of the left"—a label he wore with pride, indeed insisted upon—Cardoso's new emphases were bound to be criticized by some Marxists. For example, Carlos Nelson Coutinho (1980, p. 40) charged that Cardoso's acceptance of the legitimacy of negotiated resolutions of conflicts within capitalist society constituted an acceptance of capitalist hegemony. For Coutinho this was an example of the "assimilation by contemporary social democracy of liberal thought," and he was very critical of it—although he also tempered his criticism by adding that "At several other points in his rich reflection . . . Cardoso overcomes the limits of liberalism." Non-Marxists also noticed the changes; a skeptic said that "Marxist liberals" was a contradictory label for a phenomenon he compared to *sorvete fervido,* boiled ice cream (Tabosa Pessoa, 1983).

Were the new liberal elements in Cardoso's political thought, and Marxist thought more generally, inconsistent with Marxism, as Coutinho, Tabosa Pessoa, and others maintain, or were they merely an evolution within Marxism, as many theorists and activists in Brazil,

Western Europe, the United States, and other parts of Latin America contend? There seems little doubt that Marxist categories are able to expand enough to absorb liberal notions. However, they can also contract in ways that make liberal political institutions, protections, and processes inconsistent with them and thus illegitimate from a Marxist viewpoint. This property of being able both to expand and contract, often in somewhat arbitrary ways, is a major reason why the new social democratic thought is controversial among both Marxists and non-Marxists. It is also why it is difficult to know how firmly it is really committed to the liberal principles.

In any event Cardoso's political writings clearly stress the liberal-Weberian side of his thought substantially more than his dependency writings do. This difference may reflect in part the difference between dealing as a sociologist mainly with intellectuals and students from the elite and dealing as a political activist with broader strata in Brazilian society. Explaining why he did not favor a Socialist party in Brazil at the time, Cardoso (1978, p. 84) says, "I am not in favor of a Socialist party of intellectuals, of the elite. What good is there in people running around saying, 'I am a socialist,' 'I understand Marxism-Leninism,' and 'bla-bla-bla'? This doesn't change anything." Referring to the style of his meetings with factory workers and labor leaders during his Senate campaign, Cardoso says (1978, p. 105), "They gave us a fantastic reception. It was a lot easier dealing with them, they were more open than if one went to speak to students."

Political Liberals

A second type of interpretation that gained increased prominence in the middle and late 1970s and the 1980s may be called, for lack of a better term, the political-liberal interpretation. Political liberalism is not definitionally associated with any particular type of economic or social system. Political liberalism emphasizes basic rights and freedoms—of association, thought and speech, religion, assembly and the press—and the rule of law. In this sense of an "assemblage of basic freedoms," political liberalism is part of "the heritage of civilized life" that cannot be located exclusively in any particular political, economic, social, or religious creed (W. G. dos Santos, 1978, p. 67).

In this sense various liberal interpretations of Brazilian politics have manifested themselves in recent decades. In order to understand the significance of this development, and before describing it more specifically, it is necessary to say a word about the traditional place of liberal ideas in Brazil, and indeed most of Latin America, where they have suffered a double blow. On the one hand, liberalism is associated historically with elitism and capitalist exploitation. On the other hand, it is also associated with development and modernization theories of the fifties and sixties that were discredited by the 1964 coup and other events. As a result the very term "liberal" is an ambiguous, tainted symbol in Brazilian political discourse, as it is throughout Latin America and most of Western Europe. Historically, liberal political parties have usually been conservative and sometimes reactionary. Political liberalism is often thought to be inseparable from economic and social liberalism and therefore, in this view, from elitism and capitalist exploitation, U.S. culture and foreign policy. In short, liberalism is seen as both antidemocratic and antinationalist.

Students of Brazilian intellectual history with varying perspectives have thus concurred in minimizing the impact of liberal ideas on Brazilian society and intellectual traditions. For example, Bresser Pereira (1982, p. 298) states flatly that "a liberal interpretation does not exist in Brazil." He attributes this lack to the "theoretical poverty" of the interpretation and to the "lack of intellectuals with the ability to formulate it." W. G. dos Santos (1978) offers a rather different set of reasons to explain why political liberalism does not thrive in Brazilian society.

It is probably correct to say that political liberalism does not have deep roots in Brazilian society. But this is also true of Marxism. The Marxist hegemony of which Bresser Pereira and others speak is exercised within intellectual circles, not the society at large. And with respect to those intellectual circles, is it accurate to say that there is no liberal interpretation? Or that no liberals have had the capacity to formulate such an interpretation? I want to suggest that a number of types of investigation, cogitation, and theorizing call into question the proposition that there is no significant liberal or neoliberal interpretation of Brazilian *politics*. The authors writing in this category have differed among themselves on many things, but not on their commitment to *political* liberalism.

Political liberals have their roots not only in the academy but also law, journalism, and diplomacy. Jurist-scholars Raimundo Faoro (1958) and Victor Nunes Leal (1948) and the historian Sérgio Bu-

arque de Holanda (1956) were innovators in Brazilian political analysis and staunch defenders of democratic political values against
authoritarianisms and totalitarianisms of either the right or the left.
More recently, academic social scientists such as Bolivar Lamounier
and Wanderley Guilherme dos Santos have also worked in this broad
tradition. For example, Lamounier (1981) has stressed that certain
"liberal" mechanisms, such as competitive elections, are not merely
"formalisms" but genuine, vital institutional protections. He has also
argued (1984, p. 168) that "it is legitimate, within certain limits, to
speak of degrees of democracy." W. G. dos Santos (1978a, 1978b,
1979, 1981, 1984, 1985, 1986, 1988), who was a Marxist in the
late fifties and the early sixties, since then has been trying to work
out a theoretical position that simultaneously honors liberal political
values, principles of social justice, and the specificities of "the Brazilian reality," while avoiding the errors and abuses committed by
Brazilian liberals in the past.

A rather different manifestation of political liberalism in this sense
has been the writings of exceptionally able journalists such as Fernando Pedreira or Carlos Castello Branco. Consider Pedreira. Some
of his books have been extended essays on a single political theme,
for example, *Março 31: Civis e Militares no Processo da Crise Brasileira* (1964). Others have been collections of shorter journalistic
essays, such as *Brasil Política, 1964–1975* (1975), *A Liberdade e a
Ostra* (1976), and *Impávido Colosso* (1982). All of them have, in a
style unmatched for clean, simple elegance, gone well beyond pun-
ditry to serious, subtle political analysis. Pedreira's themes have included a constant defense of political democracy, aversion to dogma
of all kinds, and a relentless attack on the corrupting and stultifying
effects of bureaucracy. As a review (anonymous, 1982) said, "The
threads which tie these essays together are antidogmatism, liberalism,
and the conviction that despite all its flaws democracy is still the best
way to solve human problems." According to the late Tristão de
Athayde (dust jacket of Pedreira, 1982), Pedreira is "the most brilliant, the most cultivated, and the most openminded of our political
commentators."

Another author in this category, a little different in certain ways
from the two previously mentioned (who also differ among themselves), is José Guilherme Merquior. Merquior has written fifteen
books in a variety of fields ranging from literary criticism to structural
anthropology to political theory. For our purposes the most relevant

are perhaps *A Natureza do Processo* (1982) and *O Argumento Liberal* (1983). For Merquior (1983, back cover), "Modern liberalism is a social-liberalism, a liberalism which avoids the ingenuousness and innocence regarding the complexity of social phenomena that characterized classical liberalism. Modern liberalism does not have the kinds of anxieties or complexes regarding social questions which classical liberalism had. And it is this modern version of liberalism to which I link my own thinking." Merquior (1983, p. 12) names Celso Lafer, Candido Mendes de Almeida, Marcílio Marques Moreira, Luís Navarro de Brito, Francisco de Araújo Santos, Sérgio Paulo Rouanet, and Vamireh Chacon as "other essayists" with whom he has been trying "to define an area of national reflection about the psychological, ethical and historical meaning of freedom, in a line of thought which is seen not as the superseding of the great tradition of liberal thought but rather as its unfolding."

The recent prominence of liberal political ideas (again, of greatly varied shades) may be seen in debates during the process of political *abertura* in Brazil. Consider, for example, a series of articles published in the *Caderno de Leituras* of the *Jornal da Tarde* in São Paulo between 1977 and 1981, many of which appeared in a collection entitled *A Conquista do Espaço Político* (de Oliveira, 1983). The purpose of the series was to debate political themes related to the *abertura*. Among the participants were Raimundo Faoro, Tércio Sampaio Jr., Evaldo Amaro Vieira, Oliveiros S. Ferreira, José Eduardo Faria, Roque Spencer Maciel de Barros, Lenildo Tabosa Pessoa, Eduardo Seabra Fagundes, Fernando Pedreira, Wanderley Guilherme dos Santos, Gerard Lebrun, Marçal Versiani, Leôncio Martins Rodrigues, and Fabio Konder Comparato. This is a very diverse group. Some of them would reject the label "political liberal." Yet on the whole they were able to agree on the notion of democratization as "an apprenticeship and application of a method of living together with conflicts" (de Oliveira, 1983, p. 14). Whatever else one may say about this notion of democratization, it is not one that would have had the same support among intellectuals in the late sixties and the early seventies that it has had in the last decade. As Pedreira (1983a, p. 117) put it, "After 14 years of a military regime even the infantile left, even our submarxists (who are so numerous) seem reconciled with the value of liberalism and bourgeois freedoms. Let us hope that the return of full democracy (if it comes) does not make us quickly unlearn what we learned at such cost during those painful years."

In the earlier period, the focus of discussion about the Brazilian political model was the question of legitimacy. In the late seventies and eighties, the focus began to be on the question of how to submit any power, whatever its basis of legitimacy, to societal control (de Oliveira, 1983, pp. 15–16). In addressing this theme, the authors were not necessarily optimistic about the prospects for installing a representative democracy on liberal foundations, but they tended strongly to agree on the need to preserve political liberalism in some form as a way for society to check state power. Political liberalism was not seen as a sufficient condition for the democratization of power but as a necessary condition (W. G. dos Santos, 1983; Lamounier, 1981).

In sum, ideas of the kind propounded by these and other authors about political liberalism are now very important in the Brazilian intellectual community, and also among political, media, and other elites. They were much less important before the mid-seventies. They need to be included in any survey of recent trends, and they challenge Bresser Pereira's thesis that no liberal interpretation exists in Brazil.

The New Social Scientists

A third set of interpretations of Brazilian politics outside the earlier Marxist patterns also includes several—diverse in many ways—that derived from the explosion in the number of Brazilians with advanced training in political science, anthropology, sociology, economics, and other social science disciplines in the sixties and early seventies. In 1964 Fernando Pedreira could still write that "the only advanced training institute in the social sciences that Brazil has had during the past three decades has been the Communist Party" (p. 177). Possibly (although it is not entirely clear) Pedreira was speaking metaphorically; even at the metaphorical level the statement was debatable in 1964. But at that time it was a legitimate, serious, plausible argument. It would be impossible to make that kind of argument today.

According to Trindade (1982, pp. 14–15), there is a growing tendency among social scientists of various methodological and theoretical tendencies "to approach concrete manifestations of social reality, whether political or economic, with more humility and without the comfortable protection of the universalizing generalizations of classical theories or of other forms of ethnocentrism." Trindade even cites the *autocríticas* (self-critiques) of figures such as Fernando Henrique Cardoso and Celso Furtado as evidence of this growing resistance to the attractions of sweeping theoretical generalizations. And what are the origins of this process? For him, aside from the complexity of social reality itself, the roots lie in the substantial and rapid development of the social sciences in the last twenty years.

Perhaps nowhere in Latin America, or indeed the entire Third World, has the growth in quantity and quality of the social sciences been so dramatic as in Brazil. Bolivar Lamounier (as recounted in Velho, 1983, p. 246; also see Lamounier, 1982) has recently noted that almost the entire structure of post-graduate social science education now in place in Brazil was erected after 1965. Until that date, in the areas of sociology, political science and history, only the University of São Paulo maintained regular masters and doctoral programs. Even so, a recent study of the fields of anthropology, sociology, and political science shows that between 1945 and 1965 (inclusive) only 41 master's, doctoral, and *livre docencia* theses were defended—that is, an average of two per year. In the same institution from 1966 to 1977, by contrast, 158 theses were defended—that is, an average of 13 per year. If one looks at the current production of advanced degrees at all postgraduate levels throughout Brazil in these same three fields, one finds that the *annual* production is equal to at least half the total production at USP from 1945 to 1977.

Moreover, the quantitative change has been accompanied by various kinds of qualitative changes. One such qualitative change in social science, according to Lamounier (in Velho, 1983, pp. 247) is away from what he calls a "bureaucratic-mandarin model" toward a "pluralist and flexible model" that reflects a "coming of age" of a new generation of professional social scientists in Brazil. Taking these ideas and other analyses and data as points of departure, the anthropologist Otávio Velho (1983, pp. 251–261) has elaborated a detailed profile of some social processes involved in the evolution of the advanced social sciences in Brazil during the last two decades or so. Among the features he finds to be associated with this process are a stress on professionalization in contrast to the traditional intelligentsia, institutionalization rather than just the creative individual, "training" rather than "education in the classical sense," specialization rather than a totalizing or global vision, "research" rather than integrated general interpretations, operational concepts rather than intuitive concepts, internal democracy rather than hierarchical decision-making in social science organizations, mass-oriented rather than elitist-oriented scholars, and so on.

This is not the place to document the degree to which all these changes actually did occur, how they all played themselves out in concrete terms, where they are going next, and whether they are good or bad—although in a moment we shall come back to the last point. It can be suggested, however, that some such changes did occur and have had significant implications for the kinds of interpretations that are made of Brazilian politics. Take just the point about increased pluralism. Increases in diversity are manifest not only in the greater number of centers of advanced social science training and research but also in the increasing variety of types of education and training of the faculty who teach and do research in these organizations. In political science, for example, all of the permanent faculty at the oldest facility for graduate training in Brazil, the University of São Paulo (USP), received their highest graduate degree from the same place, that is, from USP. At the three newer centers for graduate training in political science, in contrast, the percentage of the permanent faculty receiving their highest graduate degree from the same place were 25 percent, 29 percent, and 50 percent, (see table 9.1). Similar patterns obtain in other areas in the social sciences such as sociology and anthropology (CAPES, 1982).

No social science discipline was more affected by these quantitative and qualitative changes in graduate training than political science. The new political scientists included Alexandre de Souza Barros, Amaury de Souza, Antônio Otávio Cintra, Benício Schmidt, Bolivar Lamounier, Celso Lafer, Edmundo Campos Coelho, Edson Nunes de Oliveira, Eli Diniz, Elisa Reis, Fábio Wanderley Reis, Gláucio Soares, Hélgio Trindade, José Murilo de Carvalho, Maria do Carmo Campello de Souza, Maria Helena Moreira Alves, Maria Herminia Tavares de Almeida, Malori Pompermayer, Olavo Brasil de Lima Junior, Paulo Sérgio Pinheiro, Renato Boschi, Sérgio Abranches, Simon Schwartzman, Vilmar Faria, and Wanderley Guilherme dos Santos. This list does not claim to be comprehensive.

These new political scientists studied almost everything: interest groups, bureaucracies, the military, legislatures, elections, political parties, political machines, public policy, science and government, urban politics, rural politics, neighborhood movements, unions and politics, business and politics, technocracy and politics, political thought in Brazil, Brazilian ideologies, political clientelism, and so on. Still others worked in the area of Brazil's foreign relations (see below). The scholars doing these studies varied greatly in the kinds

Table 9.1   Unity and diversity of training of permanent faculty in four Brazilian Master's and Ph.D. programs in political science, 1979–1980

Program	Total number of permanent faculty (1)	Number of universities granting the highest degrees of permanent faculty (2)	Greatest number of faculty trained in any single university (3)	Unity of training index (3)/(1) (maximum unity = 1.00)	Diversity of training index (2)/(1) (maximum diversity = 1.00)
IUPERJ[a]	12	8	3 (U. of Chicago)	.25	.67
UFMG	14	8	4 (UFMG)	.29	.57
USP	13	1	13 (USP)	1.00	.08
UNICAMP	6	4	3 (USP)	.50	.67

Source: CAPES, 1982, pp. 73–84.

a. IUPERJ stands for University Research Institute of Rio de Janeiro; UFMG stands for Federal University of Minas Gerais; USP stands for University of São Paulo; UNICAMP stands for University of Campinas.

of theoretical, methodological, epistemological, and ideological tools they used in their work. The expansion of the number and diversity of educational and training paths made for greater variety in these respects than had obtained before.

The practitioners of these new approaches were different from those who used the earlier approaches in other ways as well. First, they stressed "systematic empirical research" more than general and abstract theorizing (Velho, 1983, p. 245; also Trindade, 1982; Lamounier, in Velho, 1983). Second, they were political scientists who regarded political institutions and processes as subjects worthy of scholarly investigation. This contrasted with the earlier approaches in which political institutions and processes were mainly interpreted by sociologists or economists as derivative from or expressions of vast social and economic forces and therefore not really worthy of intensive study or emphasis in their own right. Third, they tended to take a somewhat different posture than their predecessors with regard to classic dilemmas of balancing "detached" scholarship and "committed" scholarship. Velho (1983, p. 260) states this important point extremely well:

> Surely today it is obvious, even banal, to note that all thought is compromised. The liberal idea of purely neutral thought explains little; it only describes the appearance of an eventual field of forces which occasionally can be crystallized. However, it is not necessary to make an abstract virtue out of an inescapable necessity. One can imagine a kind of thinking whose "interest" is precisely the search for objectivity, whose compromise and potential are precisely in the affirmation of that search. Probably this is the kind of "person" in the scientific community that ought to be developed. Perhaps this is the best reading of Mannheim's intuition.

On the whole, these changes have been positive in their consequences. Serious political studies in Brazil today are more numerous, more varied, more empirical, more systematic, and more respectful of the possible autonomy and integrity of the political sphere than they were twenty or even ten years ago. In consequence they also open up possibilities not only for still more and better empirical research but also for types of creative theoretical, normative, and policy analysis that were not possible before. In a country such as Brazil—where the political present is clearly better than the recent past but still far from what it might be; where democratic political values, processes, and institutions remain precarious; and where the political future remains open, fluid, and at least in part amenable to skillful, wise political innovation and invention—in such circumstances opening up possibilities is of no small importance.

It should not be assumed, of course, that these changes, mainly positive, came without any costs. Like the earlier modes of analysis, the new political science has its own irrational totems and taboos. The stress on information, training, and operational concepts puts less stress on interpretation, classical education, and creative innovation. The new emphasis on disaggregated parts may make it harder for some to see the aggregated whole. In sum, the capacity to be creative and to theorize may diminish in some ways in the new political science (Velho, 1983, pp. 249–261).

These costs are real but not crippling. Under the best of circumstances and with the most careful mechanisms of quality control, all scientific institutions still certify and reward some people who are dull, or foolish, or afraid. That is true everywhere. But it does not mean the end of creative political science. Far from it. A political science that can claim such works as Bolivar Lamounier's "Representação Política: A Importância de Certos Formalismos" (1981), José Murilo de Carvalho's *A Construção da Ordem* (1980), Simon Schwartzman's *As Bases do Autoritarismo Brasileiro* (1982), or Wanderley Guilherme dos Santos's *Kantianas Brasileiras* (1984), just to name a few examples, does not have to worry that its scholars are unable to address challenging theoretical questions in a creative way.

Interpretations of Brazil's International Political Economy

Other categories of interpretations of Brazilian domestic politics beyond the ones treated here might also be discussed profitably, but here we will only say a brief word about the study of Brazil's international political economy in recent years.

All three of Bresser Pereira's interpretations of the sixties and seventies (the functional-capitalist, imperialist superexploitation, and new-dependency interpretations) related Brazil to the international capitalist system mainly in terms of Marxist theoretical, methodological, and conceptual approaches. In the last twenty years or so, several new lines of investigation and interpretation have not been linked so heavily to that tradition. Thus there has been an increase in concrete, empirical studies of different aspects of Brazil's foreign policy and its place in the international system. This trend regarding studies of Brazilian foreign relations is roughly analogous to the one just noted regarding the new political science in the domestic sphere, although it has occurred on a smaller scale and began from a smaller base. The study of foreign policy and international relations does not have a strong academic tradition in Brazil. Traditionally such work has been essayistic and sometimes polemical, and often the line between academic and nonacademic work has been blurred (Moura and Soares de Lima, 1982, p. 5).

The more recent studies have tended to be more academic, more focused thematically, and less theoretically ambitious than they used to be. Their authors are younger. I have in mind such people as Alexandre de Souza Barros, Carlos Estevam Martins, Celso Lafer, Gerson Moura, Maria Regina Soares de Lima, Mônica Hirst, and Walder de Góes. A detailed bibliographical essay on these matters is given in Moura and Soares de Lima (1982.) The authors in this group have varied considerably in their political and methodological orientations and substantive emphases. Most of them do not challenge Marxist interpretations directly; indeed, some are Marxists themselves. But most of them differ from the earlier Marxist authors in the sense that their works tend to be more systematically empirical and more precisely focused in substantive terms.

Other small groups of more established authors have also challenged some of the Marxist arguments directly and explicitly. These groups have been extremely diverse on a number of dimensions, including the right-left ideological dimension. On the one hand, they offer geopolitical and psychodynamic interpretations of Brazil's international role (Golbery do Couto e Silva, 1967; Carlos de Meira Mattos, 1975; José Osvaldo de Meira Penna, 1972, 1974, 1983). On the other hand, they include interpretations of Brazilian dependency by such authors as Helio Jaguaribe (1973, 1974, 1978) and Celso Furtado (1982). Jaguaribe had for years made heretical dependency arguments, but for Furtado such views were rather different from his earlier writings. Now he was arguing that it is futile to resist the cultural unification of the world being brought about by modern communications and the example of high standards of living in industrialized countries. He thought Third World countries should use such elements of economic power as they had to gradually reduce dependency. He was thus challenging directly the fundamental premises of holistic dependency.

Conclusion

Any analysis of social science approaches necessarily involves the use of categories and labels. Thus Bresser Pereira (1982) has six categories to classify all major interpretations of Brazilian social formations during the last sixty years; those of the last twenty years he classifies as all-Marxist or under strong Marxist influences; and he says that a liberal interpretation does not exist in Brazil. The categories "functional-capitalist," "imperialist superexploitation," "new dependency," "Marxist," and "liberal" used by Bresser Pereira are labels no less than the categories "Marxist," "Marxist-liberal," "political-liberal," and "new academic social scientists" that are used in the present study.

People often react negatively to labels. This is true everywhere, not just in Brazil. It is not hard to see why: categories and labels simplify. They focus on some differences and similarities and ignore others. The theoretical and ideological perspectives passed down from previous centuries are limited in their function as guides to solve today's complex problems. There are also specific reasons why Brazilians are particularly averse to labels. Imported labels conflict with nationalism. Beyond this, Brazilians are world-renowned as improvisers (as witness the institution of *jeito,* a knack for circumventing formal categories and procedures), and they are very good at it. (Alas, not only democrats but also nondemocrats are good at it.) If Roberto da Matta (1978, 1987) is right, and I think he is, Brazilians also prefer implicitness to explicitness and indirection and ambiguity to directness and clarity. They are very good at that, too. Finally, like others, Brazilians want to keep the future open-ended and to use new concepts, theories, ideologies, and labels to deal with it.

There is no disagreeing with the foregoing. But it is only half the story. If one cannot live with labels, it is equally the case that one cannot live without them. Even geniuses at improvisation and ambiguity cannot escape this law. To begin with, language, and thus communication, are impossible without labels. This is an obvious but not a banal fact. It is a critical constraint on the objections to labels. Moreover, one needs the theoretical insights and conceptual tools that the great ideologies provide, despite their manifold, manifest flaws. As Brazilian intellectuals have long recognized, some insights from Marx are useful. And as they have come increasingly to argue in recent years, some of the concepts and theoretical perspectives of political liberalism, whether or not the explicit terminology is used, are also useful.

In the foregoing spirit, then, we suggest—again with apologies to Antonil—that whereas in the very recent past the Brazilian intellectual community was a paradise for Marxists and a hell for liberals, today it is a purgatory for both. For Marxists, the recent trends are a demotion; for liberals, a promotion. Perhaps both developments are salutary.

Ex-Consumers and Nonconsumers in Other Countries

Studies of recent intellectual and scholarly trends in other Latin American countries besides Brazil are scarce but not entirely lacking. Surveying all the major social sciences (sociology, anthropology, political science, economic and social history) except economics in Latin America as of about 1980, Balán (1982, pp. 213, 243–244) found significant changes in research styles: greater emphasis on small-scale, intensive, qualitative studies; growing "heterodoxy" of research methods ("there is no research procedure that is not used effectively by someone"); and "greater pluralism in social research and in its definition as an instrument for knowledge." Mainwaring (1984, p. 429) observes that "The best social science in South America has shifted gears significantly since the late 1960s and early 1970s. The strongest work has moved away from dependency and class analysis inspired in the Marxist tradition. Marxism, with its frequently critical attitude towards 'formal democracy,' has declined, although its influence is still significant. Most South American intellectuals have reassessed the importance of democratic institutions and have moved to new forms of social science which emphasize political values, culture, and institutions."

In a detailed review of works by César Aguiar and others on Uruguay, Andrés Fontana on Argentina, Manuel Antonio Garretón on Chile, and Luis Eduardo González on Uruguay and Chile, among others, Gillespie (1987, p. 166) finds "an intellectual sea-change . . . among Latin American scholars and leaders . . . they have fundamentally reappraised the value of liberal democracy as a system worthy of protection." There is also, he reports, "renewed concern about political processes and institutional forms" and "a corresponding turn away from simple economic reductionism and crude social determinism." Comparable trends are also to be found in Mexico and Peru (Paz, 1979; Krauze, 1986; Zaid, 1987; Levy and Székely, 1987, pp. 257–258; Vargas Llosa, 1986; de Soto, 1986).

New tendencies have also been discovered in the related fields of political economy and public policy. On the basis of interviews and field observations in Brazil, Argentina, Chile, and Mexico and other sources, Hirschman (1987, passim, esp. pp. 13, 22–29) reports that younger economists and policymakers in Latin America "are not talking nearly as much as their elders did about wholly new directions or solutions, yet they are actually coming forward with a number of original ideas and practices," such as the "heterodox shock" therapy for fighting inflation in Argentina and Brazil. He describes (p. 30) a

> shift from total confidence in the existence of a fundamental solu-
> tion for social and economic problems to a more questioning, prag-
> matic attitude—from ideological certainty to more open-ended,
> eclectic, skeptical inquiry . . . It is probably true that [previously]
> many Latin Americans have tended to take 'ideological' positions
> (both left and right) on such matters as planning, the market mech-
> anism, foreign investment, inflation, the government's role in eco-
> nomic development, and so on.
>
> But signs of substantial change in this picture have recently ap-
> peared, largely as a result of bitter experience . . . In Argentina,
> perhaps the most conflict-ridden Latin American society over the
> past fifty years, the idea of 'social concertation,' a process involving
> much give and take on the part of various social groups, has
> achieved considerable prestige. I was told that no one today would
> proudly bestow the name *intransigente* upon a political party, even
> though a minor party with that name (dating, as might be expected,
> from the sixties) is still functioning. At the same time, the spectac-
> ular miscarriage of ideology-driven economic policies (of the left
> and the right) has given rise to a new experimental spirit among
> Latin American economists, intellectuals, and policymakers. This
> spirit, with its readiness to draw on a wide variety of insights, was
> strongly evident in the monetary reforms enacted in Argentina and
> Brazil.

The foregoing trends are most visible, and appear to be strongest, in countries such as Argentina, Brazil, Chile, and Mexico, which have the largest and most differentiated social science communities (Balán, 1982; Mainwaring, 1984; Gillespie, 1987; Hirschman, 1987). However, there is evidence of similar trends in other countries as well (Gillespie, 1987; Torres-Rivas, 1987). With significant exceptions, the pattern is more pronounced among younger scholars (this point is stressed by Hirschman, 1987, pp. 13, 19–22, 25–29). The new trends have probably occurred more often among those social scientists and intellectuals who have the greatest resources, training, and other positive conditions for scholarly work—the counterparts in other Latin American countries of the "high clergy" in Brazil. Many other social scientists in Latin America remain untouched by these trends. But—and this is the most important point—they are a smaller and less influential proportion of the intellectual community today than they were thirty or twenty or even ten years ago.

Broadly speaking, then, the theoretical, conceptual, methodological, and institutional changes described for Brazil also seem to obtain, in varying degrees, throughout most of the region. On the whole the evidence tends to support the judgment of Richard Morse (1985) that "Latin America has come to a threshold in its history, a time when one senses disenchantment throughout the hemisphere with existing ideologies, intellectual strategies, and even the language in which they are cast." Morse also refers to "the swift expansion and maturation of the Latin American intellectual establishment." Two questions remain to be addressed. Why have these changes occurred? What consequences might they have?

Ideas and Democracy in Latin America

The trends just described are of interest for their own sake but also for other reasons. Ideas are influenced by political events; they also can influence political events. Let us consider each of these kinds of influence.

How Political Events Influenced Ideas

In the sixties and early seventies, political and intellectual trends throughout the world tended to discredit liberal, pluralist, and capitalist perspectives on development, and to replace them with various kinds of Marxist, dependency, and even corporatist perspectives. But history kept moving. In the last half of the seventies and the eighties, these trends began to reverse themselves. Marxist regimes started to look worse than before and pluralist democracies started to look better. Thus in the seventies the fall of the Gang of Four in China, the rise and fall of the Pol Pot regime in Cambodia, the rise and decline of Eurocommunism, the fading (though not the disappearance) of the appeal of the Cuban Revolution, the Soviet invasion of Afghanistan, the fate of Solidarity in Poland, and other events in Latin America, Africa, and elsewhere in their turn raised new doubts about the Marxist approaches. Marxism as a compelling intellectual orientation declined even in France—*especially* in France—where it had once been dominant. This example was particularly significant for Latin American Marxist intellectuals, so sensitive to French influences.

As a development model, corporatism was not generally attractive to intellectuals in Latin America. Nor were any forms of traditional conservatism. Despite the manifest conservatism of many Latin American societies, and notwithstanding the pervasive influence of corporatist, organic-statist institutional forms in the region's political history, these theoretical traditions have weakened rather than strengthened as prescriptive models among Latin American intellectuals and scholars.

What happened instead is that the previously discredited "pluralist democracy," so badly battered both as an empirical model and as a prescriptive model in the sixties and early seventies, began to make a comeback, as it were, albeit in slightly different form in some cases. Political democracy began to look more attractive and feasible again, not only in Spain and Portugal but also in Argentina, Brazil, Chile, Uruguay, Peru, and Ecuador—to say nothing of Costa Rica, Venezuela and Colombia, where political democracies had already been in place. In Argentina, the election in 1983 of President Raúl Alfonsín and the reemergence of political democracy seemed a near-miracle after seven years of harsh military rule and fifty years of political pain. Few observers viewed that development with anything but satisfaction; cavils about the imperfections of bourgeois democracy were much less numerous than before. In countries as diverse as El Salvador, Guatemala, Nicaragua, Panama, and Paraguay—not to mention Cuba—stable pluralist democracy, for all its faults, began to look attractive indeed.

None of the trends we have described, in politics or ideas, is irreversible. There are factors working against each of them and rendering them precarious (Packenham, 1986b, pp. 159–163). The new democracies are fragile. The intellectual trends may continue; they may also slow down, stop, or even reverse themselves again, as they have in the past. A unilinear view of the growth of the social sciences is erroneous. So is the idea that the end of ideology has arrived among serious students of Latin American politics. The principles that are today rather widely shared and respected were, only a few short years ago, savaged as bourgeois mystifications and formalisms. Such criticism found eager listeners then. They could again.

Marxism is endlessly recuperative, especially among intellectuals in capitalist countries. Its key concepts expand and contract to meet any contingency. The dialectic can be used to justify just about anything (W. G. dos Santos, 1984, pp. 13–14). It can include almost everybody, but it can also exclude almost anybody. One day, for example, Brazilians were told that the only solution to the country's ills was Marxist socialism and that "Socialism within the framework of capitalism is not socialism" (Cardoso, 1978, p. 84). Another day the platform is, "more democracy and less socialism" (Cardoso as quoted in "Lições da Política," 1984). It is an extraordinary turnaround. If the wheel can turn that far that fast in one direction, one should not rule out completely the possibility that it might keep turning, or turn equally far and fast in the opposite direction. It does not seem likely now, but it is certainly not impossible.

Whatever the future may hold, the record of the past is clear. The liberalization and democratization of Latin American political regimes in recent years, in the context of broader worldwide trends, helped to make possible the new types of discourse among intellectuals that are discussed in this chapter. Those events are by no means the only explanations for these trends. Other factors, such as endogenous changes in the size, quality, and institutional features of Latin American intellectual communities, also helped to shape the new modes of analysis. Yet the political contexts, both domestic and foreign, were significant. In this sense the changing discourse of scholars and intellectuals has been the object of study—if you will, the dependent variable which we have been describing and explaining.

But the causal arrow can also run in the opposite direction. Not only does politics influence the discourse; the discourse can also influence politics. The ways intellectuals think about politics can be an independent variable as well as a dependent variable.

How Ideas Influence Political Events

Surprisingly little is known about the influence of intellectuals on politics in general and democracy in particular. Although it is often assumed that intellectuals favor democracy and tend to support it, this assumption is not always justified by any means. Linz (1978, pp. 47–49, 114) writes suggestively, and with chilling Western European examples, of what he rather charitably calls "the ambivalence of intellectuals toward liberal democracy."

The present analysis suggests two sets of hypotheses. On the one hand, if intellectuals, whose influence in Latin American politics is greater than that of their U.S. counterparts on American politics, refer to elections, political parties, and legislatures as mere "formalisms" that are irrelevant or even damaging to "substantive democracy," then those institutions are diminished as mechanisms for dealing with the problems of Latin American societies. If any capitalist state, even a formally democratic one, is disparaged as merely a device by which elites dominate and exploit popular classes, then the new democratic regimes will have even greater problems of legitimacy than they already have. If any group, individual, or class fraction that has ties with capitalism can at any time be arbitrarily called an internal "expression" of external (capitalist) interests, or stigmatized as the "anti-nation inside the nation," then it will be impossible to recognize the legitimacy of divergent, conflicting interests or of bargaining about, negotiating, and reconciling them in a democratic fashion.

If, on the other hand, the intellectuals use different kinds of discourse, such as the ones that have become prominent recently, then the prospects for the new civilian regimes are improved (Packenham, 1986b, pp. 156–159). Recently some Marxists who were used to seeing the capitalist state and its bourgeois accoutrements of elections as merely the instruments of class oppression have come to see them as means for pursuing the goals of justice and human dignity. As a result they have been able to work intellectually and politically within the electoral and legislative frameworks. The writings of political liberals, and of many of the new academic social scientists of greatly varied ideological and theoretical hues, also reinforced the new tendencies in the political system to legitimate electoral and other democratic political mechanisms, respect minority rights, honor divergent interests, and maintain civility and mutual tolerance in political interactions.

The awesome economic, social, political, and international problems that Latin American countries face put enormous strains on the new democracies. It seems likely that some of them will falter. How many will be able to hold? No one can say. What is suggested is that the way people think, talk, and write about politics will be one factor affecting the fate of democracies, and that intellectuals will continue to play an important role in shaping that factor. In recent years they have been a positive factor. This trend is surely not decisive in its consequences, but it seems to be significant.

Among intellectuals in the United States, however, the trend has been in the opposite direction. Hirschman (1987, p. 34) describes what he calls "that strange switch: North Americans, so proud not long ago of their pragmatism, have taken an ideological turn while Latin Americans have become skeptical of their former sets of certainties and 'solutions' and are naturally exasperated by the neophytes from the North who pretend to teach them yet another set." The evidence presented in this chapter confirms this hypothesis regarding Latin American trends. In the next two chapters, we present evidence that is consistent with his hypothesis about the United States—or, more precisely, an extended version of that hypothesis. Whereas Hirschman refers explicitly only to the U.S. government, the point he makes also applies, as we shall see, to North American intellectuals outside the government.

10 The Consumption of Dependency Ideas in the United States

The dependency movement in the United States has been a scholarly movement. It has changed the substantive and epistemological parameters of scholarly thinking about Latin American politics, development theory, and other topics. One can debate the merits of these changes, but it would be wrong to ignore the facts of the scholarly activities themselves.

The dependency movement has also weakened the conventional distinction between scholarly and political vocations. It has thus contributed to the politicization and theatricalization of U.S. scholarship. On these points as well, one can debate the merits of the changes, but it would be wrong to ignore the facts of the politicizing activities themselves.

The Dependency Movement as Scholarship

The Evolution of Dependency Scholarship in the United States

In the late sixties and early seventies a series of books and articles in English introduced the dependency approach to U.S. scholars (Frank, 1967; Petras and Zeitlin, 1968; Sunkel, 1969, 1972, 1973; Bonilla and Silva Michelena, 1967–71; T. dos Santos, 1968b, 1968c, 1970; Ianni, 1970; Stein and Stein, 1970; Bodenheimer, 1971; Galtung, 1971; Cockcroft, Frank, and Johnson, 1972; Cardoso, 1973a, 1973b; Jaguaribe, 1973; Chilcote and Edelstein, 1974). The Spanish edition of Cardoso and Faletto (1969) was also widely cited though perhaps less often read. In these works the dependency approach was a critical perspective on, and alternative to, the so-called modernization school for the analysis of Latin American development. A few of these early works were empirical studies of single countries, but most were theoretical statements or broad-brush treatments of the entire region. In these writings orthodox, unorthodox, and heretical dependency approaches were all prominently represented; orthodox dependency was perhaps most visible. At that time, however, distinctions among dependency sub-approaches, although noted, were not emphasized as strongly as they were later.

In the mid-seventies the influence of dependency ideas in the United States continued to grow and evolve. North American scholars proceeded along the lines just noted and others as well. The bargaining approach was used in pioneering books by Moran (1974) on Chilean copper and Tugwell (1975) on Venezuelan oil. Early versions appeared of what later would be called analytic dependency (Ray, 1973; Packenham, 1976). A number of scholars used cross-national, aggregate-data, quantitative techniques to attempt to test dependency ideas (Tyler and Wogart, 1973; Kaufman, Geller, and Chernotsky, 1975; Chase-Dunn, 1975; Rubinson, 1976; McGowan and Smith, 1978; Bornschier, Chase-Dunn, and Rubinson, 1978; Walleri, 1978).

In the late 1970s, partly as a result of the proliferation of different kinds of studies, the issue of distinctions among dependency approaches and sub-approaches became salient. An influential document in this regard was a paper by Fernando Henrique Cardoso, "The Consumption of Dependency Theory in the United States" (1977a). Cardoso endorsed unorthodox dependency but criticized orthodox dependency and almost all other approaches. He rejected cross-sectional quantitative tests of dependency ideas on the grounds that they were ahistorical, formal, and positivist; he characterized the authors of such studies as "arbitrary . . . empirical and objective cultivators of science" (p. 23). He repudiated analytic dependency on epistemological and political grounds. Bargaining studies were not deemed worthy of mention; for example, the books by Moran and Tugwell were not cited.

Cardoso's article was followed just one year later by the publication of a spate of other papers in North American journals, mostly by U.S. scholars, that reinforced, elaborated, and extended Cardoso's themes (Caporaso, 1978a, 1978b; Duvall, 1978; Fagen, 1978a; Domínguez, 1978a; Palma, 1978; Valenzuela and Valenzuela, 1978). All but one of these articles affirmed in the strongest terms that unorthodox dependency was superior to orthodox dependency and all other types of dependency analysis—even though they disagreed about what unorthodox dependency really was and differed on a number of other points. Most of them also sharply criticized quantitative studies and tended to dismiss or ignore heretical, analytical, and bargaining approaches. These approaches continued in some quarters but tended thereafter not to find the same degree of attention and support within Latin American and development studies as the holistic approaches.

The overall result of the debates of the late seventies was that holistic dependency, especially its unorthodox version, became the most highly valued, prestigious approach to the study of Latin American politics and society and, increasingly, of development theory more generally as well. Unorthodox dependency's hegemony was partly substantive and methodological but also symbolic. Influential as the articles by Palma, Caporaso, Duvall, Domínguez, Fagen, and the Valenzuelas were, none of them was an empirical work; all were exhortatory and prescriptive. Their recommendations were uniform: dependency ideas needed to move into the mainstream of U.S. scholarship and dominate it. But how, in specific terms?

Now the dependency movement in the United States was about to enter a new phase. In 1979 Evans's study of Brazil appeared; it was the first detailed country case study in English using unorthodox dependency consistently as a theoretical framework. Nineteen seventy-nine was also a landmark year on account of the publication of the revised and expanded English edition of Cardoso and Faletto. For the first time readers of English had access to the major text of the leading unorthodox dependency authors. And if the seventies had witnessed the emergence of the dependency approach as a powerful challenge to mainstream views, the eighties would witness its movement into the mainstream itself.

In the eighties there was an explosion of dependency scholarship: research monographs (Sanderson, 1981, 1985, 1986; Hamilton, 1982; Humphrey, 1982; Monteón, 1982; T. F. O'Brien, 1982; Vaughn, 1982; Gereffi, 1983; Pérez, 1983; Friedman, 1984; Gentleman, 1984; Bennett and Sharpe, 1985; Weeks, 1985; Kofas, 1986; Bergquist, 1986; Stephens and Stephens, 1986; Adler, 1987; Kline, 1987; Rock, 1987; Gootenberg, 1989), readers and symposia (Godfrey, 1980; Muñoz, 1981; Seers, 1981a; Chilcote, 1982; Bienefeld and Godfrey, 1982; "Symposium on Dependency Writings," 1982; Chilcote and Johnson, 1983; Doran, Modelski, and Clark, 1983; Seligson, 1984; Abel and Lewis, 1985; "Business in Latin America," 1985; Fagen, Deere, and Coraggio, 1986; Arbena, 1988), articles and review essays (Caporaso, 1980; Snyder, 1980; Portes and Canak, 1981; Freeman, 1982; Halperín-Donghi, 1982; Duvall and Freeman,

1983; Fagen, 1983; Martz and Myers, 1983; Migdal, 1983; Roxborough, 1984; Wood, 1984; Hall, 1984; Evans, 1985, 1987; P. J. O'Brien, 1985; T. F. O'Brien, 1985; T. Smith, 1985a, 1985b; Taylor, 1985; Westman, 1985; McGovern, 1986; Walton, 1987; Stern, 1988a, 1988b; Wallerstein, 1988), broad interpretative syntheses (Weaver, 1980; Munck, 1983; Chilcote, 1984; LaFeber, 1984; Sheahan, 1987), and the leading mainstream textbook in Latin American history and politics (Skidmore and Smith, 1984, 1989), among other forms of scholarly attention.

Most of these works championed the dependency approach, in one or another of its variants, as the most appropriate way to analyze Latin American politics, economics, and society. There was much, of course, on which they disagreed. Like Latin American dependency authors, U.S. consumers of dependency approaches agreed on some things, disagreed on others. A few U.S. scholars affirmed the politicized-scholarship premise of holistic dependency explicitly; many more accepted it implicitly and/or with reservations; many others used only various substantive and methodological features of the different approaches while staying clear of the politicizing features of some of them.

At the substantive and methodological levels the writings of U.S. authors ranged across the spectrum of dependency and dependency-related approaches: from straight bargaining studies (Grieco, 1982, 1984; Adler, 1987; Kline, 1987) outside the Marxist tradition, on one end, to straight class, modes-of-production, and world-systems studies (Becker, 1983; Hall, 1984; Chilcote and Johnson, 1984; Stern, 1988a) that elaborated and criticized dependency ideas from Marxist premises, at the other. The majority of works adopted the mantle of unorthodox dependency, which was interpreted in many different ways. To cite just a few examples, unorthodox dependency was used without major modifications by Evans (1979) as the framework for his detailed study of multinational, state, and local capital in Brazil and by Bergquist (1986) to orient his comparative analysis of export workers in Chile, Argentina, Venezuela, and Colombia. It was combined with the bargaining approach in studies of Latin American states and multinational corporations (Gereffi, 1983; Bennett and Sharpe, 1985). It was combined with straight class analysis in studies of the Mexican state, Brazilian automobile workers, and Mexican rural laborers (Hamilton, 1982; Humphrey, 1982; Sanderson, 1986). It was combined with bargaining, class, modernization, and other approaches in surveys of Latin American history (Skidmore and Smith, 1984, 1989) or development issues (Sheahan, 1987). Indeed, the variety of work done under this rubric was almost endless, as we shall see presently.

U.S. scholarly consumers included eminent senior scholars, green beginners, and all categories in between. They wrote everything from narrowly specialized research studies to broad-ranging academic best-sellers. Skidmore and Smith's textbook on modern Latin American history, LaFeber's interpretative survey of the United States in Central America, and the English edition of Cardoso and Faletto's classic were all used widely in college and university courses. Skidmore and Smith and LaFeber even made the lists of national book clubs. An Argentinian political scientist (Cavarozzi, 1982, p. 152) teaching at Yale University observed that "the [1979] English edition [of Cardoso and Faletto] . . . has become an obligatory reference for all [North American] courses dealing with society and politics in Latin America." Systematic evidence confirms his point, which also applies to courses on other topics (Kornberg, 1981, 1989). Leading dependency works, especially Cardoso and Faletto (1979) and Evans (1979), were also required reading for Ph.D. comprehensive examinations in most U.S. universities.

To characterize the influence of dependency ideas in the field of Latin American studies as of the early 1980s, the following comment by the editor of the *Latin American Research Review,* the main journal of Latin American studies in the United States, is typical: "What has occurred or is occurring is a gradual convergence of theoretical perspectives. We can observe it in the selection of research topics, in the questions we ask in organizing our research, in the adoption and adaptation of analytic concepts from one intellectual tradition to another, even in the emergence of a common vocabulary to discuss our research interests" (Tulchin, 1983, p. 89). In a similar vein an expert on the Caribbean region (Pastor, 1986, p. 486) stated that the dependency perspective, "which was just beginning to emerge in the early 1970s . . . clearly has become the dominant theoretical approach today" for understanding U.S. policy toward the Caribbean and Central America.

Political science and history were by no means the only fields thus affected. In sociology the dependency movement represented "one of the most significant shifts in the history of intellectual exchange between an advanced country and a less-developed region. In essence, the lines of teaching and learning have been inverted as U.S. scholars doing field work in the region have learned about novel theoretical perspectives informing contemporary Latin American sociology . . . [This] re-socialization process . . . is reflected in almost every major sociological work on the region published in the United States during the last five years" (Portes and Canak, 1981, pp. 228–229).

In economics, Hirschman (1979, p. 83) ranked dependency writings just below Latin American fiction ("the boom") in his estimate of Latin American impact on world culture in the sixties and seventies. Other economists who like Hirschman were somewhat critical but acknowledged the influence of dependency writings and praised their innovativeness included Thorp and Bertram (1978), Reynolds (1982), Berry (1987), and Sheahan (1987). In the field of the international political economy of North/South relations, "for at least the past two decades dependency and world systems theory have dominated scholarly inquiry" and "dependency theory" was "the prevailing orthodoxy" (Lake, 1987). Wood (1986) supports Lake's claims. Quantitative studies of dependency and its concomitants, although dismissed by holistic dependency scholars, continued to be an active research field for specialists such as Bornschier, Chase-Dunn, Jackman, Kaufman, Mahler, Russett, and Weede in the 1970s and 1980s (for a survey with citations, see Russett, 1983). In addition, dependency ideas had significant influences in anthropology, communications (Sarti, 1981; Straubhaar, 1981, 1984), comparative literature, and comparative legal studies (Snyder, 1980), among other fields.

The influences of dependency writings also extended well beyond Latin American area studies. Most important, they profoundly influenced the broad field of development theory. A British political scientist (Payne, 1984, p. 1) wrote, only a little too strongly, that "dependency thinking has come to dominate the study of society, politics, and economics in the modern Third World." A North American development theorist and expert on Southern Asia (Weiner, 1981) perceived that influence from still another perspective: "The most innovative scholarship in recent years by Marxists and neo-Marxists in development theory has dealt with the issue of dependency . . . The most influential Marxist writings of our time on development have thus not come from the Soviet Union or, for that matter, China or even Cuba, but from intellectuals in the capitalist countries of Latin America." Virtually every survey confirms that during the 1970s and 1980s dependency writings massively influenced the fields of comparative politics and political development (Chilcote and Johnson, 1983; Chilcote, 1984; Migdal, 1983; Seligson, 1984; T. Smith, 1985a, 1985b; Wiarda, 1985; Klarén and Bossert, 1986; Walton, 1987; Weiner and Huntington, 1987).

In addition, dependency ideas directly affected research on other regions besides Latin America. Their influences in the study of Africa—where African authors such as Samir Amin, Walter Rodney, Arghiri Emmanuel, and Issa G. Shivji were prominent—are widely acknowledged; First World scholars who used dependency perspectives to analyze Africa include Leys (1971), Sklar (1975), Shaw and Heard (1979), and Biersteker (1987). Less well known is the use of dependency concepts and theories in analyses of East Asia (Winkler, 1981), Singapore (Beng, 1980; Deyo, 1981), South Korea (Luedde-Neurath, 1980; Mitchell, 1982; Lin, 1987; also Chira, 1986), Taiwan (Gold, 1986), Southeast Asia (Mortimer, 1973; Weinstein, 1976a, 1976b; Amarshi et al., 1979; Ozawa, 1979; Crone, 1983), Bangladesh (Banerjee, 1987), India (Byres, 1982; Grieco, 1984), Ireland (Coughlan, 1982), Portugal (Holland, 1979), Iran (Hakimian, 1980), the Middle East (Hajjar, 1984), Egypt (Waterbury, 1983), the Arab OPEC states (Luke, 1983), and Turkey and the Ottoman Empire (Rosenthal, 1980), among other places and times.

How faithful these applications of dependency perspectives to non-Latin American settings are to the intent and content of the original writings is a complex question. Dependency authors frequently have suggested that their ideas are meant for application exclusively to Latin America and excoriated those who applied them elsewhere. They have also stated the reverse: that the fundamental categories involved did not originate in Latin America, are not limited to Latin America, and could be applied wherever similar structural conditions exist.

On this issue as on others, dependency writings are contradictory. One can sympathize with dependency authors when their ideas are applied badly in the study of other countries and areas—or, for that matter, when they are applied badly in the study of Latin America. On the other hand, the contradictory and ambiguous character of dependency ideas invites distortions and perceived distortions. Also, it seems inconsistent to object to the application of a methodology for the analysis of concrete situations of dependency in non-Latin American settings when—as Cardoso, Palma, and many others have accurately stressed—the key elements of that methodology were developed in Germany, France, and England, more than a century ago, to understand mid-nineteenth century European industrialization.

The Influence of Dependency Scholarship in the United States

Four major hypotheses have been advanced about the magnitude and direction of influence of dependency ideas on U.S. and other First World scholarship. At one extreme is the view that North Americans have paid little or no attention to dependency ideas (Fagen, 1978a; Valenzuela and Valenzuela, 1978; Seers, 1981b; Caporaso, 1980; McDonough, 1980; Stern, 1988a). Thus Seers (1981b, p. 13) wrote that "The theory of dependency, or *dependencia,* has still scarcely made much impression on the social scientists of Europe or North America. This reflects our parochialism . . . It is hard to resist the conclusion that most of us just do not care, assuming tacitly that nothing of intellectual significance is produced in backward continents, a hangover from the colonial period." As late as 1988, in a lead article in the *American Historical Review,* the historian Steve Stern (1988a, pp. 871–872) lamented that the ideas of Latin American dependency authors were still "largely neglected in the United States."

This first hypothesis is untenable. In the late sixties and early seventies the first wave of dependency studies appeared in English and the approach has been un-ignored and un-ignorable ever since.

At the opposite extreme, almost two decades ago Andre Gunder Frank (1974) declared that dependency ideas, having already been influential, were now dead. At periodic intervals since then, other scholars have also sounded a death knell for the approach (Godfrey, 1980; Levine, 1988). The evidence here presented shows that this hypothesis is no more tenable than the first. The dependency approach did not die in 1974, or 1980, or even 1988. In the U.S. its appeal did decline as an explicit, overt theory in the late 1980s and early 1990s, but even then as a theoretical baseline it remained the dominant perspective in Latin American and development studies (Evans, 1985a; Walton, 1987; Skidmore and Smith, 1989).

According to the third hypothesis, dependency ideas are not merely alive in the United States but have entered the mainstream, dominated it, and left a massive residue for future generations. In this view, what began as a minority critique of "establishment" (modernization) approaches itself became the principal standard against which competing approaches were measured (Portes and Canak, 1981; Cavar-rozzi, 1982; Migdal, 1983; Tulchin, 1983; Skidmore and Smith, 1984; Evans, 1985a; T. Smith, 1985a, 1985b; Pastor, 1986; Lake, 1987; Sheahan, 1987; Walton, 1987). Most of those who advance this hypothesis applaud the situation; one or two lament it; all say it existed at the time they wrote.

The evidence overwhelmingly supports this third view as against the first two views. Orthodox dependency is frequently criticized from all sides, but unorthodox dependency has been criticized much less seriously and frequently, and then mainly by others in the Marxist tradition (Warren, 1980; Becker, 1983). Unorthodox dependency has been in the mainstream since the seventies in the United States. It remains there today, although increasingly without the dependency label (Evans, 1985a, p. 157; Dosal, 1987, 1988) and even though some authors (Becker, 1987, p. 204) make a distinction between "Cardoso's historical-structural method" and "the dependency approach" as if the one had nothing to do with one the other.

Perhaps the most significant scholarly effect of the dependency movement was to end the liberal consensus and to create space for radical hypotheses, methods, and premises. The dependency movement changed the parameters of scholarly debates. Before the advent of dependency and world-systems approaches, Marxism occupied little space in Latin American studies and still less in development theory. Not until the publication of Barrington Moore's *Social Origins of Dictatorship and Democracy* (1966) did the vast literature on political development contain a single influential Marxist work. After the dependency movement, radical perspectives occupied a great deal of intellectual space. They were legitimate. They established much of the intellectual agenda and terminology of discourse. Before, radicalism and revolution were almost always rejected; now, they were usually said to be good. The dependency movement was by no means the only influence on this sea-change in U.S. scholarship, but it was one of the most important influences. Whether this was good or bad or mixed, it was a fact.

There is a fourth and final hypothesis about the magnitude of the influence of dependency ideas on U.S. scholarship. It says that dependency and dependency-related ideas, including various class and world-systems approaches, are now the only scholarly approaches to Third World and Latin American development that merit serious attention. Thus Becker (1987, p. 204) writes that "Those who want a progressive theory of development have been left with two contenders: what Peter Evans has called 'Cardoso's historical-structural method'—and postimperialism." "Postimperialism" is Becker's version of a classical Marxist approach applied to the contemporary Third World. According to Schoultz (1987, pp. 22–23), conservative and reformist theories of Latin American development have been "deserted" by the U.S. academic community, whereas scholars supporting a revolutionary view akin to dependency and dependency-related ideas "have won hands down the intellectual debate." For many other scholars on the left virtually the entire debate occurs in the band of the spectrum between Marxist and unorthodox dependency approaches (Chilcote and Johnson, 1983; Chilcote, 1984; Stern, 1988a, 1988b; Corbridge, 1990).

This fourth hypothesis goes too far. Modernization theories, for all their influence in the fifties and sixties, never were completely dominant; neither were dependency and dependency-related approaches in the seventies and eighties. Various kinds of corporatist, statist, rational-choice, neomodernization, liberal democratic, social-democratic, Marxist, and other approaches swam in the mainstream (for surveys with citations, see Martz and Myers, 1983; Migdal, 1983; Wiarda, 1985; Klarén and Bossert, 1986; Weiner and Huntington, 1987). There were also various kinds of political-economy approaches (Seligson, 1984; Hartlyn and Morley, 1986). In the late 1980s there was a significant increase in scholarship on political liberalization and democratization (Huntington, 1984; O'Donnell, Schmitter, and Whitehead, 1986; Selcher, 1986; Malloy and Seligson, 1987; Diamond, Linz, and Lipset, 1988–; Stepan, 1988, 1989; Mainwaring, 1988; Bermeo, 1990). These writings owed little or nothing to the dependency approach; although they often did not say so most of their premises and hypotheses were sharply at odds with those of dependency writings.

The Dependency Movement as Politics

Although many have commented on the *engagé* quality of the consumption of dependency writings in the United States, there is still much confusion about it. Broadly speaking, two interpretations, a weak version and a strong version, have been given by U.S. social scientists.

In the weak version, the distinctive feature of dependency ideas was that they transcended naive assumptions about "value-free," "neutral," and "objective" social science that allegedly characterized the earlier modernization and development literatures: "While political engagement is hardly unique to dependencistas, their explicitly normative concern with the political and social outcomes of development was one characteristic that set them apart from their 'value neutral' predecessors" (Evans, 1985a, p. 157). "Thanks in good measure to the dependency perspective . . . moral advocacy is no longer taboo in the name of an 'objective' social science" (T. Smith, 1985a, p. 560).

Such formulations obscure more than they reveal. In the first place, contrary to these claims normative concerns were explicit in most of the earlier development literature. Lipset (1960, 1981) drew on Aristotle, Tocqueville, Marx, and Weber, among others, to make his explicit normative case for democracy. Huntington (1965, 1968) drew on Plato, Hobbes, and even Lenin and the novelist William Golding to bolster his explicit normative argument that "the public interest is the interest of public institutions." Authors such as Almond, Coleman, Verba, Hagen, Lerner, Pye, Apter, and Eisenstadt did not think of themselves as completely "value free." Their works were informed by explicit concerns for democracy, development, and other normative objectives. Indeed, I have never read or met any of these authors (or anyone else for that matter) who thinks he is "value free." The overwhelming majority of modernization and development theorists knew, as did Mannheim and Weber before them, that "full objectivity, full detachment from one's social and cultural biases, is an impossibility" (Almond, 1987, p. 451). They knew that to seek a measure of scholarly objectivity is neither to claim to have fully achieved it nor to abandon all normative concern. Claims to the contrary are caricatures.

The second major problem with these formulations is that they impute to dependency writings a sophistication in moral discourse that they do not have. While some claims to scholarly virtue may plausibly be made on behalf of the dependency approach, excellence in quality of ethical argument is not among them. What sort of "moral advocacy" is in fact to be found in the dependency literature? Is it a carefully constructed philosopher's argument about justice, à la the treatises of John Rawls, Robert Nozick, Michael Walzer, and others that transformed political theory in the 1970s and 1980s? Is it a clear definition and empirically grounded description of socialism on the periphery and the conditions sustaining it à la the definitions and descriptions of Dahl or Lipset on democracy? Is it a systematically elaborated concept of the public interest under socialism à la Huntington's argument that the public interest is the interest of public institutions? Is it a formal, testable approach to political economy à la the rational choice approaches of Samuel Popkin, Mancur Olson, and others? Does the moral advocacy of the dependency approach allow for and encourage fruitful scholarly debates between different schools—of the sort, for example, that occurred between classical Marxists and rational-choice Marxists like Jon Elster and John Roemer; between Popkin and James Scott; between statists, Marxists, and liberals in international relations theory?

The evidence is clear that in the dependency literature there is little or no moral advocacy in the scholarly senses just indicated. Instead there is a polemic against capitalism combined with a vague prescription for socialism. Actual capitalisms are compared to idealized socialist utopias. Whatever their virtues in other respects, as treatments of normative questions dependency works have virtually none of the intellectual qualities that make the other approaches and debates important scholarly contributions. The claim that the dependency literature offers more searching and sophisticated moral arguments than those in the other writings just mentioned is not sustainable.

This brings us to the second, stronger version of the thesis of the politicizing effect of the dependency movement. In this second version, the dependency movement turned away from the Weberian notion of trying to separate scholarly and political vocations and toward the notion of fusing them. Did this happen, and if so, how much and in what ways? Three main types of evidence show that it did happen to an extent and in ways that were different from earlier times: direct evidence from individuals, indirect evidence from individuals, and direct evidence at the level of an institution, the Latin American Studies Association (LASA).

One of the most comprehensive and sympathetic statements of the politicizing character of the dependency movement by a North American scholar is Tony Smith's (1985a) influential article in *World Politics*. It is simultaneously a positive summary of dependency ideas, including the way they fuse scholarship and political struggle, and an account of their effects in the United States. It also illustrates the kind of ethical argument claimed for the approach. Smith's earlier writings showed a much narrower, more superficial knowledge of dependency ideas; in them he was mostly critical (T. Smith, 1979, 1981). His later writings (T. Smith, 1985a, 1985b) display a surer grasp of the holism, nonfalsificationism, and politicization of the approach; they are mostly favorable.

From the very first sentences Tony Smith uses the tone, style, and method of holistic dependency. What one paragraph giveth, another paragraph taketh away. "For the unity of the movement to be irredeemably shattered intellectually," he says at one point, "it is not necessary . . . to maintain that dependency is always and everywhere mistaken, but only that it is no better than a partial truth" (p. 557). However, "piddling criticism of the dependency school is a waste of time . . . These writers have ways of deflecting attacks and maintaining their conceptual unity . . . the political interests served by such an ideology will insist on the veracity of this way of understanding the world whatever the objections" (pp. 557, 558). Smith is wrong about holistic dependency the first time, right the second time. But what is notable here are the attempt, *pace* holistic dependency, to have it both ways, and the linkage of the epistemological points to an assertion about the political interests of scholarship.

Although at several points Smith creates an impression of an evenhanded, symmetrical assessment of "developmentalism" (his term for nondependency approaches to development) compared to the dependency approach, in fact his evaluation is highly asymmetrical: a harsh critique (with a dollop of praise) of the former, and a ringing endorsement (with a dollop of criticism) of the latter. While he repeatedly endorses the "demise" of developmentalism, his account of the dependency approach concludes as follows:

> The coherence, complexity, flexibility, and self-confidence of the dependency approach should be clear. When we add the important consideration that it can serve as a powerful ideological force uniting Marxism ideologically with Third World nationalism—as is clear in the case of Liberation Theology in Latin America—we must recognize that dependency thinking has established itself as an intellectual force with which we must reckon. Quite unlike developmentalism—which lives on in the wide variety of studies it spawned earlier, but which today lacks a center of gravity in a well-anchored, broad-based theory of change—the dependency school is in its prime. (p. 553)

Besides describing and evaluating the impact of dependency ideas "within American academia" (p. 545), Smith also sought to explain why he and others find it so appealing. His remarkable answer goes to the heart of the politicizing features of the dependency movement. Dependency ideas are appealing, he writes, because they show that developmentalism was "the ideological handmaiden of imperialism and the ruling elites in the Third World . . . the very categories with which American academics analyzed the South were . . . instruments in the subjugation of Africa, Asia, and Latin America" (p. 550). He elaborates as follows:

> It should thus be understandable that, in the eyes of the dependencistas, developmentalists in the United States were responsible for much more than inadequate model building with respect to affairs in the Third World. This very "inadequacy" was nothing more than an ideological smokescreen behind which North American imperialism freely operated . . . In their work, the developmentalist intelligentsia of American universities had given the lie to all their protestations of academic freedom and value-free or progressive theorizing, revealing instead their true character as apologists for the established international division of wealth and power. The attack was now complete: the dependency school not only had established a paradigm for the study of the Third World, but it had provided an explanation of its rival, developmentalism, powerful enough to complete the latter's disintegration. (p. 552).

This is the type of "moral advocacy . . . no longer taboo" that in Smith's judgment so commends the dependency approach. For Smith, ideas are not merely discarded; they are "angrily discarded." Scholars with views different from his own are not merely wrong, but "betrayers," "emperors who wear no clothes," occupants of "charmed circles" who wrote "as much to ensure their professional standing as to advance the discipline" (pp. 532, 543, 532, 532, 540, respectively). By conventional standards of scholarly discourse this kind of argumentation would be inadmissible in a serious social science journal on the grounds that it is ad hominem and focused on motives. But by the mid-1980s traditional standards were sufficiently weakened that such arguments were made in a leading journal in the mainstream of U.S. scholarship.

Other observers with more critical evaluations have also documented these politicizing attitudes and practices. A former editor of the *Latin American Research Review* (Tulchin, 1983, pp. 89–90) observes that, partly because of the rise of dependency thinking, "Extreme proponents [of different views] were at war over the issue of whether scholarship is possible at all within or without an *engagé* posture . . . [This] polarization . . . is especially tiresome to an editor trying to secure Solomonic judgments from referees on a submission to his journal." A political scientist (Pastor, 1986, p. 486), writing a detailed analysis of books published in the 1980s on U.S. policy toward the countries of the Caribbean Basin, also finds that politicization and theoretical polarization accompanied the rise to dominance of the dependency perspective. "Compared to the literature of the 1960s and 1970s," he notes, "recent work appears more passionate and argumentative . . . there have been few attempts to build on the previous literature . . . history is used selectively, often for advocacy purposes."

Clearly the politicizing effect of the dependency movement involved more than the modest and unexceptionable notion that scholars can have normative concerns and the possibility of moral advocacy. It weakened or eliminated—in practice and, much more important, in principle—the traditional prohibition against politicized, ad hominem, and personal arguments and activities in scholarly discourse. Sometimes the politicization was blatant and consistent, as in the examples just given and many LASA activities (see below). More often the politicization endorsed and practiced by U.S. and other First World scholars was more ambivalent and conflicted. Consider, for example, the following assessment of dependency writings by a British scholar, the political scientist Philip J. O'Brien (1985, pp. 43–44):

> One of the main reasons for the passion surrounding the debate on dependency theory has been the politically "committed" stance of its principal proponents, who have set out to analyze the past and present in order to draw the kind of conclusions useful to those trying to change the future. Writers in the developed world have sometimes reacted violently to the whole [dependency] school, disliking its assumption that capitalism—"our" capitalism—has failed to develop the Third World in a satisfactory manner, and that existing relationships between developed and underdeveloped coun-

tries must be changed. On the other hand, those who share the basic political judgments of the dependency school may still want to rewrite it in terms of their own, slightly different, political programmes, dismissing other writers out of hand, not for reasons of intellectual clarity or coherence, but because of their suspicions about the "really revolutionary" character of those involved. The dependency debate has taken place in the middle of a political mine-field. But that does not mean that its writers are not serious social scientists, nor does it justify those who prefer exploding their own political passions to serious intellectual criticism, dismissing out of hand the serious work which has accumulated.

It is instructive to parse this statement. Without ever actually stating the politicized-scholarship axiom in its accurate second version, O'Brien here gives a fine example of practicing it. In the first sentence, he offers a rendition—with quotation marks around "committed"—of the weak first version of the *engagé* hypothesis. After that one sentence he switches the focus from dependency ideas to alleged, unnamed critics of dependency ideas. Ignoring substantive issues, he uses ad hominem and political criteria to evaluate them: non-Marxist critics are "writers in the developed world" (as if there were none in the developing world) whose "violent reactions" are rooted not in scholarly concerns but rather in a self-interested defense of capitalism ("their" capitalism). These ad hominem attacks on non-Marxist critics are followed by a parallel ad hominem attack on Marxist critics. None of this is documented; it is all merely asserted. O'Brien laments that the dependency debate has occurred "in a political mine-field," as if dependency premises had nothing to do with it. He concludes with a plea for the very principles—independent scholarship, dispassionate criticism, cumulative knowledge across scholarly traditions—for which holistic dependency has the deepest contempt.

O'Brien's statement illustrates two phenomena that are not unusual in the consumption of dependency ideas in First World countries: ambivalence about the politicization of scholarship and theatricalization of the issues raised by the dependency movement. Many scholars want it both ways. They are drawn to many features of the approach, including the politicization, and reluctant to criticize, especially unorthodox dependency ideas, but also ambivalent about embracing them completely. Conversely, they are reluctant to defend or endorse conventional approaches and standards when dependency authors attack them but also reluctant to abandon those standards completely.

These two phenomena are related. The less the ambivalence, the more direct is the politicization. But the greater the ambivalence, the more indirect, implicit, and theatrical is the politicization. O'Brien is well down this scale from Tony Smith; here is another example still farther down than O'Brien's. It is from a North American political scientist, Thomas Biersteker (1987, pp. 287–288):

> Too much contemporary academic work is littered with narrow considerations of issues and sham put-downs of alternative theoretical perspectives. The recent spate of attacks on dependency approaches is one of the latest manifestations of this tendency. Dependency approaches are certainly not flawless, needed some careful scrutiny, and were themselves polemical in their treatment of modernization theorists a decade and a half ago. There is, however, little point in reversing the polemic and dismissing the entire approach out of hand, however fashionable it may be at present. This is not a way toward the cumulation of knowledge. It would be far more constructive to integrate some of their insights into contemporary analysis, rather than scoring cheap victories, reverting to the past, or rediscovering the wheel (a point dependency writers themselves should have considered in the past).

Like O'Brien, Biersteker focuses on alleged violations of conventional academic rules by critics of dependency, rather than the critics' substantive and methodological ideas. The image he offers is of an intolerant, polemical U.S. academic community dogmatically closed to new ideas from an approach that seeks only to offer insights and contribute to the cumulation of knowledge. He is full of accusations: "cheap victories," "sham put-downs," intellectual "narrowness," "dismissive attitudes." The documentation he offers for these charges is thin and vague ("a number of recent Ph.D. dissertations in political science"). He repeats the myth that early dependency works were politicized but later ones were not. He makes no reference to holistic dependency's denunciations of cumulative social science. He says nothing to acknowledge or suggest that his own analysis might be touched by the politicizing imperatives of holistic dependency.

Biersteker *says* he favors unorthodox dependency over any other approach: "I have employed a quasi-dialectical, historical analysis of a concrete situation, obviously borrowing heavily from the method of the three radical approaches (especially of sophisticated dependency writers)" (p. 287). In his study, however, Biersteker uses a bargaining approach to examine the relations between the Nigerian state and multinational corporations. He says he opposes "narrow consideration of issues," yet he himself focuses mostly on state/MNC relations and says relatively little about the central issues—distorted development, political authoritarianism, internal class relations, and the need for socialism—of the unorthodox approach upon which he says he most relies. Although he does not seem to realize it, his work fits best into the bargaining-study tradition, and in that genre it is a good study. Yet his typology of approaches (pp. 11–51) excludes the approach that his own work most closely approximates, the bargaining orientation. The classic bargaining studies of Moran and Tugwell are nowhere cited in his book.

What is going on here? Why does Biersteker make the melodramatic allegations and appeals of the paragraph reproduced above? Why does he say he mainly uses the unorthodox dependency approach when plainly that is not his main orientation at the substantive level? To answer these questions one needs to consider the concept of scholarship as theatre, ritual, and symbol and its crucial importance for understanding the consumption of dependency writings in the United States.

The Dependency Movement as Theatre

The Concept of Scholarship as Theatre

The notion that many different kinds of people, groups, and activities can be usefully perceived and analyzed in terms of a theatrical metaphor is not new. Interpretations of social units ranging from individuals in everyday social intercourse to large collectivities like states have been made in various important scholarly studies (Goffman, 1959; Geertz, 1980; also Carvalho, 1988, 1990). From this perspective it is even possible—a view that would go further than my own—to see all social actors at all times as at once performers and spectators in a drama (Schechner, 1985).

Until recently this mode of analysis has seldom, if ever, been applied to *scholars* as social actors. This should not be very surprising. Traditionally, scholarship has been seen as a sphere of human activity where reason, logic, and evidence are considered the only *legitimate* tools for carrying on debates and resolving disputes. Especially since Mannheim, it has been well understood that other considerations can affect debates, but even then these have been viewed essentially as obstacles to be overcome or minimized rather than as legitimate parts of the enterprise itself. In the conventional view there would be little reason therefore to interpret scholarly processes as theatrical.

If the boundaries between scholarship and politics were to break down, however, then it would not be surprising if scholarship became theatrical as well. Scholarship would then be political not only directly, as we have just seen (and will see again in the next chapter), but also indirectly, as theatre, drama, symbolism, ceremony, ritual, and melodrama. In fact, politics and theatre overlap and interlace a great deal. Drama is by far the most social and political form of art (Esslin, 1977, passim, esp. p. 23); politics is (among other things) highly symbolic, ritualistic, ceremonial, theatrical, and melodramatic. It may be inevitable, then—it is surely very likely—that when scholarship fuses with politics, it perforce also fuses with theatre.

That has happened in the case of the dependency movement. It was a scholarly movement but it was also a melodrama, a ritual, a set of symbols. Geertz (1980) has argued that in nineteenth-century Bali the state was not merely an allocator of values which also had a symbolic aspect; sometimes the state in Bali *was* ceremony and ritual, period. In a more or less parallel way the dependency movement in the United States not only had a symbolic aspect; sometimes it ceased being primarily scholarship and became primarily theatre, ceremony, ritual. Without addressing this aspect of the phenomenon it is impossible to have an adequate understanding of the consumption of dependency ideas in the United States.

The Dependency Movement as Melodrama

To understand the theatrical uses of dependency scholarship, let us begin with an apparent puzzle.

Buried in an appendix of Domínguez's article articulating the distinction between orthodox and unorthodox dependency is the statement that "the two dependency perspectives clearly derive from the same intellectual source and continue to have common methods and concerns; their differences are similar to a family quarrel, not a divorce" (1978a, p. 117). In a book published the same year Domínguez again wrote, also in an appendix, that the "basic propositions" of unorthodox dependency "are not drastically different from those of the orthodox perspective" (1978b, p. 513).

These are strong statements. Taken seriously, they obviously cast the frequent discussions of the differences between these two approaches, and of the alleged significance of these differences, in a drastically different light than if one were to consider these discussions independently. But the statements in Domínguez's appendixes are never elaborated, emphasized, or discussed in any detail in the texts of these two works (or anywhere else in Domínguez's writings). It is the differences that are regarded as significant. Thus Domínguez gives the strongest possible endorsement to the unorthodox dependency perspective as a guide to research and policy, and the strongest possible condemnation of orthodox dependency for such purposes. As we have seen (Chapter 1 above) this same pattern is found again and again in the writings of the great majority of scholarly commentators on dependency ideas in the United States.

But if the "basic propositions" of orthodox and unorthodox dependency are the same, and if the differences between them are more like a "family quarrel" than a divorce, then how can it make sense to base entire programs of research and policy on the one while simultaneously regarding the other as totally unsuitable to guide either research or policy? If the latter is totally unsuitable, why is the former so suitable? Intellectually and scientifically this would appear to make little sense. In terms of the notion of the dependency movement as theatre or melodrama, it makes a lot of sense.

Dependency ideas arose and spread in the United States in the context of the war in Vietnam and its aftermath, urban conflicts, campus tumult, Watergate, and other political and cultural upheavals of the sixties and seventies. The dependency movement was at the center of a major reassessment in the field of development studies. Central values of the Western liberal tradition were challenged. Self-doubt and guilt were widespread, especially among intellectuals. In the sphere of epistemology, realism and the idea of objective truths and cumulative knowledge were out; antirealism and the notion of subjectivism and scientific revolutions were in (Kuhn, 1962). Hermeneutic, interpretive, critical, and deconstructionist modes of thought became influential in the social sciences and humanities (Miller, 1987). Reflecting on these changes, Sutton (1985, p. 64) was reminded "of the Romantic revolt at the beginning of the 19th century. There came in the turbulence of the late 1960s and early 1970s a passion for direct experience and a reaction against rational deliberation that was like the Romantic turn against the grand visions of the Enlightenment. We still feel the force of this tide."

In these contexts, dependency ideas were associated with developing countries, the South, and popular classes. Support for these ideas was widely seen as support for the Third World and poor classes. Criticism of them by non-Marxist scholars was widely rejected by the new defenders of dependency ideas in the First World. They tended to see such criticism as an expression of hostility to developing countries and popular classes, and as support for capitalist imperialism and exploitation. The scientific and philosophical issues were posed in analogous fashion and linked to the other divisions. The propositions and intellectual standards associated with non-Marxist thinkers in the North (that is, First World, "developed" countries at the center of capitalism) were suspect among First-World proponents of depending ideas. Propositions and intellectual standards associated with thinkers from the South (that is, Third World, "developing" countries on the periphery of capitalism) were favored.

In this setting it was awkward, however, that the first person to make a big splash with these ideas was a Berlin-born, U.S.-educated Ph.D. from the University of Chicago named Andre Gunder Frank. The new ideas of the periphery had to have a more authentic representative than that. Fernando Henrique Cardoso became that representative, and he was perfect for the role. A Brazilian man of the left, he could represent the periphery more authentically than Frank. A rising star in Brazilian and Latin American intellectual circles in the late fifties and sixties, he also was a respectable (later eminent) member of the international social science establishment. Cardoso could plausibly represent the have-nots, the South. Moreover, Cardoso had formidable political instincts and skills which he used brilliantly both within the academy and, later, in practical politics. In contrast to Cardoso's dazzling use of ambiguity and subtle contradiction, Frank had a genius for exaggeration and over-simplification and no predisposition or talent for practical politics. In the melodrama of good guys and bad guys, and so far as symbolism, politics, styles, and personalities were concerned, it was no contest.

By conventional scholarly criteria the contradictory, ambiguous, and unfalsifiable features of unorthodox dependency were defects. But conventional criteria were not much in favor. To the contrary, they were highly suspect. In unorthodox dependency U.S. scholars found a way to embrace a "sophisticated, subtle, nonvulgar" approach while simultaneously dividing the world into just two categories: the "progressive" forces in the Third World and their allies, and the "antiprogressive" forces in the First and Third worlds and their allies. It represented a way to embrace the critical perspective offered by the dependency approach without seeming to "go to extremes." One could reject Western capitalism in favor of Third World socialism, yet avoid the initially fashionable but soon-to-be-taboo thesis of the development of underdevelopment. Most of all, in the drama of Center-Periphery, North-South scholarly relations, one could be on the side of the just.

All of this affected how the dependency books by Frank and by Cardoso and Faletto were received. That there were forms of industrial development in Latin America, supported by foreign capital and technology with production for the internal market, were facts apparent to anyone with eyes to see. These were phenomena perfectly consistent not only with capitalist economics but also with the visions and hypotheses of Marx and Lenin. Frank saw these phenomena clearly and reported them at length. But no one paid attention. It did not fit the scenario. Soon the myth became gospel that Frank did not perceive correctly what everyone, including Frank, could plainly see. Soon Cardoso's notion of "associated-dependent development" was hailed as a theoretical breakthrough of global significance—a "world-class" intellectual event.

But the theatrical use of unorthodox dependency has involved much more than exaggerating the differences and minimizing the similarities between orthodox and unorthodox dependency. More important still, it has also involved the invocation of the unorthodox dependency symbol to decorate, justify, and legitimate almost every conceivable kind of dependency approach and even a number of nondependency approaches.

The Dependency Movement as Symbol and Ritual

Merquior (1982, pp. 65–66) has described dependency writings as "an etiquette used to decorate an analysis," "an ideological pass-word," and an "'in-phrase' for the Marxist or Marxisant culture which dominates the intellectual circles and the universities." He was referring to the situation in Brazil, but the same phenomenon was also observable in the United States, and by no means only in the Marxist subculture. Thus Tulchin noted (1983, p. 92) that "Not long ago it was rare to receive a manuscript at LARR [the *Latin American Research Review*] that did not have 'dependency' in its title, no matter what the ostensible subject of the paper." Few who reviewed manuscripts and evaluated research proposals at the time will fail to recall the pattern.

Scholars who cited unorthodox dependency works as the inspiration and guide for their studies often seemed to have relatively little knowledge of what the works actually said. Or else they drew upon them in highly selective ways. Manifestly they derived very different, often incompatible ideas and methods from the same textual sources of inspiration. Consider, for example, the following passage in which Domínguez (1978b, pp. 513–514) states what he saw in unorthodox dependency that so much commended it to him:

> First, [in unorthodox dependency] a much more substantial degree of autonomy is afforded to the client state by competition among major foreign powers in international affairs, by the limitations and incompetence of imperial powers, and by the client's shrewdness in using resources. Autonomy is explicitly created by political action; it is what a Marxist might call a "subjective condition" that can repeatedly overcome the "objective condition" of dependency. Second, external economic penetration is politically differentiated, by the type of imperial power, by the type of client state, and by the form of penetration. Third, the role of client states is viewed in the same way as in the orthodox perspective. Fourth, the creation of client states is not peculiar to capitalist states but may occur in any situation where power is asymmetrical. Fifth, only certain sorts of development, not all, are prevalent in the client state; what F. H. Cardoso has called "associated-dependent development" may occur. This is not an optimal pattern for development, but it is development nonetheless. Sixth, there is no necessary assumption of rationality, coherence, or unified imperial policy.

In fact only two of Domínguez's six points, the third and fifth, are accurate; and one of these, the third, is about similarities instead of differences. Each of the other four points is consistent with Domínguez's own approach but either flatly at odds with unorthodox dependency texts or irrelevant to them. Cardoso has explicitly and repeatedly rejected the idea of analyzing dependency and autonomy in terms of degrees. He makes no "political differentiation" of types of imperial powers and no assumptions or claims either way about the rationality, coherence, or unity of imperial policy; his only claim in this regard is that as a category imperialism is subordinate to capitalism which he regards as coherent in its own terms. Cardoso condemns the idea of defining dependency in terms of power. He insists on framing dependency ideas in the context of Marx's theory of capitalism. He has repeatedly showered contempt and vilification on those—non-Marxists and Marxists alike—who failed to understand these points; he sees such misunderstandings as stemming not only from ignorance but also, in line with the premise of politicized scholarship, from willful misrepresentation for political purposes. Nonetheless, Domínguez claims that the best exponent of his approach is Cardoso.

Domínguez is by no means the only U.S. scholar to attribute his own views to unorthodox dependency. Many others of greatly varying views have also done so. Here is a passage from an article by the sociologist Alejandro Portes (1985, pp. 7–8):

> This article will attempt to "map" the class structure of Latin American societies . . . This formal exercise should help clarify existing class structures by reducing a large and complex list of designations to a manageable number . . . As Brazilian sociologist Fernando Henrique Cardoso (1979) has noted, dissimilarities in Latin American political regimes and other variables should not obscure the fact that all these countries, with the exception of Cuba, are capitalist and occupy a subordinate position in the international economic order. This shared position as dependent capitalist societies is reflected in a series of internal social, cultural, and political characteristics. Class structure is easily one of the most important. Although the proportions of each country's population belonging to different classes vary significantly, the same basic configuration is present everywhere and tends to exhibit a similar historical development.

Again, one sees Cardoso's name being invoked on behalf of views that he has attacked repeatedly.

Bennett and Sharpe (1985, p. 9) claim that unorthodox dependency is the best methodological, conceptual, and theoretical guide to their bargaining study of multinational corporations and the Mexican automobile industry. But unorthodox dependency texts (Cardoso, 1977a; Cardoso and Faletto, 1969, 1979; Palma, 1978) disdain the bargaining approach because it does not address the patterns of internal development, underdevelopment, distortion, and exploitation (social inequality, political authoritarianism, distorted economic development, and the like) that are essential postulates and foci in holistic dependency. The subtitle of Evans's unorthodox dependency study of Brazil is *The ALLIANCE of Multinational, State, and Local Capital in Brazil;* by contrast, the title of Bennett and Sharpe's bargaining study of the Mexican automobile industry is *Transnational Corporations VERSUS the State.* Yet both books claim to be inspired by, and written within the premises of, the unorthodox dependency approach.

In terms of the actual central contents and methods of these two books these contrasting wordings are accurate and appropriate: holistic dependency assumes the alliance of the interests of multinational, state, and local capital; bargaining studies assume conflicts of interest between multinational and state capital. But just for those reasons the title and substantive focus of Bennett and Sharpe's book are much less accurate and appropriate in terms of unorthodox dependency premises, if indeed they fit at all. Bennett and Sharpe put Cardoso and Faletto together with Moran and Tugwell as examples of authors who "use the dependency approach but do begin to focus on state action to alter aspects of dependent development" (pp. 15–16). But putting holistic and bargaining studies together in the same box does far greater violence to the texts of these two approaches than the grouping together of orthodox and unorthodox dependency writings which is so often criticized.

What emerges from these and other examples is that U.S. scholarly consumers attached the label or symbol of unorthodox dependency to almost every imaginable approach. The "associated-dependent development" model—orginally formulated to describe an unacceptable and undesirable form of capitalist development in Brazil—has been invoked to characterize or explain everything from the "miraculous progress" of Taiwanese capitalism (Gold, 1986, pp. vii, passim) to the more mundane and uneven progress of Cuban socialism (Domínguez, 1989, pp. 101, 103). A few authors maintain that unorthodox dependency's epistemology invites "crucial-case tests" or "test cases" of its hypotheses (Gereffi, 1983; Bennett and Sharpe, 1985). Walton (1987, p. 198) praises the "clarity and testability" of dependency theories.

Of course, with its abundant ambiguities and contradictions, unorthodox dependency was well suited to be different things to different scholarly consumers. But that feature alone cannot account for these patterns, and to rely on it alone would be quite misleading. For one thing, many of the claims made about unorthodox dependency—that it has a falsificationist epistemology, or favors analyzing degrees of dependency, or can be considered independent of the Marxist tradition of the analysis of capitalist society, or is oriented toward the use of cross-sectional aggregate data—are at odds with so many dependency texts, as well as the weight and logic of the approach as a whole, that to make the claims without reference to any of the contrary texts is not explicable in scholarly terms alone.

If the multifaceted quality of unorthodox dependency writings were in itself a sufficient explanation for these contradictory interpretations, then at least some of the time the references and citations to the many facets would have been critical. Unorthodox dependency would have been cited as an approach with which commentators disagreed as well as one with which they agreed. In other words, logically the contradictions and ambiguities that scholars seized upon to praise it also left unorthodox dependency vulnerable to criticism. As we have seen, Marxists perceived this and criticized unorthodox dependency much more freely.

However, except for those Marxist critiques—which in any case focused most strongly on orthodox dependency—this logical vulnerability seldom mattered. With rare exceptions the contradictions and ambiguities helped unorthodox dependency but did not hurt it in the eyes of its U.S. consumers. Almost no one criticized unorthodox dependency for the features opposed to the ones they praised; almost everyone just praised the features they liked and ignored the rest. If the desired feature was not there, some still cited unorthodox dependency as support for it anyway. The operational code among U.S. consumers was that diverse readings of unorthodox dependency, accurate or inaccurate, plausible or implausible, were all permissible so long as the reference was positive.

Critical references to unorthodox dependency, by contrast, were discouraged as much as positive ones were encouraged. When unorthodox dependency writings were said, inaccurately, to represent heretical dependency, or a bargaining approach, or falsificationism, or a formal exercise in analyzing the class structure of Latin America, or a methodology for the celebration of capitalist development, and the citation was favorable, then there were few if any complaints. If, however, anyone characterized unorthodox dependency writings in any of those ways and was critical, then the roof fell in. Then complaints were frequent, loud, and harsh. Then commentators had much to say about the holistic, nonfalsificationist, antiformal, anticapitalist features of unorthodox dependency and they skewered interpretations that ignored or minimized them.

What was at work here was a totem/taboo phenomenon. It was permissible to read unorthodox dependency texts almost any way one chose if one praised them; but critical references were quite another matter. What drove the diverse kinds of citations of those texts was not only that they were susceptible of different readings; even more, it was the imperative to identify positively with unorthodox dependency. This imperative virtually eliminated criticism of unorthodox dependency by non-Marxists. Tony Smith wrote (1985a, p. 554) that "no one closely related with developmentalism has demonstrated an ability to do more than thumb his nose ineffectively at the *dependencistas*." By reducing substantive and methodological criticism to the level of personalistic nose-thumbing, and consigning all non-Marxist criticism and critics to the category of leprous "developmentalism," Smith delegitimates criticism even before it starts and thus avoids any issues it might raise.

The most powerful taboo in the U.S. academic culture related to criticism of Cardoso's work. The code was that only others on the left could legitimately criticize it. Criticism of it by non-Marxists was taboo. Violations of this rule rarely occurred. The idea that such criticism could derive from scholarly concerns, rather than from illegitimate political, personal, or ideological concerns, was inadmissible.

This taboo corroded elementary scholarly standards, values, and processes. Frank's first book on dependency was published in 1967. The first edition of Cardoso and Faletto's book was published in 1969. These are facts. They are unambiguous. But they did not fit the melodramatic scenario; they were to be ignored; if they could not be ignored then they had to be neutralized, put "in context," delegitimized. Thus Stern (1988a, p. 836) writes as follows: "The co-authored book of Cardoso and Faletto on dependency and development (first published in 1969 but circulating in mimeographs and oral form since the mid-1960s) and Andre Gunder Frank's study of capitalism and underdevelopment (first published in 1967) are the landmarks to which assessments of dependency perspectives inevitably return." By comparing the year when Frank's book was published to the years when Cardoso and Faletto's book was drafted, without saying anything about the years when Frank drafted his book, Stern is able to maintain the proposition that Cardoso and Faletto got there first. Now, it happens that Frank wrote his manuscript "between 1963 and 1965" (Frank, 1974, p. 89). Yet Stern (1988a, p. 837) claimed that to note that fact and its relevance to the issue of priority, as he did regarding the years when Cardoso and Faletto were writing their draft, was evidence of "tendentious hostility toward Cardoso and Faletto."

The taboo on non-Marxist criticism of unorthodox dependency has been highly effective. Authors who had endorsed unorthodox dependency arguments in the 1970s did not criticize those arguments when they changed their views in the 1980s. The operational code manifestly was: if you cannot praise it, be silent, but do not criticize. Thus Domínguez (1987) wrote an essay comparing theories to realities regarding Latin American politics in the period from about 1960 to the mid-1980s. He explicitly criticized (pp. 81, 91) almost all the theories that were prominent in this period: Lipset's late-1950s/early-1960s version of modernization theory, Frank's 1967 version of orthodox dependency, O'Donnell's early 1970s bureaucratic authoritarianism. But he said nothing about Cardoso's unorthodox dependency. The most influential theoretical perspective of the period, which a decade earlier he said was indispensable, is now ignored. Cardoso's work is not cited and his name is not mentioned. The only mention of an unorthodox dependency work is a passing, favorable, inaccurate reference (p. 69) to Evans's book on Brazil as positing the "autonomy" [*sic*] of the Brazilian state from business and labor.

Other authors who had made luxuriantly positive references to unorthodox dependency writings in earlier times also were silent about them during the period of political liberalization; now they linked dependency ideas to different authors from those cited favorably before (O'Donnell and Schmitter, 1986, pp. 18, 74). Major dependency writers were newly cited as authorities on the dangers of dependency thinking (Collier and Collier, forthcoming, manuscript chapter 8, p. 25). The international environment, seen as a powerful and indispensable part of the explanation when bad things happened, was said to be weak and irrelevant when relatively good things happened (O'Donnell and Schmitter, 1986).

These totem-and-taboo norms and practices set up a lethal crossfire. On the one hand, anyone who criticized the overall dependency perspective without giving detailed attention to unorthodox dependency texts was excoriated for failing to address the most sophisticated writings. On the other hand, anyone who did give detailed attention to unorthodox dependency texts and found it necessary to be critical was accused of being motivated by political or personal concerns (P. O'Brien, 1985, pp. 43–44; T. Smith, 1985a, pp. 540, 554; Biersteker, 1987, pp. 287–288; Stern, 1988a, p. 837). It was a game in which criticism, no matter how accurate or cogent, could not even be considered, let alone be effective. If the critic ignored unorthodox dependency, he was damned; if he addressed it, he was also damned. Unorthodox dependency became a virtually untouchable perspective on Latin American development. It was a no-win situation for any effort at objective scholarly assessment.

The game was played selectively and asymmetrically. Those who used it to assault critics of unorthodox dependency did not inquire whether their own arguments had some of the features they attributed to others. They did not ask, for instance, whether any of the numerous defenses of unorthodox dependency, critiques of modernization theory and orthodox dependency, or attacks on non-Marxist critics of unorthodox dependency might themselves be rooted in political or personal interests analogous to those they said animated work they did not like. To the contrary, not only were ad hominem and politicized attacks permissible when used against critics of the dependency movement, they were morally obligatory. The traditional conventions prohibiting such attacks were invoked to protect dependency proponents but ignored when dependency proponents did the attacking.

All of this inverted (and from his point of view would have debased) the insight of Mannheim on the sociology of knowledge. Mannheim wanted to use the sociology of knowledge as an instrument of enhanced self-awareness and sensitivity, not as a weapon with which to bludgeon one's critics. The idea was to strengthen the community of scholars, not destroy it. In other words, his message was: be self-critical; assume that others are also; do not challenge the motives of critics and scholarly adversaries. Those who treated dependency writings as politics and theatre reversed that formula: assume (and vigorously assert) the worst about the motives of critics and scholarly adversaries; assume that the motives of oneself and one's political allies are above reproach; avoid self-criticism except among political allies. The result was scholarship as aggressive politics and, in its theatrical form, as totem and taboo.

If our argument is correct it follows that the politicizing effects of the dependency movement will have been felt not only on individuals, as suggested in this chapter, but also on scholarly organizations. In the next chapter, we have a chance to test this hypothesis by studying the largest U.S. scholarly organization for the study of Latin America, the Latin American Studies Association (LASA).

11 Politicizing the Academy: The Dependency Movement and LASA

The Latin American Studies Association (LASA) is the major scholarly organization for the study of Latin American affairs in the United States (and the largest such organization in the world). If, as we have argued, the dependency movement has been influential in the United States, it must have influenced LASA as well as individual scholars. Did LASA continue to follow its original classical conception in which scholarly activities are separated, to the extent possible, from political causes and pressures? Or did it move toward the holistic dependency premise of politicized scholarship, in which the fusion of academic work and political struggles is considered to be desirable and necessary?

LASA's Early History

LASA was founded in 1966. By 1984–85 the organization had 2,079 individual members, mainly in the social sciences and the humanities, and 87 institutional memberships. Most members (about 85–90 percent) were from the United States. Like other scholarly associations, LASA has elected and appointed officers, holds periodic scholarly meetings, publishes a scholarly journal and a newsletter, and has various standing and ad hoc committees, task forces, and study groups. (For LASA's constitution and bylaws, committees and task forces, membership, and a list of past officials, see LASA, 1985a; a revised version of the constitution and bylaws is published in LASA, 1988c.)

LASA's "founding fathers" were members of a generation of Latin Americanists who regarded scholarship and politics as separate vocations: scholars such as Richard Adams, John Augelli, Howard Cline, Federico Gil, John Johnson, Richard Morse, and Kalman Silvert. All the organization's first presidents—Silvert, 1966, 1967; Adams, 1968; Augelli, 1969; Johnson, 1970—were drawn from this group. As individuals they had quite varied political outlooks and propensities for political activity, but they agreed on the appropriateness and necessity of the classical separation between scholarly and political enterprises. In their view the main purpose of LASA, ahead of all its other purposes, was "strictly academic": it was to promote scholarship about Latin American affairs through scholarly meetings and publications. In their view LASA was supposed to be open to all points of view held by qualified scholars; it was not supposed to take sides on political questions. (For more on LASA's early history, see Johnson, 1984; Gil, 1985; Safa, 1985. The phrases "founding fathers" and "strictly academic" are from Safa, 1985.)

Although the views of the founders guided LASA in its earliest days, they were not decisive in shaping LASA's identity, institutional features, and informal ethos. Their views were replaced by assumptions that came out of the dependency movement and other changes in American society and culture in the early seventies. Rarely have intellectual innovations, organizational changes, and political trends come together more completely and consistently. The appearance of the first dependency writings in the late sixties coincided precisely with the early years of LASA. Dependency ideas gained momentum just at the moment when virtually every aspect of North American culture, politics and social life was called into question. North American universities and conventional scholarly values were especially vulnerable. Many U.S. academicians, especially in the social sciences and humanities, began to harbor grave doubts about the enterprise in which they were engaged. Students and young faculty, in particular, were shaken, doubting, confused, and eager to find radically new ideas and approaches. Under these circumstances, dependencia ideas gained a breadth and depth and intensity of influence that were extraordinary.

The period from the early sixties to the mid-seventies was also one of great expansion in the numbers of scholars entering Latin American studies. LASA reflected these trends. From its founding in 1966 it grew to include more than two thousand members by the mid-1970s. LASA was a young organization with an unusually young membership. Its officials were also quite youthful compared to those in most scholarly organizations. Between 1966 and 1989, inclusive, more than half of LASA's presidents (Kalman Silvert, Richard Adams, Thomas Skidmore, Paul Doughty, Richard Fagen, Riordan Roett, Carmelo Mesa-Lago, Peter Smith, Jorge Domínguez, Wayne Cornelius, and Paul Drake) were forty-five or younger when they assumed office. (The others were John Augelli, John Johnson, Federico Gil, Henry Landsberger, Evelyn Stevens, William Glade, Helen Safa, Cole Blasier, and Jean Franco.) The first LASA president over sixty (Blasier) came in the 1986–87 term. These ages are unusual for presidents of national or international scholarly organizations. LASA officers below the level of president—elected members of the executive council, appointed members of committees, task forces and study groups—appear on average to be even younger, although complete data are not available. The significance of these demographics is that the appeal of dependency norms was strongest among younger persons trained and socialized into academic life during the late sixties and early seventies (for the names of LASA presidents, see LASA, 1985a, p. xx, and post-1985 issues of the *LASA Forum;* birthdates are given in Hispanic Division, Library of Congress, 1986).

All these changes—in political and cultural context, academic values, demographic characteristics—were about to be reflected in changes in LASA's organizational norms and practices. The overall result would be a classic case of "punctuated equilibrium": ideas and practices implanted at a crucial turning point would live on over a long period of time and affect structures and behaviors to a far greater extent than they could have under more settled historical-structural conditions. After its response to this "critical juncture," LASA would emerge as an organization that incorporated norms and practices significantly at odds with conventional scholarly norms and practices. (The term "punctuated equilibrium" is from Krasner, 1984. An earlier version of it is the notion of "fragment" cultures in Hartz et al, 1964. A valuable, comprehensive, well-documented review of the literature on this idea under the rubric "critical juncture" is in Collier and Collier, forthcoming.) LASA was not unique in going through politicizing experiences; in varying degrees and ways many scholarly societies in the social sciences and humanities had experienced them. However, whereas most of these organizations, especially in the disciplines (economics, history, political science), emerged with their commitment to conventional scholarly values and processes still intact, others moved toward other norms and practices that were more critical of the traditional ones. LASA was in the latter group.

A major turning point for LASA seems to have been the second national meeting in Washington, D.C., on April 16–18, 1970. According to participants, the business meeting and some of the panels were emotional, raucous, and politicized. For those who did not agree with the majority views, an atmosphere of intimidation and threat prevailed. The founding generation of LASA leaders and the classical idea of the separation of scholarship and political struggle were vilified. During the business meeting and at some of the panels persons in the audience came forward, surrounded presenters as they spoke, and shouted epithets. A distinguished historian, the late Howard Cline, was shouted down when he tried to argue that Cuba was authoritarian. After these events, attendance at national meetings and other forms of participation in LASA activities by senior members of the field, who already were a small and ever-declining proportion of it, fell off even more sharply.

The eroding away of conventional academic norms and practices continued in the seventies. A significant event in this process was a conference on inter-American relations in Lima in 1972 (Cotler and Fagen, 1974a). Sponsored by the Joint Committee on Latin American Studies of the Social Science Research Council and the American Council of Learned Societies, the conference highlighted much that would be institutionalized in Latin American studies, and especially LASA, in the 1970s. As the organizers and editors of the conference volume noted, most of the participants "subscribe[d] to a *dependencia* paradigm in one of its many variations." While some of the papers were "quite close to 'conventional' scholarly analyses . . . others [were] more polemical." Much of the conference ("the dominant tone") was given over to critical assaults on traditional notions of academic community, social science cumulation, and insulating scholarship from politics. Considerable stress was placed on "the dangers that inhere in much North American empirical research on Latin America." What made it "dangerous" was "the imbalances in power and malevolence of purpose" between the United States and Latin America. Instead of conventional scholarship, what was needed was "struggle" to create new types of social science work and organizational forms (Cotler and Fagen, 1974b, pp. 14–16).

In more specific scholarly and institutional terms this meant "a critical, anti-status-quo social science" and social science organizations linked "more directly to social action" than in the past (Cotler and Fagen, 1974b, pp. 15–16). One of the organizers of the Lima meeting urged the adoption of a "progressive" agenda for U.S. scholars: "given the immense . . . power of the United States, and the historic misuse of that power, there is a clear responsibility to participate in what might be called 'documented denunciation'—essentially muckraking and informational activity, often less than scholarly by conventional definitions, but absolutely vital if the worst excesses of the exercise of North American power, whether perpetrated by the Marines or by the multinationals, are to be held in check. It is an activity for which North Americans with academic and intellectual pretensions are particularly well suited and well situated" (Fagen, 1974, pp. 263–264).

The philosophy that dominated the Lima conference soon found institutional expression in LASA. Fagen was shortly thereafter elected president of LASA. In his end-of-term remarks he commented on what had been accomplished during his presidential year: "Perhaps most importantly—and most controversially—I think we have demonstrated that serious Association concern for public issues (Latin American academic refugees, U.S. newsreporting on Latin America, immigration and visa questions, U.S. policy toward repressive regimes) is not incompatible with our scholarly pursuits. In fact, I would hope that we have gone a step further and demonstrated at least to some that our scholarly interests and our concerns as citizens of the Americas are intimately related—and properly so" (1976).

As it turned out, his statement could have been even stronger. LASA has been even more politicized than Fagen's account suggested. A decade later, LASA's President Helen Safa wrote as follows (1985) in her own end-of-term remarks:

Some see [LASA] as a purely academic organization, designed to bring together scholarship on Latin America through our congresses and publications. Certainly, this is a central function of LASA, and was probably the central function of the founding members of the association . . . At the same time, however, some members of LASA feel that we need to take a more activist position regarding events in Latin America. They feel we should not simply study events and issues in Latin America, but attempt to assist and participate in the process of social change . . . My LASA presidency has clearly been activist rather than purely academic . . . I am prepared to defend this policy against charges of partisanship and politicalization [*sic*]. As an academic, I have always felt committed to speaking out on issues of concern to me, particularly where I felt I had some special expertise. As president of LASA, I felt this need even more deeply, because of the visibility and respect the association enjoys in most Latin American scholarly circles, both in the United States and abroad. If we wish to continue to earn this respect, especially in Latin America, we must support the principle of self-determination and return to civilian democracy in all the countries of our hemisphere . . . I am confident that my successors in the LASA presidency will uphold these standards as fervently as I do.

President Safa's confidence was well-placed. Not only did her successor as president, Wayne Cornelius, head the official LASA delegation to study the Nicaraguan election of 1984 (see below), but, more important, by the last half of the eighties the question whether LASA was "activist" rather than "purely academic" had long since been settled. The answer did not depend, as Safa supposed it might, on which persons occupied LASA offices. Although different individuals have had different views, the organization rejected the purely academic concept. The activist concept became firmly ingrained in LASA's culture, practices, and structures, no matter who its officers were. LASA's institutional premises about scholarship and politics were now closer to those of holistic dependency than to the conventions that have historically underlain the idea of the university and the academic community in the West.

The new equilibrium that emerged in LASA in the late sixties and early seventies, and that has been firmly embedded in the life of the organization ever since, can be seen in three main types of activities: resolutions, panels, and task-force and committee reports.

Resolutions

At least since 1970, LASA national and international meetings have been occasions, in the business meeting, to pass resolutions on "matters of public concern," which in practice has mainly meant political questions. Since 1973, about seven resolutions have been passed on average at each meeting (see Table 11.1). In 1979 the process by which these resolutions were considered and adopted was described as follows: "The motions tend to be hastily prepared. Often they are internally contradictory, flawed in drafting, and even ungrammatical . . . Rarely does informed and illuminating debate take place" (Lowenthal and Jaquette, 1979). Subsequently, a few reforms were made in this process. Some resolutions are now considered before the business meeting; all are reviewed by the executive council; if they pass the business meeting and the executive council all are now

Table 11.1 Resolutions passed at LASA national meetings, 1973–1988

National meeting	Number of resolutions	LASA Newsletter or *Forum*
4th, Madison, May 1973	6	5:1 (March 1974), pp. 9–12; 6:1 (March 1975), p. 30
5th, San Francisco, November 1974	—	No report made
6th, Atlanta, March 1976	9	7:2 (June 1976), pp. 6–10
7th, Houston, November 1977	9	8:4 (December 1977), pp. 9–12
8th, Pittsburg, April 1979	9	10:2 (June 1979), pp. 7–9
9th, Bloomington, October 1980	2	11:4 (December 1980), pp. 2–3
10th, Washington, March 1982	4	13:1 (Spring 1982), pp. 41–45; 13:2 (Summer 1982), p. 1
11th, Mexico City, September 1983	9	14:4 (Winter 1984), pp. 2–4; 15:1 (Spring 1984), pp. 3–4
12th, Albuquerque, April 1985	13	16:2 (Summer 1985), pp. 3–5
13th, Boston, October 1986	5	17:4 (Winter 1987), pp. 24–26
14th, New Orleans, March 1988	7	19:1 (Spring 1988), pp. 12–15; 19:2 (Summer 1988), p. 10
Total	73	

Source: Newsletters of LASA (originally called *LASA Newsletter*, later called *LASA Forum*). Specific issues are given in column three above. It was not possible to find sources (if any exist) for resolutions passed (if any) at the first three national meetings. If, as seems likely, resolutions were passed at the 5th national meeting, they were not reported in any issue of the *LASA Newsletter*.

submitted to mail ballots of the LASA membership. A very few resolutions passed in the business meeting have been rejected by the council. However, no resolution passed by the business meeting and the council has ever been rejected by the membership as a whole. Most important, the tradition of politicized resolutions remains. It is inviolable no matter what the preferences of individual LASA members and officers might be; in fact, there has been relatively little demand within LASA to change it. For instance, the executive director of LASA notes that "Of the more than 1,000 LASA members who mailed in ballots [following the thirteenth meeting in Boston in 1986], only 11 members wrote in comments critical of the resolutions and/or of LASA's activist role" (Reading, 1987, p. 13n).

A few resolutions have been on matters of interest strictly to scholars, but the vast majority have concerned political questions in the United States and Latin America (see Table 11.2). The distinction between topics affecting scholars as scholars and political topics in the broadest senses is ignored. The most difficult empirical, ethical, and theoretical questions are treated as political issues to be resolved by majority vote. Votes are typically overwhelming. At the twelfth meeting in Albuquerque, for example, 13 motions were presented at the business meeting. Seven were passed unanimously; of the other six, none had more than two dissenting votes. Mail ballots produce slightly less overwhelming but still very strong majorities. In mail balloting a three to one majority would be a very close vote that happens infrequently. More typical are votes of 455 to 27, 442 to 43, and so on. For example, in the mail ballots that ratified the votes taken during the 1988 LASA meeting in New Orleans, the most hotly contested issue, regarding the Latin American debt, had a vote of 436 affirmative, 44 negative, and 32 abstentions (LASA, 1988b).

This breakdown of the distinction between the academic and political enterprises is a clear and serious manifestation of the politicization of LASA. As Lowenthal and Jaquette (1979) put it, in a praiseworthy but rare instance of public protest within LASA against this tradition, "collective violation of professional norms in pursuit of other aims, however laudable, cannot be positive." Such violations of the integrity of scholarship are always wrong, even if they come from a wide variety of political and ideological orientations.

In LASA, however, the violations do not come from a wide variety of perspectives. They come from a clearly delimited range of "permissible" perspectives. This range is seen in Table 11.2. Criticisms

Table 11.2 Types of resolutions passed at LASA national meetings, 1973–1988

Type of resolution	N
Criticisms of U.S. policies in Latin America (35)	
Regarding Cuba	7
Regarding Nicaragua (Sandinistas)	6
Regarding visa policies	4
Regarding Guatemala	3
Regarding Central America, Chile, El Salvador, Latin American policies generally, and various individuals (2 each)	10
Regarding refugee policy, Puerto Rico, Mexican border policy, Haiti, and amnesty (1 each)	5
Criticisms of Latin American governments (27)	
Chile (post–1973)	6
Guatemala	4
Brazil	4
Paraguay	3
Argentina, Peru (2 each)	4
El Salvador, Latin America (in general), Nicaragua (Somoza), Uruguay, Haiti, Colombia (1 each)	6
Academic issues (some mixed with human rights issues)	7
Miscellaneous (U.S. press coverage of Latin America, Women's Coalition of Latin Americanists, Latin American Studies at California State University-Los Angeles, Equal Rights Amendment, Simpson-Mazzoli Bill)	5
Propose alternative U.S. policies (debt, Central America, Cuba)	3
Pro-U.S. policy (Panama Canal treaties)	1
Total	78

Source: Same as Table 11.1. Total (78) is higher than in Table 11.1 (73) because a few resolutions (5) dealt about equally with more than one topic and thus were counted in more than one category.

are made of the United States but never of any other major power; of repression and exploitation in capitalist countries of Latin America but never in any socialist country of Latin America or anywhere else; of "violations of freedom of the press" in Paraguay and of academic freedom in Guatemala and El Salvador, all capitalist countries, but never of violations of freedom of the press or academic freedom in socialist Cuba, where the violations are even more serious. Cuba, and Nicaragua under the Sandinistas, are explicitly supported and never criticized. Capitalist authoritarian regimes are frequently criticized; communist and socialist regimes are never criticized. Over a period of two decades LASA has passed dozens of resolutions critical of capitalist countries and their policies; it has never passed a single resolution critical of any communist or socialist country or policy.

Further, the theatricalization of scholarship at the individual level that we saw in Chapter 10 also occurs in LASA. There is little evidence that LASA's politicized resolutions have the desired effects in Washington. Not even LASA itself has taken them very seriously except as cathartic or ritualistic kinds of activities (which, of course, have serious consequences of their own). In 1983, when a LASA committee attempted to obtain a compilation of the resolutions and motions that had been approved by LASA since its founding, it was advised by the Executive Director that no such collection existed. It turned out that the records contained only the resolutions that had been passed since 1981, when the Secretariat moved from the University of Illinois to the University of Texas, Austin (LASA Report, 1984, p. 9). Astonishingly, although LASA had for many years justified politicized resolutions on the grounds that the policy, ethical, and humane benefits outweighed the serious costs to conventional scholarly principles, not even LASA itself took the resolutions seriously enough to keep a working record of them.

In summary, LASA's resolutions are profoundly and overwhelmingly politicized. This politicization manifests the holistic dependency premise of politicized scholarship and rejects the Weberian premise of scholarship and politics as separable vocations. The substantive content of the politicized LASA resolutions is in all respects consistent with the main substantive claims of holistic dependency. In fusing scholarship and politics, LASA resolutions also fuse scholarship and theatre.

Panels

Politicization its also apparent in LASA's panels. The breakdown of conventional academic norms has taken a variety of forms. One of these is the low incidence of written papers, which in turn is related to the panels' politicization. For example, LASA's panels as of 1982 are described as follows: "Papers prepared and written in advance are the exception rather than the rule. There is often no intention of ever writing a paper, even though nothing in the program suggests that this is a discussion workshop rather than a regular panel. The oral presentation of remarks is, at times, little more than a polemical diatribe without the presentation of reasoned argumentation or empirical evidence. Panel commentators, who have received no paper in advance, often have no option but to join in the unfocused and unprofessional expression of opinion" (Domínguez, 1982, p. 2). Although this description may not necessarily be his own, it seems clear from Domínguez's phraseology and subsequent remarks (p. 3) that he believes it to be accurate.

Efforts to change the pattern of oral presentations without written papers have had limited success. At the 12th meeting in 1985 there was an "extensive" effort to correct the situation but still "more than half" the papers were not provided. According to the chairman of the program committee (Mitchell, 1985, p. 13), "It seems doubtful that all the explanation can lie in college budget cutbacks for duplication, since disciplinary meetings like that of the American Political Science Association routinely receive almost every paper programmed."

An even more direct mode of politicization of LASA panels and debates is blatantly intolerant, disruptive, uncivil behavior toward speakers who present views that lie outside the boundaries of LASA orthodoxies. This mode has a long history in LASA. The events of the second national meeting in Washington in April 1970 have already been described. During the sixth national meeting in Atlanta in 1976, the program committee surveyed participants about their reactions to the proceedings. Twenty percent of the respondents criticized chairpersons of panels for "not stopping personal attacks on panelists by other panelists as well as by members of the audience." Sixteen percent of the respondents also criticized the presentations for being "polemical, biased, and given to attacking strawmen" and for the "lack of courtesy and offensiveness of some panelists toward other panelists and the audience" (LASA, 1976, pp. 27–28).

At the ninth meeting in Bloomington in 1980 one of the main events was the plenary session on Nicaragua. An invited speaker was James Cheek, then Deputy Assistant Secretary of State for Inter-American Affairs. His appearance and remarks induced a continuing, widespread barrage of hostile screams, shouts, and insults. As Domínguez (1982, p. 3) noted later, it was scandalous behavior for any group, let alone a scholarly organization. Speakers who happened to agree with U.S. government policies tended not to be heard in LASA in any case; when they did appear they ran the risk of this kind of reception. The Cheek episode occurred during the presidency of Jimmy Carter. LASA's hostility to views that could be associated with the administrations of Lyndon Johnson, Richard Nixon, Gerald Ford, Ronald Reagan, or George Bush was greater still.

The counterpart of uncivil, intolerant behavior toward unpopular views is uncritical, sloganistic, and emotional behavior in support of views that are popular within LASA. This too has been widespread. Very rarely it has been criticized by LASA members or officials. Mostly it has been tolerated and even praised as one of the appeals and strengths of the organization. For example, at the seventh meeting in Houston in 1977, held jointly with the African Studies Association, the best attended session—more than a thousand persons—was the plenary on "Marxist Perspectives on the Political Economy of Africa and Latin America." The four speakers were all Marxists. Three of them said not one word about socialism after the revolution; they talked exclusively about capitalism and its evils. Their remarks were met with resounding applause. In the question period one brave soul asked the Cuban speaker, Oscar Pino Santos, to define socialism. He replied, "We do not have to define socialism; we know what it is." This produced even louder and more prolonged applause. The fourth speaker was the only one to speak of socialism after the revolution. He made a thoughtful case for liberty as an indispensable criterion of development under socialism. His remarks elicited some support (but nothing like the others) and also some open hostility. For what appears to have been a very small minority the session created a deep sense of unease because of its emotionalism, theatricality, and pressures for conformity. For what appears to have been the overwhelming majority the session was very satisfying because it was "marked by provocative presentations, spirited discussion among panelists and members of the audience, and a general sense of intellectual excitement and community which is all too rare at professional meetings of any type" (Cornelius, 1978, p. 10).

Even the minority that criticizes LASA's politicization tends to qualify the criticisms excessively and minimize their importance. Thus it has been said that polemics, diatribes, and other "grossly unprofessional" activities are ideologically symmetrical within LASA: "Yes, it is true that [such activity] can happen at LASA meetings among 'leftists' but I have witnessed it among 'rightists' at LASA meetings, too" (Domínguez, 1982, p. 3). This verbal pairing—it "can happen" among leftists, but "I have witnessed it" among rightists—implies an asymmetry exactly opposite to the one that in fact occurs. Certainly the ideological parameters of LASA are far more "leftist" than "rightist"; obviously the breakdown of academic culture expresses itself much, much more in the former terms than the latter.

The atmosphere in LASA is hardly one that welcomes "open opposition" to resolutions and to the politicized premises and affirmations of the organization. Nor is it accurate to say that "there is no reason to remain silent" (Domínguez, 1982, p. 4). Many practices and traditions within LASA reward conformity and silence rather than dissent. Members who see what happens to U.S. government officials—who are, after all, morally and legally obliged to defend unpopular views when they are invited to speak at LASA meetings— do not have to be told what would happen to them if they voluntarily voiced unpopular views. Members of LASA who hold unpopular views can be "reluctant publicly to criticize progressive movements illegitimately threatened by U.S. might" (Levy, 1986, p. 26n). The politicized atmosphere also has implications for other aspects of Latin American studies such as scholarly recruitment and promotion. To the extent that senior evaluators regard the politicization of scholarship as a moral duty, junior scholars who agree have unfair advantages over those who disagree, and the latter are vulnerable to terrible pressures. The opportunity costs of all this—potential contributors to knowledge who decide not to enter Latin American studies because of its politicization—are not precisely calculable but should not be ignored and might be quite high.

It is important to establish these last two points about asymmetry and atmosphere because they relate to other aspects of the politicized character of LASA, visible in the activities of LASA task forces and ad hoc committees.

Task Forces and Ad Hoc Committees

Important LASA activities are carried on by task forces and ad hoc committees. Authorized by LASA's by-laws, these groups have their charges, membership, and duration established by the executive council. Ad hoc committees are relatively few in number and appear, as their designation suggests, from time to time in response to specific needs: for example, the Ad Hoc Committee to Investigate the Publication of a CIA Employment Advertisement in the *LASA Forum*

(LASA Report, 1984). More numerous are the task forces. In 1988, for example, LASA listed six task forces. Their areas of concern were: academic freedom/human rights, the media, Spain, Cuba, Nicaragua, and the USSR (LASA, 1988a).

From time to time LASA's committees and task forces issue reports (LASA Report, 1984, 1985, 1986; Safa, Valdés, and Sinkin, 1984; Schoultz, 1985; Jaksic, 1985; Whiting, 1986; Diskin et al., 1986). These reports vary in length, depth, and quality. Some are commendable in scholarly terms. Others are politicized. In general they show great concern about repression and injustice under capitalism but, with rare exceptions, indifference to or support for repression and injustice under socialism. This asymmetry goes to the heart of LASA's refusal as an organization to address certain important theoretical, ethical, and political questions in a nonpartisan, scholarly fashion.

An important example of this refusal is the standard LASA has applied to Cuba. Nowhere in Latin America are restrictions on freedom of the press and academic freedom as great as in Cuba. By the standards that LASA routinely uses to assess capitalist countries, Cuba ought logically to be one of the countries most criticized by LASA task forces. Yet there is very little of this. Very infrequently LASA task force reports have mentioned the abuse of human rights in Cuba (for example, Whiting, 1986, p. 33). But these instances are rare, and LASA does not make much of them or of abuses in other communist or socialist countries. Indeed, far from criticizing and condemning such violations, as they do when they occur in capitalist countries, LASA's task forces in effect encourage and legitimate the abuses and their perpetrators through formal agreements, exchanges with Cuban academic organizations, and promotion of positive relations with the Cuban scholarly community and government (Safa, Valdés, and Sinkin, 1984; Whiting, 1986; LASA Report, 1986).

In 1976 LASA passed a resolution stating that U.S. organizations should "take all necessary steps to dissociate themselves from any actions and relationships with countries in which it is evident that massive and systematic violations of academic freedom have occurred in order that such actions and relationships might not appear to condone these violations" (LASA Resolution, 1976). LASA has honored this resolution in the case of capitalist countries but ignored it in its dealings with socialist and communist countries. Indeed, "actions and relationships" with such countries are encouraged.

The politicization of LASA's task forces and committees can best be seen by examining the report on the Nicaraguan election of 1984.

Report on the Nicaraguan Election of 1984

On August 15, 1984, the Supreme Electoral Council of Nicaragua invited LASA to observe the electoral campaign and general election to be held on November 4 of that year. In mid-September the LASA executive council accepted the invitation. It asked the co-chairs of the LASA Task Force on Scholarly Relations with Nicaragua, Richard Fagen and Thomas Walker, to "make preparations and assemble a delegation." The official LASA delegation had fifteen members: eight political scientists, two economists, two anthropologists, and one each from history, Latin American studies, and sociology. The delegation head and spokesperson was Professor Wayne Cornelius, Political Science, University of California, San Diego, who also was president-elect of LASA. Professors Michael Conroy, Economics, University of Texas, Austin, and Thomas Walker, Political Science, Ohio University, Athens, were coordinators. (The names, disciplines, and universities of the other members are given in the report.) The delegation arrived in Managua on October 28 and departed on November 5. Its report was officially published on November 19, 1984 (Cornelius, 1986a, p. 23n), and distributed to all LASA members early in 1985 (LASA Report, 1985).

The report on the Nicaraguan election that gave victory to President Daniel Ortega is by a wide margin the best known task force report in LASA's history. It has been reprinted, used widely as a text in college and university classes, and discussed publicly by prominent government officials in Nicaragua and the United States. LASA presidents since 1984 have singled it out for laudatory comment. For these reasons, and because it raises directly the questions about politicized scholarship that are central in this book, we examine it in detail here.

Substantive Conclusions

The main substantive conclusions of the report are three. First, the election "by Latin American standards was a model of probity and fairness (at least to all candidates who chose to register and submit themselves to a popular test)" (LASA Report, 1985, p. 40). Second, the election was not manipulated by the Sandinistas but was manipulated by the United States. As the report put it (p. 39): "Clearly, the Nicaraguan electoral process in 1984 was manipulated, as the U.S. Government has so often charged. However, the manipulation was not the work of the Sandinistas—who had every interest in making these elections as demonstrably fair, pluralistic, and competitive as possible—but of the Reagan administration, whose interest apparently was in making the elections seem as unfair, ideologically one-sided, and uncompetitive as possible."

Third, the main constraints on the democratic process came not from the Sandinistas but from the United States. This third conclusion is summarized in the final passage (p. 42) of the report: "We submit . . . that the future of freedom and democracy in Nicaragua rests primarily in the hands of the United States. As it has been almost continuously since 1909, the United States remains the principal maker of Nicaragua's political options. Our fact-finding mission leads us to believe that if the pressures of a war economy and war psychology are relieved, there is a good chance that political liberalization will proceed. Despite U.S. interference, the elections of November 4, 1984, were an impressive beginning." In other words, the report concludes that if Nicaragua does not become a political democracy, the United States will be responsible; if it does become a political democracy, the Sandinista regime will be responsible. The United States, which is given a great deal of attention in the report, is seen almost entirely as a force for repression, destruction, and injustice. Cuba, the Soviet Union, and other communist countries with close ties to the Sandinista regime are scarcely mentioned. Antidemocratic forces within Nicaragua are interpreted almost exclusively as legacies of the pre-Sandinista past. Authoritarian and totalitarian features of Sandinismo are mentioned infrequently, and the weight and significance of such features are always minimized.

Thus at the substantive level the report is an almost-perfect holistic dependency interpretation of the Nicaraguan polity. In other words, if one were to imagine an ideal-type dependency way of characterizing the 1984 election and analyzing the Sandinista polity, it would would look very much like this report. The only obvious difference between the actual report and a hypothetical ideal-type holistic dependency report is the presumption in the former that autonomy from the United States in Nicaragua would produce political liberalization rather than a socialist polity as required by holistic dependency.

A number of questions have been raised about these conclusions, the adequacy of the evidence on which they are based, the degree to which alternative explanations were considered, and other matters (Levy, 1985, 1986; Fretz, 1985; Reilly, 1985; Becker, 1986; responses are given in Cornelius, 1986a, 1986b, 1988). For example, Levy, a political scientist, raised important questions about the mode of presentation, methodology, consideration of alternative explanations, and balance and fairness of the report. Fretz, the U.S. Consul General in Managua, said that the report "borders on being a fairy tale. There is no wrong which the Sandinistas have committed for which your group was unable to find an excuse." A social scientist might question the standards of falsification used by the LASA delegation. Nothing that happened before, during, or after the election had any negative impact on the conviction expressed repeatedly by the delegation that the Sandinistas were deeply committed to liberal political institutions. The question arises whether any conceivable evidence could have altered the delegation's conviction. The LASA report on Nicaragua appears to fit some of the patterns described and analyzed in the work of Hollander (1981, 1988) on the impressions of other Western intellectual travelers to countries with similar regimes.

The foregoing substantive and epistemological questions are interesting, legitimate, and important, but we need not go into them further here. Our concern is politicization. Although a case could reasonably be made that the report's substantive conclusions about Nicaragua are politicized, that is not the sort of argument we wish to make. By themselves, substantive conclusions do not necessarily indicate politization. The features of the report most relevant for present purposes are the manifestations of politicization within the report itself and the organizational context in which it was written.

Evidence of Politicization

LASA's and the delegation's own statements, their own structuring of the task, and their own standards and procedures show that the task force report was politicized not only in the eyes of its critics but *in its own terms.*

Prereport resolutions. When the delegation was formed and its charge was issued, LASA had already passed resolutions in support of the Sandinistas and against opposition groups and their claims. For example, a resolution passed at the 11th meeting in 1983 stated that the Sandinistas were "representatives of the people of Nicaragua"; it opposed U.S. aid to the Contras "and other anti-Sandinista forces" (LASA Resolution, 1984). Related resolutions were passed at the eighth and tenth national meetings (see Table 11.1). The issue of whether or not the Sandinistas were a popularly based government had already been decided—officially, repeatedly, and unambiguously—by LASA. For the delegation to have reached a conclusion seriously critical of the Sandinista handling of the 1984 election would have been to contradict LASA's own established policy. This was extremely unlikely if not impossible. At the very least it profoundly conditioned the context for the delegation's activities.

This point is even stronger if one uses the criterion the delegation used for assessing whether observers of the elections had prejudged it. According to delegation head Wayne Cornelius, the principal drafter of the report and the group's spokesperson, "U.S. editorial opinion on the Nicaraguan elections had been set before the first ballot was cast, and our findings were unwelcome in most editorial boardrooms" (Cornelius, 1986a, p. 26). Cornelius's generalization is asserted without evidence. It is unclear whether it is accurate or not. By contrast, if one applies his standard to LASA—had LASA's official and unofficial "editorial opinion" on Nicaragua been "set" before the ballots were cast and before the delegation went to Nicaragua?— the answer is clear. It can be determined not by subjective impression but concretely from official LASA resolutions.

Framing the report. The delegation itself explicitly framed the Nicaragua report as a political document: "any deliberate effort to write a consistently 'pro- ' or 'anti-Sandinista' report on the 1984 elections would have torn the LASA delegation apart and prevented us from issuing a unanimously-agreed-upon report. This was an ideologically diverse delegation consisting of strongly independent-minded scholars. Half of the members were not Nicaraguan specialists, and had no vested professional interests to defend" (Cornelius, 1986a, pp. 22–23). If half the delegation had no "vested interests" to defend, then by that standard the other half of the delegation, and all of the members of the task force on Nicaragua who appointed the delegation, did have vested interests to defend. Once one uses this political criterion of vested interests, moreover, other things necessarily follow. For instance, by this standard specialists on neighboring countries whose scholarly communities and governments took an anti-Sandinista or a pro-Sandinista position also had a vested interest in doing the same.

The delegation put an extremely high priority on the objective of an "unanimously-agreed-upon" report. This objective is not a scientific criterion; it is a political criterion. This political objective was manifestly considered much more important than communicating publicly any scholarly diversity of opinion that may have existed within the delegation about the election and its meaning. The political objective of total unanimity within the delegation has been completely achieved; remarkably, at least so far as the public written record is concerned, every member agreed with every sentence of the report and with all of the responses by delegation-head Cornelius to the published commentaries on it.

The comments quoted earlier also imply a political or ideological symmetry in the potential for the delegation to be "torn apart" if it were to write either a pro-Sandinista or an anti-Sandinista report. This implication is misleading. On the one hand, a consistently and deliberately anti-Sandinista report was unthinkable in the LASA context. LASA's history, official resolutions, and informal culture made any kind of anti-Sandinista report, whether "consistent and deliberate" or not, hard to imagine. Any anti-Sandinista report would assuredly have created an explosion within the delegation and LASA. LASA's normal mechanism for investigating incorrect behavior, an ad hoc commission, would almost certainly have been named to see what happened. On the other hand, the LASA report that was in fact issued was about as favorable to the Sandinistas as one can conceive a report to be, and it manifestly did not tear the delegation apart. Quite the contrary, it had total unanimity.

In assessing the impact and "accomplishments" of the publication of the report, delegation-head Cornelius (1986a, p. 26) explicitly included as a criterion the degree to which it might have helped congressional opponents of President Reagan. When the *LASA Forum* published responses to the report, it framed the discussion explicitly in political rather than academic terms. For example, the introduction to those responses said that the report "has generated many responses from the entire length of the political spectrum" (LASA, 1985b, p. 8). A scholarly framing would have said something like, "The report generated responses from the entire length of the spectrum of theoretical and methodological perspectives on revolutionary regimes, national-international linkages, electoral behavior, and the like." But there was none of this.

Origin of the report. The report was not the fruit of a scholarly research program but of a political initiative taken by the Supreme Electoral Council of Nicaragua, "the fourth branch of the Government of National Reconstruction," which issued the invitation to LASA to observe the electoral campaign and general election. It issued similar invitations to various other organizations—of the sort characterized by Cornelius as "advocacy groups"—which also accepted them; but so far as is known LASA is the only scholarly society invited to send observers or that did send them. This was the first time in LASA's history that an official LASA delegation was sent to observe an election in Latin America. LASA's executive council accepted the invitation, the report says, because of "the unusual international circumstances surrounding this particular election, and the paucity of information from academic (rather than journalistic and governmental) sources concerning these matters" (LASA Report, 1985, p. 9).

What these unusual circumstances were is not stated explicitly. The Salvadoran elections of 1982 and 1983, for example, would seem to have been equally compelling ones to study by the criteria of "unusual international circumstances" and "paucity of information." Moreover, in the Salvadoran case the prospects for pluralism, while very uncertain and precarious, nevertheless appear to have been no less promising than the prospects, which the report evaluates so positively absent the influence of the United States, for pluralism in Nicaragua. Yet the Salvadoran elections were not studied. In contrast to its attitude toward Nicaragua, LASA has several times taken a critical attitude in its resolutions and other activities toward the Salvadoran political system (resolutions at 10th, 11th, and 12th LASA national and international meetings cited in Table 11.1).

Normal scholarly standards? In the report and articles by Cornelius the claim is made repeatedly that normal scholarly standards were fully observed in preparing the study (LASA Report, 1985, p. 9; Cornelius, 1986a, pp. 22–24, and 1986b). This claim is untenable. It is flatly at odds with facts that Cornelius himself emphasizes when justifying omissions in the report but ignores when claiming that no scholarly standards were compromised. For example, Cornelius (1986a, p. 24) says that "optimally" the delegation would have given more space to the consideration of "alternative explanations . . . But that would have required significantly more time than we had at our disposal . . . It must be recalled that the report was written, edited, typeset, and published within two weeks of the delegation's return to the United States. This production schedule . . . mandated both by our charge from the Executive Council and by the emergency situation that prevailed in the two weeks following the elections . . . left little time for the kind of textual elaboration that Levy—as well as our delegation—might have preferred."

These were truly severe constraints, and they are not the only ones under which the LASA group labored. Given them, the report is a considerable achievement of a certain kind. But it is still very far indeed from adhering to the highest scholarly standards or even normal scholarly procedures. In particular, anonymous peer review—a fundamental requirement of standard scholarship—was not used. So far as one can tell, it was never contemplated. The article was published without it, although Cornelius (1986a, p. 25) reports that there was extensive consultation ("more than 500 changes") within the delegation during the two weeks the report was being written, edited, typeset, and published in the United States. The authors of the report justified the omission of anonymous peer review by refering to the LASA mandate and the production schedule. These constraints flowed entirely from policy considerations. In no sense did they reflect scholarly concerns; these would have constrained the authors in the opposite direction, that is, toward a less frantic publication schedule and a more scholarly report.

The authors make no attempt to set the report in the context of any body of scholarly literature—on elections, revolutions, regime types, national-international linkages in Latin American development, U.S.-Latin American relations, and so on. No references to such literatures are made in the conclusions to the report or the replies by Cornelius to comments on it published later in the *LASA Forum*. Rather, throughout the report and the published defenses of it the central points of reference for the discussion are official U.S. government and journalistic interpretations of events in Nicaragua and their alleged inadequacies and distortions. The "hypotheses" examined and tested are not those of other scholars but those of the Reagan administration (versus, implicitly, those of the Sandinistas). In general, the report and the commentaries engage in debates and polemics at that level rather than scholarly debates and polemics in the context of scholarly literatures. This pattern continued after the report itself was published. For example, most of Cornelius (1988) is devoted to reprinting in the *LASA Forum* a piece of "investigative journalism" from *The Nation* that agrees with the report.

The delegation claimed that "There are numerous advocacy groups, not constrained by the usual standards of evidence and inference, that can and do report on critical elections in Latin America. The role that LASA can potentially play in illuminating such events is qualitatively different" (Cornelius, 1986b). However, except for the fact that its authors were academics, the LASA report on Nicaragua is not distinguishable—is not "qualitatively different"—from the sort of policy-relevant, applied research done by the "numerous advocacy groups" to which Cornelius refers.

Selective and inaccurate use of advocacy-group and journalistic sources. Although the delegation report and Cornelius repeatedly claim that the LASA study was necessary as an alternative to non-scholarly sources of information, Cornelius (1986a, pp. 25–26n) nonetheless cites several nonscholarly studies—by advocacy groups—as sources of "corroborating" evidence. But if other studies were done and are now cited as corroborating evidence, why was the LASA study necessary in the first place, as the report contended so strongly in its justification of the Nicaragua mission? Some of the studies cited as corroborating evidence were done by advocacy groups and applied research organizations—the Washington Office on Latin America, the International Human Rights Law Group, the Institute for Food and Development Policy. If such studies were irrelevant because they are "not constrained by the usual standards of evidence and inference," as Cornelius asserts, why did they cite them as corroborating evidence? On the other hand, if they were relevant, then why did the report ignore or disdain studies in similar genres and genres even closer to scholarly ones that come to conclusions at odds with those of the delegation—such as, for example, Shirley Christian's *Nicaragua: Revolution in the Family* (1985) or David Nolan's *The Ideology of the Sandinistas and the Nicaraguan Revolution* (1984), respectively?

Christian's book was not available when the report was written, but Nolan's was. In his post-report comments Cornelius (1986a, p. 28) again ignored Nolan's monograph but referred to Christian's book critically as an example of a narrow, unicausal explanation of Sandinista behavior in terms of "rigid ideological preconceptions." In the report, however, Cornelius and his colleagues had used precisely the kind of narrow, unicausal explanation to explain U.S. policy that they reject when others used it to explain Sandinista behavior. Thus the Nicaragua report argues (p. 39) that "The most plausible explanation for [U.S. policies], in our view, is the deep, ideologically grounded hostility of the Reagan Administration toward the Sandinista government."

Similar questions arise regarding the use of journalistic sources. Although the LASA authors make many critical references to alleged biases of journalists and editors against the Sandinistas and for the Reagan administration, they draw frequently on journalistic sources of information and ideas that support their own arguments (LASA Report, 1985, pp. 18, 28, 32, 37–41; Cornelius, 1986a, pp. 23, 27). By contrast, they explicitly disparage journalistic sources that present information or arguments contrary to their position. This is overwhelmingly the dominant pattern in the report as well as in Cornelius's follow-up comments. Consider just one prominent example, the treatments of journalistic articles by Philip Taubman (1984), a reporter for the *New York Times*, and Robert Leiken (1984b), an analyst of Latin American affairs from the Carnegie Endowment for International Peace writing in *The New Republic*.

Taubman's article is cited in the LASA report (p. 37) as a principal factual source for the report's contention that U.S. policy was to prevent opposition candidates from running, or to make them withdraw if they were running, in order to delegitimize the election. The report quotes statements of officials from Taubman's article that support this point. It does not quote, or mention the existence of, other statements in Taubman's article from U.S. officials and from Arturo Cruz, a principal opposition candidate, refuting this point. In his response to Levy and others Cornelius (1986a, p. 23) again refers sympathetically to "the investigative reporting of Philip Taubman of the *New York Times* alleging U.S. Government interference in the Nicaraguan electoral process." Cornelius and the LASA report do not refer to the contrary evidence in Taubman's article. In short, both the report and Cornelius's responses to criticisms of it convey the idea that Taubman's article supports the report's interpretation. It does not. Taubman's article does not say that one interpretation was correct, but that conflicting interpretations existed. Taubman says nothing about which view or set of facts, if either, was correct; his reportial point was that two interpretations existed, period. His article is accurate; Cornelius's account of it is not.

Now consider the report's and Cornelius's treatments of Leiken's article. Leiken based it on a trip to Nicaragua in August 1984, his sixth since the revolution. He had edited and coauthored a major book on Central America (Leiken, 1984a) that was widely regarded as "the Democratic alternative to the Kissinger Report." The theme of Leiken's article was disparities between the claims and realities of the revolution. "For one who has sympathized with the Sandinistas, it is painful to look into the house they are building, but it is unwise not to . . . This visit convinced me that the situation is far worse than I had thought [when he wrote the introduction to his book on Central America], and it disabused me of some of the remaining myths about the Sandinista revolution" (Leiken, 1984b, p. 16). The body of the piece is a wide-ranging and detailed account, within the limits of the journalistic format, of economic, political, church, media, and union activities.

How is this article treated in the LASA report? It is cited under this single sentence: "Reports published in the United States have implied that all of the Coordinadora's rallies were violently disrupted by FSLN thugs, while the Sandinista police stood by doing nothing to restrain them." After rendering this one-sentence version of Leiken's article the report goes on to cite and quote at length a letter, also published in the United States, from an individual who witnessed one Coordinadora rally and had a different view of it from the "generalization" about rallies the report attributed to Leiken (LASA Report, 1985, p. 32). Later Cornelius (1986a, p. 22) refered to Leiken's article as "another 'sins-of-the-Sandinistas' exposé, of the sort that has been so fashionable among U.S. newspaper editorial writers and disgruntled liberals since mid-1984."

Both journalistic accounts are good ones by able reporters. But the LASA report and Cornelius's article give an extremely negative, ad hominem treatment of the story that reports inconvenient facts and an extremely positive, laudatory treatment of the one that is congenial to their own claims. Manifestly, their criticism of journalistic sources is applied inconsistently; manifestly, journalistic sources and criticisms of them are used politically. Other examples of the LASA report's asymmetrical, politicized usage of positive and pejorative terminology are given by Levy (1985, p. 8, and 1986, p. 26).

If advocacy-group and journalistic sources are inappropriate or inadequate, they should not be used. If they are appropriate they should be used in a consistent way rather than only when they support one side, and all sources should be treated with respect rather than as objects of ad hominem characterizations if they report inconvenient facts.

A Scholarly Report?

In describing their report the delegation and its spokesperson repeatedly used words such as "academic," "balanced," "dispassionate," "fair," "impartial," "judicious," "objective," and "scholarly" (each of the foregoing adjectives is their own; see LASA Report, 1985, p. 9; Cornelius, 1986a, pp. 22–24, and 1986b). They state that there was absolutely no compromise of scholarly standards in the Nicaragua report and that to say otherwise is "ludicrous" (Cornelius, 1986b).

These claims are not sustainable, as LASA's and the delegation's own terms of reference, criteria, and procedures plainly show. The report resulted from a political invitation, not an academic research program. LASA and the Nicaragua delegation explicitly framed the report as a political document. LASA was on record in support of the Sandinistas and their claims before the delegation was even assembled. Many of the procedures employed to review and publish the report were sub-standard in scholarly terms. Advocacy-group and journalistic sources were employed selectively and inaccurately to support one side of the argument rather than systematically, accurately, and in a balanced fashion.

If the intent of the report on Nicaragua was a kind of Latin American Studies version of a report by the National Academy of Sciences (NAS) on an important national problem—as Cornelius implies when he says that LASA studies are "qualitatively different" from those of advocacy groups, or as Safa implies with her remarks about applying the expertise of LASA members to important public problems—then the effort was a failure. The quality of the work was not nearly at the scholarly level of NAS reports. Analogies to reports of other kinds of high-quality policy-analysis groups, such as the Inter-American Dialogue reports, the Kissinger Commission report, or the earlier Linowitz commission reports, would also fail. Although the LASA report is more precisely focused, more detailed, and more empirical on a few questions, it is also less balanced, less sensitive to broader dimensions of its problem, much narrower in reporting diversity of views about the election and its meaning, more polemical, and more intolerant of the views of others than the kinds of publications issued by these other groups.

The closest analogy to the LASA report is certainly not normal scholarly work, as its authors maintain. It is not even NAS reports or the other kinds of policy-oriented reports mentioned. Rather, the closest analogy is precisely the work of advocacy groups that the LASA authors initially disdain but then cite to corroborate their conclusions. According to Cornelius (1986b), "If 'scholarship' and 'impact' cannot be pursued simultaneously in observing and reporting an election, with no compromise of scholarly norms, then LASA should not undertake such missions." The principle is correct, but the Nicaragua report is not the sort of work that could be done by a scholarly association following the conventional model of the relations between scholarship and politics. It is the sort of work that could be done by a scholarly association following the politicized-scholarship premise of holistic dependency.

Institutionalized Politicization and the Sounds of Silence

Latin American studies is a much larger and more consequential field today than it was when LASA was founded. In some areas and subfields the quality of the work has improved compared to earlier times. This achievement has mostly been the work of individuals, but LASA has helped with its journals and in other ways.

But something is very wrong in LASA and the field of Latin American studies generally. It has long been a commonplace among scholars that the so-called economic miracles in countries such as Brazil (1968–1980) and Mexico (1940–1970) had a "dark underside" of inequality, authoritarianism, and exploitation that was less appealing than the record of economic achievement suggested. An analogous point must now be made about LASA and the field of Latin American studies. LASA's growth in size and achievements in quantitative terms has also been accompanied by a dark underside—the pervasive, persistent violation of fundamental academic principles in the service of political ends.

Moreover, in one respect the situation in LASA is worse. Whereas even defenders of the development models of Brazil and Mexico concede that the social inequalities are a major negative feature, LASA and its defenders make no such concession regarding its manifest and pervasive politicization. They refuse to acknowledge that a problem exists. Either they justify LASA's politicization on the grounds that the ends justify the means (Safa, 1985; Reading, 1987), or they remain silent about it even as they condemn politicization when in their view others engage in it (LASA Resolution, 1976; P. Smith, 1982b; Cornelius, 1986a, 1986b).

If LASA members or officials consistently passed resolutions criticizing socialist governments but never capitalist governments, or screamed insults at speakers who used Marxist perspectives but enthusiastically applauded those who used capitalist perspectives, or used extra-scholarly criteria and procedures to publish hastily prepared official reports supporting capitalist authoritarian regimes, then most of the membership would rise up in righteous indignation against the manifest politicization of the scholarly enterprise. They would be correct to do so. But there has been no uprising against the patterns that have actually occurred. To the contrary, protests have been extremely rare. Although LASA sees itself as a critical organization, it abhors dissent outside the parameters of its resolutions and task force reports. In LASA's normative culture the legitimate responses to LASA's violations of traditional academic norms are approval and justification, or silence.

LASA's reforms in the 1980s were laudable so far as they went. Procedures regarding resolutions were altered to require more careful drafting, more scrutiny by the executive committee, and better coordination between the executive committee, the business meeting, and mail votes by members. An award, the Kalman Silvert Prize, was established to honor distinguished senior scholars. The Bryce Wood Award for an outstanding book on Latin America in the social sciences and the humanities was presented for the first time in 1989. After two decades recognition of scholarly distinction had finally become a part of the collective life of the association with a ritualistic and symbolic importance comparable to the politicized resolutions of the business meeting.

But fitting as each of these reforms was, none corrected the main elements of LASA's politicization. Resolutions on political questions remained a cherished, untouchable feature of LASA practice and culture. Politicized panels and task forces—"putting knowledge at the service of social justice," as one of LASA's presidents (Safa, 1984, p. 1) put it somewhat charitably—continued to be central, valued parts of the life and identity of the organization. In 1987, after the reforms had been made, the executive director of LASA continued publicly to acknowledge LASA's politicization in all the areas described in this chapter and in other areas such as lobbying government officials and the choice of topics for panels. He vigorously defended LASA's politicization as an appropriate response to the policies of the Reagan administration, the need to defend "underdogs," the need to "defend freedom of speech in our democratic system" against "the latest phase of witch-hunting" by "elements of the far right," and for other reasons. As he saw it, the issue was not LASA's sins but the sins of others; it was not a scholarly or educational question but a political question (Reading, 1987). Even if in the future further reforms should change LASA's politicization, the record of the last two decades would stand.

What happened was that after about 1970 or so LASA's politicization became institutionalized. After that critical juncture in the late sixties/early seventies, its politicization no longer depended on individuals alone. It became embedded in the organization's traditions, normative culture, and institutional practices. Individual members of LASA were affected by this organizational context. What they did within the organization was not necessarily what they did outside it— where, among other things, the norms of academic disciplines constrained tendencies toward politicization. Over time LASA evolved a specific set of organizational tenets or guidelines, consistent with holistic dependency, that have informed, facilitated, and justified its institutionalized politicization. These tenets of LASA culture can be inferred and abstracted from resolutions, statements by LASA officials, and task force reports. The citations below merely illustrate some of the more articulate and explicit formulations of these tenets; other sources can be identified easily in the earlier parts of the chapter.

LASA1. It is possible to pursue a political and a scholarly agenda at the same time without any cost to the latter (Fagen, 1976; Safa, 1984, 1985; Cornelius, 1986b).

LASA2. The basis of the scholarly community concerned with Latin America is not only mutual interest and competence in the subject but also agreement on basic substantive and political propositions (Safa, 1985; Reading, 1987). The tradition of politicized resolutions draws much support from this premise.

LASA3. The U.S. media are biased; their distortions must be corrected; LASA has a special responsibility to make these corrections. The U.S. government and larger political system unduly restrict academic specialists on Latin America. The combination of media bias and government constraints on U.S. scholars necessitates LASA activism (P. Smith, 1982b; Safa, 1984, 1985; Cornelius, 1986a; Reading, 1987; Walker, 1987).

LASA4. The pursuit of truth is a social responsibility and the academic community is therefore accountable "to the whole society, national and international" (LASA Resolution, 1976). LASA has a "responsibility to the people of Latin America" which propels it into an activist role (Safa, 1984, 1985).

LASA5. Work on Latin America done by North American scholars before the late sixties was not only wrong but profoundly exploitative, repressive, and evil; work produced by North American scholars since the late sixties has transcended those earlier ills. Therefore, when the earlier scholarship informed U.S. policy, that was bad; but if more recent scholarship, endorsed by LASA, were to inform U.S. policy, that would be good. This premise informs and underlies many LASA resolutions and task force reports; it is well articulated by Schoultz (1987, esp. pp. 22–23).

LASA6. The goodness of LASA's political ends justifies the politicization of scholarship as a means (Safa, 1984, 1985; Reading, 1987).

These tenets may be questioned. For each of them an opposite tenet is at least equally plausible and desirable as a guide for scholarly organizations.

ALT1. Pursuing political and scholarly agendas simultaneously is costly if not disastrous for the scholarly vocation—particularly when, as often happens, the two agendas diverge and the former triumphs over the latter.

ALT2. It is in the nature of scholarship always to be uncertain whether or not the ideas prevailing among most scholars at a particular time and place are true and just. Scholarly organizations must protect, preserve, and encourage conditions in which scholars have space to search for truths, even if their views are unpopular.

ALT3. Scholarly organizations should not promote this or that version of the truth in political arenas or in the media.

ALT4. The social and ethical responsibilities of scholars and the ways they are accountable before "national and international society" are complicated issues. The first social and ethical responsibility of scholars should be to pursue truth. "National and international society" is an extremely vague concept; the actual and desirable mechanisms for accountability before national and international society are unclear. Accountability is not the same as partisanship; appeals for accountability should not be used as means to carry on partisan activities within scholarly fora.

ALT5. Scholars tend to exaggerate the contributions they can and should make to policy and policymakers. Scholars have had misguided policy preferences and theoretical understandings in the past; their present and future preferences and interpretations may also be flawed. Scholarly organizations do well to facilitate good scholarship in all its glorious uncertainty and diversity; they should not seek to promote particular policies allegedly based on scholarly expertise.

ALT6. The ends do not justify the means.

LASA's norms, traditions, and policies hold that scholars have ethical obligations and that, as P. Smith (1982b, p. 12) put it in his farewell statement as LASA president, they "speak through their silence as well as their words." In this view silence on political issues is morally indefensible; this perception contributes to LASA's politicization. But the first ethical obligation of scholarship is to pursue truths wherever facts, logic, and reason lead, and to foster an environment congenial to that goal. LASA's principles about ethical obligations and the moral costs of silence are applied selectively and one-sidedly. Although the association is sensitive to threats to liberty, justice, and the pursuit of truth from some sources, its awareness of threats to those values from other sources, including LASA itself, is weak or nonexistent. Scholars do indeed speak through their silences. So does LASA.

12 The Dependency Movement and the Impasse in Development Scholarship

In this effort to describe and analyze the dependency movement, my own perspectives and values have inevitably affected the work. But my goal has been to convey as accurately as possible the origins of the dependency approach, its main features and internal variations, and the influences it has had in Latin America and the United States. Even in the two chapters on analytic dependency as an alternative to holistic dependency, one of the main goals was to give sharper focus to holistic dependency ideas themselves.

In this concluding chapter, I want to shift the emphasis. I will first summarize my own views about the contributions and costs of the dependency movement for scholarship in the fields of Latin American studies, comparative politics, and development theory. Then I broaden the focus by offering a few hypotheses about the relationship of the dependency movement to the crisis in the field of development scholarship. Finally, I summarize what this study suggests about a fundamental choice facing development scholars and others.

Contributions and Costs of the Dependency Movement

Understood in certain ways, the dependency literature has made positive contributions to the study of development. This was especially so in the late sixties and the seventies. The emphasis on the external sources of national development, the focus on class linkages across national boundaries, the attention to equality as well as productivity, the merging of politics and economics into political economy studies, and other ideas that flowed *or seemed to flow* from the dependency perspective, had been insufficiently explored by earlier approaches. To be sure, not all of these ideas were novel or exclusive to the dependency approach. Sometimes they were carried too far. Other qualifications might be entered. Nevertheless, understood in the foregoing terms, the dependency approach offered a number of ideas and hypotheses that were interesting and useful and remain so today.

These contributions and others have been widely acknowledged. Even scholars who do not themselves use holistic dependency affirm them. The notion that the virtues of the dependency approach have been unduly neglected in the scholarly literature is not tenable. To the contrary, the prevailing view of it is on balance favorable both in Latin American studies and other scholarly fields (P. Smith, 1982a, 1983; Migdal, 1983; Seligson, 1984; Skidmore and Smith, 1984, 1989; Evans, 1985a; T. Smith, 1985a, 1985b; Wiarda, 1985; Klaren and Bossert, 1986; Walton, 1987; Weiner and Huntington, 1987; Stern, 1988a, 1988b; Palmer, 1989).

Although the prevailing assessments are correct up to a point, they are deficient in at least two important respects. First, they are incomplete, unclear, imprecise, or flat-out inaccurate about the central substantive claims of holistic dependency writings. In particular, scholars frequently state or assume that the dependency approach is mainly about external influences on internal development—that it is, as the term dependency implies, about (national) dependency versus (national) autonomy. For instance, in their comprehensive survey of the political development literature Huntington and Domínguez (1975, pp. 93–94) dealt briefly with dependency ideas as follows: "A situation thus existed in which, to oversimplify, establishment political science ignored a phenomenon, while radical political theory exaggerated it . . . Subtle psychological factors may have been at work on both sides. American political science may have avoided external influences because they themselves were, in some measure, one of those influences. Third World theorists may have exaggerated the role of external influences, on the other hand, in order to rationalize and justify their own failures to develop their societies." In assessing the same literature more than a decade later, Weiner (1987, p. xxiv) again concluded that dependency writers "have raised important questions about the impact of the global economy on economic and political development and normative questions about the effects of U.S. policies on the third world." Similar characterizations appear frequently in the literatures of international political economy and political development (Haggard, 1989; Palmer, 1989, p. 296).

We have seen, however, that the dependency approach is not fundamentally about dependency versus autonomy; it is fundamentally about capitalism versus socialism. The idea that internal development is conditioned significantly by external factors seemed to be one of the valuable innovations of the dependency way of thinking. But holistic dependency rejects any consistent usage of the distinction between external and internal used in the passages just quoted or in a hundred others that could be cited. It uses that distinction only when the facts of a concrete case or series of cases fit its substantive hypotheses. When such facts contradict its hypotheses, the internal/external distinction is said to be mechanical, positivist, and not at all what holistic authors have in mind. The nominally internal factors are actually external if they are doing the wrong (capitalist) kinds of things and genuinely internal only if they are doing the right (socialist) kinds of things. To fail to understand that is to miss the most important substantive claim of holistic dependency.

The second major weakness in the prevailing scholarly descriptions and assessments of holistic dependency is that they tend not to go beyond its substantive claims, particularly its empirical arguments about dependent capitalism. These are important, but the utopian, unfalsifiable, and politicized features of the approach are even more important. These features reduce, outweigh, and often destroy the benefits the dependency approach seemed to bring to the analysis of development.

The open-endedness and utopianism of holistic dependency with regard to political development opens the door to the most serious abuses of political power. Holistic dependency categories of thought have an inherent logic and symbolic and emotional thrust toward political polarization and repressive political regimes. They dichotomize interests. Positive-sum relations between these interests are impossible by definition. Thus the only possibility for "real" justice and "genuine" development is elimination of capitalist interests, groups, and classes or class fractions. This leads to the rhetoric, symbolism, and psychology of struggle, conflict, and disdain for critics so common in holistic dependency writings. It is why socialist regimes informed by dependency thinking disdain competition and individual rights and freedoms. It is why Salvador Allende said, "I am not President of all Chileans." It is why believing that Cuba is or can become democratic under its brand of socialism is like believing in the Easter Bunny.

The logical implications of what some of its proponents like to call "the dependency way of framing the question of development" could be illustrated by what happened in Cambodia during the regime of Pol Pot: "A group of modern intellectuals, formed by Western thought, primarily Marxist thought, claim to seek to return to a rustic Golden Age, to an ideal rural and national civilization. And proclaiming these ideals, they are systematically massacring, isolating, and starving city and village populations whose crime was to have been born when they were, the inheritors of a century of historical contradictions during which Cambodia passed from paternalistic feudalism, through colonization, to a kind of precapitalism manipulated by foreigners" (Lacouture, 1977, p. 9). It is all there: the "anti-nation inside the nation" that must be destroyed; the self-righteousness and intolerance; the elitism of intellectuals who claim to know the interests of the whole society; the contempt for liberal standards of responsibility, guilt, and innocence; the clarity about what is evil, the murky utopianism about what is good.

Although he does not develop it analytically, Lacouture makes an important distinction: "Of course it is horrible when Pinochet tortures his prisoners, Amin strangles his enemies, and the extreme Franco-ist guerrillas massacre theirs . . . [But] what has taken place in Cambodia . . . is of a different historical order. Here the leaders of a popular resistance movement, having defeated a regime whose corruption by *compradors* and foreign agents had reached the point of caricature, are killing people in the name of a vision of a green paradise." Nothing like Cambodia, fortunately, has ever been implemented in Latin America. It is, however, due less to the weakness of holistic dependency ideas than to the strength of other intellectual and political currents in the region and the common sense of its peoples, leaders, and thinkers. If, as has happened, the articulators and defenders of holistic dependency have recoiled in horror from its totalitarian implications, they did so not because of dependency ideas but in spite of them.

From a social-scientific point of view, the crucial feature of holistic dependency is its resistance to falsification. It does not allow for the possibility of data that reject or revise fundamental premises; it accepts only data that confirm its premises and hypotheses. It can be confirmed, or put "on hold," but never be self-correcting.

Holistic dependency is structural functionalism turned on its head. It uses the same epistemological principles as structural functionalism but with a completely different set of values. Both dependency analysis and structural functionalism posit a set of "needs" and "interests" that must be served in society. Unless these needs are met, the societies will not survive. In both kinds of analysis, it is the analyst who determines what these needs and interests are and whether data confirm or disconfirm hypotheses. In both cases, the premises and the main hypotheses of the approach are always preserved, no matter what the data are. Structural functionalism tends to value stability, equilibrium, and preservation of the system; dependency analysis favors (for capitalist systems) instability, conflict, and the destruction of the system. Structural functionalism says that there are certain "functional requisites" in all societies which, if not performed, will result in the destruction of the society; dependency says that certain capitalist groups, classes, class-fractions, and the like have certain interests that must be protected or their social order will be destroyed. In short, the social values of the two perspectives are very different, but the essential scientific methodology is the same.

From the valid point that some other approaches besides holistic dependency, such as structural functionalism, are nonfalsificationist, many dependency authors and defenders have drawn the invalid conclusion that *all* social science approaches have central hypotheses that are not rejectable with data (Caporaso, 1978a, p. 7; Duvall, 1978, passim; Gereffi, 1983, pp. 40–43). It is true, of course, that all approaches begin with concepts and definitions. That is inevitable. But that is very different from the idea that in all approaches the central *hypotheses* are nonfalsifiable. This idea is false. Modernization theories—the ideas of such writers as Lerner, Lipset, and Cutright—were revised or rejected in the late sixties and early seventies not only because of their values but also because of the ways in which empirical evidence seemed to falsify them. So was Rostow's "take-off" theory. In order for this to happen, falsificationist criteria had to exist. Most of the modernization theories contained hypotheses that were correctable or rejectable with data. So do a number of other influential theoretical approaches, such as studies of bureaucratic authoritarianism (O'Donnell, 1973; Collier, 1979). Holistic dependency does not.

The differences between these two types of social science are significant. The first can be rejected with data, and in large part it was. The second can be rejected only by emotion and force. The first, when it is wrong, can be discarded. The second has no mechanism for knowing whether it is wrong except political power. The first produces many types of scientific failure and a few successes. The second may produce a scientific success, but there is no way to know that, either. This uncertainty can have extremely high costs in human terms. As L. G. Thomas (1984, p. 713) rightly states, "By obfuscating the true causes of legitimate and often pressing LDC problems, dependency theorists hamper rather than promote effective and just solutions."

A final problem associated with holistic dependency is an ethical one. It is related to the politicization of social science work already described, but it is broader and deeper.

The idea of an intellectual community implies a shared ethic of open discussion based on mutual respect, trust, and candor. It assumes that despite social distortions and pressures, social science can be relatively independent from politics. It implies that the ideal of objectivity and dispassionate analysis is worth striving for even though it is never achieved. It implies that all parties in the community seek to play by these rules and confront conflicting logics and data openly and respectfully. Perhaps most of all, it values the very idea of a social-scientific and intellectual community that, while never free of cultural, national, political, and social influences, nevertheless seeks to transcend those distorting influences in some measure.

To put it mildly, the last two decades have not been kind to that idea. Up to a point, criticism of the more conventional social science models has been appropriate. But the criticism, and the counterproposals and counterethics to supplant the earlier models, have gone too far—in some cases much too far. Nowhere is this more true than in the intellectual circles in the United States that deal with Third World, particularly Latin American, politics and development.

During the last two decades, instead of trying to promote a community of scholars dealing with these problems, many leading figures have tried to keep it fragmented, polarized, and politicized. The idea of autonomous social science has been widely disparaged as not even a worthy ideal but as a disguised form of repression. The idea of balanced social science presenting both supporting and conflicting arguments and data has been explicitly rejected by some scholars in favor of an adversary or forensic model in which only supporting data should be presented.

The idea of an independent intellectual community implies that an individual within that community may pursue an idea wherever reason, logic, and evidence lead, no matter how unpopular or unfashionable this journey may be politically. By contrast, holistic dependency and those who agree with it contend that it is illegitimate even to discuss the approach unless one accepts its basic premises. Thus a dialogue between believers and nonbelievers is rendered impossible. Moreover, according to this view, the problem is not with those who refuse to enter the dialogue, but rather with those who want a dialogue but refuse to agree beforehand on the answers to the important questions.

Thus Duvall (1978, p. 57) writes that "Dialogue between systematic empiricism and dependencia theory is possible if empiricists recognize the fundamentally historical and historicist character of the particular substance of dependencia theory." He is right that dependency ideas are historicist (in his sense) but very wrong to imply that knowing this will necessarily make a dialogue possible. Later in his article he alludes to this problem in a footnote (p. 68n, emphasis in original): "Meaningful dialogue will not occur if dependencia theorists are adamantly opposed to rigorous empiricism in principle, as there is indication that some of them may be. See, for example, Cardoso and Faletto. All that can be done is to provide the *possibility* of dialogue." But he never develops this point or allows it to inform his basic argument. Given the importance of Cardoso and Faletto in the literature, this is quite an important omission.

The degree to which accepting the dependencista rules of discourse has suffused the subculture of scholars in the United States who deal with development in Latin America and other parts of the Third World is remarkable. Pressures to conform to these norms have been powerful. The invocation of political criteria and claims to justice as justifications for violations of basic academic standards has occurred with remarkably little comment or resistance. If it were true that all scholarly approaches are equally intolerant of dissenting views and data, then the criteria for evaluating theories would indeed have to be political. Our view is very different and can be stated succinctly. Different approaches are not equally intolerant. Some are much more intolerant and resistant to conflicting data and interpretations than others. Holistic dependency is antischolarly, antiscientific, and more intolerant of dissenting views and data than the social-scientific tradition it seeks to replace. The central problem is not the difficulty of communication across different scholarly traditions, "language communities," or "scripts" (Caporaso, 1978a, p. 7, and 1978b, pp. 19–20, 43; Duvall, 1978); it is that one scholarly tradition uses evidence to test ideas and the other refuses to do so both in practice and in principle.

The differences between these ways of doing scholarly work are vast. They have profound moral and political implications. A social-scientific community that freely and rigorously explores ideas is a good thing in its own right. In addition, it has instrumental values for the quality of life, of politics, and other good things. Some of the prohibition on critical analysis of dependency writings by anyone except others in the Marxist tradition, and some of the efforts to intimidate those who violate the prohibition, seem to be based upon the idea that the political end justifies the means. In fact, these prohibitions are rarely if ever justified, and certainly not in these cases.

Beyond this, these taboos and pressures also seem to be based on desires to participate in a cultural and political melodrama, a kind of politico-academic morality play, and to show respect and esteem for a group of innovative social scientists. One can understand these wishes and honor some of them, but still question whether the means serve the ends. Who shows greater respect: the commentator who suspends critical judgment in order to applaud, or the one who evaluates scholarly work seriously, on its merits as social science, without reference to who wrote it?

The Impasse in Development Scholarship

For some years development scholarship has been in crisis. This fact is widely acknowledged (Higgott, 1983; T. Smith, 1985a; Wiarda, 1985; Weiner and Huntington, 1987; Apter, 1987; "A World to Make," 1989). But there is little agreement about the specific nature of the crisis, its causes, and potential cures for it. In our view, to understand the crisis one must understand the dependency movement that emerged just ahead of it. Along with other influences, the dependency movement eroded the idea that scholars were required to go where facts, reason, and logic led them. It weakened the principle that they should report their results independently of the claims of political agenda. The spread of the nonfalsificationist and politicized-scholarship premises of holistic dependency is a major reason for the crisis in the development field.

To see how this is so, contrast the fates of the modernization and dependency perspectives, respectively, when each of them at different times encountered disconfirming historical trends. In the late sixties and most of the seventies, an avalanche of disconfirming events assaulted modernization theories: political instability and coups d'etat throughout the Third World; bureaucratic authoritarian regimes, coupled with persisting or growing socioeconomic inequalities, in Latin America; the seeming success of socialist mobilization regimes in China and Cuba; the installation and seeming viability of radical regimes in Vietnam, Ethiopia, Mozambique, Angola, Grenada, and Nicaragua, among other examples. A number of trends in the First World also tended to weaken, directly or indirectly, the premises and claims of modernization theories: the Vietnam War, student revolts, revolutions in community, family, and personal values, Watergate, the cultural and political "malaise" of the late seventies, widespread doubt throughout the West about its core values and institutions, the rise of "limits to growth" and "small is beautiful" movements, and much more.

Confronted by those trends and the bodies of research and theory critical of modernization theories to which they gave rise, the scholarly establishments in the United States and other Center or Northern countries generally behaved the way scholars are supposed to behave according to the classical standards. They allowed the facts to alter their views. They credited the new scholarship even when doing so challenged established views and clashed with earlier political orientations. When new scholars presented data and reasoning that challenged the older ideas and values, and offered interesting and promising new theories, they were admitted into the game. Any scholar who did not play by these rules was, given the academic norms then in force, in the wrong. He was liable to criticism and even sanctions. But most scholars did play by those rules.

In consequence, the development field was transformed. There were new perspectives, new theories, new people. By the end of the seventies, as we have seen, the old mainstream was the mainstream no longer. The challengers had become the new mainstream. The avalanche of facts countering modernization theories led to a corresponding avalanche of studies critical of those theories, now widely applauded and accepted. The conventional scholarly system worked as it said it should.

Now consider what happened to the *new* mainstream when subsequent events, in their turn, cast doubt on *its* substantive premises, hypotheses, and prescriptions. After the late seventies there was another turn of the historical wheel and another avalanche of new facts. Socialist regimes did very badly. In the two biggest and most important cases, China and the USSR, socialist performance was so poor that new leaderships began major reforms to incorporate elements of the previously loathsome liberal capitalist models. In the name of socialism, Cambodia perpetrated one of the horrors of the twentieth century, or any century. The bloom was off the rose of Fidelista socialism in Cuba. Afghanistan was invaded and Solidarity in Poland was suppressed. Eurocommunism fizzled. Socialism had almost no significant successes in the development field.

In the same period liberalism and capitalism were doing relatively well, however. Democratic regimes returned to most of Latin America and the Philippines. They were imperfect and fragile, but there was a new and broader determination to try to avoid military rule. Analogous pressures for democracy built up in South Korea and Taiwan. Economically, the East Asian NICs (Newly Industrializing Countries: South Korea, Taiwan, Singapore, and Hong Kong) were spectacular successes. In Japan, the United Kingdom, Western Europe, and the United States, capitalist dynamism showed itself anew. In general, on the historical record the case for capitalism was stronger than it had been in decades.

Today, the dependency prescription for socialism is not very persuasive if one takes into account the record of economic, political, cultural, and even social performance of actual socialist systems. Even its theoretical champions are not eager to defend socialist performance on the empirical record. The events of the late seventies and the eighties were even more damaging to holistic dependency and its prescription for socialism than the earlier trends had been to modernization theories. Now it was the substantive premises, hypotheses, and prescriptions of holistic dependency that were cast into doubt by the emerging trends and that logically should have been confronted with its own round of scholarly criticisms.

But the fate of holistic dependency, especially its unorthodox version, has been very different. Scattered criticisms of it do not come to anything resembling in volume and intensity the earlier critical literature about modernization theory. Scholarly acknowledgment of the failures of holistic dependency and other radical literatures—which have been if anything even greater than those of modernization theory—is a small trickle by comparison to the torrent of critical writing about modernization theory that flowed in the sixties and seventies. Even in the eighties—by which time the evidence supporting modernization theory had again strengthened (Lipset, 1981, pp. 459–476; Huntington, 1984, pp. 198–205, and 1987, pp. 7–11)—the scholarly current critical of it continued to flow as if it were fresh and new (T. Smith, 1985a; Grendzier, 1985; Kohli, 1986). When Kohli (1986, pp. 8–14) refered to modernization theory as one of the "hitherto prevailing approaches" that "reduce politics to social and economic forces," he was making the same point that Apter, Eisenstadt, Halpern, Hirschman, Huntington, and others had made two decades earlier and that has been repeated in dozens if not hundreds of studies since then.

By contrast, theoretical writings on the political economy of development still refrain from negative assessment of socialism or the theoretical perspectives that prescribe it. The powerful critiques written many years ago by classical liberals such as Friedrich Hayek, Ludwig von Mises, and Milton Friedman are either ignored or vilified by most contemporary development theorists. More recent works by authors such as Peter Bauer, Peter Berger, and Michael Novak, which connect those traditions to contemporary development theories, usually meet a similar fate. Although capitalist societies have performed better than socialist ones, and liberal principles are being incorporated into a number of hitherto socialist systems, these facts rarely enter the theories of mainstream development scholars.

By traditional standards, then, scholars have not behaved as one would expect given the events of the last fifteen years or so. Why is the scholarly system no longer working as it did before? Part of the explanation may be that conventional scholarly standards are much less widely accepted today than they were twenty years ago. New standards, which the dependency movement embodies, seem to be much more prominent. The nonfalsificationism, politicization, and theatricalization of holistic dependency now occupy much of the intellectual "space" previously held by the conventional approaches, and this has constrained critiques of the prescription for socialism. These features may have similarly impeded the consideration and incorporation by development scholars of substantive alternatives to those sanctioned by the dependency movement's agenda. Thus, although by the old standards scholars are behaving strangely, by the new standards they are behaving as they should.

The overall result is the present impasse. On the one hand, it is hard to go "forward" to socialism because socialist systems have performed so poorly. On the other hand, it is hard to go "backward" to nonsocialist alternatives because the nonfalsificationist, politicized, and theatricalized premises of the newly dominant approaches discredit capitalism and liberalism in all their forms. Development theory cannot go "ahead" and it cannot go "backwards." It is stuck.

Breaking the Impasse

Some scholars have offered solutions to the impasse at the substantive level. Thus Huntington (1987, p. 4) proposes a "return to empirical analyses of subjects that have not received much attention since the mid-1960s." P. O'Brien (1985, p. 44) states that the best dependency work "is concerned with interpretation, and can only be superseded by a better interpretation." Walton (1987, p. 198) makes a similar argument to the effect that only an alternative "substantive logic" can displace dependency's current hegemony.

More empirical studies, better interpretations, and better substantive logics are always welcome, of course, so these things are certainly worth doing. If our analysis is correct, however, they alone cannot resolve the central problems and break the impasse. The biggest problems with holistic dependency are not and never have been its substantive propositions, but rather its insistence on a nonfalsificationist epistemology and the fusion of scholarship and political struggle. These are the problems that have contributed the most to the impasse in the development field. They are the problems which must be addressed if the impasse is to be broken.

At the substantive level, there already are a number of plausible alternative interpretations and substantive logics. But to the extent the nonfalsificationist and politicized-scholarship premises of holistic dependency are in place, these substantive alternatives are not admissible to the debate. Rather, they are taboo interpretations which are either ignored or attacked on nonsubstantive, extra-scholarly grounds. To see how these constraints work concretely, consider recent scholarly writings on capitalist and socialist development models, Cuba, and democracy. Each of these literatures deals with central issues posed by the dependency movement. The story would be similar in almost any substantive area touched by it—which is to say, any other area of development scholarship.

Consider first the issue of socialism versus capitalism. In the 1970s, when capitalism looked weak, many studies called for socialism as the only solution. The events since the late seventies laid bare the many debilities of socialism and the continuing possibilities of capitalism. In an undogmatic, comprehensive, scholarly review of evidence and theory the sociologist Peter Berger (1986) recently found the empirical arguments for the capitalist models to be overwhelming. Today, as Berger noted (1984) with prescience, the real question would seem to be not whether capitalism or socialism but how to achieve the more humane and dynamic forms of capitalism.

But that has not been a strong line of inquiry in the field of development scholarship. Part of the reason is that the two alternatives are not evaluated in substantive terms alone. Instead, symbolic factors impede scholarly consideration of this substantive question. Even if the substantive case for capitalism compared to socialism seems overwhelming, the "mythic" appeals of socialism remain strong while those of capitalism are still weak (Berger, 1986, pp. 194–209). Some of the people who state that dependency can only be superseded by a better interpretation respond to the suggestion of capitalism as an alternative with an attack on the motives of those who offer it (P. O'Brien, 1985, pp. 43–44). Those who suggest that capitalism and liberal democracy may be superior to socialism are vulnerable to the charge of being "consumed by . . . cold war passion" (Kohli, 1986, p. 3).

Among Latin Americanists the idea that capitalism is evil is so deeply embedded that often it is not open to discussion. When things go reasonably well, as in the sixties and seventies, capitalism is attacked because they did not go better. When things go badly, as in the eighties, capitalism is again blamed. The premise is always that there was too much capitalism and not enough socialism. The possibility that there might have been too little capitalism is hard to raise and discuss. It might be true, but anyone saying it is vulnerable on political and symbolic grounds.

Evidence of political and symbolic factors impeding consideration of alternative substantive interpretations is also abundant in studies of Cuba. (The Cuban experience is extremely important to the development field because it offers the opportunity to explore the crucial question of capitalist versus socialist models.) Although interpretations of Cuba at odds with those of holistic dependency exist, frequently they are ignored or vilified on extra-scholarly grounds. For example, the British historian Hugh Thomas and other scholars (Thomas, Fauriol, and Weiss, 1984) have argued that Cuba since 1959 has fallen under a new form of dependency no less constraining and exploitative than the earlier forms. This is a principal theme of Thomas's magisterial *Cuba: The Pursuit of Freedom* (1971), which concludes, hauntingly: "Perhaps even Cubans, for all their gifts, cannot escape Goethe's dictum: 'In vain will undisciplined spirits strive to attain pure freedom. For the Master first reveals himself in limitation and only Law can give us liberty'" (p. 1494).

But most U.S. and European scholars ignore or disdain such interpretations. A leading authority who surveyed the literature in 1988 reported complete agreement among U.S. academic specialists that Cuba's foreign policy "stands on its own," "autonomous" from the influences of the USSR. Cuba is repeatedly described without qualification as "autonomous." No "knowledgeable analyst" thought differently; only uncited "columnists," "U.S. government officials," and "shrill partisan polemicists" could think so. Cuba's dependency relations with the USSR were sometimes mentioned but never given any theoretical or policy importance (Domínguez, 1988, pp. 196–197, 201, 202, 204). By contrast, the dominant scholarly image of capitalist countries in the region was that of dependent societies ruled by an alliance of U.S. and local capital, state and private. In short, in the U.S. scholarly consensus Cuba was autonomous but other Latin American nations were dependent.

Scholarship alone, conventionally defined, cannot account for these images and reactions to dissenting interpretations. In dependency and development writings there is often greater preoccupation with what claims might "mean" or "symbolize" or "imply" or "justify" than whether the claims are true. Authors frequently use the terms "true" and "truth" only in quotation marks. Ideas and facts whose "implications" and "interests" are thought to be politically incorrect are ignored or vilified. The possibility that the "politically correct" ideas might themselves be false, oppressive, or dogmatic is not explored or even raised. Scholars pass these norms along to students, and the patterns deepen and expand accordingly.

Consider the analysis of Cuba in Skidmore and Smith's *Modern Latin America* (1984), a widely used textbook on Latin American history and politics which in many respects is admirable. At the substantive level it uses holistic dependency as its main conceptual and theoretical framework. Thus the authors begin with the observation that while their book "is a survey of modern Latin American history, not a formulation of social theory," nevertheless "we cannot escape the need for concepts in approaching our material." This rightly avoids the fallacy that one can study "concrete situations" without a theoretical perspective. They summarize the basic arguments that guide their inquiry as follows: "political outcomes in Latin America derive largely from the social class structure . . . the class structure derives largely from each country's position in the world economy . . . a comparative perspective on these phenomena can help elucidate the variations and the regularities in Latin American society and politics" (pp. 9–12, 362).

Skidmore and Smith apply the framework loosely and eclectically—not unlike Cardoso and Faletto themselves. Much of their material on individual countries could stand alone, without the dependency apparatus. They claim (pp. 11–12) to borrow from other theoretical perspectives as well, and they do. At some points (pp. 351, 280–285, 368–369) they implicitly commit heresies—treating national dependence as a continuous variable to be analyzed as a question of degree, citing diversification as a legitimate and important indicator of declining dependence, giving the notion of waning U.S. influence significant theoretical weight, and acknowledging the alliance between Cuba and the USSR and the dependence of the former on the latter. Such heresies are noticed; a reviewer (Eakin, 1988, p. 252) found Skidmore and Smith's textbook to be "much more critical" of the Cuban revolution than one of its main competitors.

But holistic dependency is their main conceptual-theoretical guide and it profoundly affects their historical descriptions and comparative analyses. During the occupation of Cuba in the early 1900s, North Americans built schools, roads, sewers, and telegraph lines; their reasons and motives were complex. In the authors' account, however, "it was all in service of integrating the now 'civilized' Cubans more closely into the U.S. orbit" (Skidmore and Smith, 1984, p. 258). Cuba's reliance on sugar was not an unmixed blessing, but it did bring prosperity to much of the Cuban population. But Skidmore and Smith say it brought prosperity "only for a tiny fraction of the people as a whole" (p. 263). By his own account, Fidel Castro was not treated harshly during his imprisonment after the Moncada attack. To the contrary, he had a large patio, his own library, and a cleaning service provided by the prison; he gave interviews to the opposition press, which was permitted to publish them; and, he reported at the time, "we [he and his brother Raul, with whom he shared the prison quarters] don't have to get up until we want to . . . we have plenty of water, electric light, food and clean clothes— all free . . . we don't even pay rent" (Castro as quoted in Szulc, 1987,

p. 342). In Skidmore and Smith, by contrast, Fidel and Raúl "rotted" in prison, period (p. 266).

Fidel was captured after the Moncada attack (Szulc, 1987, pp. 293–298), but in Skidmore and Smith he "surrender[ed], in hopes that would stop the killing" (p. 266). The fighting in 1956–58 involved a remarkably small number of casualties; it was more a militarized political campaign than a regular military operation. Fidel lost only 40–50 men in his guerrilla army in the entire period, and Batista no more than 300. Casualties from civil resistance in the cities and towns were much higher, but even so it appears likely that only about 1,500 to 2,000 persons were killed in the Civil War—a terrible toll in individual terms, of course, but a very small number compared to most revolutions, civil wars, or insurrections. "Castro operated as much as a politician seeking to influence opinion as he did a guerrilla leader seeking territory. The Cuban Civil War had really been a political campaign in a tyranny, with the campaigner being defended by armed men" (Thomas, 1977, pp. 256–262). In Skidmore and Smith, however, the guerrilla war was "savage" (p. 268).

The dependency sensibility also shapes their interpretations of the political and social coalitions undergirding fifteen state-regimes in Cuba and six other countries of Latin America. Skidmore and Smith contend (pp. 360–371) that in post-1959 Cuba every political and social group is in a "strong alliance" with the state. In their analysis, all of the other state-regimes had or now have only partial class support; in Cuba, they say, the regime has the strong support of every social class—peasants, workers, rural and urban middle classes. "To achieve this Fidel has had to rely heavily on foreign support . . . from the Soviet Union. The bonds of dependency continue to exist." But in their comparative analysis, that is the only cost; it would seem a worthwhile trade-off. In this framework it is not pertinent to note that these political and class alliances, if they exist, are inextricably linked to the closest approximation to a totalitarian state in Latin America, with the same maximum leader for more than three decades, absolutely controlled media and educational systems, a massive intelligence and security apparatus, and much more.

In short, holistic dependency shapes descriptions and explanations and filters out alternative interpretations. Even where alternative scholarly interpretations are considered, they are vulnerable to attacks rooted in the politicizing imperatives of holistic dependency. Recently, for example, political scientists have been revitalizing, reformulating, and replenishing earlier perspectives on liberalization and democratization (Huntington, 1984; Przeworski, 1985; O'Donnell and Schmitter, 1986; Stepan, 1988, 1989; Falcoff, Valenzuela, and Purcell, 1988; Diamond, Linz, and Lipset, 1988–). Although the authors of these studies disagree about many things, explicitly or (more often) implicitly they all break with the kind of Marxism embedded in holistic dependency. Precisely for this reason, they are the objects of politicized and ad hominem attacks. Thus Petras (1988a) attacks their alleged "adaptation to the needs of capital" and their alleged defenses of "civilian-terrorist cohabitation." He contends that such "neoliberalism . . . resonates with the . . . ambitions of upwardly mobile intellectuals (fast-approaching middle age) . . . [Neoliberals] have tied their personal fortune to the survival of these regimes . . . The problem is that what is decisive for their personal fortune is not tied to the destiny of the great majority of its population."

By conventional standards of scholarly civility, such attacks are clearly not legitimate. Yet public protests or reprimands by other scholars against them are rare. The only published objection to Petras's ad hominem comments came not from a scholar working mainly in the field of Latin American studies but from Przeworski (1988) who has excellent credentials as a Latin Americanist but whose major scholarly experiences and work have been in other fields that have different norms. Petras's (1988b) reply to Przeworski was, in toto, that "Professor Przeworski's comments are inappropriate to a scholarly discussion. The issue is, and continues to be, the Latin American state and the transition to democracy." Like P. O'Brien (see above), Petras disdains conventional scholarly standards in making ad hominem attacks on others but invokes them to defend himself.

The examples in this section illustrate that a solution to the impasse in development scholarship cannot be found at the substantive level alone. At this level, the treatment of alternative interpretations in recent scholarly discourse is asymmetrical. When holistic dependency interpretations are consistent with the facts, they are said to be confirmed. They are not vulnerable to attack on political and ad hominem grounds. If such attacks occur, scholars invoke the conventional sanctions, which are observed, as they should be. Interpretations that fall outside the dependency substantive agenda, by contrast, have to fight a three-front battle: they have to fit the facts, have the politically and symbolically "correct" meanings and implications, and contend with politicized and ad hominem attacks.

The result is a kind of scholarly ratchet effect. The substantive propositions of holistic dependency can be affirmed, or set aside temporarily, but not rejected. Substantive propositions outside holistic dependency can be rejected, either by facts or by their alleged political meanings; but when they fit the facts they are vulnerable to attacks on political, personal, and theatrical grounds in ways dependency propositions are not. The effects of this on the development field are inexorable. One set of propositions can be accepted, or put "on hold," but never really rejected. Another set can be rejected but never really accepted. Therefore the impasse cannot be broken by focusing only on the substantive level. It can be broken only by going to its roots.

The Options Before Us

Those who support the premise of politicized-scholarship often argue that the only alternative to it is to achieve full freedom from values. In fact, however, almost nobody argues—certainly I do not—that a completely value-free social science is possible. Extra-scholarly considerations such as national values, cultures, class backgrounds, generations, ideologies, and the like, doubtless influence scholarship—although where, how often, how strongly, and in what ways is much more difficult to determine than is often supposed. In those senses, there is inevitably a certain amount of overlapping and intertwining among scholarly and extra-scholarly influences and values. No human being can escape them. The question is not whether those things ever happen, but what if anything to do about them.

Essentially there are two options. The first is to "relax and enjoy it": to accept and encourage the fusion of scholarship, politics, and theatre. The other is to try to optimize scholarly values in the conventional sense and minimize the distorting effects of politics and theatre that will always be present.

The first option has been chosen by many not only in the dependency movement, as we have seen, but also in other areas of contemporary scholarship and culture. Miller (1987, pp. 4–5) refers to the "vitality" throughout the social sciences of hermeneutic approaches and other forms of "antirealism" which base the study of human conduct "on distinctive forms of explanation and justification, immune from criticism by the standards dominating the natural sciences." A related and equally powerful trend in the humanities is what some have called interpretation theory. According to this approach, knowledge is always a function of power. The scholar's proper role is to demystify knowledge and offer a new and more appropriate interpretation-synthesis. In this perspective, it is self-deluding for scholars to seek to be detached or objective. Texts must be understood first and foremost as political documents. The class, ethnic, and gender interests served by texts are always paramount issues. The first question to be asked of texts and arguments is not, "Is it true?" but "Whose 'hegemony' is it designed to perpetuate?" Interpretation theory has had major effects on research and teaching in the humanities in the United States in recent years (sympathetic accounts include Levine et al., 1989; Gless and Herrnstein Smith, 1990; Lindenberger, 1990, Chapter 7; Graff, Herrnstein Smith, and Levine, 1991; critical discussions include Cheney, 1988, 1989; Kernan, 1990; Kimball, 1990; Searle, 1990, 1991).

Preoccupation with the political and symbolic meanings and implications of scholarly claims more than with their truth or falsity is also manifest in the criterion of "political correctness" in U.S. universities. "PCness" refers to "a cluster of opinions about race, ecology, feminism, culture, and foreign policy" that is the "'correct' attitude toward the problems of the world, a sort of unofficial ideology of the university." "PCPs" (politically correct persons) enforce "a growing intolerance, a closing of debate, a pressure to conform to a radical program or risk being accused of . . . thought crimes: sexism, racism, and homophobia" (Bernstein, 1990; also Barchas, 1989–90; Kimball, 1990; Rabinowitz, 1990; D'Souza, 1991).

As James David Barber of Duke University (quoted in Rabinowitz) noted in 1990, "what's going on in universities now threatens everything that a university is supposed to be about . . . Students' minds are supposed to be trained, not converted politically." While PCness is parallel in many ways to the McCarthyism of the 1950s, there are also important differences. In the fifties attacks on politically "incorrect" ideas in the university came mostly from individuals and organizations outside it and from the political right, and faculty and administrators tended strongly to resist such attacks. PCness since the late sixties, by contrast, has mostly come from faculty and administrators themselves, and from the political left; and until very recently there has been little resistance to it by most sectors within the university.

Our own preference is for the second of the two major options before us. (If one understands these options not as a dichotomy but as opposing points on a continuum, the point would be that scholars have moved too close to the first pole and ought to move in the direction of the second pole.) Following the second option, we believe, would advance and preserve values that are extremely important even to some of those who say they favor the first.

Our preference is rooted in the traditions of Popper and Lakatos on falsification and Weber on the separateness of the scholarly and political vocations. The basic principles of those traditions are well known; it is unnecessary here to give a detailed discussion at the abstract philosophical level about them. Rather, the alternatives we propose appear throughout the book in ways and at moments that we think are right for understanding them. Thus in describing and analyzing holistic dependency, Chapters 1 through 5 say much both implicitly and explicitly about alternatives to it. Chapters 6 and 7 are entirely about an alternative to holistic dependency and how to apply it in the study of concrete situations. Chapters 8 through 10 say much about alternatives at cultural, psychological, theoretical, and methodological levels; so does Chapter 11, which includes a specific alternative to LASA's politicized code. Most of the present chapter in various ways is also about alternatives. In short, the specific features of the second option as it applies to the subject areas of the dependency movement have been indicated throughout the book.

A Concluding Word

In considering holistic dependency and its alternatives, it is vital that the focus not be limited to substantive propositions. They are important, obviously. They convey what we want to know. But *how* we know, and are permitted to know, are more basic questions.

Two issues are paramount. The first is how to evaluate substantive propositions: whether by falsificationist criteria, or by the criteria of political power and melodrama. The second issue is what norms shall guide and constrain scholarly practice: those that encourage scholars to go where evidence, logic, and reason lead them, or those that oblige scholars to engage or acquiesce in acts and threats of vilification and politicization.

Since scholars are fallible human beings, some violations of conventional scholarly standards will occur in any case. But they will be much more frequent under the norms of holistic dependency than under the conventional norms. Even more important, there is all the difference in the world between a situation in which politicized and ad hominem attacks and threats are violations of norms, and one in which such attacks give positive expression to norms that justify and encourage them. In the first case, we are all constrained to be scholars and criticized if we slip into unscholarly behavior. In the second case, scholarship is an extension of politics, struggle on another level.

Some of the substantive propositions of holistic dependency have been innovative, interesting, and correct in some circumstances. This should be acknowledged; on the whole it has been. But some of its key propositions are also incorrect. Other hypotheses, outside holistic dependency, often seem to be much more plausible. It must be possible to acknowledge and defend these or other ideas, right or wrong, and to remain free from threats, attacks, and symbolic constraints. Scholarly norms ought to discourage and punish politicized attacks and pressures. Holistic dependency justifies and rewards them. That has been the biggest cost of the dependency movement in the past. It remains its most disturbing legacy to the present and future.

References

Index

References

"A World to Make: Development in Perspective." *Daedalus*, 118:1 (Winter 1989), entire issue.

Abel, Christopher, and Colin M. Lewis, eds. 1985. *Latin America, Economic Imperialism and the State: The Political Economy of the External Connection from Independence to the Present*. London: Athlone Press.

Adler, Emanuel. 1987. *The Power of Ideology: The Quest for Technological Autonomy in Argentina and Brazil*. Berkeley: University of California Press.

Aguilar, Luis E., ed. 1978. *Marxism in Latin America*. Rev. ed. Philadelphia: Temple University Press.

Alker, Hayward R., Jr. 1978. "Learning How to Do Analysis in Political and Social Science." Paper delivered at American Political Science Association Annual Meeting, New York, August 30–September 3.

Allende, Salvador. 1972. "Against All Forms of Dependence." *Review of International Affairs* (Belgrade), 24:562 (September 5), pp. 1–2.

Almond, Gabriel. 1987. "The Development of Political Development." In Weiner and Huntington, eds., 1987. pp. 437–490.

Amarshi, Azeem, et al. 1979. *Development and Dependency: The Political Economy of Papua New Guinea*. Melbourne: Oxford University Press.

Anonymous. 1982. "A Política com Humor." *Jornal do Brasil*, March 28, p. 4.

Antonil, J. A. 1711. *Cultura e Opulência do Brasil*.

Apter, David. 1987. *Rethinking Development: Modernization, Dependency, and Postmodern Politics*. Beverly Hills: Sage.

Araújo Castro, J. A. de. 1972. "O Congelamento do Poder Mundial." *Revista Brasileira de Estudos Políticos*, 33 (January), pp. 7–30.

Arbena, Joseph L., ed. 1988. *Sport and Society in Latin America: Diffusion, Dependency, and the Rise of Mass Culture*. Westport, Conn.: Greenwood Press.

Ayres, Robert. 1972. "Economic Stagnation and the Emergence of the Political Ideology of Chilean Underdevelopment." *World Politics*, 25:1 (October), pp. 34–61.

——— 1976. "The 'Social' Pact as Anti-Inflationary Policy: The Argentine Experience since 1973." *World Politics*, 28:4 (July), pp. 473–501.

Baer, Werner. 1976. "The Brazilian Growth and Development Experience, 1964–1975." In Roett, 1976, pp. 41–62.

Baer, Werner, Isaac Kerstenetzky, and Annibal V. Villela. 1973. "The Changing Role of the State in the Brazilian Economy." *World Development,* 1:11 (November), pp. 23–34.

Balán, J. 1982. "Social Sciences in the Periphery: Perspectives on the Latin American Case." In L. D. Stifel, Ralph K. Davidson, and James S. Coleman., eds., *Social Sciences and Public Policy in the Developing World.* Lexington: Lexington Books, pp. 211–247.

Balbus, Isaac. 1971. "The Concept of Interest in Marxian and Pluralist Analysis." *Politics and Society,* 1:2, pp. 151–177.

Baldwin, David A. 1980. "Interdependency and Power: A Conceptual Analysis." *International Organization,* 34:4 (Autumn), pp. 470–506.

Banerjee, Sanjoy. 1987. "Explaining the American 'Tilt' in the 1971 Bangladesh Crisis: A Late Dependency Approach." *International Studies Quarterly,* 31, pp. 201–216.

Baran, Paul. 1957. *The Political Economy of Growth.* New York: Monthly Review Press.

Barchas, Isaac D. 1989–90. "Stanford After the Fall." *Academic Questions,* 3:1 (Winter), pp. 24–34.

Barros de Castro, Antonio, and Francisco Eduardo Pires de Souza. 1985. *A Economia Brasileira em Marcha Forçada.* Rio de Janeiro: Paz e Terra.

Bath, C. Richard, and Dilmus D. James. 1976. "Dependency Analysis of Latin America." *Latin American Research Review,* 11:3, pp. 3–54.

Becker, David G. 1983. *The New Bourgeoisie and the Limits of Dependency: Mining, Class, and Power in 'Revolutionary' Peru.* Princeton: Princeton University Press.

———— 1986. "LASA's Election Coverage: An Effort Misplaced?" *LASA Forum,* 17:3 (Fall), pp. 7–9.

———— 1987. "Postimperialism: A First Quarterly Report." In David G. Becker, et al., 1987, pp. 203–225.

Becker, David G., et al. 1987. *Postimperialism: International Capitalism and Development in the Twentieth Century.* Boulder: Lynne Rienner.

Beng, Cheah Hock. 1980. "Export-Oriented Industrialization and Dependent Development: The Experience of Singapore." In Godfrey, 1980, pp. 35–41.

Bennett, Douglas. 1984. Book review, in *American Political Science Review,* 78:2 (June), pp. 530–531.

Bennett, Douglas C., and Kenneth E. Sharpe. 1985. *Transnational Corporations versus the State: The Political Economy of the Mexican Auto Industry.* Princeton: Princeton University Press.

Berger, Peter L. 1984. "Underdevelopment Revisited." *Commentary,* July, pp. 41–45.

——— 1986. *The Capitalist Revolution: Fifty Propositions about Prosperity, Equality, and Liberty.* New York: Basic Books.

Bergquist, Charles. 1986. *Labor in Latin America.* Stanford: Stanford University Press.

Bermeo, Nancy. 1990. "Rethinking Regime Change." *Comparative Politics,* 22:3 (April), pp. 359–377.

Bernstein, Richard. 1990. "The Rising Hegemony of the Politically Correct." *New York Times,* October 28, "The Week in Review," pp. 1, 4.

Berry, Albert. 1987. "Poverty and Inequality in Latin America." *Latin American Research Review,* 22:2, pp. 204–208.

Bienefeld, Manfred, and Martin Godfrey, eds. 1982. *The Struggle for Development: National Strategies in International Context.* New York: Wiley.

Biersteker, Thomas J. 1987. *Multinationals, the State, and Control of the Nigerian Economy.* Princeton: Princeton University Press.

Binder, Leonard. 1986. "The Natural History of Development Theory." *Comparative Studies in Society and History,* 28:1 (January), pp. 3–33.

Blasier, Cole. 1983. *The Giant's Rival: The USSR and Latin America.* Pittsburg: University of Pittsburg Press.

Bodenheimer, Susanne. 1971. "Dependency and Imperialism: The Roots of Latin American Underdevelopment." In K. T. Fann and Donald C. Hodges, eds., *Readings in U.S. Imperialism.* Boston: Porter Sargent Publisher, pp. 155–181.

Boff, Leonardo. 1978. *Jesus Christ Liberator: A Critical Christology for Our Time.* Maryknoll, N.Y.: Orbis Books.

Bonilla, Frank, and José A. Silva Michelena, eds. 1967–1971. *The Politics of Change in Venezuela.* 3 vols. Cambridge, Mass.: MIT Press.

Bornschier, Volker, C. Chase-Dunn, and R. Rubinson. 1978. "Cross-National Evidence of the Effects of Foreign Investment and Aid on Economic Growth and Inequality: A Survey of Findings and a Reanalysis." *American Journal of Sociology,* 84:3 (November), pp. 651–683.

Bresser Pereira, Luís Carlos. 1982. "Seis Interpretações sôbre o Brasil." *Dados,* 25:3, pp. 269–306.

Brundenius, Claes. 1984. *Revolutionary Cuba: The Challenge of Economic Growth with Equity.* Boulder: Westview.

Buarque de Hollanda, Heloísa. 1980. *Impressões de Viagem: CPC, Vanguarda e Desbunde: 1960/1970.* São Paulo: Brasiliense.

Buarque de Holanda, Sérgio. 1956. *Raízes do Brasil.* Rio de Janeiro: José Olympio.

Burstin, Luis. 1985. "A Few Home Truths about Latin America." *Commentary,* February, pp. 46–53.

"Business in Latin America." 1985. *Business History Review,* 59:4 (Winter), pp. 543–562, 663–669, 711–712.

Byres, T. J. 1982. "India: Capitalist Industrialization or Structural Stasis?" In Bienefeld and Godfrey, 1982, pp. 135–164.

Cammack, Paul. 1987. Book review, in *Journal of Latin American Studies,* 19:1 (May), pp. 215–218.

Campos, Roberto. 1979. "Sôbre o Conceito de Dependencia." *Veja,* February 21, p. 114.

Cândido, Antonio. 1980. "Universidade e Política." *Encontros com a Civilização Brasileira,* No. 27 (3:9), p. 11–22.

CAPES (Coordenação de Aperfeiçoamento de Pessoal de Nível Superior), Ministério de Educação e Cultura. 1982. "Pós-Gradução: Catálogo de Cursos, 1980," Vol. 4. *Ciências Sociais,* pp. 25–70. Brasília: CAPES.

Caporaso, James A. 1978a. "Introduction: Dependence and Dependency in the Global System." *International Organization,* 32:1 (Winter), pp. 1–12.

——— 1978b. "Dependence, Dependency, and Power in the Global System: A Structural and Behavioral Analysis." *International Organization,* 32:1 (Winter), pp. 13–44.

——— 1980. "Dependency Theory: Continuities and Discontinuities in Development Studies." *International Organization,* 34:4 (Autumn), pp. 605–628.

Cardoso, Fernando Henrique. 1962. *Capitalismo e Escravidão no Brasil Meridional.* São Paulo: Difel.

——— 1964. *Empresário Industrial e Desenvolvimento Econômico no Brasil.* São Paulo: Difel.

——— 1971a. "'Teoria da Dependência' ou Análises Concretas de Situações de Dependência?" *Estudos I,* pp. 25–45. CEBRAP, São Paulo. Published in Spanish in *Revista Latinoamericana de Ciencia Política,* I:3 (December 1970), pp. 402–414. Reprinted in Cardoso, 1973c, pp. 123–139.

——— 1971b. *Política e Desenvolvimento en Sociedades Dependentes: Ideologias do Empresariado Industrial Argentino e Brasileiro.* Rio de Janeiro: Zahar.

——— 1972. "Notas sobre el Estado Actual de los Estudios sobre la Dependencia." *Revista Latinoamericana de Ciencias Sociales* (Santiago de Chile), (December), pp. 3–31. Also in Cardoso, 1980, pp. 57–87.

——— 1973a. "Associated-Dependent Development: Theoretical and Practical Implications." In Stepan, 1973, pp. 142–176.

——— 1973b. "Imperialism and Dependency in Latin America." In Frank Bonilla and Robert Girling, eds., *Structures of Dependency.* Stanford: Institute of Political Studies, pp. 7–16. Also in Cardoso, 1973c, pp. 186–203.

——— 1973c. *O Modelo Político Brasileiro e Outros Ensaios.* São Paulo: Difel.

———— 1973d. "Cuba: Lesson or Symbol?" in David P. Barkin and Nita R. Manitzas, eds., *Cuba: The Logic of the Revolution*. Andover, Mass.: Warner Modular Publications, pp. 1–9.

———— 1974. "O Inimigo de Papel (The Paper Enemy)." *Latin American Perspectives*, 1:1 (Spring), pp. 66–74.

———— 1977a. "The Consumption of Dependency Theory in the United States." *Latin American Research Review*, 12:3, pp. 7–24. Published in Portuguese in Cardoso, 1980, pp. 89–108.

———— 1977b. "Um Cientista do Ar." *Folha de São Paulo*, January 7, 1977, p. 3.

———— 1978. *Democracia Para Mudar: 30 Horas de Entrevistas*. Coleção Documentos da Democracia Brasileira, 4. Rio de Janeiro: Paz e Terra.

———— 1979a. "On the Characterization of Authoritarian Regimes in Latin America." In Collier, ed., 1979, pp. 33–57.

———— 1979b. "The Originality of the Copy: The Economic Commission for Latin America and the Idea of Development." In *Toward a New Strategy for Development*, 1979, pp. 53–72, 312–316. Published in Portuguese in Cardoso, 1980, pp. 17–56.

———— 1980. *As Idéias e Seu Lugar: Ensaios Sôbre as Teorias do Desenvolvimento*. Petrópolis: Vozes.

———— 1981. "PMDB: Um Partido de Massas?" *Revista do PMDB*, 1:1 (July), pp. 25–55.

Cardoso, Fernando Henrique, and Enzo Faletto. 1967. "Dependencia y Desarrollo en América Latina." Lima: Instituto de Estudios Peruanos, Serie Documentos Teóricos No. 1 (March). Mimeographed. 37 pp.

———— 1968. "Dependencia e Desarrollo en América Latina." In Helio Jaguaribe, et al., *La Dominación de América Latina*. Lima: Francisco Moncloa, pp. 177–221.

———— 1969. *Dependencia y Desarrollo en America Latina: Ensayo de Interpretación Sociológica*. México: Siglo Veintiuno.

———— 1970. *Dependência e Desenvolvimento na América Latina: Ensaio de Interpretação Sociológica*. Rio de Janeiro: Zahar.

———— 1979. *Dependency and Development in Latin America*. With a new Preface and Post-Scriptum. Berkeley: University of California Press.

Cardoso, Fernando Henrique, and Octávio Ianni. 1960. *Côr e Mobilidade Social em Florianópolis*. São Paulo: Editora Nacional.

Cardoso, Fernando Henrique, and Francisco Weffort, eds. 1970. *America Latina: Ensayos de Interpretación Sociológico-Política*. Santiago de Chile: Editorial Universitaria.

———— 1970. "Introducción." In Cardoso and Weffort, 1970.

Carvalho, José Murilo de. 1980. *A Construção de Ordem: A Elite Imperial*. Rio de Janeiro: Campus.

————— 1988. *Teatro de Sombras: A Política Imperial.* São Paulo: Vértice.

————— 1990. *A Formação das Almas: O Imaginário da República no Brasil.* São Paulo: Editora Schwarcz, Companhia das Letras.

Castañeda, Jorge G., and Enrique Hett. 1979. *El Economismo Dependentista.* México: Siglo Veintiuno.

Cavarozzi, Marcelo. 1982. "El 'Desarrollismo' y las Relaciones entre Democracia y Capitalismo Dependiente en *Dependencia y Desarrollo en América Latina.*" *Latin American Research Review,* 17:1, pp. 152–171.

Chase-Dunn, Christopher. 1975. "The Effects of International Economic Dependence on Development and Inequality: A Cross-National Study." *American Sociological Review,* 40:6 (December), pp. 720–738.

————— 1982. "A World System Perspective on Dependency and Development in Latin America." *Latin American Research Review,* 17:1, pp. 166–171.

Chauí, Marilena. 1984. *Cultura e Democracia: O Discurso Competente e Outras Falas.* São Paulo: Moderna.

Cheney, Lynne V. 1988. *Humanities in America.* Washington, D.C.: National Endowment for the Humanities.

————— 1989. "Point of View." *The Chronicle of Higher Education,* February 8, p. A40.

Chilcote, Ronald. 1974. Book review, in *Annals of the American Academy of Political and Social Science,* No. 415 (September), p. 232.

————— ed. 1982. *Dependency and Marxism: Toward a Resolution of the Debate.* Boulder: Westview.

————— 1984. *Theories of Development and Underdevelopment.* Boulder: Westview.

Chilcote, Ronald, and Joel Edelstein, eds. 1974. *Latin America: The Struggle with Dependency and Beyond.* Cambridge, Mass.: Schenkman.

Chilcote, Ronald, and Dale L. Johnson, eds. 1983. *Theories of Development: Modes of Production or Dependency?* Beverly Hills: Sage.

Christian, Shirley. 1985. *Nicaragua: Revolution in the Family.* New York: Random House.

Chira, Susan. 1986. "Korea Is Breeding a New Kind of College Radical." *New York Times,* June 17, p. 4.

Cirincione, Joseph, and Leslie C. Hunter. 1984. "Military Threats, Actual and Potential." in Leiken, ed., 1984a, pp. 173–192.

Cline, William R. 1975. "Distribution and Development: A Survey of the Literature." *Journal of Development Economics,* 1, pp. 359–400.

————— 1976. "Brazil's Emerging International Economic Role." In Roett, 1976, pp. 63–88.

Cockcroft, James D., Andre Gunder Frank, and Dale L. Johnson. 1972. *Dependence and Underdevelopment: Latin America's Political Economy.* Garden City, N.Y.: Doubleday.

Cole, Jonathan R., and Stephen Cole. 1973. *Social Stratification in Science.* Chicago: University of Chicago Press.

Collier, David, ed. 1979a. *The New Authoritarianism in Latin America.* Princeton: Princeton University Press.

———— 1979b. "Introduction." In David Collier, ed., 1979, pp. 3–16.

Collier, Ruth Berins, and David Collier. Forthcoming. *Shaping the Political Arena: Critical Junctures, the Labor Movement, and Regime Dynamics in Latin America.* Princeton: Princeton University Press.

Cooper, Richard N. 1979. "Developed Country Reactions to Calls for a New International Economic Order." In *Toward a New Strategy for Development,* 1979, pp. 243–274, 343–347.

Corbridge, Stuart. 1990. "Post-Marxism and Development Studies." *World Development,* 18:5, pp. 623–639.

Cornelius, Wayne A. 1978. "Final Report, Seventh National Meeting, Houston." *LASA Newsletter,* 9:1 (March), pp. 7–13.

———— 1986a. "The 1984 Nicaraguan Elections Revisited." *LASA Forum,* 16:4 (Winter), pp. 22–28.

———— 1986b. "Response by Wayne Cornelius." *LASA Forum,* 17:1 (Spring), p. 27.

———— 1988. "The 1984 Nicaraguan Election Observation: A Final Comment." *LASA Forum,* 19:2 (Summer), pp. 16–19.

Cosío Villegas, Daniel. 1967. "De la Necesidad de Estudiar a Estados Unidos." *Anglia,* 1, pp. 9–17.

Cotler, Julio. 1979. "State and Regime: Comparative Notes on the Southern Cone and the 'Enclave Societies.'" In Collier, ed., 1979, pp. 255–282.

Cotler, Julio, and Richard R. Fagen, eds. 1974a. *Latin America and the United States: The Changing Political Realities.* Stanford: Stanford University Press.

———— 1974b. "Introduction." In Cotler and Fagen, 1974a, pp. 1–20.

Coughlan, Anthony. 1982. "Ireland: Sustained Growth Through Foreign Capital and Manufactured Exports?" In Bienefeld and Godfrey, 1982, pp. 241–264.

Coutinho, Carlos Nelson. 1980. *A Democracia como Valor Universal: Notas sobre a Questão Democrática no Brasil.* São Paulo: Ciências Humanas.

Couto e Silva, Golbery do. 1967. *Geopolítica do Brasil.* Rio de Janeiro: José Olympio.

Crone, Donald. 1983. *The ASEAN States: Coping with Dependence.* New York: Praeger.

Cruz Sequeira, Arturo. 1984. "The Origins of Sandinista Foreign Policy." In Leiken, ed., 1984a.

Cueva, Augustín. 1976. "A Summary of 'Problems and Perspectives of Dependency Theory.'" *Latin American Perspectives,* 3:4 (Fall), pp. 12–16.

Dahl, Robert A. 1968. "Power." *International Encyclopedia of the Social Sciences,* 12, pp. 405–415. New York: Free Press.

Dahl, Robert A. 1971. *Polyarchy: Participation and Opposition.* New Haven: Yale University Press.

da Matta, Roberto. 1978. *Carnavais, Malandros, e Heróis: Para uma Sociologia do Dilema Brasileiro.* Rio de Janeiro: Zahar.

———— 1987. "The Quest for Citizenship in a Relational Universe." In John D. Wirth, Edson de Oliveira Nunes, and Thomas Bogenschild, eds., *State and Society in Brazil: Continuity and Change,* pp. 307–335. Boulder: Westview.

del Aguila, Juan M. 1984. *Cuba: Dilemmas of a Revolution.* Boulder: Westview.

de Meira Mattos, Carlos. 1975. *Brasil: Geopolítica e Destino.* Rio de Janeiro: José Olympio.

de Oliveira, Maria Lucia, ed. 1983. *A Conquista do Espaço Político.* São Paulo: Jornal da Tarde.

de Soto, Hernando. 1986. *El Otro Sendero.* Lima: Ed. el Barranca.

Deyo, Frederic C. 1981. *Dependent Development and Industrial Order: An Asian Case Study* [Singapore]. New York: Praeger.

Diamond, Larry, Juan Linz, and Seymour Martin Lipset, eds. 1988– . *Democracy in Developing Countries.* 4 vols. Boulder: Lynne Rienner.

Diskin, Martin, et al. 1986. "Peace and Autonomy on the Atlantic Coast of Nicaragua: A Report of the LASA Task Force on Human Rights and Academic Freedom." *LASA Forum,* 17:1 and 2 (Spring and Summer), pp. 1–19 and pp. 1–16.

Dix, Robert. 1987. *The Politics of Colombia.* New York: Praeger.

Domínguez, Jorge I. 1978a. "Consensus and Divergence: The State of the Literature on Inter-American Relations in the 1970s." *Latin American Research Review,* 13:1, pp. 87–126.

———— 1978b. *Cuba: Order and Revolution.* Cambridge, Mass.: Harvard University Press.

———— 1982. "The President's Corner." *LASA Newsletter,* 13:2 (Summer), pp. 1–4.

———— 1987. "Political Change: Central America, South America, and the Caribbean." In Weiner and Huntington, 1987, pp. 65–99.

———— 1988. "Cuba in the International Arena." *Latin American Research Review,* 23:1, pp. 196–206.

———— 1989. *To Make a World Safe for Revolution: Cuba's Foreign Policy.* Cambridge, Mass.: Harvard University Press.

Doran, Charles F., George Modelski, and Cal Clark, eds. 1983. *North/South Relations: Studies of Dependency and Dependency Reversal.* New York: Praeger.

Dosal, Paul J. 1987. "Dependency, Revolution, and Industrial Development in Guatemala, 1821–1986." Ph.D. diss., Tulane University.

———— 1988. "The Political Economy of Guatemalan Industrialization, 1871–1948." *Hispanic American Historical Review,* 68:2 (May), pp. 321–358.

dos Santos, Theotonio. 1968a. "El Nuevo Carácter de la Dependencia." *Cuadernos del Centro de Estudios Socio-Económicos,* no. 10 (Santiago de Chile).

———— 1968b. "The Changing Structure of Foreign Investment in Latin America." In Petras and Zeitlin, 1968, pp. 94–98.

———— 1968c. "Foreign Investment and the Large Enterprise in Latin America: The Brazilian Case." In Petras and Zeitlin, 1968, pp. 431–453.

———— 1970. "La Crisis de la Teoría del Desarrollo y las Relaciones de Dependencia en América Latina." In Jaguaribe, et al., 1970, pp. 147–187.

———— 1970. "The Structure of Dependence." *American Economic Review,* 60:2 (May), pp. 231–236.

———— 1980. *Imperialismo y Dependencia.* México: Ediciones Era.

dos Santos, Wanderley Guilherme. 1978a. *Ordem Burguesa e Liberalismo Político.* São Paulo: Duas Cidades.

———— 1978b. *Poder e Política: Crônica do Autoritarismo Brasileiro.* Rio de Janeiro: Forense-Universitária.

———— 1979. *Cidadania e Justiça: A Política Social na Ordem Brasileira.* Rio de Janeiro: Campus.

———— 1980. "A Ciência Política na América Latina: Notas Preliminares de Autocrítica." *Dados,* 23:1. pp. 15–27.

———— 1981. "Reflexões sôbre a Questão do Liberalismo." In Bolivar Lamounier, Francisco Weffort, and Maria Victória Benevides, eds., pp. 155–188.

———— 1983. "A Quem Sirvirão as Instituições Liberais?" In de Oliveira, 1983, pp. 117–120.

———— 1984. *Kantianas Brasileiras: A Dual-Ética da Razão Política Nacional.* Rio de Janeiro: Paz e Terra.

———— 1985. "A Pós-'Revolução' Brasileira." In Jaguaribe et al., 1985, pp. 223–335.

———— 1986. *Sessenta e Quatro: Anatomia da Crise.* São Paulo: Vértice.

———— 1988. *Paradoxos do Liberalismo.* São Paulo: Vértice.

D'Souza, Dinesh. 1991. *Illiberal Education: The Politics of Race and Sex on Campus.* New York: Free Press.

Duncan, W. Raymond. 1985. *The Soviet Union and Cuba: Interests and Influence.* New York: Praeger.

Duvall, Raymond B. 1978. "Dependence and Dependencia Theory: Notes toward Precision of Concept and Argument." *International Organization,* 32:1 (Winter), pp. 51–78.

Duvall, Raymond D., and John R. Freeman. 1983. "The Techno-Bureaucratic Elite and the Entrepreneurial State in Dependent Industrialization." *American Political Science Review,* 77:3 (September), pp. 569–587.

Eakin, Marshall C. 1988. "Surveying the Past: Latin American History Textbooks and Readers." *Latin American Research Review,* 23:3, pp. 248–257.

Elguea, Javier. 1984. "Scientific Revolutions, Paradigms and Textbooks in Development Theories." *International Journal of Education Development,* 3:1, pp. 1–5.

———— 1989. *Las Teorías del Desarrollo Social en América Latina: Una Reconstrucción Racional.* México: El Colegio de México.

Elster, Jon. 1985. *Making Sense of Marx.* Cambridge: Cambridge University Press.

———— 1986. *An Introduction to Karl Marx.* Cambridge: Cambridge University Press.

Erisman, H. Michael. 1985. *Cuba's International Relations: The Anatomy of a Nationalistic Foreign Policy.* Boulder: Westview.

Esslin, Martin. 1977. *An Anatomy of Drama.* New York: Hill and Wang.

Evans, Peter B. 1979. *Dependent Development: The Alliance of Multinational, State, and Local Capital in Brazil.* Princeton: Princeton University Press.

———— 1980. *A Tríplice Aliança.* Rio de Janeiro: Zahar.

———— 1985a. "After Dependency: Recent Studies of Class, State, and Industrialization." *Latin American Research Review,* 20:2, pp. 149–160.

———— 1985b. "State, Capital, and the Transformation of Dependence: The Brazilian Computer Case." Working Paper No. 6, Brown University, Department of Sociology.

———— 1987. "Foreign Capital and the Third World State." In Weiner and Huntington, eds., 1987, pp. 319–352.

Fagen, Richard R. 1969. *The Transformation of Political Culture in Cuba.* Stanford: Stanford University Press.

———— 1974. "Commentary on Einaudi," in Cotler and Fagen, 1974a, pp. 256–265.

———— 1976. President's Statement. *LASA Newsletter,* 7:1 (March), p. 1.

———— 1977. "Studying Latin American Politics: Some Implications of a *Dependencia* Approach." *Latin American Research Review,* 12:2, pp. 3–26.

———— 1978a. "A Funny Thing Happened on the Way to the Market: Thoughts on Extending Dependency Ideas." *International Organization,* 32:1 (Winter), pp. 287–300.

———— 1978b. "Cuba and the Soviet Union," *The Wilson Quarterly,* 2:1 (Winter), pp. 69–78.

———— 1983. "Theories of Development: The Question of Class Struggle." *Monthly Review,* 34:10 (September), pp. 13–24.

Fagen, Richard R., Carmen Diana Deere, and José Luis Coraggio, eds. 1986. *Transition and Development: Problems of Third-World Socialism.* New York: Monthly Review Press.

Falcoff, Mark. 1980. "Latin America." In Peter Duignan and Alvin Rabushka, eds., *The United States in the 1980s,* pp. 797–826. Stanford: Hoover Institution Press.

Falcoff, Mark, Arturo Valenzuela, and Susan Kaufman Purcell. 1988. *Chile: Prospects for Democracy.* New York: Council on Foreign Relations.

Faoro, Raimundo. 1958. *Os Donos do Poder.* Rio de Janeiro: Globo.

Faria, Vilmar. 1971. "Dépendance et Idéologie des Dirigeants Industriels Brésiliens." *Sociologie du Travail,* 3 (July–September), pp. 264–281.

Fernández, Raúl A., and José F. Ocampo. 1974. "The Latin American Revolution: A Theory of Imperialism, Not Dependence." *Latin American Perspectives,* 1:1 (Spring), pp. 30–61.

Finifter, Ada W., ed. 1983. *Political Science: The State of the Discipline.* Washington, D.C.: American Political Science Association.

Francis, Michael. 1980. "Studying Latin American Politics: Methods or Fads?" *Review of Politics,* 42:1 (January), pp. 35–55.

Frank, Andre Gunder. 1967. *Capitalism and Underdevelopment in Latin America: Historical Studies of Chile and Brazil.* New York: Monthly Review Press.

———— 1969. *Capitalism and Underdevelopment in Latin America: Historical Studies of Chile and Brazil.* Rev. and enlarged ed. New York: Monthly Review Press.

———— 1972. *Lumpenbourgeoisie, Lumpendevelopment: Dependence, Class, and Politics in Latin America.* New York: Monthly Review Press.

———— 1974. "Dependence is Dead, Long Live Dependence and the Class Struggle: A Reply to My Critics." *Latin American Perspectives,* 1:1 (Spring), pp. 87–106.

———— 1975. *On Capitalist Underdevelopment.* Bombay: Oxford University Press.

———— 1979. *Dependent Accumulation and Underdevelopment.* New York: Monthly Review Press.

Freeman, John. 1982. "State Entrepreneurship and Dependent Development." *American Journal of Political Science,* 26, pp. 90–112.

Fretz, Robert. 1985. "Letter to the Editor." *LASA Forum,* 16:1 (Spring), p. 11.

Friedman, Douglas. 1984. *The State and Underdevelopment in Spanish America: The Political Roots of Dependency.* Boulder: Westview.

Fuentes, Carlos. 1984. "Are You Listening, Henry Kissinger?" *Harper's Magazine* (January), pp. 30–31, 34–37.

———— 1985. Remarks on receiving Mexico's Premio Nacional en Literatura y Lingüística. *New York Times Book Review*, March 31, p. 25.

Furtado, Celso. 1982. "Dependence in a United World." *Alternatives*, 8, pp. 259–284.

Gabeira, Fernando. 1979. *O Que é Isso, Companheiro?* Rio de Janeiro: Condecri.

Gall, Norman. 1976. "Atoms for Brazil, Dangers for All." *Foreign Policy*, 23 (Summer), pp. 155–201.

Galtung, Johan. 1971. "A Structural Theory of Imperialism." *Journal of Peace Research*, 8:2, pp. 81–117.

———— 1972. "A Structural Theory of Imperialism." *The African Review* (Dar es Salaam), 1:4 (April), pp. 93–108.

Geertz, Clifford. 1980. *Negara: The Theatre State in Nineteenth-Century Bali*. Princeton: Princeton University Press.

Gentleman, Judith. 1984. *Mexican Oil and Dependent Development*. New York: Peter Lang.

Gereffi, Gary. 1983. *The Pharmaceutical Industry and Dependency in the Third World*. Princeton: Princeton University Press.

Gil, Federico G. 1985. "Latin American Studies and Political Science: An Historical Sketch." *LASA Forum*, 16:2 (Summer), pp. 8–12.

Gilbert, Guy J. 1974. "Socialism and Dependency." *Latin American Perspectives*, 1:1 (Spring), pp. 107–123.

Gillespie, Charles. 1987. "From Authoritarian Crises to Democratic Transitions." *Latin American Research Review*, 22:3, pp. 165–184.

Gleijeses, Piero. 1984. "Nicaragua: Resist Romanticism." *Foreign Policy*, 54 (Spring), pp. 122–138.

Gless, Darryl L., and Barbara Herrnstein Smith, eds. 1990. *The Politics of Liberal Education*. Durham, N.C.: Duke University Press.

Godfrey, Martin, ed. 1980. "Is Dependency Dead?" *Bulletin* of the Institute of Development Studies, 12:1 (December), entire number.

Goffman, Erving. 1959. *The Presentation of Self in Everyday Life*. Garden City, N.Y.: Doubleday.

Gold, Thomas B. 1986. *State and Society in the Taiwan Miracle*. Armonk, N.Y.: M. E. Sharpe.

Góngora, Mario. 1983. "An Interview with Mario Góngora." *Hispanic American Historical Review*, 63:4 (November), pp. 663–675.

González, Edward. 1974. *Cuba under Castro: The Limits of Charisma*. Boston: Houghton Mifflin.

Gootenberg, Paul. 1989. *Between Silver and Guano: Commercial Policy and the State in Postindependence Peru*. Princeton: Princeton University Press.

Graff, Gerald, Barbara Hernnstein Smith, and George Levine. 1991. "'The Storm Over the University': An Exchange." *New York Review of Books*, February 14, pp. 48–50.

Grendzier, Irene. 1985. *Managing Political Change: Social Scientists and the Third World.* Boulder: Westview.

Grieco, Joseph M. 1982. "Between Dependency and Autonomy," *International Organization,* 36:3 (Summer), pp. 609–632.

——— 1984. *Between Dependency and Autonomy: India's Experience with the International Computer Industry.* Berkeley: University of California Press.

Grosse, Robert E. 1986. Book review, in *Journal of Interamerican Studies and World Affairs,* 28:4 (Winter), pp. 212–214.

Gutiérrez, Gustavo. 1973. *A Theology of Liberation: History, Politics, and Salavation.* Maryknoll, N.Y.: Orbis Books.

Haggard, Stephan. 1989. "The Political Economy of Foreign Direct Investment in Latin America." *Latin American Research Review,* 24:1, pp. 184–208.

Hajjar, Sami G., ed. 1984. "The Middle East: From Transition to Development." *Journal of Asian and African Studies,* 19:3–4, entire number.

Hakimian, Hassan. 1980. "Iran: Dependency and Industrialization." In Godfrey, ed., 1980, pp. 24–28.

Halebsky, Sandor, and John M. Kirk, eds. 1985. *Cuba: Twenty-Five Years of Revolution, 1959–1984.* New York: Praeger.

Hall, John R. 1984. "World-System Holism and Colonial Brazilian Agriculture." *Latin American Research Review,* 19:2, pp. 43–69.

Halperín-Donghi, Tulio. 1982. "'Dependency Theory' and Latin American Historiography." *Latin American Research Review,* 17:1, pp. 115–130.

Hamilton, Nora. 1982. *The Limits of State Autonomy: Post-Revolutionary Mexico.* Princeton: Princeton University Press.

Harding, Timothy F. 1976. "Dependency, Nationalism, and the State in Latin America." *Latin American Perspectives,* 3:4, (Fall), pp. 3–11.

Hartlyn, Jonathan, and Samuel Morley, eds. 1986. *Latin American Political Economy: Financial Crisis and Political Change.* Boulder: Westview.

Hartz, Louis, et al. 1964. *The Founding of New Societies.* New York: Harcourt, Brace.

Hewlett, Cynthia Ann. 1980. *The Cruel Dilemmas of Development.* New York: Basic Books.

Higgott, Richard A. 1983. *Political Development Theory: The Contemporary Debate.* London: Croon Helm.

Hirschman, Albert O. 1945, 1980. *National Power and the Structure of Foreign Trade.* Berkeley: University of California Press.

——— 1961. "Ideologies of Economic Development in Latin America." In Albert O. Hirschman, ed., *Latin American Issues: Essays and Comments,* pp. 3–42. New York: Twentieth Century Fund.

——— 1971. *A Bias for Hope: Essays on Development and Latin America.* New Haven: Yale University Press.

——— 1978. "Beyond Asymmetry: Critical Notes on Myself as a Young

Man and on Some Other Old Friends." *International Organization,* 32:1 (Winter), pp. 45–50.

——— 1979. "The Turn to Authoritarianism in Latin America and the Search for Its Economic Determinants." In David Collier, ed., 1979a, pp. 61–98.

——— 1987. "The Political Economy of Latin American Development: Seven Exercises in Retrospection." *Latin American Research Review,* 22:3, pp. 7–36.

Hirst, Mônica. 1984. "Transição Democrática e Política Externa: A Experiência Brasileira." *Dados,* 27:3, pp. 377–394.

Hispanic Division, Library of Congress. 1986. *National Directory of Latin Americanists,* 3rd ed. Washington, D.C.: U.S. Government Printing Office.

Hodara, Joseph. 1971. "La Dependencia de la Dependencia." *Aportes* (Paris), 21 (July), pp. 6–15.

——— 1983. "Demonología en la Ciencia." *Interciencia,* 8:2 (March-April), pp. 115–116.

Holland, Stuart. 1979. "Dependent Development: Portugal As Periphery." In Dudley Seers, ed., *Underdeveloped Europe: Studies in Core-Periphery Relations.* Sussex: Institute of Development Studies.

Hollander, Paul. 1981. *Political Pilgrims: Travels of Western Intellectuals to the Soviet Union, China, and Cuba 1928–1979.* New York: Oxford University Press.

——— 1988. *The Survival of the Adversary Culture.* New Brunswick: Transaction.

Horowitz, Irving Louis. 1982. *Beyond Empire and Revolution: Militarization and Consolidation in the Third World.* New York: Oxford University Press.

Humphrey, John. 1982. *Capitalist Control and Workers' Struggle in the Brazilian Auto Industry.* Princeton: Princeton University Press.

Huntington, Samuel P. 1965. "Political Development and Political Decay." *World Politics,* 17:3 (April), pp. 386–430.

——— 1968. *Political Order in Changing Societies.* New Haven: Yale University Press.

——— 1984. "Will More Countries Become Democratic?" *Political Science Quarterly,* 99:2, pp. 193–218.

——— 1987. "The Goals of Development." In Weiner and Huntington, 1987, pp. 3–32.

Huntington, Samuel P., and Jorge I. Domínguez. 1975. "Political Development." In Nelson W. Polsby and Fred I. Greenstein, eds., *Handbook of Political Science,* vol. 3. Reading, Mass.: Addison-Wesley.

Ianni, Octávio. 1970. *Crisis in Brazil.* New York: Columbia University Press.

Jaguaribe, Helio. 1966. "A Brazilian View." In Raymond Vernon, ed., *How*

Latin America Views the Private Investor, pp. 67–93. New York: Praeger.

——— 1970. "Dependencia y Autonomía en América Latina." In Jaguaribe, et al., 1970, 1971, pp. 1–86.

——— 1973. *Political Development: A General Theory and a Latin American Case Study.* New York: Harper and Row.

——— 1974. *Brasil: Crise e Alternativas.* Rio de Janeiro: Zahar.

——— 1978. *Introdução ao Desenvolvimento Social: As Perspectivas Liberal e Marxista e os Problemas da Sociedade Não Repressiva.* Rio de Janeiro: Paz e Terra.

——— 1986a. *Sociedade e Cultura.* São Paulo: Vértice.

——— 1986b. *O Novo Cenário Internacional.* Rio de Janeiro: Editora Guanabara.

Jaguaribe, Helio, A. Ferrer, M. S. Wionczek, and T. Dos Santos. 1970, 1971. *La Dependencia Político-Económica de América Latina.* México: Siglo Vientiuno.

Jaguaribe, Helio, F. Iglésias, W. Guilherme Dos Santos, V. Chacon, and F. Comparato. 1985. *Brasil, Sociedade Democrática.* Rio de Janeiro: José Olympio.

Jaguaribe, Helio, W. Guilherme Dos Santos, M. de Paiva Abreu, W. Fritsch, and F. Bastos de Ávila. 1986. *Brasil, 2.000: Para um Novo Pacto Social.* Rio de Janeiro: Paz e Terra.

Jaksic, Iván. 1985. "Task Force Report on the Mapuches of Chile." *LASA Forum,* 15:3 (Fall), pp. 16–19.

Johnson, John J. 1984. "Remarks by John J. Johnson." *LASA Forum,* 15:2 (Summer), pp. 8–11.

Johnson, Leland. 1965. "U.S. Business Interests in Cuba and The Rise of Castro." *World Politics,* 17:3 (April), pp. 440–459.

Kahl, Joseph A. 1976. *Modernization, Exploitation, and Dependency in Latin America: Germani, González Casanova, and Cardoso.* New Brunswick, N.J.: Transaction Books.

Kaplan, Marcos. 1974. "The Power Structure in International Relations." *International Social Science Journal,* 26:1, pp. 96–97.

Kaufman, Edy. 1976. *The Superpowers and Their Spheres of Influence.* New York: St. Martin's Press.

Kaufman, Robert H., Daniel S. Geller, and Harry I. Chernotsky. 1975. "A Preliminary Test of the Theory of Dependency." *Comparative Politics,* 7:3 (April), pp. 303–330.

Kernan, Alvin. 1990. *The Death of Literature.* New Haven: Yale University Press.

Kimball, Roger. 1990. *Tenured Radicals: How Politics Has Corrupted American Higher Education.* New York: Harper and Row.

Kinzer, Stephen. 1985a. "Nicaragua Says Main Oil Source Will Be Moscow." *New York Times,* May 21, pp. 1, 6.

—— 1985b. "Sandinista Curbs Aimed at Enemy at Home." *New York Times,* October 18, p. 4.

Klarén, Peter F., and Thomas Bossert, eds. 1986. *Promise of Development: Theories of Change in Latin America.* Boulder: Westview.

Kline, Harvey F. 1987. *The Coal of El Cerrejón: Dependent Bargaining and Colombian Policy Making.* University Park, Pa.: Penn State Press.

Kofas, Jon V. 1986. *Dependence and Underdevelopment in Colombia.* Tempe, Arizona: Center for Latin American Studies, University of Arizona.

Kohli, Atul, ed. 1986. *The State and Development in the Third World.* Princeton: Princeton University Press.

Konder, Leandro. 1980. *A Democracia e os Communistas no Brasil.* Rio de Janeiro: Graal.

Kornberg, Allan, ed. 1981. *Political Science Reading Lists and Course Outlines.* Durham, N.C.: Eno River Press.

—— 1989. *Political Science Reading Lists and Course Outlines.* Durham, N.C.: Eno River Press.

Krasner, Stephen D. 1973a. "Manipulating International Commodity Markets: Brazilian Coffee Policy, 1906 to 1962." *Public Policy,* 21:4 (Fall), pp. 493–523.

—— 1973b. "Business-Government Relations: The Case of the International Coffee Agreement." *International Organization,* 27:4 (Fall), pp. 495–516.

—— 1984. "Approaches to the State." *Comparative Politics,* 16:2 (January), pp. 223–246.

—— 1985. *Structural Conflict: The Third World Against Global Liberalism.* Berkeley: University of California Press.

Krauze, Enrique. 1986. *Por una Democracia sin Adjetivos.* México: Joaquín Mortiz-Planeta.

Kuhn, Thomas S. 1962. *The Structure of Scientific Revolutions.* Chicago: University of Chicago Press.

Laclau, Ernesto. 1971. "Feudalism and Capitalism in Latin America." *New Left Review,* No. 67 (May-June), pp. 19–38.

Lacouture, Jean. 1977. "The Bloodiest Revolution." *New York Review of Books,* March 31.

LaFeber, Walter. 1984. *Inevitable Revolutions: The United States in Central America.* New York: W. W. Norton.

Lakatos, Imre. 1970. "Falsificationism and the Methodology of Scientific Research Programs." In Imre Lakatos and Alan Musgrave, eds., *Criticism and The Growth of Knowledge,* pp. 91–196. Cambridge: Cambridge University Press.

Lake, David. 1987. "Power and the Third World: Toward a Realist Political Economy of North-South Relations." *International Studies Quarterly*, 31, pp. 217–234.

Lamounier, Bolivar. 1981. "Representação Política: A Importância de Certos Formalismos." In Lamounier, Weffort, and Benevides, 1981, pp. 230–257.

———— 1982. "A Ciência Política no Brasil: Roteiro para um Balanço Crítico." In Bolivar Lamounier, ed., *A Ciência Política nos Anos 80*, pp. 407–435. Brasília: Editora da Universidade de Brasília.

———— 1984. "Opening Through Elections: Will the Brazilian Case Become a Paradigm?" *Government and Opposition*, 19:2 (Spring), pp. 167–177.

———— 1989. "Inequality Against Democracy." In Diamond, Linz, and Lipset, 1988– , vol. 4, pp. 111–157.

Lamounier, Bolivar, Francisco Weffort, and Maria Victória Benevides, eds., 1981. *Direito, Cidadania e Participação*. São Paulo: T. A. Queiroz.

LASA. 1976. "Program Evaluation, 6th National Meeting." *LASA Newsletter*, 7:4 (December), pp. 26–32.

———— 1985a. Latin American Studies Association. *Handbook and Membership Directory*, 1984–85. Austin: LASA.

———— 1985b. "Nicaragua Report Stirs Controversy." *LASA Forum*, 16:1 (Spring), pp. 8–11.

———— 1988a. "Committees and Task Forces." *LASA Forum*, 19:1 (Spring), pp. 16–17.

———— 1988b. "Resolutions Ratified." *LASA Forum*, 19:2 (Summer), pp. 11–15.

———— 1988c. Revised Constitution and Bylaws. *LASA Forum*, 19:2 (Summer), pp. 11–15.

LASA Report. 1984. "Report of the Ad Hoc Committee to Investigate the Publication of a CIA Employment Advertisement in the LASA Forum." *LASA Forum*, 14:4 (Winter), pp. 8–18.

———— 1985. "Report of the Latin American Studies Association Delegation to Observe the Nicaraguan General Election of November 4, 1984." *LASA Forum*, 15:4 (Winter), pp. 9–43.

———— 1986. "Report of the Task Force on Scholarly Relations with Cuba." *LASA Forum*, 17:3 (Fall), pp. 13–16.

LASA Resolution. 1976. In *LASA Newsletter*, 7:2 (June), p. 6.

———— 1984. In *LASA Forum*, 15:1 (Spring), pp. 3–4.

Latin American Perspectives. 1974. "Dependency Theory: A Reassessment," 1:1 (Spring).

Leiken, Robert S. 1981. "Eastern Winds in Latin America." *Foreign Policy*, 42 (Spring), pp. 94–113.

———— ed. 1984a. *Central America: Anatomy of Conflict.* New York: Pergamon.

Leiken, Robert S. 1984b. "Nicaragua's Untold Story." *The New Republic,* October 8, pp. 16–22.

LeoGrande, William M. 1979. "Cuban Dependency: A Comparison of Pre-Revolutionary and Post-Revolutionary International Economic Relations." *Cuban Studies,* 9:2 (July), pp. 1–28.

Leontiev, Wassily. 1971. "The Trouble With Cuban Socialism." *New York Review of Books,* January 7, pp. 19–23.

Lerner, Daniel. 1958. *The Passing of Traditional Society.* Glencoe: Free Press.

Lévi-Strauss, Claude. 1969. *Tristes Tropiques.* Trans. by John Russell. New York: Atheneum.

Levine, Daniel. 1988. "Paradigm Lost: Dependence to Democracy." *World Politics,* 40:3 (April), pp. 377–394.

Levine, George, et al. 1989. *Speaking for the Humanities.* New York: American Council of Learned Societies.

Levy, Daniel. 1985. "Letter to the Editor." *LASA Forum,* 16:1 (Spring), pp. 8–10.

———— 1986. "LASA's Election Coverage: Reflections and Suggestions." *LASA Forum,* 17:1 (Spring), pp. 24–27.

Levy, Daniel, and Gabriel Székely. 1987. *Mexico: Paradoxes of Stability and Change.* 2nd ed. Boulder: Westview.

Leys, Colin. 1971. *Underdevelopment in Kenya: The Political Economy of Neo-Colonialism, 1964–1971.* Berkeley: University of California Press.

"Liçoes da Política." 1984. *Isto É,* 8:380 (4 April), p. 23.

Lijphart, Arend. 1984. *Democracies.* New Haven: Yale University Press.

Lin, Hyan-Chin. 1987. *Dependent Development in Korea, 1963–1979.* Honolulu: University of Hawaii Press.

Lindenberger, Herbert. 1990. *The History in Literature: On Value, Genre, Institutions.* New York: Columbia University Press.

Linz, Juan J. 1978. *The Breakdown of Democratic Regimes: Crisis, Breakdown, and Reequilibration.* Baltimore: Johns Hopkins University Press.

Linz, Juan, and Alfred Stepan, eds. 1978. *The Breakdown of Democratic Regimes.* Baltimore: Johns Hopkins University Press.

Lipset, Seymour Martin. 1960. *Political Man: The Social Bases of Politics.* Garden City, N.Y.: Doubleday.

———— 1981a. *Political Man: The Social Bases of Politics,* Expanded ed. Baltimore: Johns Hopkins University Press.

———— 1981b. "Whatever Happened to the Proletariat?" *Encounter,* 56 (June).

Liss, Sheldon. 1984. *Marxist Thought in Latin America.* Berkeley: University of California Press.

Lockwood, Lee. 1970. "Introduction to 'This Shame Will Be Welcome. . .': A Speech by Fidel Castro." *New York Review of Books*, September 24, pp. 18–20.

Löwy, Michael, ed. 1982. *El Marxismo en América Latina*. México: Ediciones Era.

Lowenthal, Abraham F. 1986. *Brazil and the United States*. New York: Foreign Policy Association.

——— 1987. *Partners in Conflict: The United States and Latin America*. Baltimore: Johns Hopkins University Press.

Lowenthal, Abraham, and Albert Fishlow. 1979. *Latin America's Emergence: Toward a U.S. Response*. New York: Foreign Policy Association.

Lowenthal, Abraham, and Jane Jaquette. 1979. "Note." *LASA Newsletter*, 10:3 (September), p. 3.

Love, Joseph L. 1980. "Raúl Prebisch and the Origins of the Doctrine of Unequal Exchange." *Latin American Research Review*, 15:3, pp. 45–72.

Luedde-Neurath, Richard. 1980. "Export Orientation to Korea: How Helpful is Dependency Thinking to Its Analysis?" In Godfrey, 1980, pp. 48–53.

Luke, Timothy W. 1983. "Dependent Development and the Arab OPEC States." *Journal of Politics*, 45:4 (November), pp. 979–1003.

Maidique, Modesto. 1983. "Fidel's Plantation." *The Stanford Magazine*, 11:4 (Winter), pp. 26–32.

Mainwaring, Scott. 1984. "Authoritarianism and Democracy in Argentina." *Journal of Interamerican Studies and World Affairs*, 26:3 (August), pp. 415–431.

——— 1988. "Political Parties and Democratization in Brazil and the Southern Cone." *Comparative Politics*, 21:1 (October), pp. 91–120.

Malloy, James M., and Mitchell Seligson, eds. 1987. *Authoritarians and Democrats: Regime Transition in Latin America*. Pittsburgh: University of Pittsburgh Press.

Mamalakis, Markos. 1987. Book review, in *Journal of Latin American Studies*, 19:1 (May), pp. 204–207.

Mandle, Jay R. 1979. Book review, in *The Annals of the American Academy*, 445, p. 178.

Mariátegui, José Carlos. 1971. *Seven Interpretive Essays on Peruvian Reality*. Austin: University of Texas Press.

Marsal, Juan Francisco. 1979. *Dependencia y Independencia: Las Alternativas de la Sociología Latinoamericana en el Siglo XX*. Madrid: Centro de Investigaciones Sociológicas.

Martins, Carlos Estevam, ed. 1977. *Estado e Capitalismo no Brasil*. São Paulo: Hucitec-CEBRAP.

Martz, John D. III, and David J. Myers. 1983. "Understanding Latin American Politics: Analytic Methods and Intellectual Traditions." *Polity*, 16:2 (Winter), pp. 214–241.

Marx, Karl. 1972. "The Future Results of British Rule in India," (1853). In Robert C. Tucker, ed., *The Marx-Engels Reader*, pp. 583–588. New York: Norton.

Mazrui, Ali. 1978. *Political Values and the Educated Class in Africa*. Berkeley: University of California Press.

McClintock, Cynthia, and Abraham F. Lowenthal, eds. 1983. *The Peruvian Experiment Reconsidered*. Princeton: Princeton University Press.

McDonough, Peter. 1980. Book review, in *American Political Science Review*, 74:1 (March), pp. 234–235.

McGovern, Arthur F. 1986. "Latin America and Dependency Theory." *This World*, 14 (Spring/Summer), pp. 104–123.

McGowan, Patrick, and Dale Smith. 1978. "Economic Dependency in Black Africa: A Causal Analysis of Competing Theories." *International Organization*, 32:1 (Winter), pp. 179–235.

McLellan, David. 1976. *Karl Marx*. New York: Penguin.

Meira Penna, José Osvaldo de. 1972. *Política Externa: Segurança e Desenvolvimento*. Rio de Janeiro: APEC.

—— 1974. *Em Berço Esplêndido: Ensaios de Psicologia Coletiva Brasileira*. Rio de Janeiro: José Olympio.

—— 1983. "The U.S. as Scapegoat: A Psychological Approach to Foreign Policy Problems." *Catholicism in Crisis*, July, pp. 30–34.

Merquior, José Guilherme. 1982. *A Natureza do Processo*. Rio de Janeiro: Nova Fronteira.

—— 1983. *O Argumento Liberal*. Rio de Janeiro: Nova Fronteira.

—— 1984. "Power and Identity: Politics and Ideology in Latin America." *Government and Opposition*, 19:2 (Spring), pp. 239–249.

Merton, Robert King. 1973. *The Sociology of Science*. Chicago: University of Chicago Press.

Mesa-Lago, Carmelo. 1981. *The Economy of Socialist Cuba: A Two-Decade Appraisal*. Albuquerque: University of New Mexico Press.

Mesa-Lago, Carmelo, and Fernando Gil. 1989. "Soviet Economic Relations with Cuba." In Eusebio Mujal-León, ed., *The USSR and Latin America: A Developing Relationship*, pp. 183–232. Boston: Unwin Hyman.

Migdal, Joel. 1983. "Studying the Politics of Development and Change: The State of the Art." In Finifter, ed., 1983, pp. 309–338.

Miller, Richard W. 1987. *Fact and Method: Explanation, Confirmation and Reality in the Natural and the Social Sciences*. Princeton: Princeton University Press.

Mitchell, Christopher. 1985. "Final Report of the Program Committee, LASA Twelfth International Meeting." *LASA Forum*, 16:2 (Summer), pp. 12–14.

Mitchell, Tony. 1982. "South Korea: Vision of the Future for Labour Surplus Economies?" In Bienefeld and Godfrey, eds., 1982, pp. 189–216.

Monteón, Michael P. 1982. *Chile in the Nitrate Era: The Evolution of Economic Dependence, 1880–1930.* Madison: University of Wisconsin Press.

Moore, Jr., Barrington. 1966. *Social Origins of Dictatorship and Democracy: Lord and Peasant in the Making of the Modern World.* Boston: Beacon Press.

Moran, Theodore. 1974. *Multinational Corporations and the Politics of Dependence: Copper in Chile.* Princeton: Princeton University Press.

Moreira Alves, Marcio. 1973. *A Grain of Mustard Seed: The Awakening of the Brazilian Revolution.* Garden City, N.Y.: Doubleday.

Morley, Samuel A., and Gordon W. Smith. 1973. "The Effect of Changes in the Distribution of Income on Labor, Foreign Investment, and Growth in Brazil." In Stepan, ed., 1973, pp. 119–141.

Morse, Richard M. 1985. "New Directions for the Latin American Program." *Newsletter,* no. 13 (Spring). Washington, D.C.: Latin American Program, Woodrow Wilson International Center for Scholars.

Mortimer, Rex, ed. 1973. *Showcase State: The Illusion of Indonesia's Accelerated Modernization.* Sydney: Angus and Robertson.

Moura, Gerson, and Maria Regina Soares de Lima. 1982. "Relações Internacionais e Política Externa Brasileira: Uma Resenha Bibliográfica." *Boletím Informativo e Bibliográfico de Ciências Sociais* (O BIB). Rio de Janeiro, Number 13 (1st Semester), pp. 5–36.

Munck, Ronaldo. 1983. *Politics and Dependency in the Third World: The Case of Latin America.* New York: Monthly Review Press.

Muñoz, Heraldo, ed. 1981. *From Dependency to Development: Strategies to Overcome Underdevelopment and Inequality.* Boulder: Westview.

Murphy, Craig. 1984. *The Emergence of the NIEO Ideology.* Boulder: Westview.

Myer, John. 1975. "A Crown of Thorns: Cardoso and Counter-revolution." *Latin American Perspectives,* 2:1. (Spring), pp. 33–48.

Nef, Jorge. 1988. "The Trend toward Democratization and Redemocratization in Latin America: Shadow and Substance." *Latin American Research Review,* 23:3, pp. 131–153.

Nolan, David. 1984. *Ideology of the Sandinistas and the Nicaraguan Revolution.* Coral Gables, Fla.: Institute of Interamerican Studies, University of Miami.

North, Liisa L. 1983. "Ideological Orientations of Peru's Military Rulers." In McClintock and Lowenthal, 1983, pp. 245–274.

Nunes Leal, Victor. 1948. *O Município e o Regime Representativo no Brasil: Contribuição ao Estudo do 'Coronelismo'.* Rio de Janeiro: Revista Forense.

Oates, Joyce Carol. 1987. "The World's Worst Critics." *New York Times Book Review,* 18 January, p. 1.

O'Brien, Philip. J. 1974. "A Critique of Latin American Theories of Dependency." Occasional paper no. 12. Institute of Latin American Studies, University of Glasgow.

—— 1985. "Dependency Revisited." In Abel and Lewis, eds., 1985, pp. 40–69.

O'Brien, Thomas F. 1982. *The Nitrate Industry and Chile's Crucial Transition: 1870–1891.* New York: New York University Press.

—— 1985. "Dependency Revisited: A Review Essay." *Business History Review,* 59:4 (Winter), pp. 663–669.

O'Donnell, Guillermo. 1973. *Modernization and Bureaucratic Authoritarianism.* Berkeley: Institute of International Studies, University of California.

—— 1974. Letter to the author, January 18.

—— 1978. "Corporatism and the Question of the State." In James Malloy, ed., *Authoritarianism and Corporatism in Latin America,* pp. 47–87. Pittsburgh: University of Pittsburgh Press.

O'Donnell, Guillermo, and Delfina Linck. 1973. *Dependencia y Autonomía: Formas de Dependencia y Estratégias de Liberación.* Buenos Aires: Amorrortu.

O'Donnell, Guillermo, and Philippe Schmitter. 1986. *Transitions from Authoritarian Rule: Tentative Conclusions about Uncertain Democracies.* Baltimore: Johns Hopkins University Press.

O'Donnell, Guillermo, Philippe Schmitter, and Laurence Whitehead, eds. 1986. *Transitions From Authoritarian Rule.* Baltimore: Johns Hopkins University Press.

Ozawa, Terutomo. 1979. *Multinationalism, Japanese Style: The Political Economy of Outward Dependency.* Princeton: Princeton University Press.

Packenham, Robert A. 1976. "Trends in Brazilian National Dependency Since 1964." In Roett, ed., 1976, pp. 89–115.

—— 1982. "Plus Ça Change . . . : The English Edition of Cardoso and Faletto's *Dependencia y Desarrollo en América Latina.*" *Latin American Research Review,* 17:1, pp. 131–151.

—— 1986a. "Capitalist Dependency and Socialist Dependency: The Case of Cuba." *Journal of Interamerican Development and World Affairs,* 28:1 (Spring), pp. 59–92.

—— 1986b. "The Changing Political Discourse in Brazil, 1964–1985." In Selcher, ed., 1986, pp. 135–173.

Page, Joseph A. 1972. *The Revolution That Never Was: Northeast Brazil, 1955–1964.* New York, N.Y.: Grossman.

Palma, Gabriel. 1978. "Dependency: A Formal Theory of Underdevelopment or a Methodology for the Analysis of Concrete Situations of Underdevelopment?" *World Development,* 6:7/8, pp. 881–924.

Palmer, Monte. 1989. *Dilemmas of Political Development,* 4th edition. Itasca, Ill.: F. E. Peacock.

Pang, Eul-Soo. 1975. "Brazil's Pragmatic Nationalism." *Current History,* 68:401, pp. 5–10, 38.

Pareek, Udai. 1968. "Motivational Patterns and Planned Social Change." *International Social Science Journal,* 20:3, pp. 464–473.

Pastor, Robert A. 1983. "Cuba and the Soviet Union: Does Cuba Act Alone?" In Barry B. Levine, ed., *The New Cuban Presence in the Caribbean,* pp. 191–209. Boulder: Westview.

——— 1986. "Explaining U.S. Policy toward the Caribbean Basin: Fixed and Emerging Images." *World Politics,* 38:3 (April), pp. 483–515.

Payne, Anthony. 1984. "Introduction: Dependency Theory and the Commonwealth Caribbean." In Anthony Payne and Paul Sutton, eds., *Dependency under Challenge: The Political Economy of the Commonwealth Caribbean.* Manchester: Manchester University Press, pp. 1–17.

Paz, Octavio. 1972. *The Other Mexico: Critique of the Pyramid.* New York: Grove Press.

——— 1979. *El Ogro Filantrópico.* México: Joaquín Mortiz.

Pedreira, Fernando. 1964. *Março 31: Civis e Militares no Processo da Crise Brasiliera.* Rio de Janeiro: José Álvaro.

——— 1975. *Brasil Política, 1964–1975.* São Paulo: Difel.

——— 1976. *A Liberdade e a Ostra.* Rio de Janeiro: Nova Fronteira.

——— 1982. *Impávido Colosso.* Rio de Janeiro: Nova Fronteira.

——— 1983a. "Dois Grandes Desafios: Um Vem do Socialismo." In de Oliveira, 1983, pp. 114–117.

——— 1983b. "Viva Pois o Consenso." *Journal do Brasil,* March 3, p. 11.

Pereira, Carlos Alberto M., and Heloísa Buarque de Hollanda. 1980. *Patrulhas Ideológicas.* São Paulo: Brasiliense.

Pérez, Louis A. 1983. *Cuba Between Empires, 1878–1902.* Pittsburgh: University of Pittsburgh Press.

——— 1985. "Toward a New Future, from a New Past: The Enterprise of History in Socialist Cuba." *Cuban Studies,* 15:1 (Winter), pp. 1–13.

Petras, James. 1988a. "State, Regime, and the Democratization Muddle." *LASA Forum,* 18:4 (Winter), pp. 9–12.

——— 1988b. Letter. *LASA Forum,* 19:2 (Summer), p. 33.

Petras, James, and Maurice Zeitlin, eds. 1968. *Latin America: Reform or Revolution?* New York: Fawcett.

Phillips, D. C. 1976. *Holistic Thought in Social Science.* Stanford: Stanford University Press.

Pike, Frederick. 1978. Book review, in *Hispanic American Historical Review,* 58:1 (February), p. 157.

Popper, Karl. 1957. *The Poverty of Historicism.* London: Routledge, Keegan Paul.

———— 1959. *The Logic of Scientific Discovery.* New York: Basic Books.

———— 1963. *Conjectures and Refutations.* London: Routledge, Keegan Paul.

———— 1976. *Unended Quest: An Intellectual Autobiography.* LaSalle, Ill.: Open Court Publishing Company.

Portes, Alejandro. 1976. "On the Sociology of National Development: Theories and Issues." *American Journal of Sociology,* 82:1 (July), pp. 55–85.

———— 1985. "Latin American Class Structures." *Latin American Research Review,* 20:3, pp. 7–39.

Portes, Alejandro, and William Canak. 1981. "Latin America: Social Structures and Sociology." *Annual Review of Sociology,* 7, pp. 225–248.

Prowess, M. Cavalcade, Tony Frank, and Harry O'Fields [pseudonyms for Richard Morse]. 1977. "McLuhanaíma The Solid Gold Hero; or, O Herói Com Bastante Carácter (Uma Fuga)." *Almanaque, Cadernos de Literatura e Ensaio,* 3, pp. 63–74.

Przeworski, Adam. 1985. *Capitalism and Social Democracy.* Cambridge: Cambridge University Press.

———— 1988. Letter. *LASA Forum,* 19:2 (Summer), p. 33.

Purcell, Susan Kaufman. 1984. Book review, in *New York Times Book Review,* February 12, p. 21.

———— 1990. "Cuba's Cloudy Future." *Foreign Affairs,* 69:3 (Summer), pp. 113–130.

Quijano D., Aníbal. 1970. "Dependencia, Cambio Social y Urbanización en Latinoamérica." In Cardoso and Weffort, 1970.

Rabinowitz, Dorothy. 1990. "Vive the Academic Resistance." *Wall Street Journal,* November 13.

Randall, Vicky, and Robin Theobald. 1985. *Political Change and Underdevelopment.* Durham, N.C.: Duke University Press.

Rangel, Carlos. 1986. *Third World Ideology and Western Reality: Manufacturing Political Myth.* New Brunswick: Transaction Books.

Ray, David. 1973. "The Dependency Model of Latin American Underdevelopment: Three Basic Fallacies." *Journal of Inter-American Studies and World Affairs,* 15:1 (February), pp. 4–20.

Reading, Reid. 1987. "On Being Targeted: Some Personal Reflections." *LASA Forum,* 18:1 (Spring), pp. 12–13.

"Reflections on Sidney Hook." 1989–90. *Academic Questions,* 3:1 (Winter), pp. 9–23.

Reilly, Robert. 1985. Letter. *LASA Forum,* 16:1 (Spring), p. 11.

Reynolds, Clark. 1982. "Notes on the State of Development Modeling." *LASA Newsletter*, 13:1 (Spring), pp. 12–14.

Ripoll, Carlos. 1982. "The Cuban Scene: Censors and Dissenters." *Partisan Review*. 48:4.

Robock, Stefan H. 1975. *Brazil: A Study in Development Progress*. Lexington, Mass.: D. C. Heath.

Roche, Marcel. 1976a. "Dependence." *Interciencia*, 1:4 (November-December), p. 200.

———— 1976b. "Early History of Science in Spanish America." *Science*, 194 (19 November), pp. 806–810.

———— 1977. "The Anti-Science Movement." *Interciencia*, 2:2 (March-April), p. 74.

Rock, David. 1987. *Argentina, 1516–1987: From Spanish Colonization to Alfonsín*. Berkeley: University of California Press.

Roett, Riordan, ed. 1976. *Brazil in the Seventies*. Washington, D.C.: American Enterprise Institute.

Roett, Riordan. 1984. *Brazil: Politics in a Patrimonial Society*. 3rd ed. New York: Praeger.

Romero, Sílvio. 1978. "Psicologia Nacional, Prejuízos de Educação, Imitação do Estrangeiro." In Antonio Cândido, ed., *Sílvio Romero: Teoria, Crítica, e História Literária*, pp. 17–24. Rio de Janeiro: Livros Técnicos e Científicos.

Rosenthal, Steven T. 1980. *The Politics of Dependency: Urban Reform in Istanbul*. Westport, Conn.: Greenwood Press.

Roxborough, Ian. 1984. "Unity and Diversity in Latin American History." *Journal of Latin American Studies*, 16, pp. 1–26.

Rubinson, Richard. 1976. "The World-Economy and the Distribution of Income within States: A Cross-National Study." *American Sociological Review*, 41 (August), pp. 638–659.

Ruddle, Kenneth, and Kathleen Barrows, eds., 1974. *Statistical Abstract of Latin America*. Los Angeles: Latin American Center, University of California.

Russett, Bruce. 1983. "International Interactions and Processes: The Internal versus External Debate Revisited." In Finifter, ed., 1983, pp. 541–570.

Safa, Helen I. 1984. "President's Corner." *LASA Forum*, 14:4 (Winter), pp. 1–2

———— 1985. "President's Corner." *LASA Forum*. 15:4 (Winter), p. 1–3.

Safa, Helen I., Nelson P. Valdés, and Richard N. Sinkin. 1984. "Report of the LASA Delegation's Visit to Cuba." *LASA Forum*, 15:3 (Fall), pp. 8–9.

Sanderson, Steven E. 1981. *Agrarian Populism and the Mexican State: The Struggle for Land in Sonora*. Berkeley: University of California Press.

Sanderson, Steven E., ed. 1985. *The Americas in the New International Division of Labor.* New York: Holmes and Meier.

Sanderson, Steven E. 1986. *The Transformation of Mexican Agriculture: International Structure and the Politics of Rural Change.* Princeton: Princeton University Press.

Sarti, Ingrid. 1981. "Communication and Cultural Dependency." In Emile McAnany, Jorge Schnitman, and Noreen Janus, eds., *Communication and Social Structure: Critical Studies in Mass Media Research,* pp. 317–334. New York: Praeger.

Schechner, Richard. 1985. *Between Theater and Anthropology.* Philadelphia: University of Pennsylvania Press.

Schoultz, Lars. 1985. "Task Force Report on Grenada." *LASA Forum,* 16:1 (Spring), pp. 12–15.

———— 1987. *National Security and United States Policy Toward Latin America.* Princeton: Princeton University Press.

Schwartzman, Simon. 1977. "As Eleições e o Problema Institucional (1): Estado e Sociedade no Brasil." *Dados,* 14, pp. 164–184.

———— 1981. *Ciência, Universidade e Ideologia.* Rio de Janeiro: Zahar.

———— 1982. *Bases do Autoritarismo Brasileiro.* 2nd ed. Rio de Janeiro: Campus.

———— 1987. "Brazil: Opportunity and Crisis in Higher Education." Berkeley: Center for Studies in Higher Education, University of California.

Schwarz, Roberto. 1977. *Ao Vencedor as Batatas: Forma Literária e Processo Social nos Inícios do Romance Brasileiro.* São Paulo: Duas Cidades.

Searle, John. 1990. "The Storm over the University." *New York Review of Books,* December 6, pp. 34–42.

———— 1991. "Reply." In Graff, Herrnstein Smith, and Levine, 1991, pp. 48–50.

Seers, Dudley. 1979. "The Congruence of Marxism and Other Neoclassical Doctrines." In *Toward a New Strategy for Development,* 1979, pp. 1–17.

Seers, Dudley, ed. 1981a. *Dependency Theory.* London: Frances Pinter.

Seers, Dudley. 1981b. "Introduction." In Dudley Seers, ed., 1981a, pp. 13–19.

Selcher, Wayne, ed. 1986. *Political Liberalization in Brazil.* Boulder: Westview.

Seligson, Mitchell A., ed. 1984. *The Gap between Rich and Poor: Contending Perspectives on the Political Economy of Development.* Boulder: Westview.

Seward, Jeffrey. Forthcoming. "The State and the Informatics Industry in Brazil, 1971–1990." Ph.D. diss., Stanford University.

Shaw, Timothy, and Kenneth Heard, eds. 1979. *The Politics of Africa:*

Dependence and Development. Essex, England: Longman and Dalhousie University Press.

Sheahan, John. 1983. "The Economics of the Peruvian Experiment in Comparative Perspective." In McClintock and Lowenthal, 1983, pp. 387–414.

———— 1987. *Patterns of Development in Latin America: Poverty, Repression, and Economic Strategy.* Princeton: Princeton University Press.

Sigmund, Paul J. 1980a. "Marxism in Latin America." In Charles F. Elliott and Carl A. Linden, eds., *Marxism in the Contemporary West,* pp. 20–35. Boulder: Westview.

———— 1980b. *Multinationals in Latin America: The Politics of Nationalization.* Madison: University of Wisconsin Press.

Silva Gotay, Samuel. 1981. *El Pensamiento Cristiano Revolucionario en América Latina y el Caribe: Implicaciones de la Teología de la Liberación para la Sociología de la Religión.* Salamanca: Ediciones Sígueme.

Singer, Marshall. 1972. *Weak States in a World of Powers.* New York: Free Press.

Skidmore, Thomas E. 1973. "Politics and Economic Policy Making in Authoritarian Brazil, 1937–1971." In Stepan, ed., 1973, pp. 3–46.

———— 1988. *The Politics of Military Rule in Brazil, 1964–1985.* New York: Oxford University Press.

Skidmore, Thomas E., and Peter H. Smith. 1984. *Modern Latin America.* New York: Oxford University Press.

———— 1989. 2nd ed. of Skidmore and Smith, 1984.

Sklar, Richard. 1975. *Corporate Power in an African State: The Political Impact of Multinational Mining Companies in Zambia.* Berkeley: University of California Press.

Smith, Peter H. 1982a. "Political History in the 1980s: A View from Latin America." In Theodore K. Rabb and Robert I. Rotberg, eds., *The New History: The 1980s and Beyond,* pp. 3–28. Princeton: Princeton University Press.

———— 1982b. "The Intellectual Integrity of Latin American Studies." *LASA Forum,* 12:4 (Winter), pp. 11–12.

———— 1983. Discussant's Comments on "Comparative Politics and Political Development: An Historical Perspective." Harvard-MIT Joint Seminar on Political Development [JOSPOD], mimeographed transcript.

Smith, Tony. 1979. "The Underdevelopment of Development Literature: The Case of Dependency Theory." *World Politics,* 31:2 (January), pp. 247–288.

———— 1981. "The Logic of Dependency Theory Revisited." *International Organization,* 35:4 (Autumn), pp. 755–761.

———— 1985a. "Requiem or New Agenda for Third World Studies?" *World Politics,* 37:4 (July), pp. 532–561.

———— 1985b. "The Dependency Approach." In Wiarda, ed., 1985, pp. 113–126.

Snyder, Francis G. 1980. "Law and Development in the Light of Dependency Theory." *Law and Society Review*, 14:3 (Spring), pp. 723–804.

Souza Barros, Alexandre de. 1976. "The Changing Role of the State in Brazil: The Technocratic-Military Alliance," paper delivered at Sixth Annual Meeting of the Latin American Studies Association, Atlanta, Georgia, March 25–28.

Springborg, Patricia. 1981. *The Problem of Human Needs and the Critique of Civilization*. London: Allen and Unwin.

Stein, Stanley J., and Barbara H. Stein. 1970. *The Colonial Heritage of Latin America: Essays on Economic Dependence in Perspective*. New York: Oxford University Press.

———— 1980. *La Herencia Colonial de América Latina*. México: Siglo Veintiuno.

Stepan, Alfred, ed. 1973a. *Authoritarian Brazil*. New Haven: Yale University Press.

Stepan, Alfred. 1973b. "Preface." In Stepan, ed., 1973a., pp. vii–xi.

———— 1978a. "Political Leadership and Regime Breakdown: Brazil." In Linz and Stepan, 1978, pp. 110–137.

———— 1978b. *The State and Society: Peru in Comparative Perspective*. Prineton: Princeton University Press.

———— 1988. *Rethinking Military Politics: Brazil and the Southern Cone*. Princeton: Princeton University Press.

———— ed. 1989. *Democratizing Brazil: Problems of Transition and Consolidation*. New York: Oxford University Press.

Stephens, Evelyne Huber, and John D. Stephens. 1986. *Democratic Socialism in Jamaica: The Political Movement and Social Transformation in Dependent Capitalism*. Princeton: Princeton University Press.

Stern, Steve J. 1988a. "Feudalism, Capitalism, and the World-System in the Perspective of Latin America and the Caribbean." *American Historical Review*, 93:4 (October), pp. 829–872.

———— 1988b. "Reply: 'Ever More Solitary.'" *American Historical Review*, 93:4 (October), pp. 886–897.

Straubhaar, Joseph. 1981. "The Transformation of Cultural Dependency: The Decline of American Influence on the Brazilian Television Industry." Ph.D. diss., Fletcher School of Law and Diplomacy, Tufts University.

———— 1984. "Brazilian Television: The Decline of American Influence." *Communication Research*, 11:2 (April), pp. 203–220.

Street, James H., and D. P. James, eds. 1979. *Technology Progress in Latin America*. Boulder: Westview.

Sunkel, Osvaldo. 1969. "National Development Policy and External Dependence in Latin America." *Journal of Development Studies,* 6:1 (October), pp. 23–48.

—— 1971. "Capitalismo Transnacional y Desintegración Nacional en América Latina." *El Trimestre Económico,* 38:2 (April-June), pp. 571–628.

—— 1972. "Big Business and 'Dependencia': A Latin American View." *Foreign Affairs,* 50:3 (April), pp. 517–531

—— 1973. "Transnational Capitalism and National Disintegration in Latin America." *Social and Economic Studies,* 22:1 (March), pp. 132–176.

Sunkel, Osvaldo, and Pedro Paz. 1970. *El Subdesarrollo Latinoamericano y la Teoría del Desarrollo.* México: Siglo Veintiuno.

Sutton, Francis X. 1985. "American Foundations and the Social Sciences." *Items,* 39:4 (December), pp. 57–64.

"Symposium on Dependency Writings." 1982. *Latin American Research Review,* 17:1, pp. 115–171.

Szulc, Tad. 1987. *Fidel: A Critical Portrait.* New York: Avon.

Tabosa Pessoa, Lenildo. 1983. "Não Encontramos Um Só Liberalismo, Mas Vários." In Maria Lucia de Oliveira, ed., 1983, pp. 102–105.

Talbott, Strobe. 1978a. "A Display of Group-Think." *Time,* June 26, p. 31.

—— 1978b. "'Comrade Fidel Wants You.'" *Time,* July 10, pp. 36–39.

Taubman, Philip. 1984. "U.S. Role in Nicaragua Vote Disputed." *New York Times,* October 21.

Taylor, John. 1979. *From Modernization to Modes of Production: A Critique of Sociologies of Development and Underdevelopment.* London: Macmillan.

Taylor, William B. 1985. "Between Global Process and Local Knowledge: An Inquiry into Early Latin American Social History, 1500–1900." In Olivier Zunz, ed., *Reliving the Past,* pp. 115–190. Chapel Hill: University of North Carolina Press.

Thomas, Hugh S. 1971. *Cuba: The Pursuit of Freedom.* New York: Harper and Row.

—— 1977. *The Cuban Revolution.* New York: Harper and Row.

—— 1987. "Coping with Cuba." In Irving Louis Horowitz, ed., *Cuban Communism,* 6th ed., pp. 719–729. New Brunswick, N.J.: Transaction.

Thomas, Hugh S., Georges A. Fauriol, and Juan Carlos Weiss. 1984. *The Cuban Revolution: Twenty-Five Years Later.* Boulder: Westview.

Thomas, Lacy Glenn. 1984. "Underdevelopment: Test of a Theory." *Science,* 224 (18 May), pp. 711–713.

Thorp, Rosemary, and Geoffrey Bertram. 1978. *Peru 1890–1977: Growth and Policy in an Open Economy.* New York: Columbia University Press.

Timerman, Jacobo. 1982. *Prisoner Without a Name, Cell Without a Number.* New York: Vintage Books.

Torres-Rivas, Edelberto. 1987. *Centroamerica: La Democracia Posible.* San José, Costa Rica: Ed. Universitario Centroamericano.

Toward a New Strategy for Development. 1979. New York: Pergamon Press.

Trilling, Lionel. 1952. "Introduction" to George Orwell, *Homage to Catalonia,* pp. v–xxiii. New York and London: Harcourt Brace.

Trindade, Hélgio. 1982. "Paradoxos da Conjuntura Política: A Sociedade Civil Sob Pressão." In H. Trindade, ed., *Brasil em Perspectiva: Dilemas da Abertura Política,* pp. 11–29. Pôrto Alegre: Sulina.

Tugwell, Franklin. 1975. *The Politics of Oil in Venezuela.* Stanford: Stanford University Press.

Tulchin, Joseph. 1983. "Emerging Patterns of Research in the Study of Latin America." *Latin American Research Review,* 18:1, pp. 85–94.

Tyler, William, and J. Peter Wogart. 1973. "Economic Dependence and Marginalization: Some Empirical Evidence." *Journal of Inter-American Studies and World Affairs,* 15 (February), pp. 36–46.

Urquidi, Victor, Vicente Sánchez, and Eduardo Terrazas. 1982. "Latin America and World Problems." *Journal of Interamerican Development and World Affairs,* 24:1. (February), pp. 3–36.

Valenzuela, Arturo, and J. Samuel Valenzuela. 1975. "Visions of Chile." *Latin American Research Review,* 10:3 (Fall), pp. 155–175.

Valenzuela, J. Samuel, and Arturo Valenzuela. 1978. "Modernization and Dependency: Alternative Perspectives on the Study of Latin American Underdevelopment." *Comparative Politics,* 10:4 (July), pp. 535–557.

Van Dyke, Vernon. 1962. "Values and Interests." *American Political Science Review,* 56:3 (September), pp. 567–576.

Vargas Llosa, Mario. 1986. *The Real Life of Alejandro Mayta.* New York: Farrar, Straus and Giroux.

Vaughn, Mary Kay. 1982. *The State, Education, and Social Class in Mexico, 1880–1924.* DeKalb, Ill.: Northern Illinois University Press.

Velho, Otávio Guilherme. 1983. "Processos Sociais no Brasil Pós-64: As Ciências Sociais." In Bernardo Sorj and Maria Hermínia Tavares de Almeida, eds., *Sociedade e Política no Brasil Pós-64,* pp. 240–261. São Paulo: Brasiliense.

Véliz, Claudio. 1980. *The Centralist Tradition of Latin America.* Princeton: Princeton University Press.

Walker, Thomas W., ed. 1987. *Reagan versus the Sandinistas.* Boulder: Westview.

Walleri, R. Dan. 1978. "Trade Dependence and Underdevelopment: A Causal-Chain Analysis." *Comparative Political Studies,* 11:1 (April), pp. 94–127.

Wallerstein, Immanuel. 1974. *The Modern World-System: Capitalist Agriculture and the Origins of the European World-Economy in the Sixteenth Century.* New York: Academic Press.

———— 1979. *The Capitalist World-Economy*. Cambridge: Cambridge University Press.

———— 1980. *The Modern World-System II: Mercantilism and the Consolidation of the European World-Economy, 1600–1750*. New York: Academic Press.

———— 1988. "Comments on Stern's Critical Tests." *American Historical Review*, 93:4 (October), pp. 873–885.

Walton, John. 1987. "Small Gains for Big Theories: Recent Work on Development." *Latin American Research Review*, 22:2, pp. 192–201.

Warren, Bill. 1980. *Imperialism: Pioneer of Capitalism*. London: Verso.

Waterbury, John. 1983. *The Egypt of Nasser and Sadat: The Political Economy of Two Regimes*. Princeton: Princeton University Press.

Weaver, Frederick Stirton. 1980. *Class, State and Industrial Structure: The Historical Process of South American Industrial Growth*. Westport, Conn.: Greenwood Press.

Weber, Max. 1958. *From Max Weber: Essays in Sociology*. H. H. Gerth and C. W. Mills, eds. New York: Oxford University Press.

Weeks, John. 1985. *Limits to Capitalist Development in the Industrialization of Peru, 1950–1980*. Boulder: Westview.

Weffort, Francisco. 1971. "Nota Sôbre a 'Teoria da Dependência': Teoria de Classe ou Ideologia Nacional?" *Estudos I*, CEBRAP, São Paulo. pp. 1–24. Also published in *Revista Latinoamericano de Ciencia Política*, 1:3 (December 1970), pp. 389–401.

———— 1984. *Por Qué Democracia?* São Paulo: Brasiliense.

Weiner, Myron. 1981. Book review, in *Journal of Politics*, 43, pp. 226–227.

Weiner, Myron. 1987. "Introduction." In Weiner and Huntington, 1987, pp. xiii–xxviii.

Weiner, Myron and Samuel P. Huntington, eds. 1987. *Understanding Political Development*. Boston: Little, Brown.

Weinstein, Franklin. 1976a. *Indonesian Foreign Policy and the Dilemma of Dependence*. Ithaca: Cornell University Press.

———— 1976b. "Multinational Corporations and the Third World: The Case of Japan and Southeast Asia." *International Organization*, 30:3 (Summer), pp. 373–404.

Werneck Viana, Luís. 1981. "Comentários." In Bolivar Lamounier, et al., eds., 1981, pp. 258–264.

Wesson, Robert. 1981. *The United States and Brazil*. New York: Praeger.

Westman, John. 1985. "Modern Dependency: A 'Crucial Case' Study of Brazilian Government Policy in the Minicomputer Industry." *Studies in Comparative International Development*, 20:2, pp. 25–47.

Whiting, Jr., Van R. 1986. "Report of the Task Force on Scholarly Relations with Cuba." *LASA Forum*, 17:1 (Spring), pp. 32–33.

Wiarda, Howard, ed. 1985. *New Directions in Comparative Politics*. Boulder: Westview.

Williams, Eric. 1982. "Dependence as a State of Mind." *The Wilson Quarterly,* 6:2 (Spring), p. 123.

Winckler, Edwin A. 1981. "Authoritarianism and Dependency in East Asia." *Items,* 35:1/2 (June), pp. 14–17.

Wolfe, Bertram D. 1965. *Marxism: One Hundred Years in the Life of a Doctrine.* New York: Dial Press.

Womack, John. 1980. "Mariátegui, Marxism, and Nationalism." *Marxist Perspectives,* 3:2 (Summer), pp. 170–174.

Wood, Robert E. 1984. "The Debt Crisis and North-South Relations." *Third World Quarterly,* 6:3 (July), pp. 703–716.

Wood, Robert E. 1986. *From Marshall Plan to Debt Crisis: Foreign Aid and Development Choices in the World Economy.* Berkeley: University of California Press.

Zaid, Gabriel. 1987. *La Economía Presidencial.* México: Vuelta.

Index